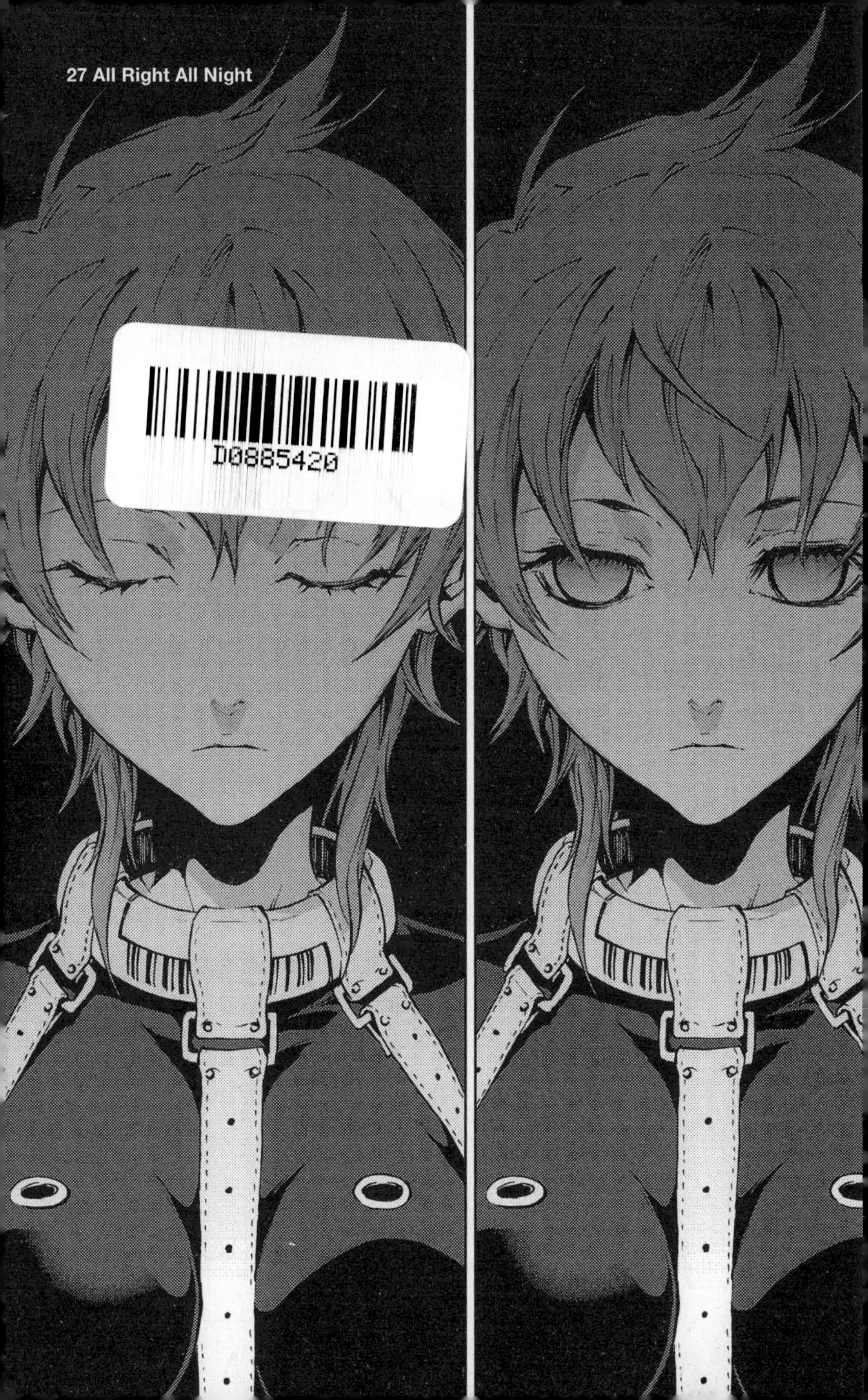
27 All Right All Night

DING

LIGHTS OUT FOR NINBEN NUMBERS ONE THROUGH TWENTY IN CLASSES B AND C.

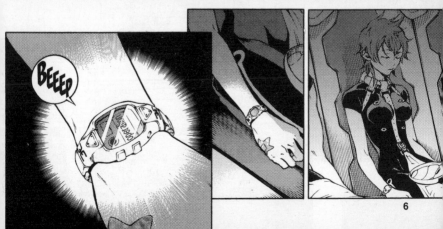

BEEEP

6

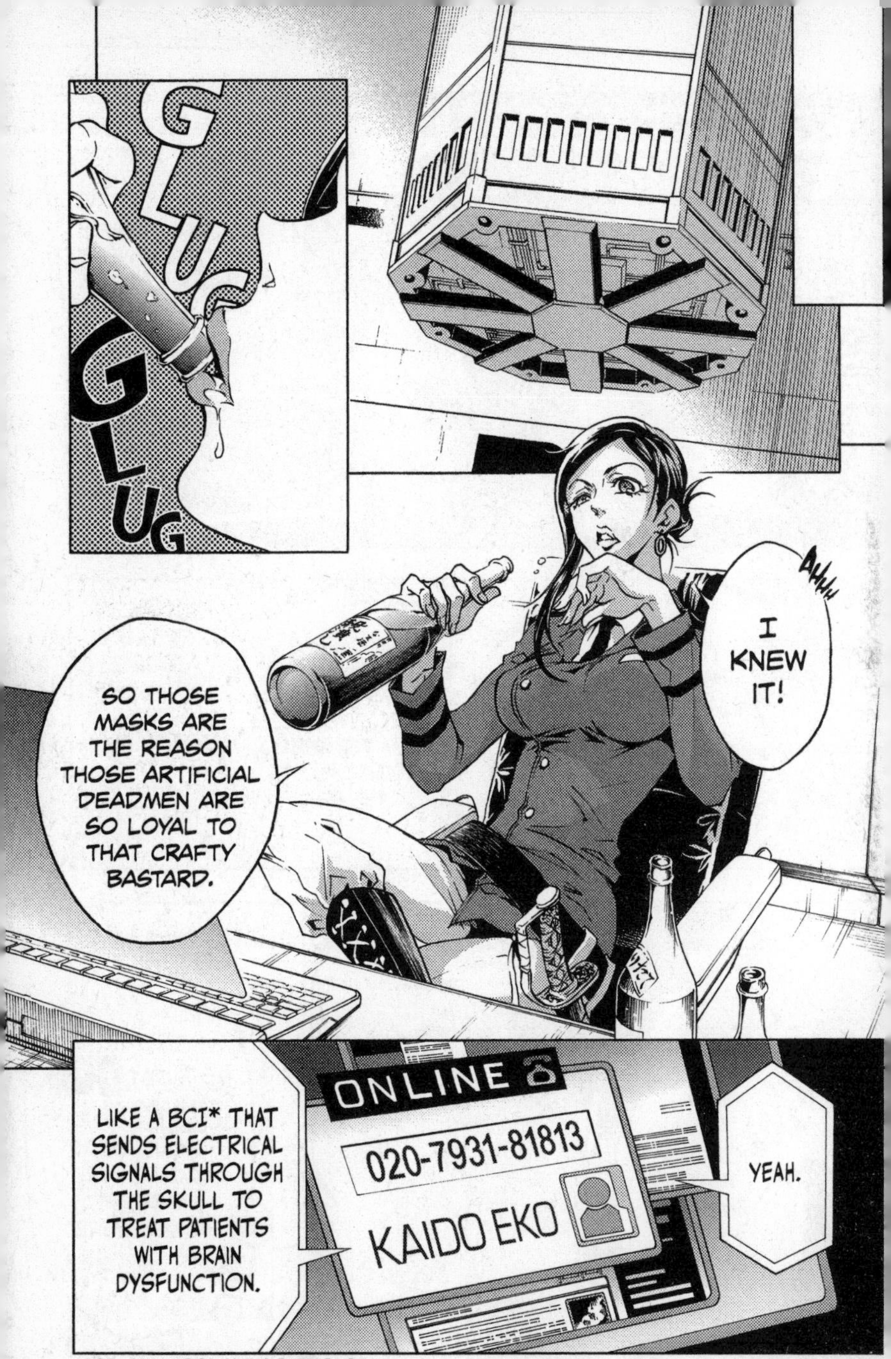
GLUG
GLUG
GLUG
AHHH
I KNEW IT!
SO THOSE MASKS ARE THE REASON THOSE ARTIFICIAL DEADMEN ARE SO LOYAL TO THAT CRAFTY BASTARD.
YEAH.
ONLINE
020-7931-81813
KAIDO EKO
LIKE A BCI* THAT SENDS ELECTRICAL SIGNALS THROUGH THE SKULL TO TREAT PATIENTS WITH BRAIN DYSFUNCTION.

*BCI = BRAIN/COMPUTER INTERFACE

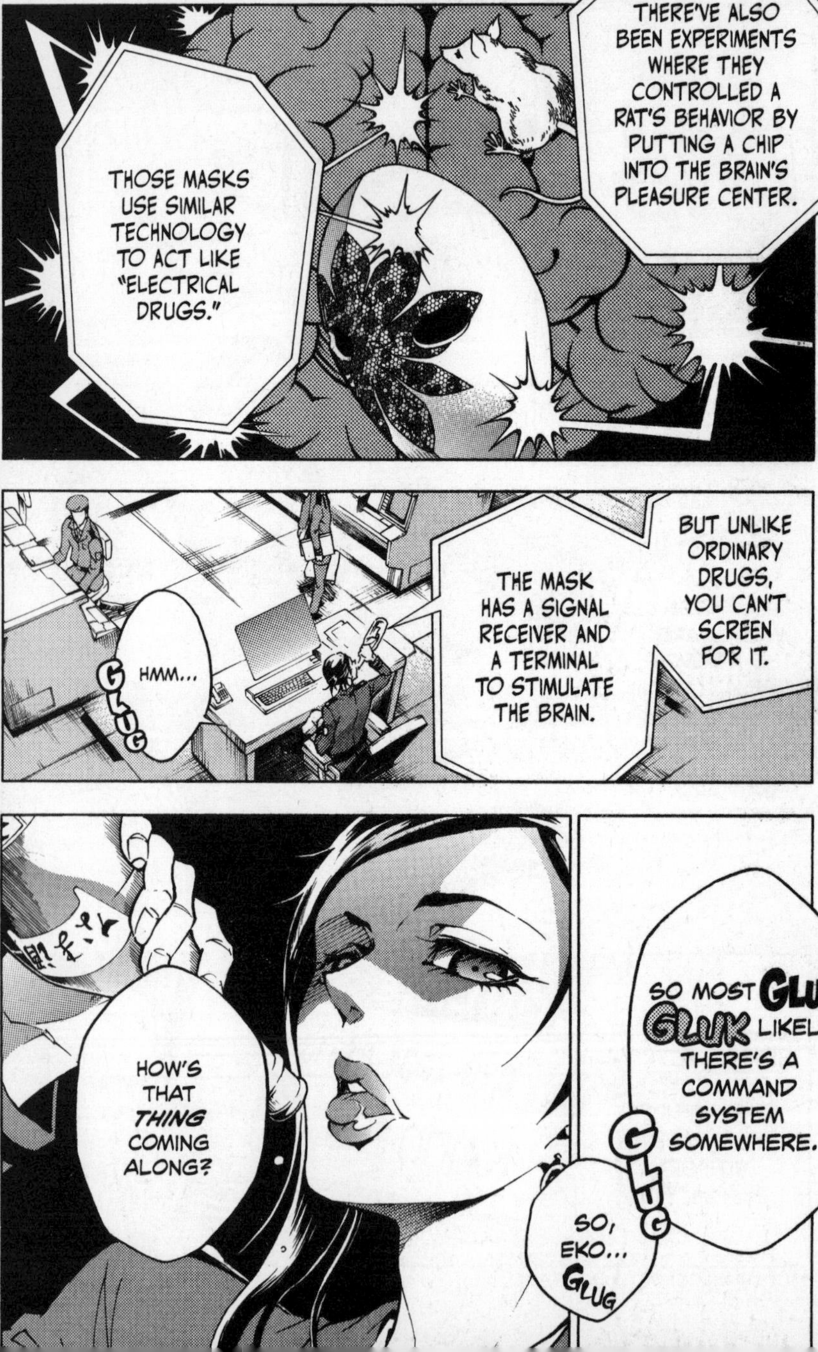

THERE'VE ALSO BEEN EXPERIMENTS WHERE THEY CONTROLLED A RAT'S BEHAVIOR BY PUTTING A CHIP INTO THE BRAIN'S PLEASURE CENTER.
THOSE MASKS USE SIMILAR TECHNOLOGY TO ACT LIKE "ELECTRICAL DRUGS."
BUT UNLIKE ORDINARY DRUGS, YOU CAN'T SCREEN FOR IT.
THE MASK HAS A SIGNAL RECEIVER AND A TERMINAL TO STIMULATE THE BRAIN.
HMM...
GLUG
SO MOST GLUG GLUK LIKELY THERE'S A COMMAND SYSTEM SOMEWHERE.
GLUG
SO, EKO...
GLUG
HOW'S THAT *THING* COMING ALONG?

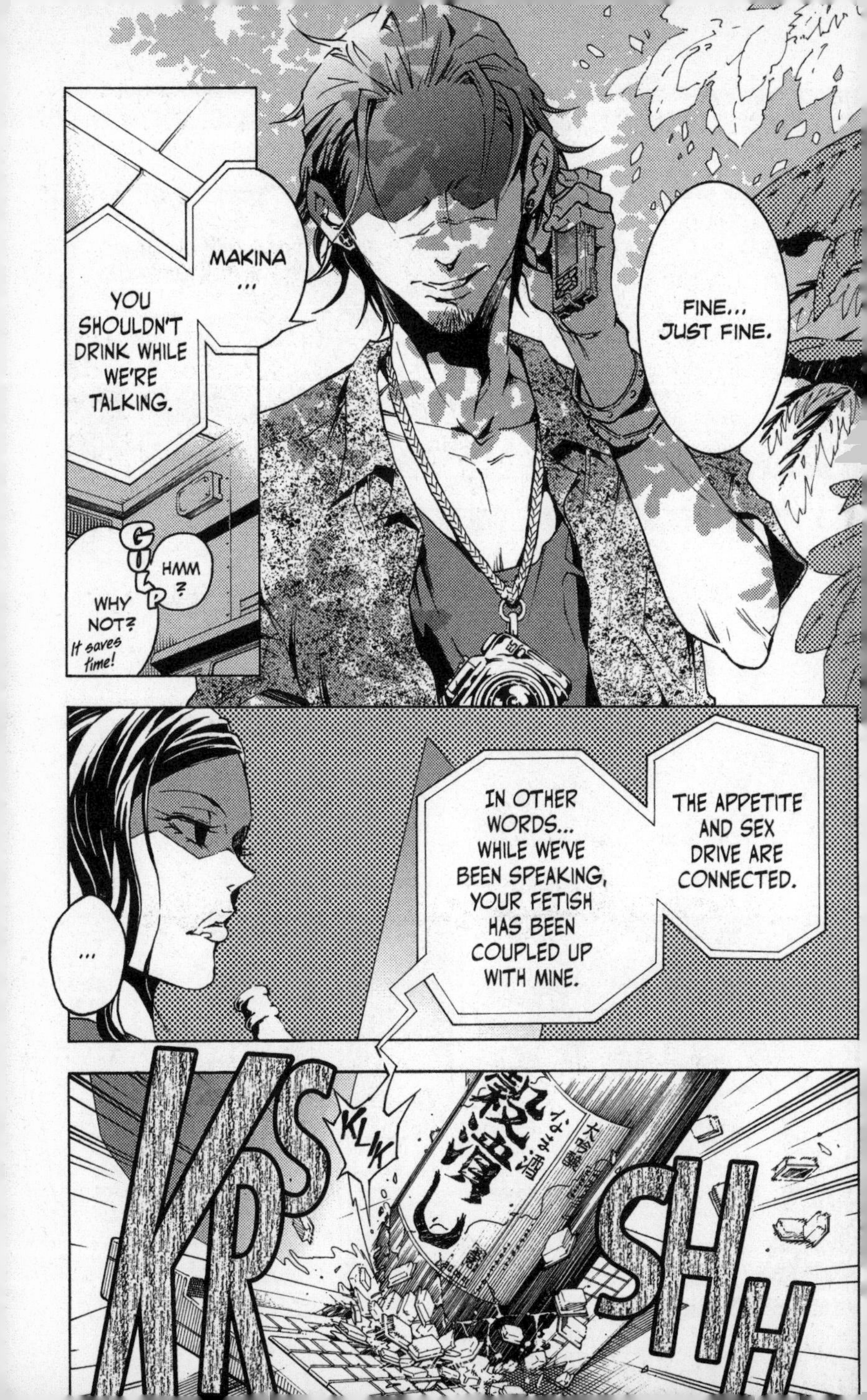
FINE... JUST FINE.
MAKINA ...
YOU SHOULDN'T DRINK WHILE WE'RE TALKING.
GULP
HMM?
WHY NOT? It saves time!
THE APPETITE AND SEX DRIVE ARE CONNECTED.
IN OTHER WORDS... WHILE WE'VE BEEN SPEAKING, YOUR FETISH HAS BEEN COUPLED UP WITH MINE.
...
KLNK
KRSSHH

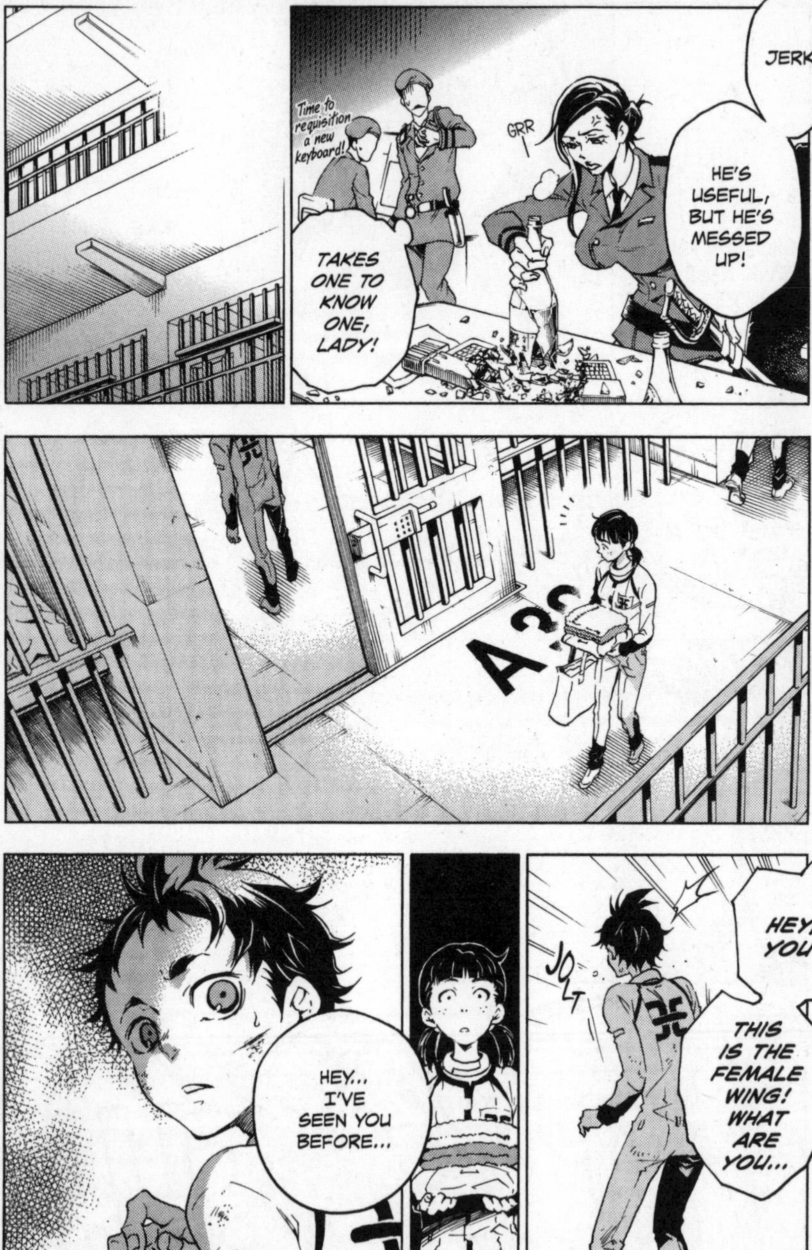
JERK!
HE'S USEFUL, BUT HE'S MESSED UP!
GRR
Time to requisition a new keyboard!
TAKES ONE TO KNOW ONE, LADY!
HEY, YOU!
JOLT
THIS IS THE FEMALE WING! WHAT ARE YOU...
HEY... I'VE SEEN YOU BEFORE...

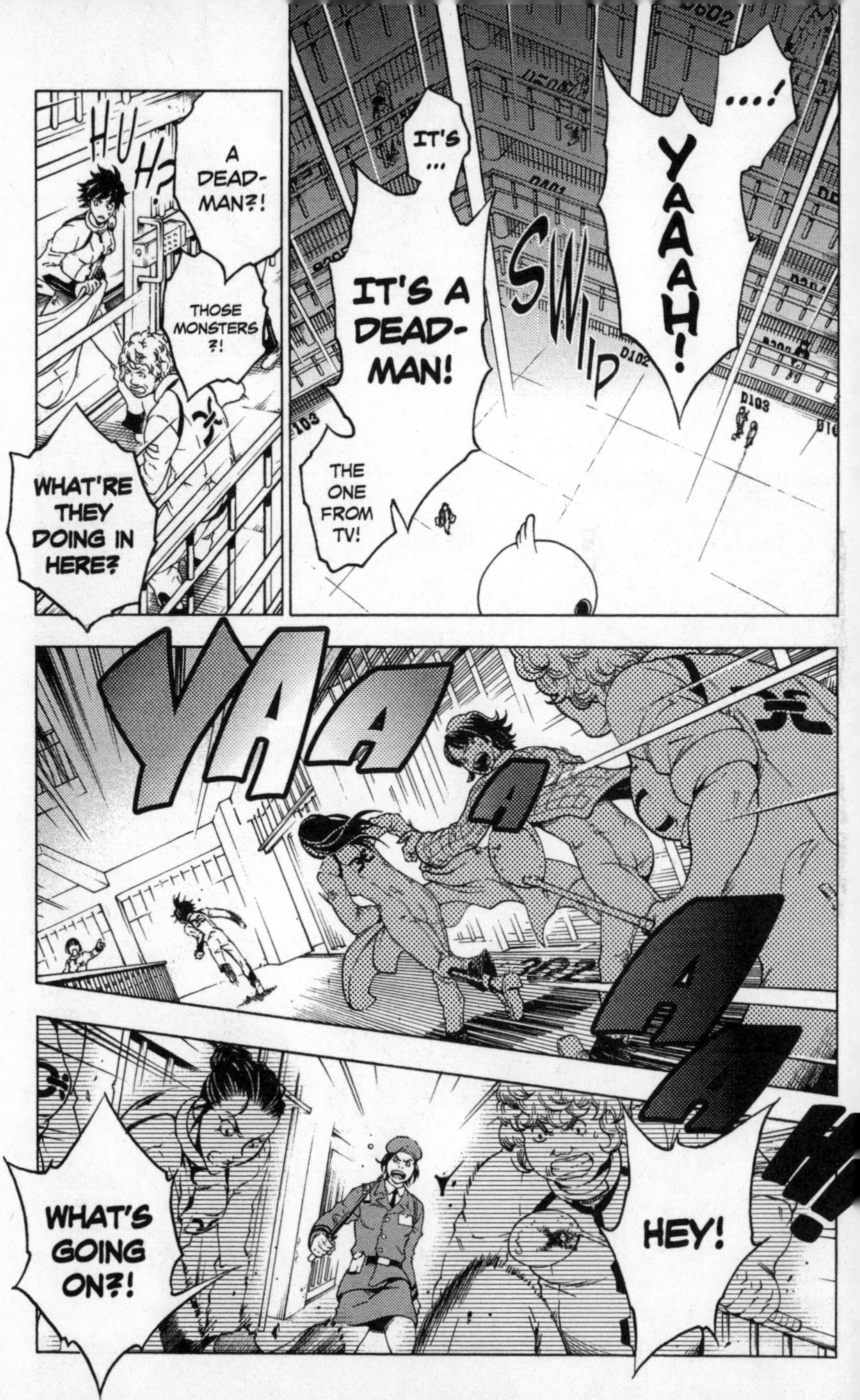

...!
YAAAH!
SWIIP
IT'S...
IT'S A DEAD-MAN!
THE ONE FROM TV!
HUH?
A DEAD-MAN?!
THOSE MONSTERS?!
WHAT'RE THEY DOING IN HERE?
YAAAAH
HEY!
WHAT'S GOING ON?!

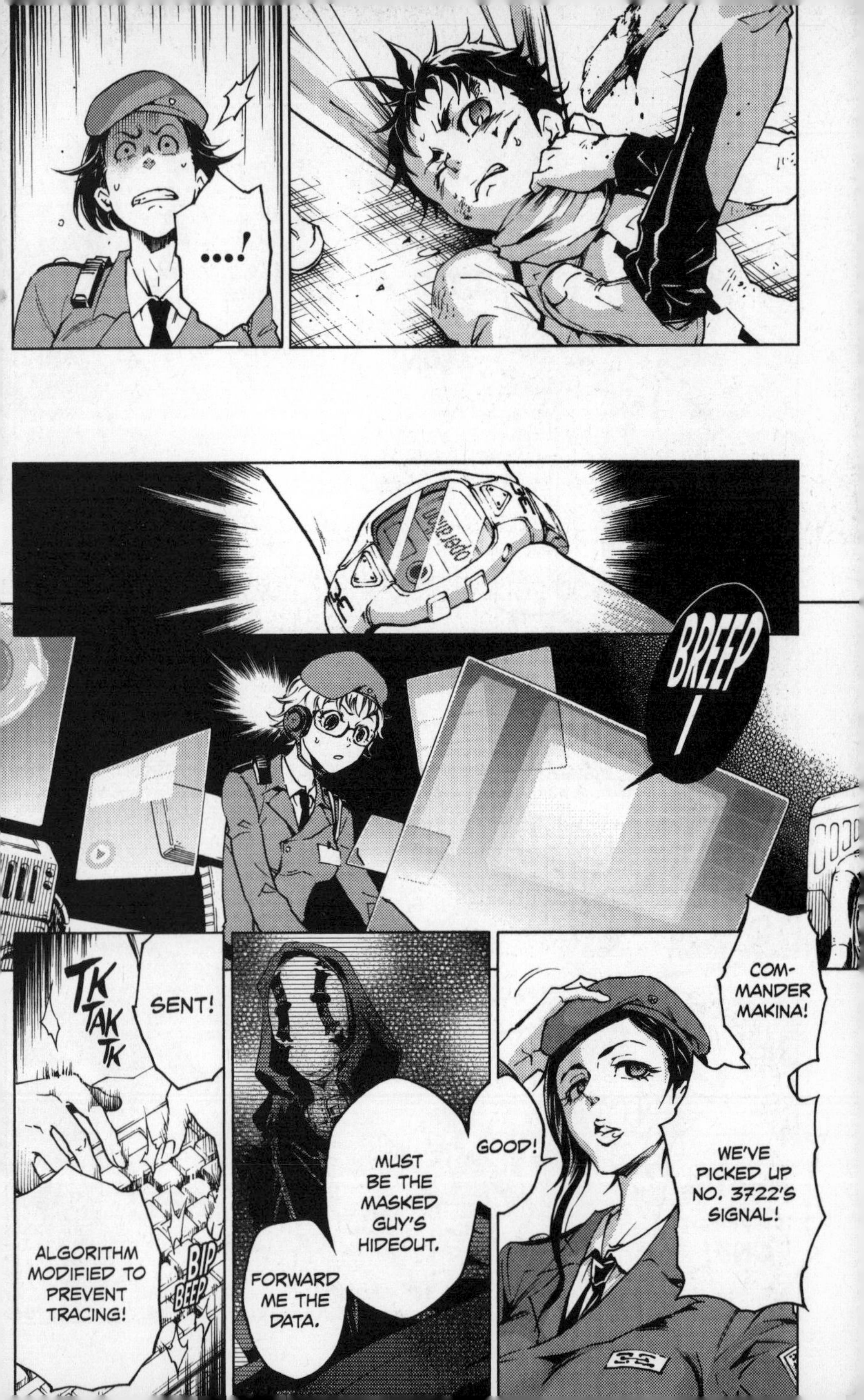
....!
BREEP!
COM-MANDER MAKINA!
WE'VE PICKED UP NO. 3722'S SIGNAL!
GOOD!
MUST BE THE MASKED GUY'S HIDEOUT.
FORWARD ME THE DATA.
SENT!
TK TAK TK
ALGORITHM MODIFIED TO PREVENT TRACING!
BIP BEEP

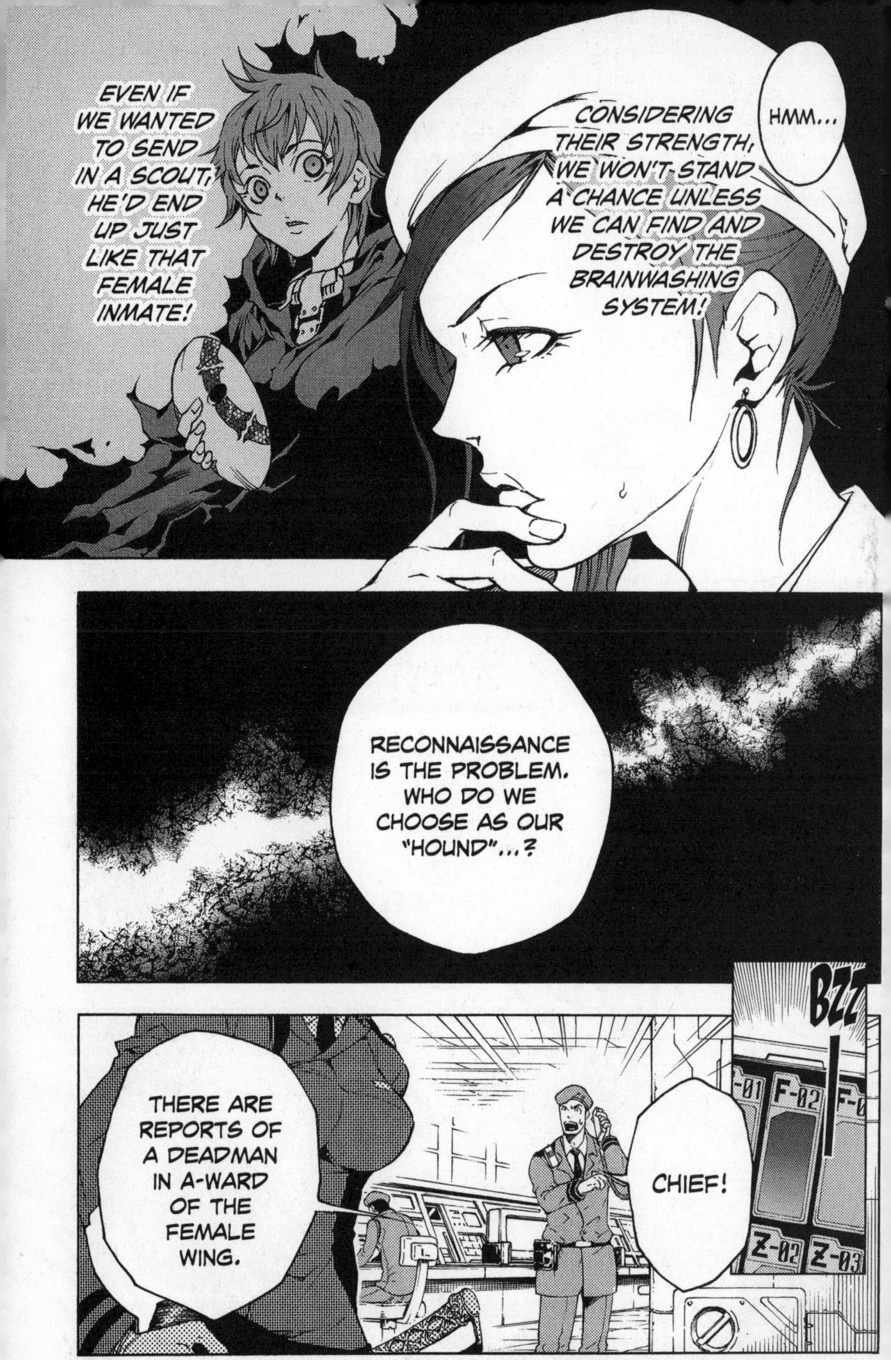
HMM...
CONSIDERING THEIR STRENGTH, WE WON'T STAND A CHANCE UNLESS WE CAN FIND AND DESTROY THE BRAINWASHING SYSTEM!
EVEN IF WE WANTED TO SEND IN A SCOUT, HE'D END UP JUST LIKE THAT FEMALE INMATE!
RECONNAISSANCE IS THE PROBLEM. WHO DO WE CHOOSE AS OUR "HOUND"...?
BZZ
CHIEF!
THERE ARE REPORTS OF A DEADMAN IN A-WARD OF THE FEMALE WING.

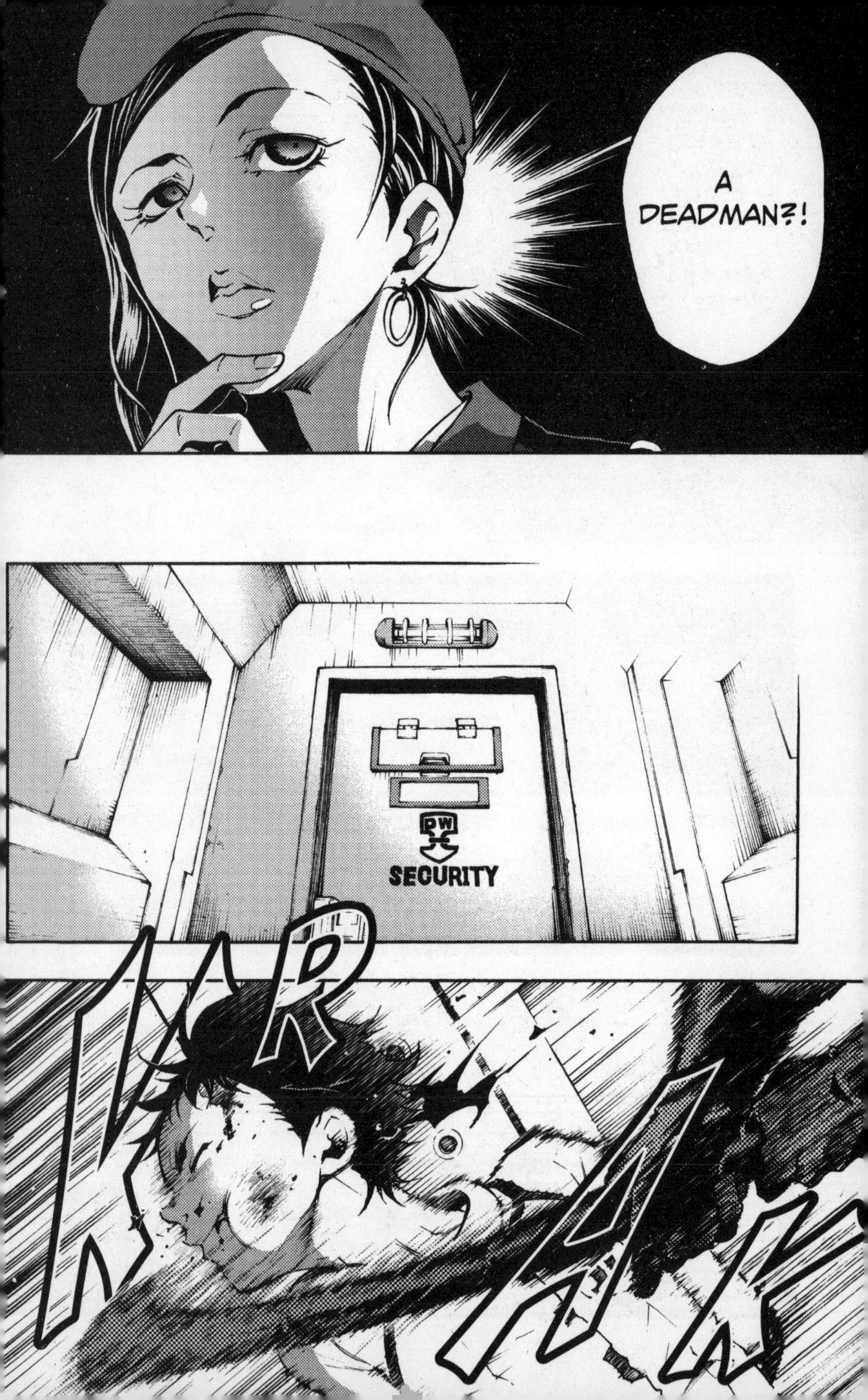
A DEADMAN?!
SECURITY

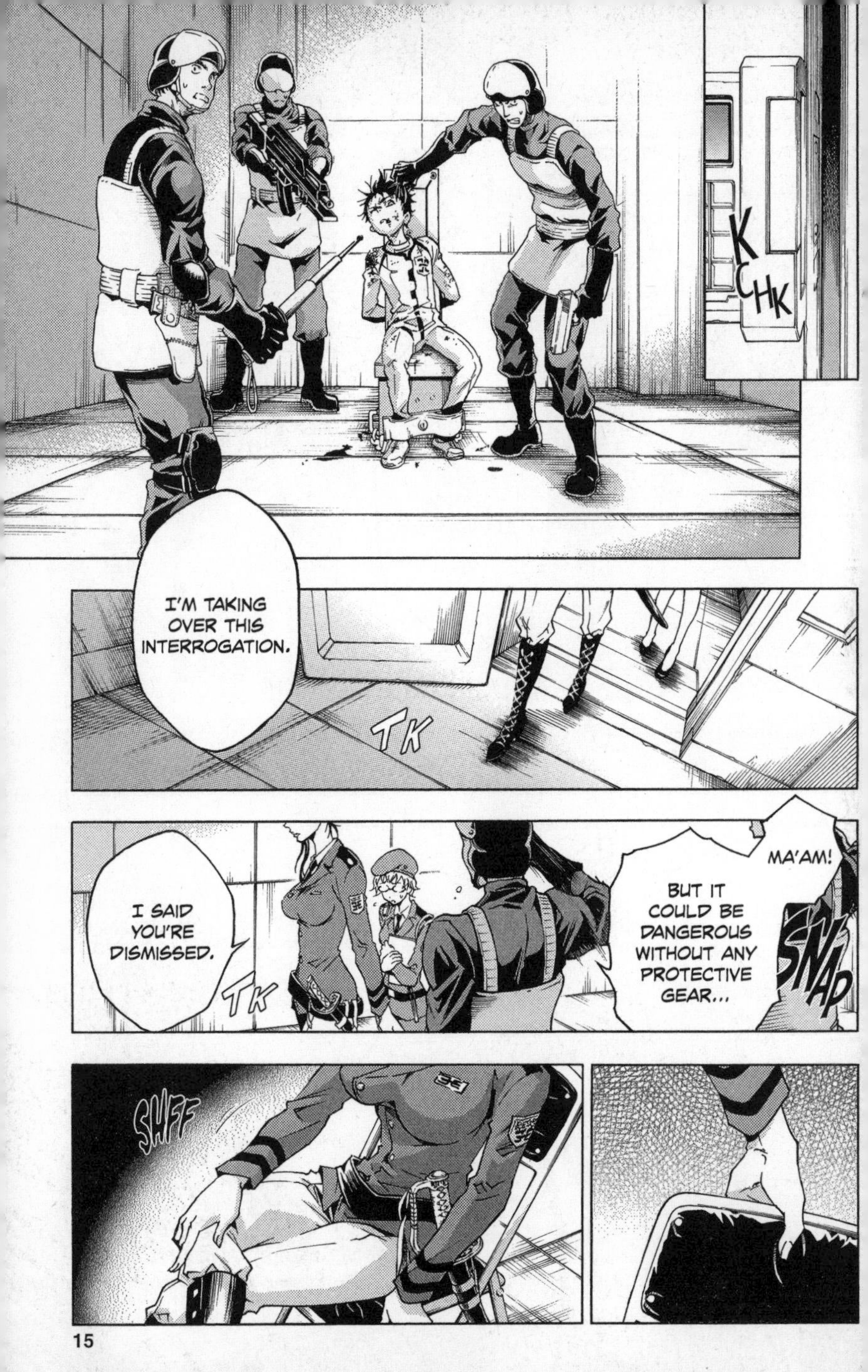
KCHK
I'M TAKING OVER THIS INTERROGATION.
TK
SNAP
MA'AM!
BUT IT COULD BE DANGEROUS WITHOUT ANY PROTECTIVE GEAR...
TK
I SAID YOU'RE DISMISSED.
SHFF

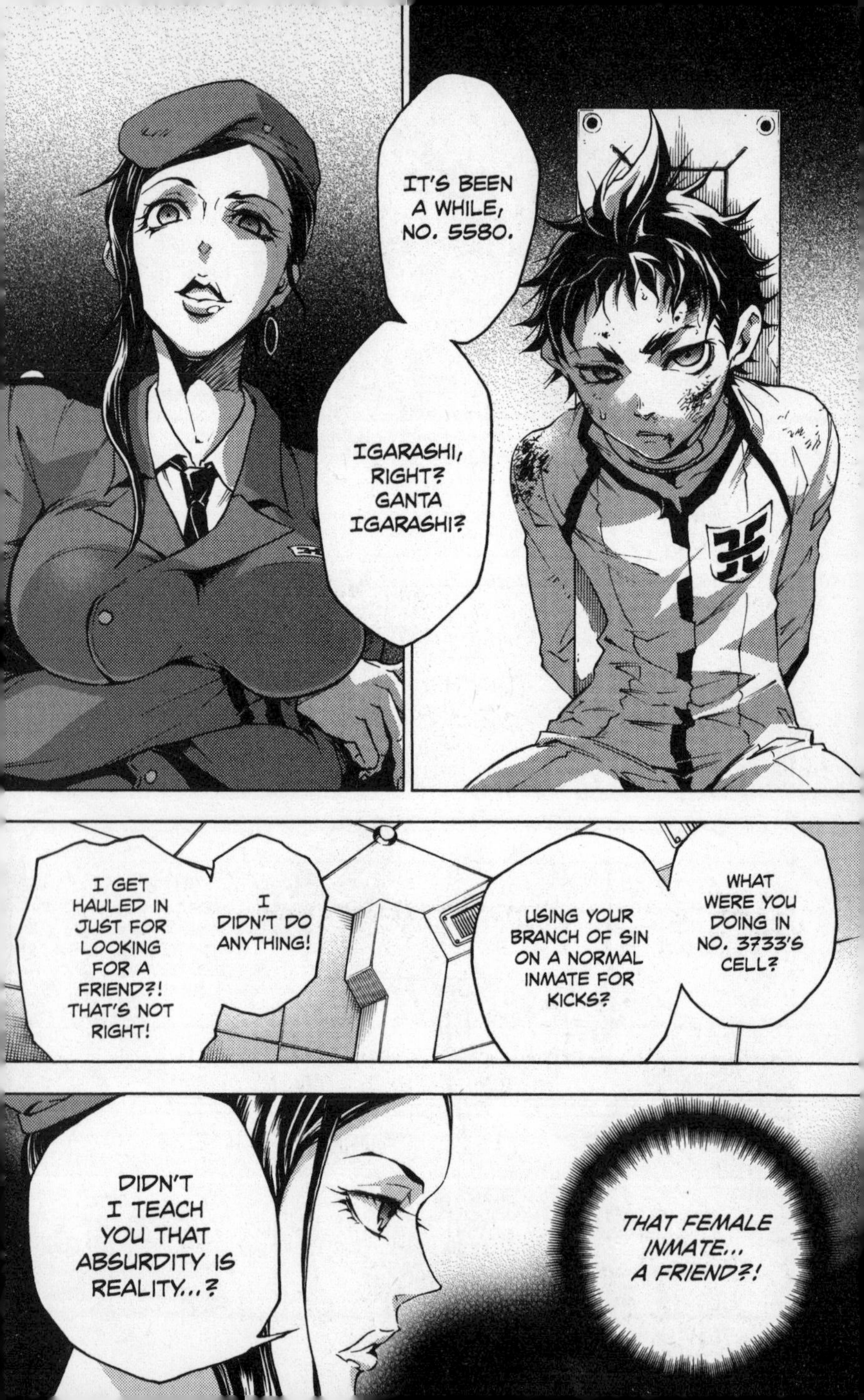
IT'S BEEN A WHILE, NO. 5580.
IGARASHI, RIGHT? GANTA IGARASHI?
WHAT WERE YOU DOING IN NO. 3733'S CELL?
USING YOUR BRANCH OF SIN ON A NORMAL INMATE FOR KICKS?
I DIDN'T DO ANYTHING!
I GET HAULED IN JUST FOR LOOKING FOR A FRIEND?! THAT'S NOT RIGHT!
THAT FEMALE INMATE... A FRIEND?!
DIDN'T I TEACH YOU THAT ABSURDITY IS REALITY...?

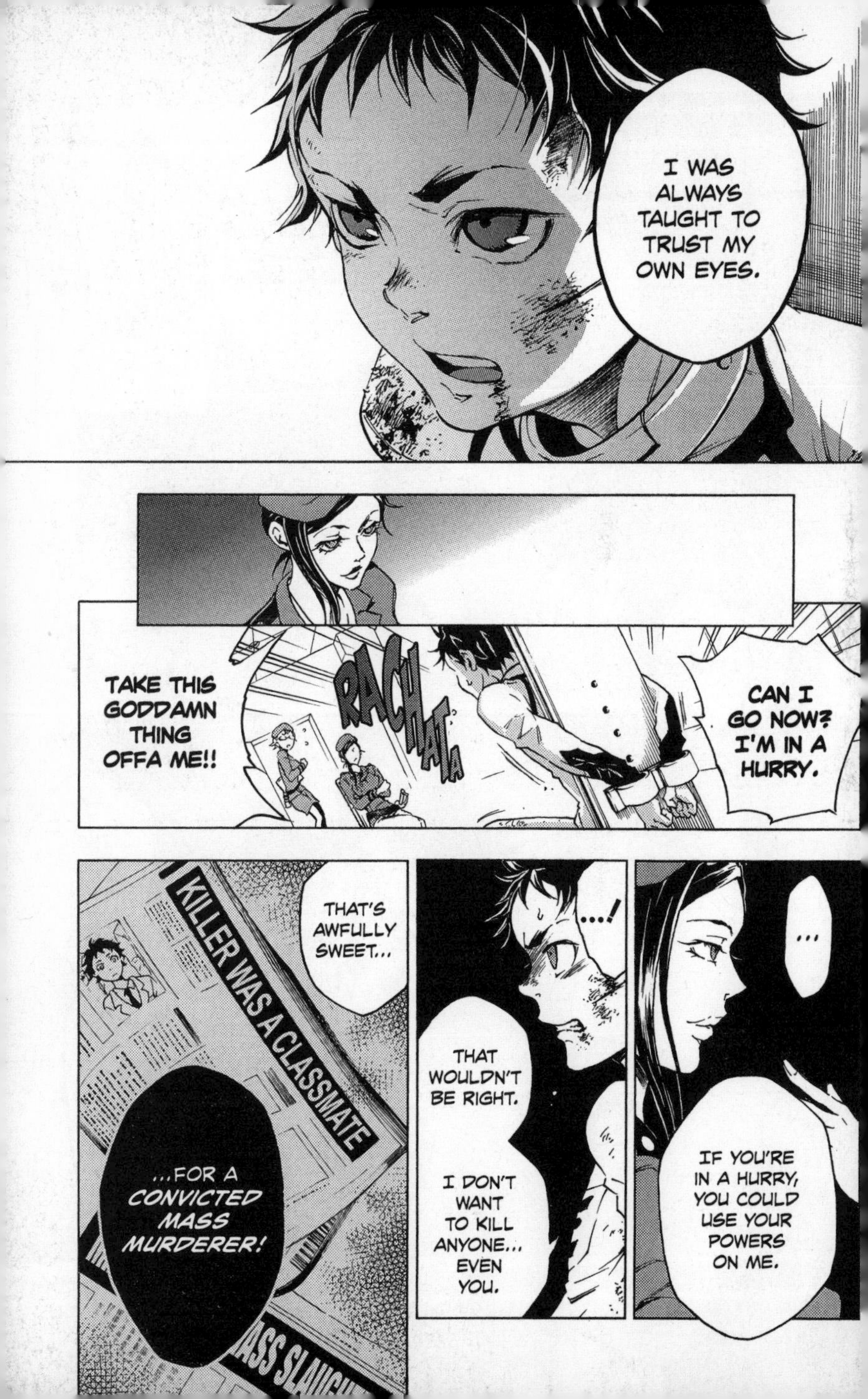
I WAS ALWAYS TAUGHT TO TRUST MY OWN EYES.
CAN I GO NOW? I'M IN A HURRY.
RACHATA
TAKE THIS GODDAMN THING OFFA ME!!
...
IF YOU'RE IN A HURRY, YOU COULD USE YOUR POWERS ON ME.
...!
THAT WOULDN'T BE RIGHT.
I DON'T WANT TO KILL ANYONE... EVEN YOU.
THAT'S AWFULLY SWEET...
KILLER WAS A CLASSMATE
...FOR A CONVICTED MASS MURDERER!

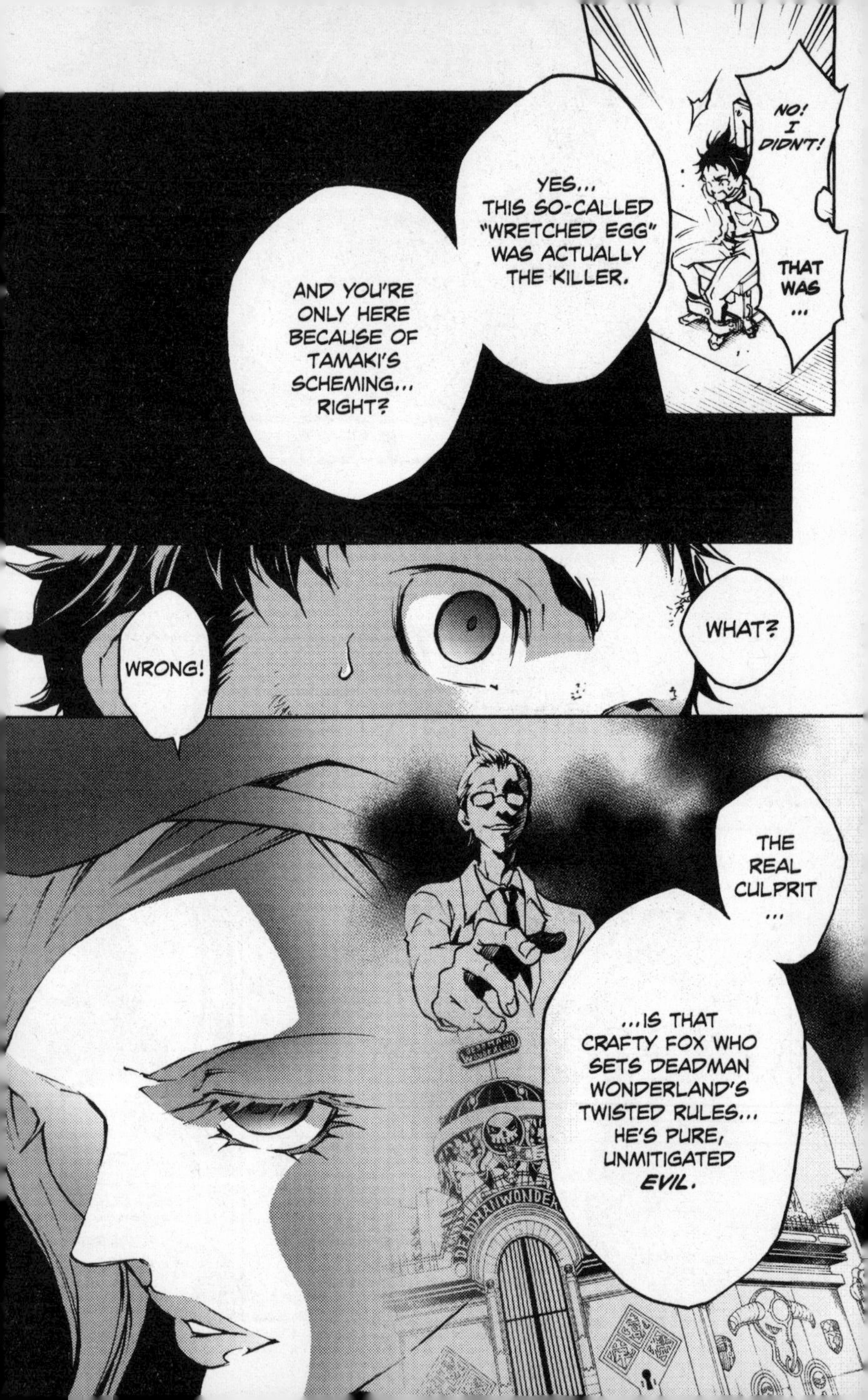

NO! I DIDN'T!
THAT WAS...
YES... THIS SO-CALLED "WRETCHED EGG" WAS ACTUALLY THE KILLER.
AND YOU'RE ONLY HERE BECAUSE OF TAMAKI'S SCHEMING... RIGHT?
WHAT?
WRONG!
THE REAL CULPRIT...
...IS THAT CRAFTY FOX WHO SETS DEADMAN WONDERLAND'S TWISTED RULES... HE'S PURE, UNMITIGATED *EVIL*.

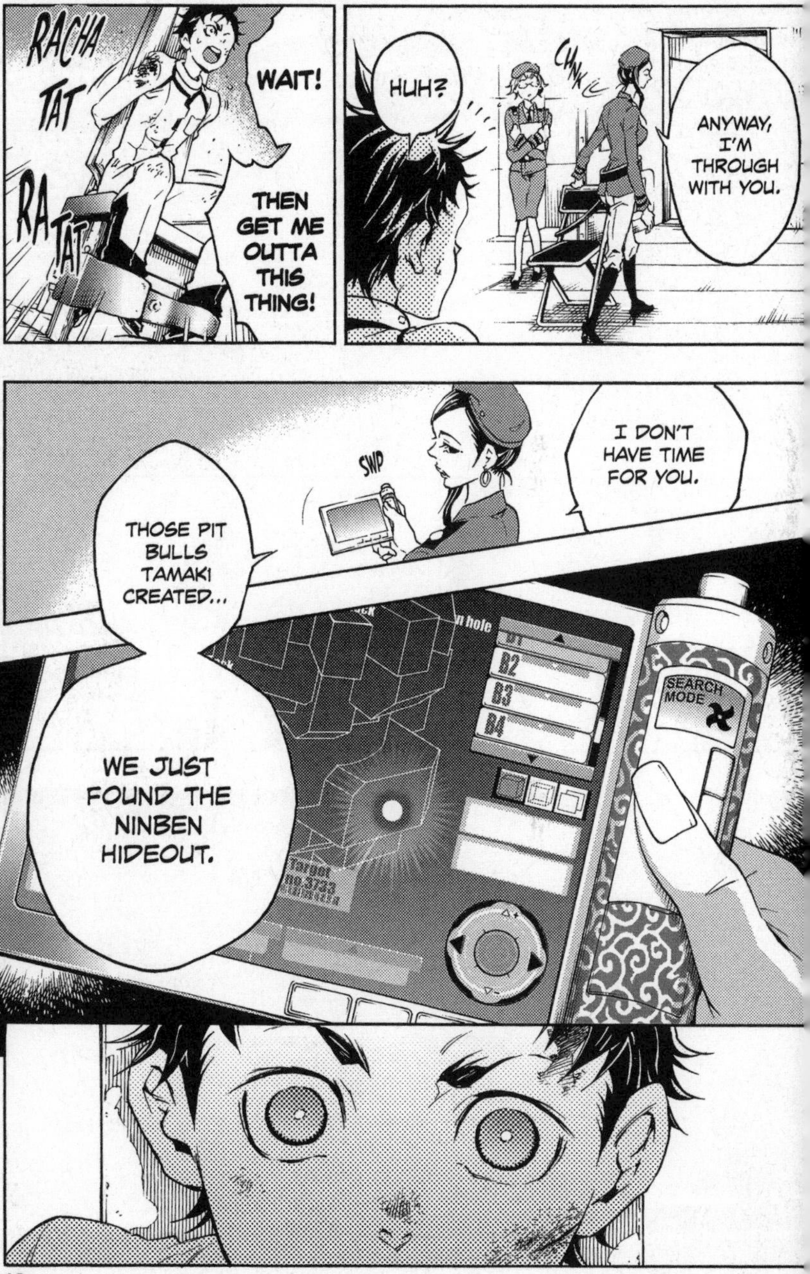
ANYWAY, I'M THROUGH WITH YOU.
CHNK
HUH?
WAIT!
RACHA TAT
RA TAT
THEN GET ME OUTTA THIS THING!
I DON'T HAVE TIME FOR YOU.
SWP
THOSE PIT BULLS TAMAKI CREATED...
WE JUST FOUND THE NINBEN HIDEOUT.
B2
B3
B4
SEARCH MODE
Target
no.3733

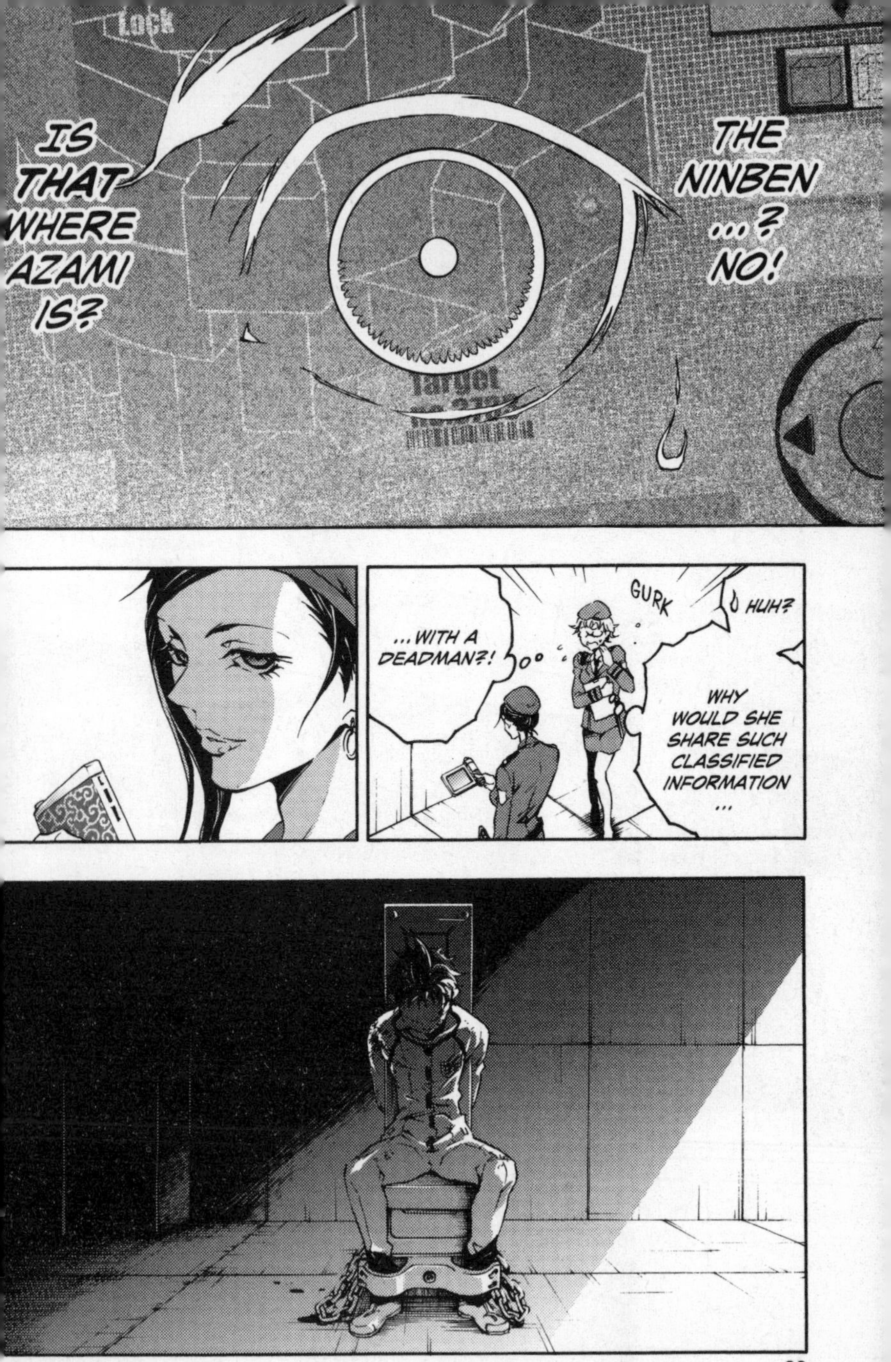
Lock
THE NINBEN ...? NO!
IS THAT WHERE AZAMI IS?
Target
HUH?
GURK
...WITH A DEADMAN?!
WHY WOULD SHE SHARE SUCH CLASSIFIED INFORMATION ...

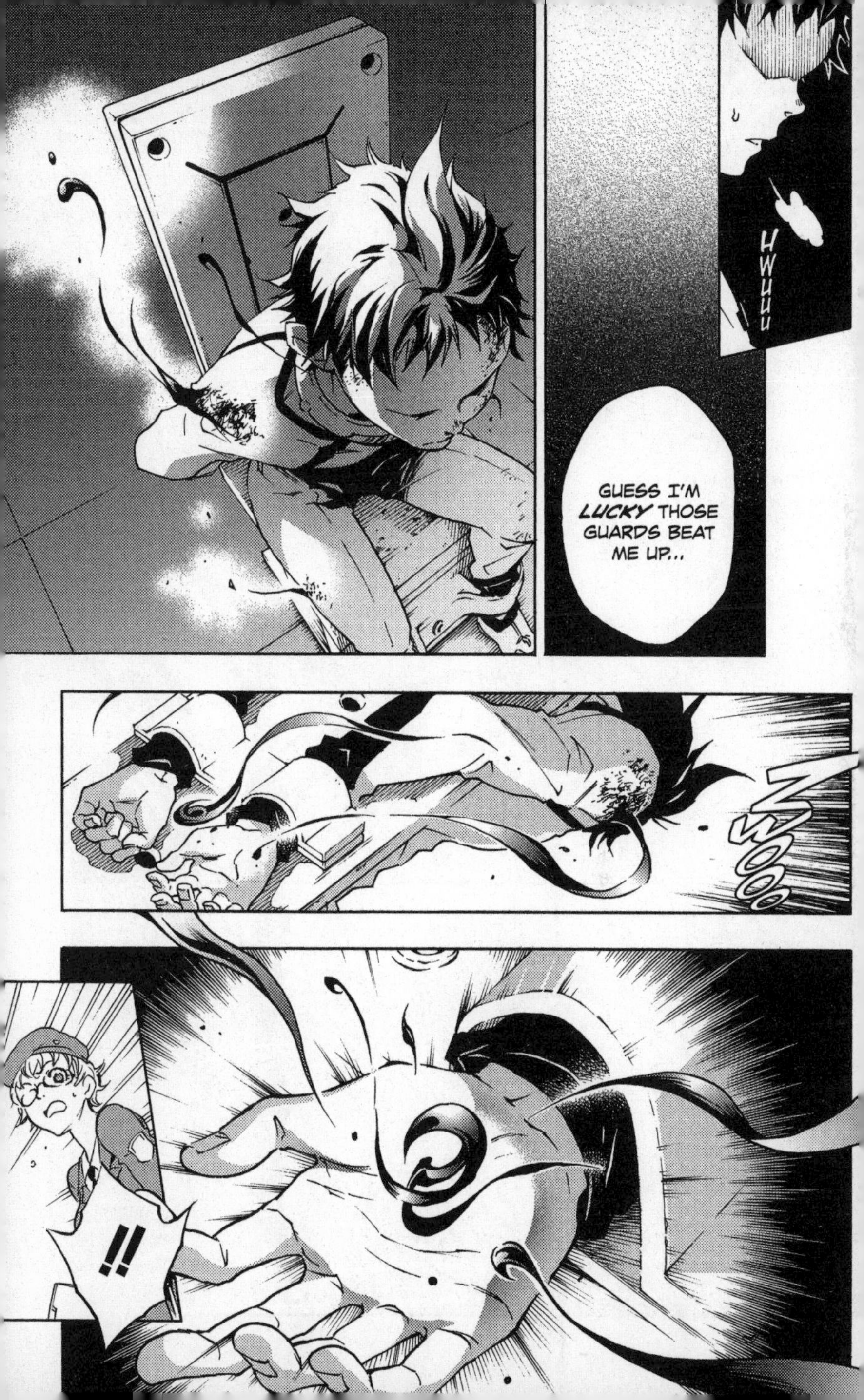
HWUUU
GUESS I'M LUCKY THOSE GUARDS BEAT ME UP...
WOOO
!!

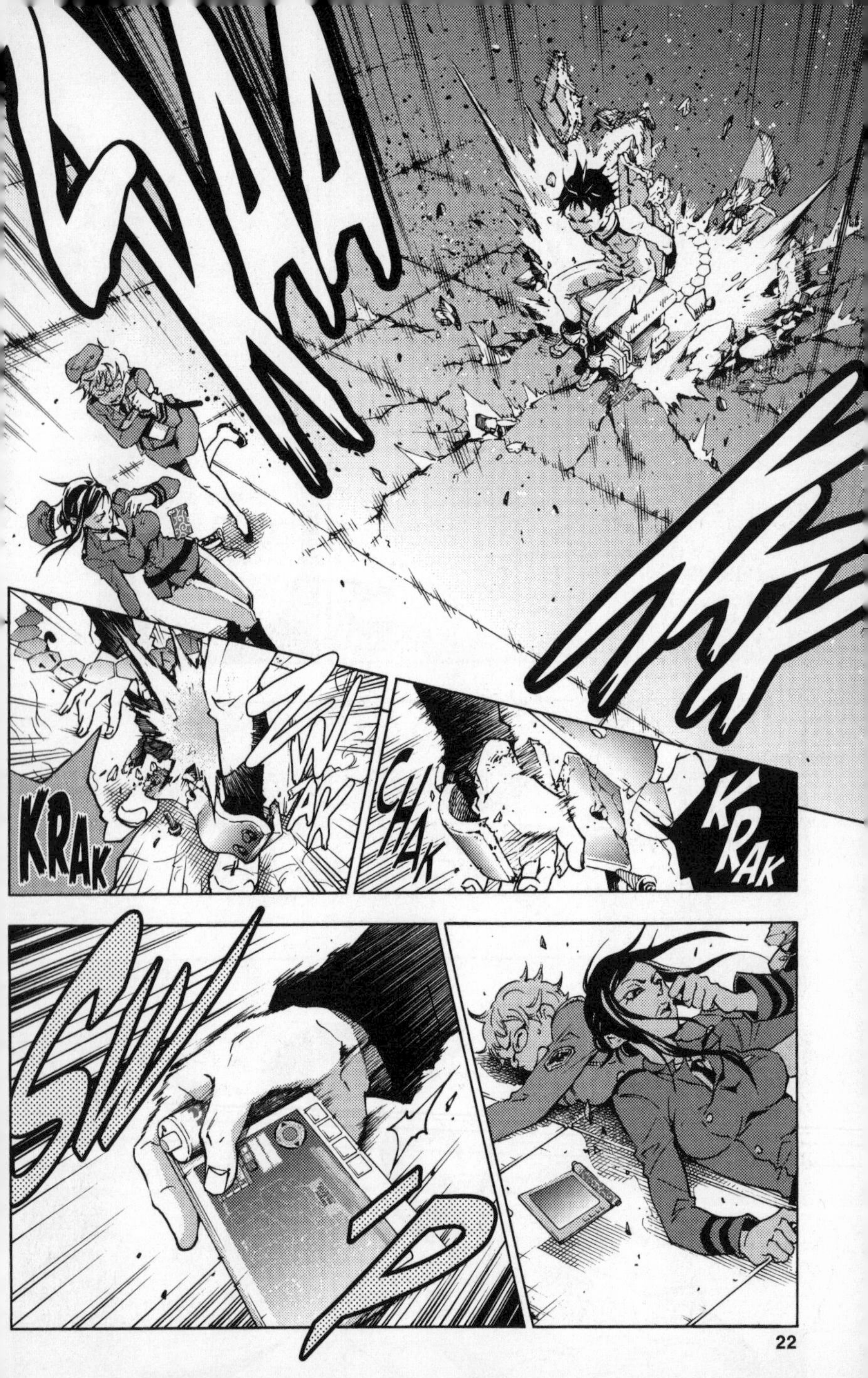
KRAK
CHAK
ZWAK
KRAK
SWIP

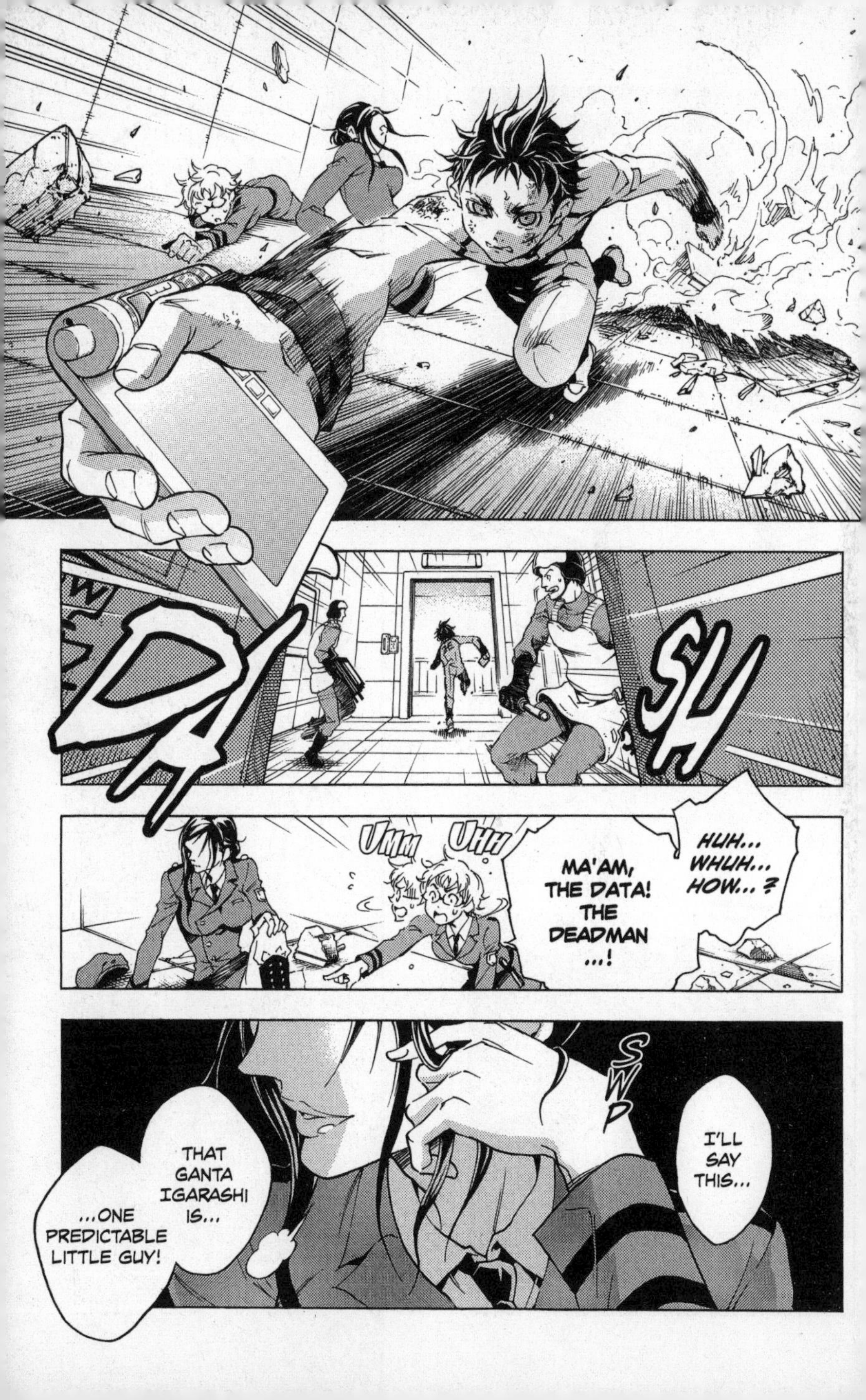
DA
SH
UHH
UMM
HUH... WHUH... HOW...?
MA'AM, THE DATA! THE DEADMAN ...!
SWD
I'LL SAY THIS...
THAT GANTA IGARASHI IS...
...ONE PREDICTABLE LITTLE GUY!

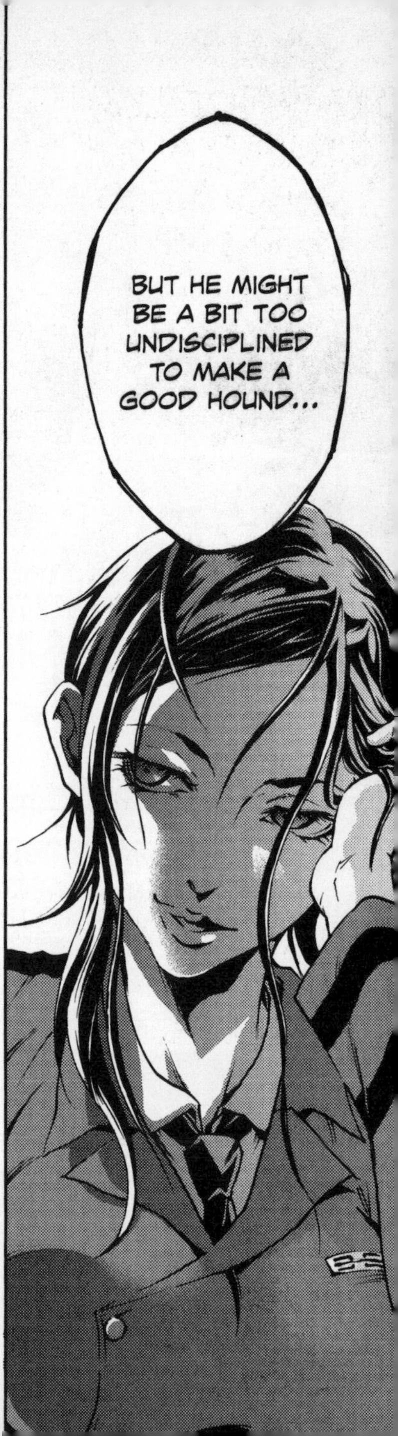
BUT HE MIGHT BE A BIT TOO UNDISCIPLINED TO MAKE A GOOD HOUND...

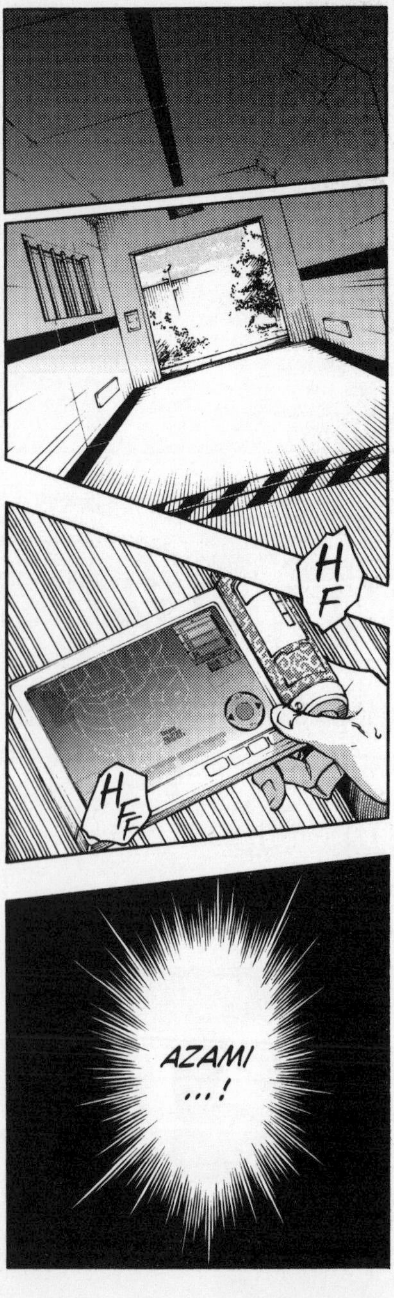
HF
HFF
AZAMI ...!

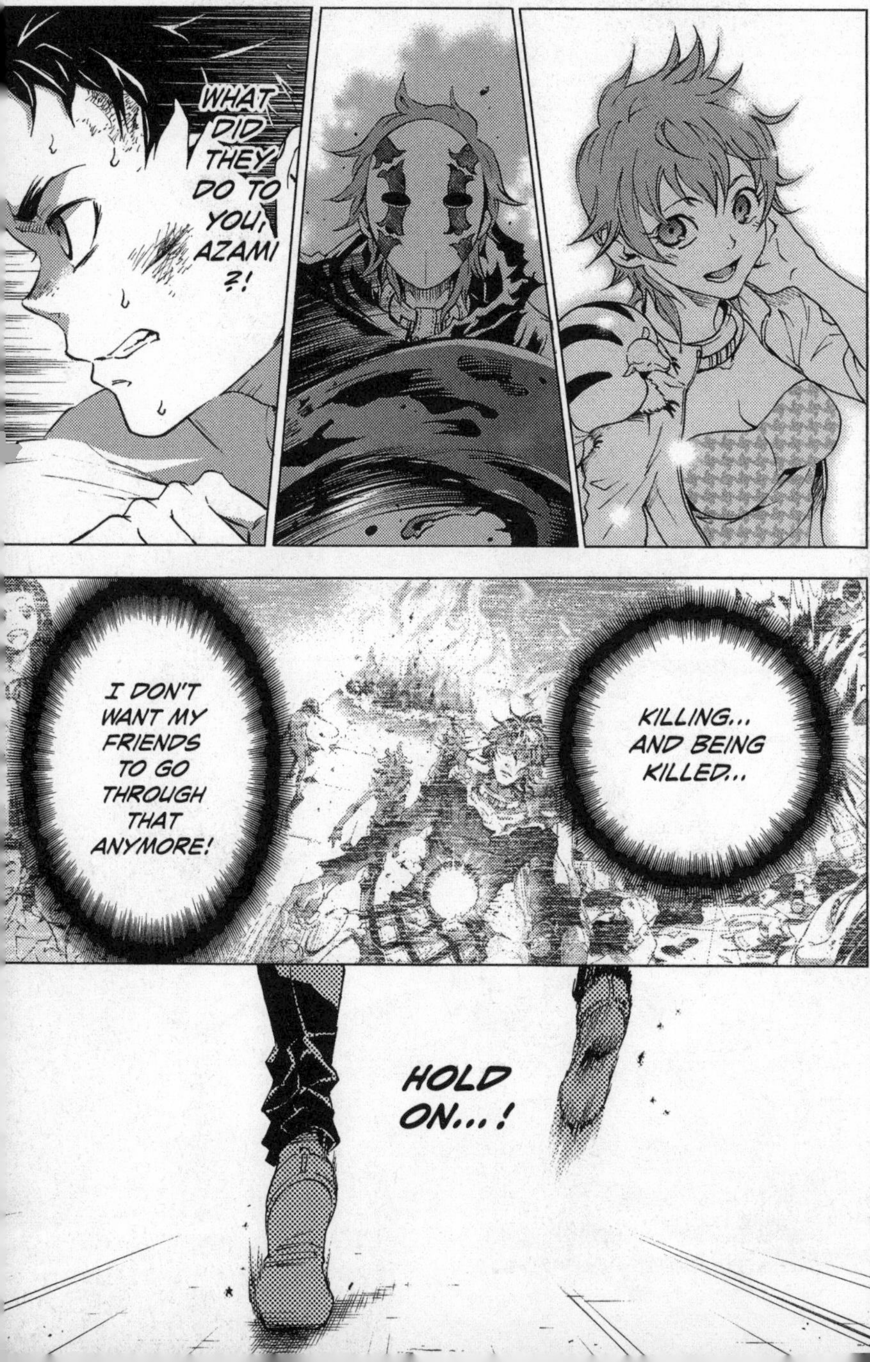
WHAT DID THEY DO TO YOU, AZAMI?!
KILLING... AND BEING KILLED...
I DON'T WANT MY FRIENDS TO GO THROUGH THAT ANYMORE!
HOLD ON...!

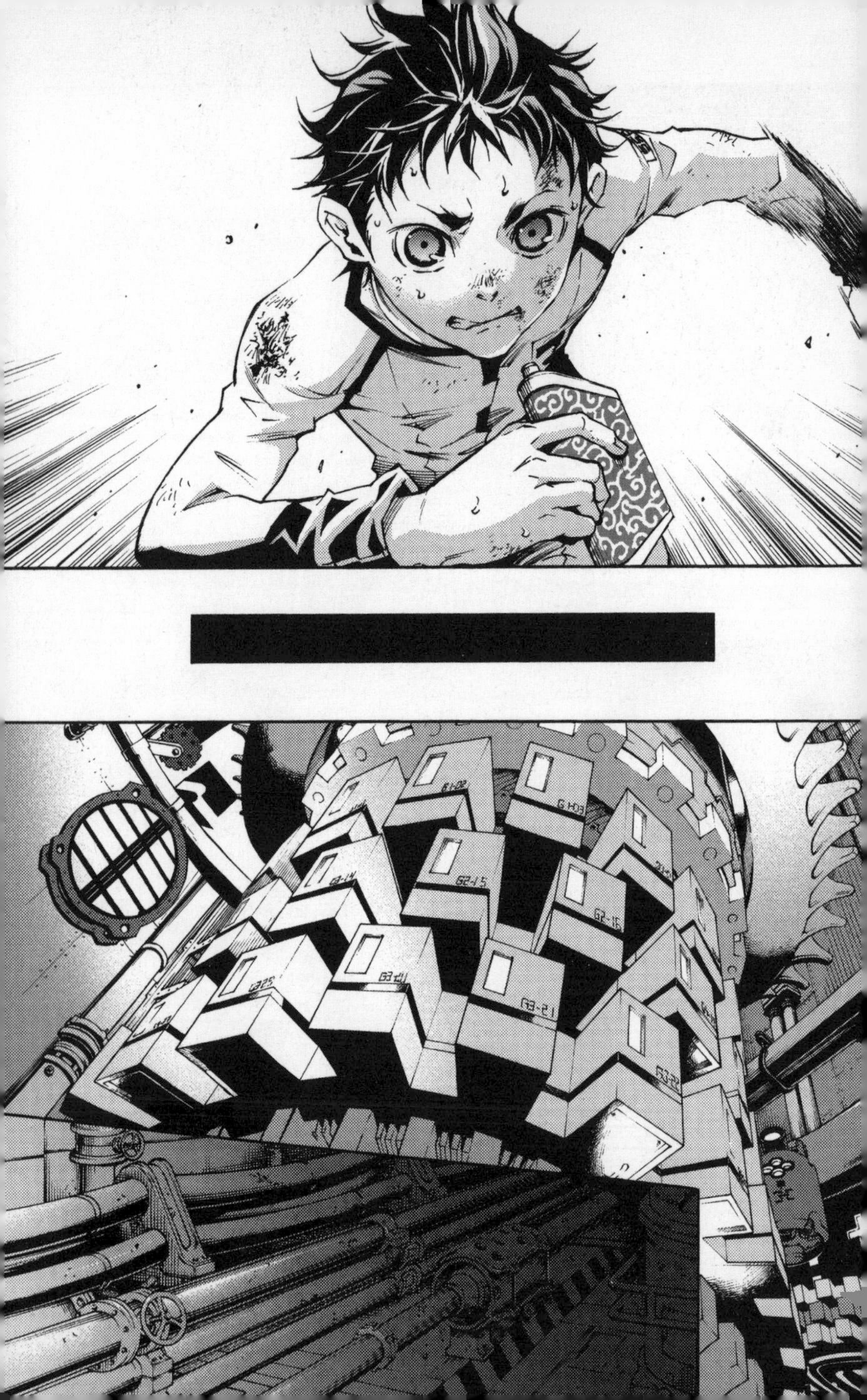
[redacted]

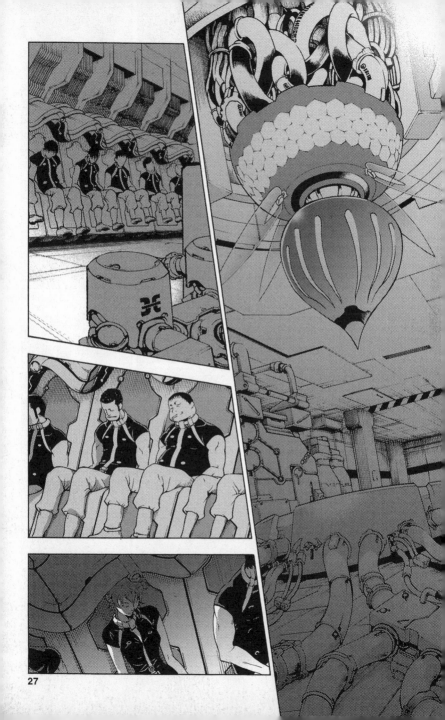

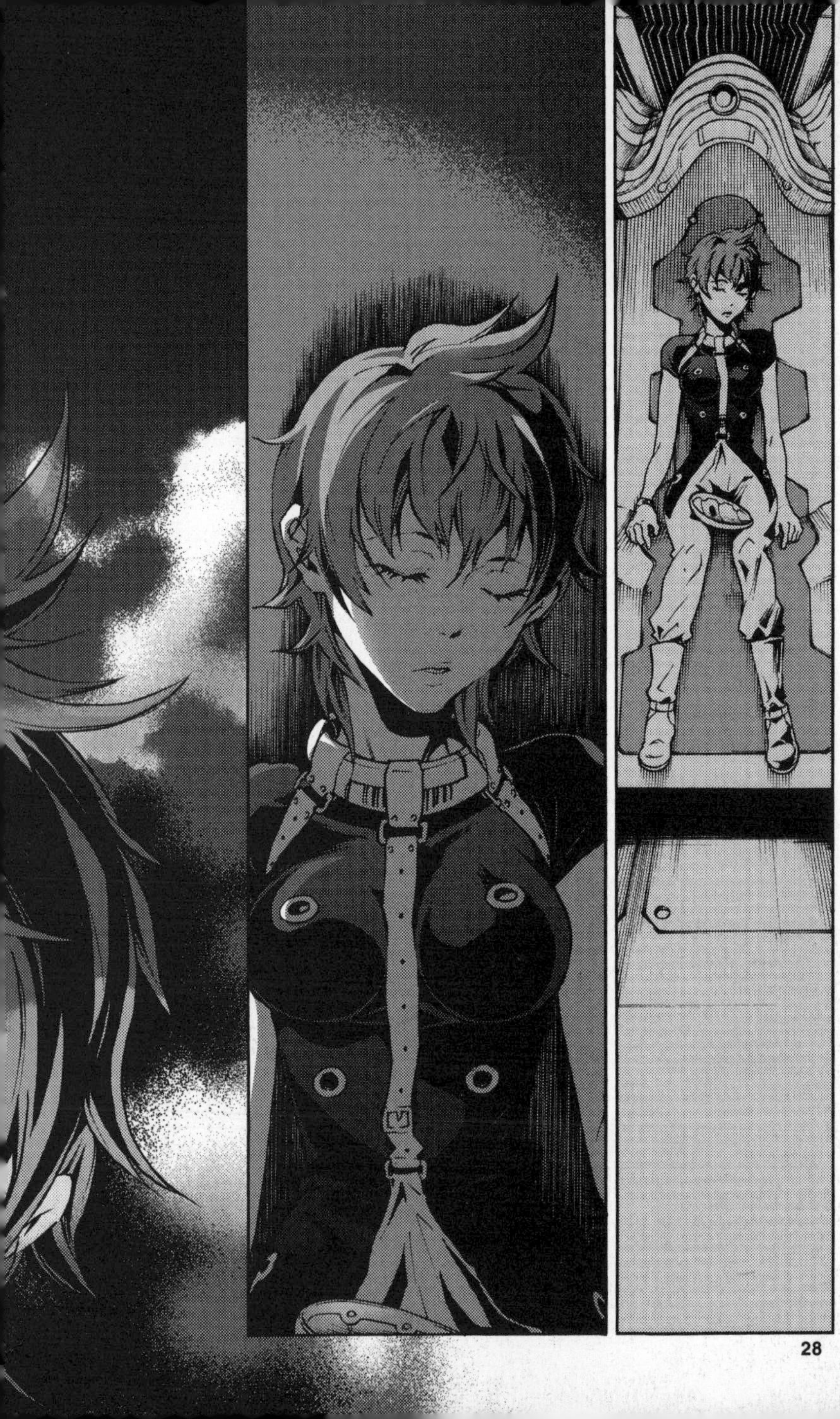

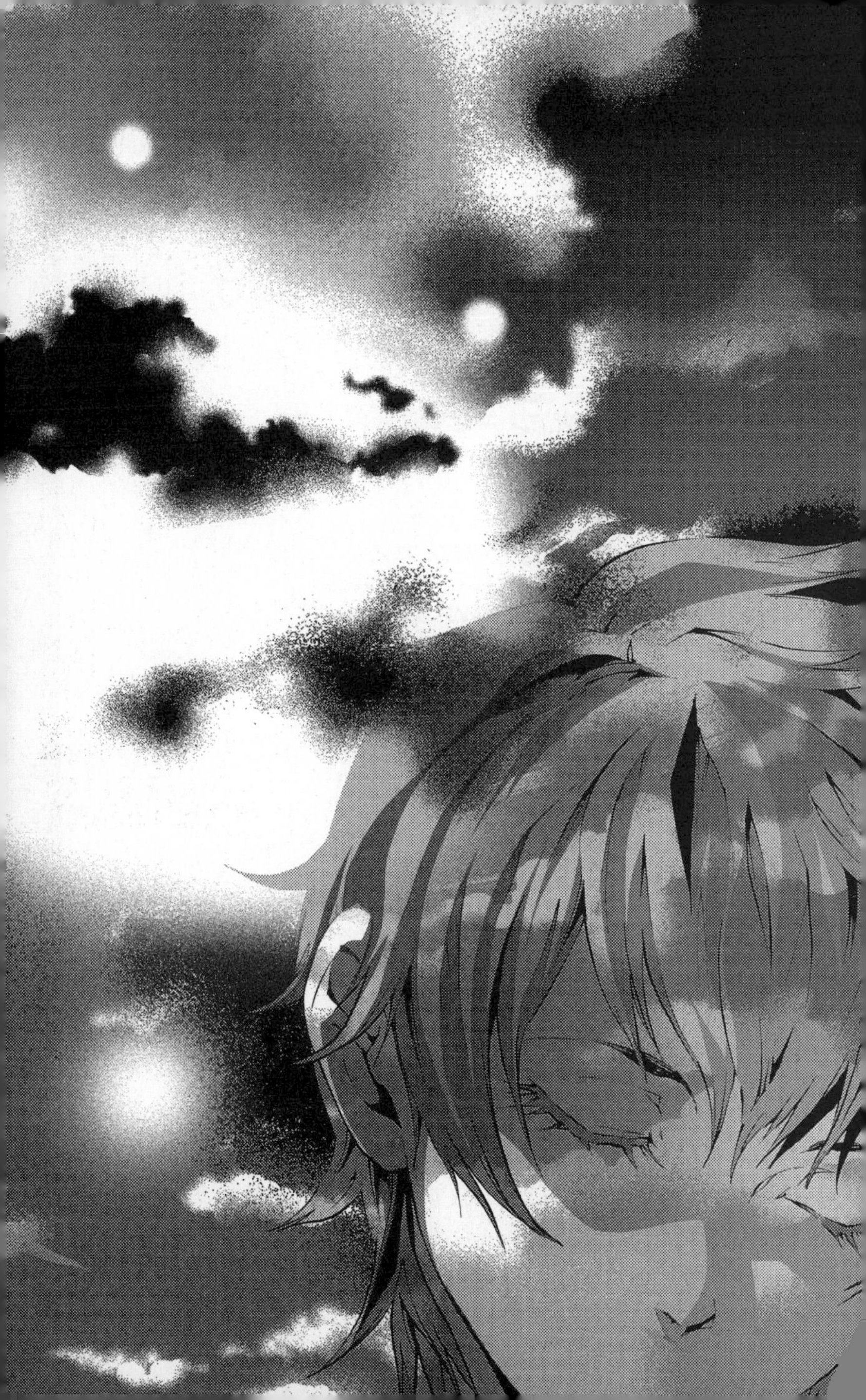

AT FIRST,
I CRIED BECAUSE
OF THE SHOCK.

THE SECOND TIME,
I CRIED FROM
THE PAIN.

THE THIRD TIME,
I CRIED BECAUSE
MOM AND DAD
DIDN'T NOTICE.

THE FOURTH TIME,
I CRIED WHEN
I REALIZED THEY
WERE IGNORING ME.

THE FIFTH TIME,
I CRIED BECAUSE
I WAS MISERABLE.

THE SIXTH TIME...

...I JUST STOPPED CRYING.

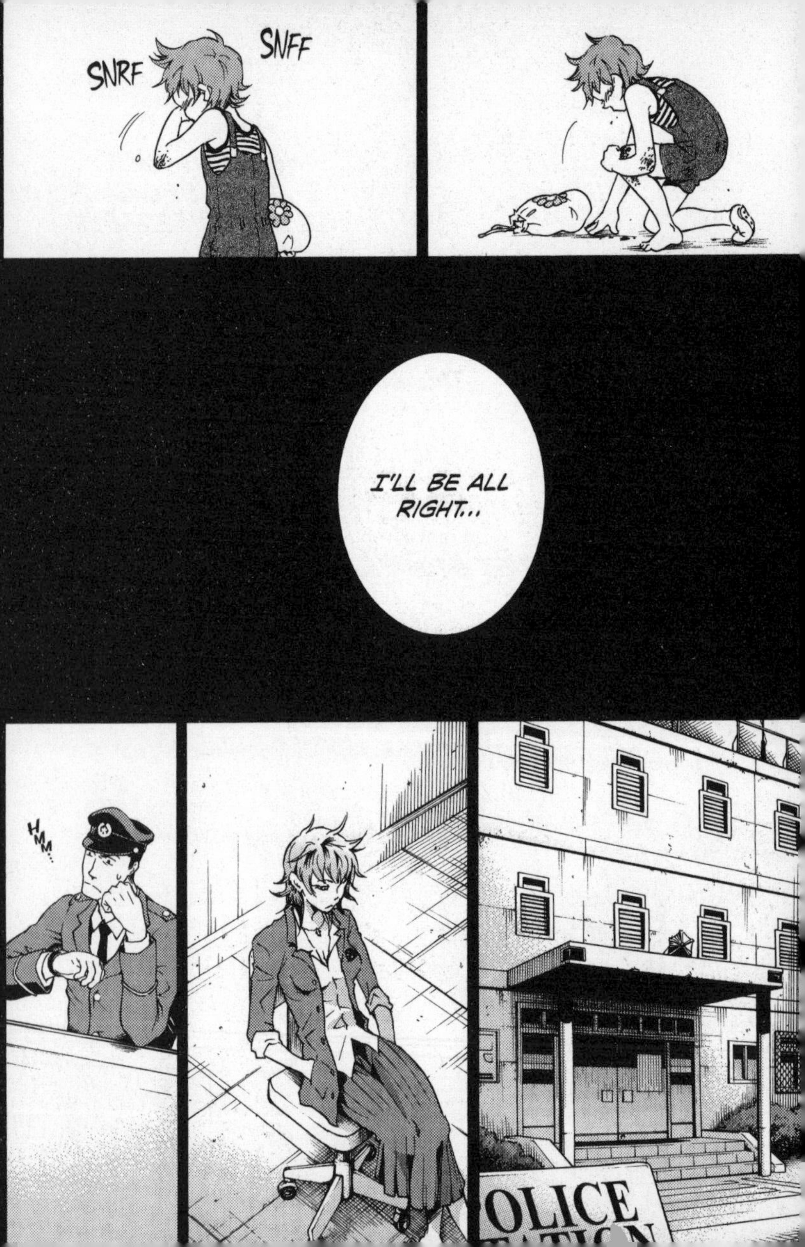
SNFF
SNRF
I'LL BE ALL RIGHT...
OLICE
HMM..

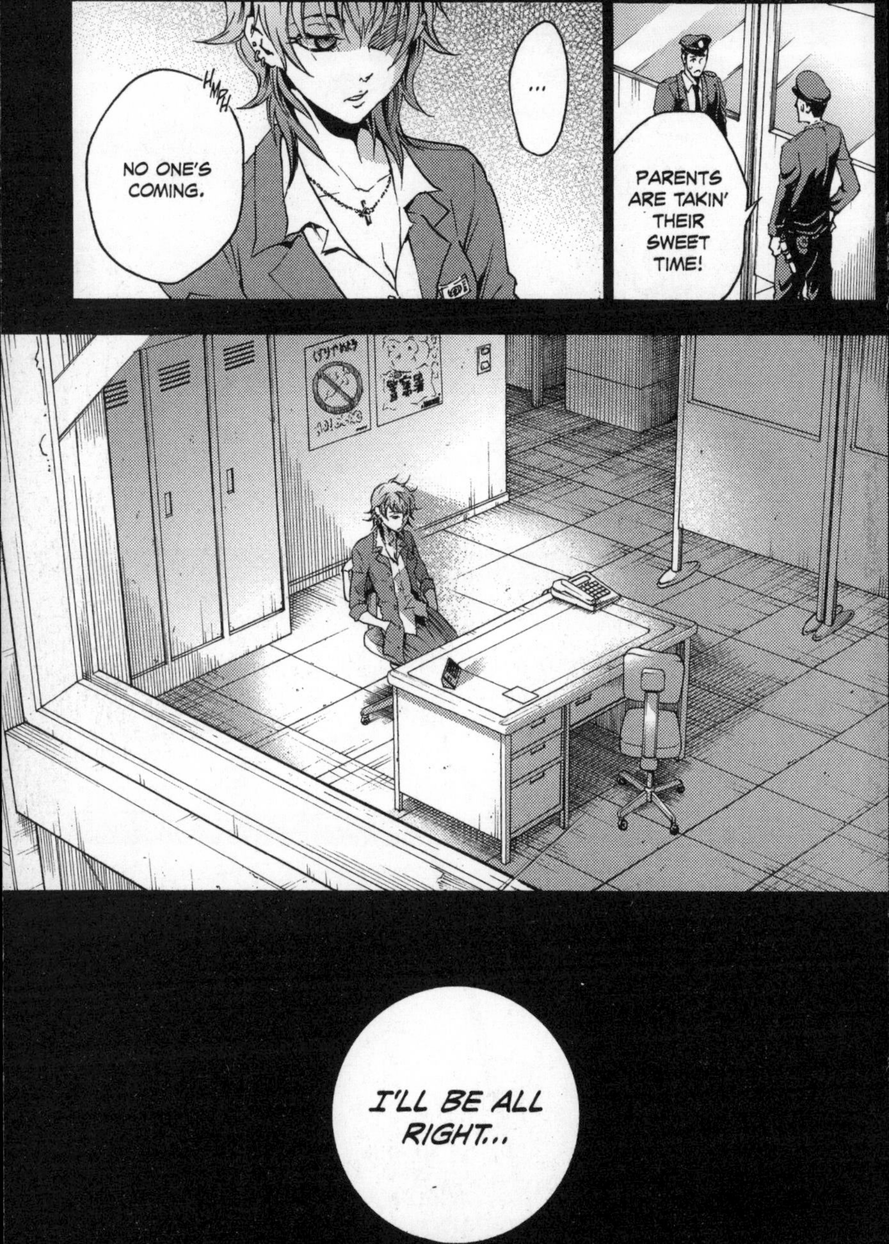
PARENTS ARE TAKIN' THEIR SWEET TIME!
...
HMPH
NO ONE'S COMING.
I'LL BE ALL RIGHT...

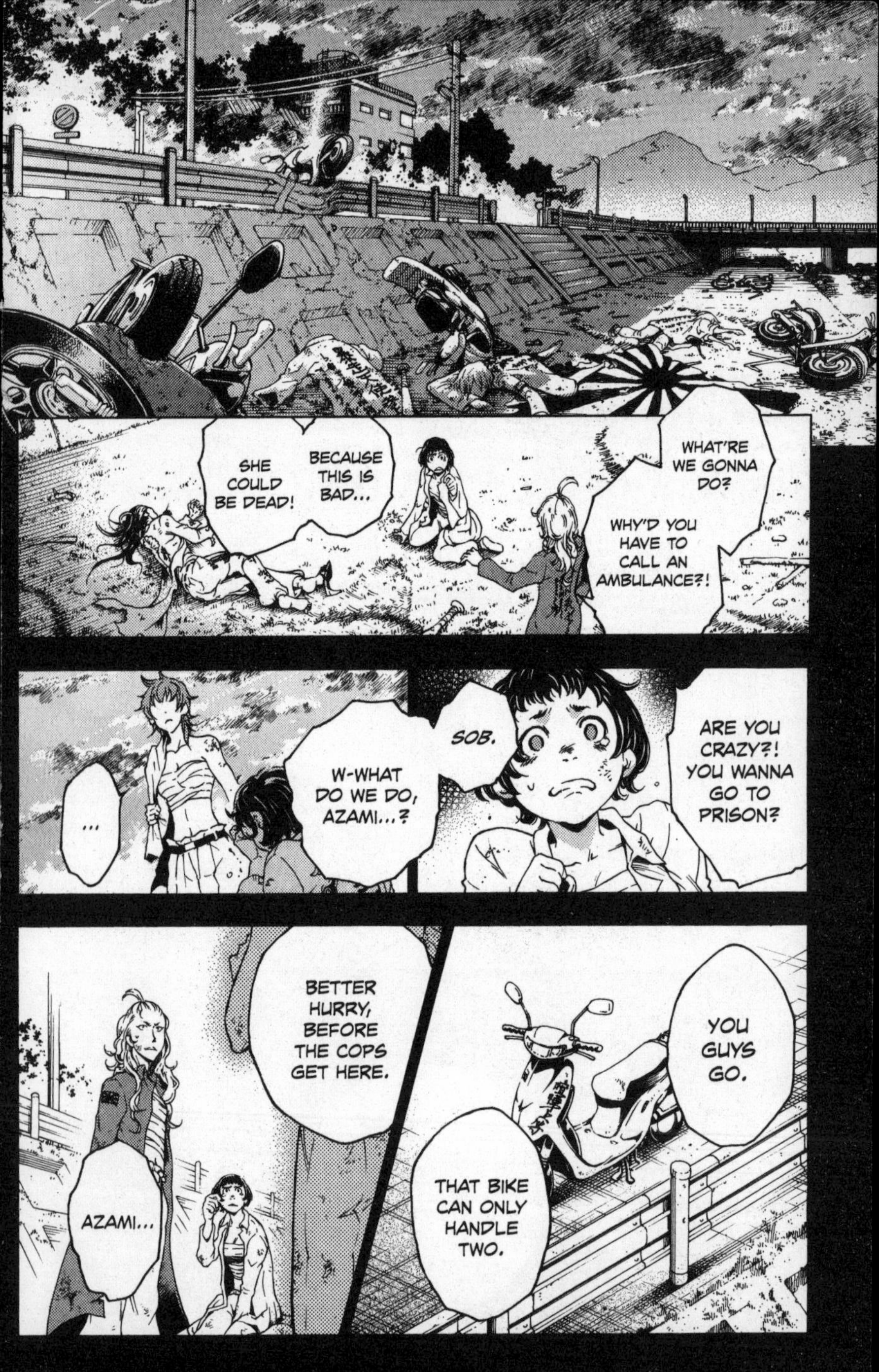
WHAT'RE WE GONNA DO?
WHY'D YOU HAVE TO CALL AN AMBULANCE?!
BECAUSE THIS IS BAD...
SHE COULD BE DEAD!
ARE YOU CRAZY?! YOU WANNA GO TO PRISON?
SOB.
W-WHAT DO WE DO, AZAMI...?
...
YOU GUYS GO.
THAT BIKE CAN ONLY HANDLE TWO.
BETTER HURRY, BEFORE THE COPS GET HERE.
AZAMI...

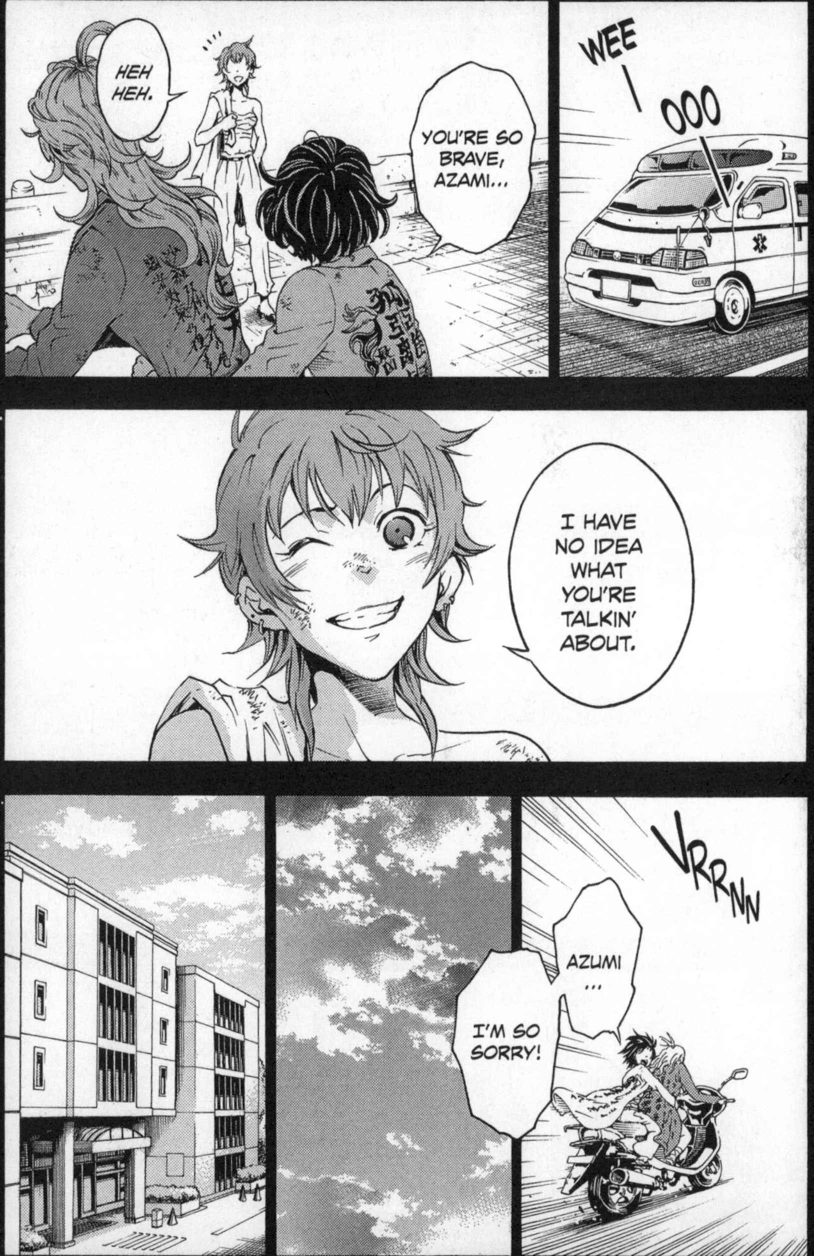
WEE-OOO
YOU'RE SO BRAVE, AZAMI...
HEH HEH.
I HAVE NO IDEA WHAT YOU'RE TALKIN' ABOUT.
VRRNN
AZUMI...
I'M SO SORRY!

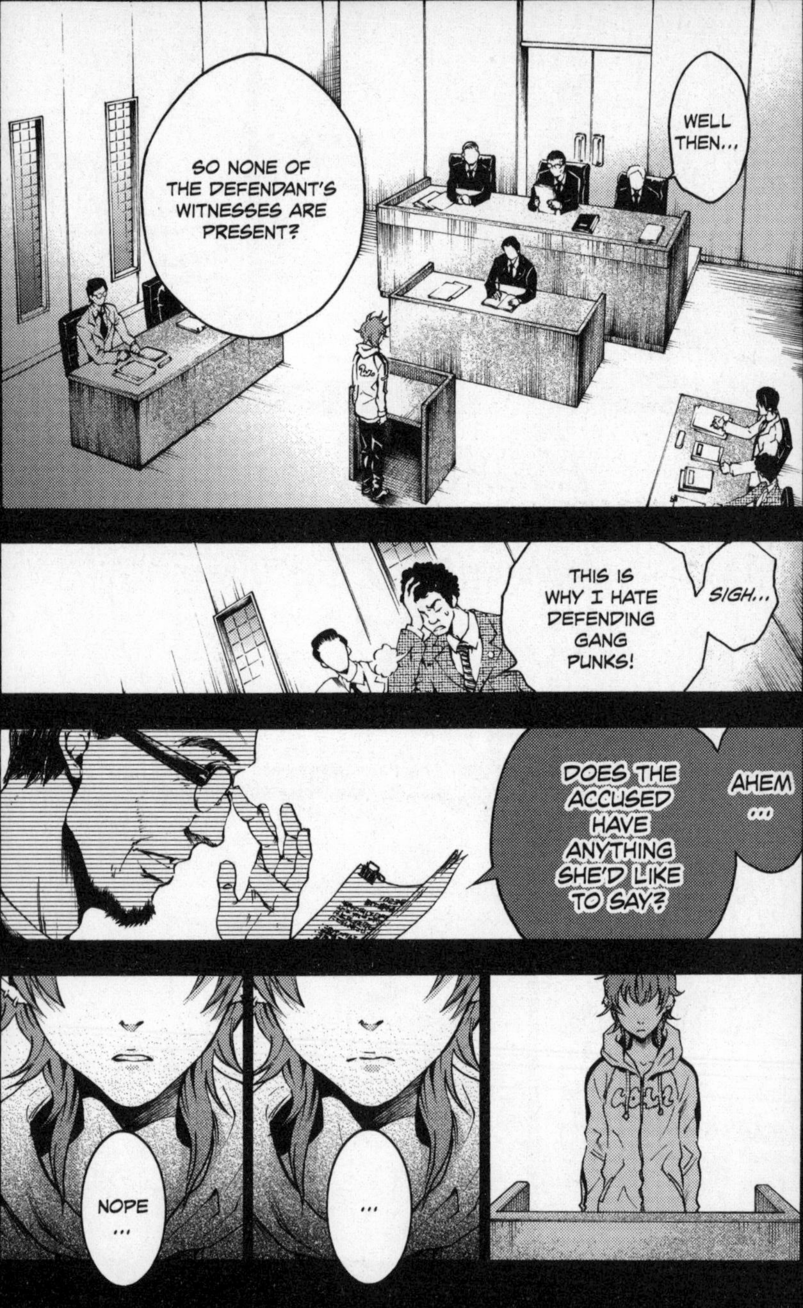
WELL THEN...
SO NONE OF THE DEFENDANT'S WITNESSES ARE PRESENT?
SIGH...
THIS IS WHY I HATE DEFENDING GANG PUNKS!
AHEM ...
DOES THE ACCUSED HAVE ANYTHING SHE'D LIKE TO SAY?
...
NOPE ...

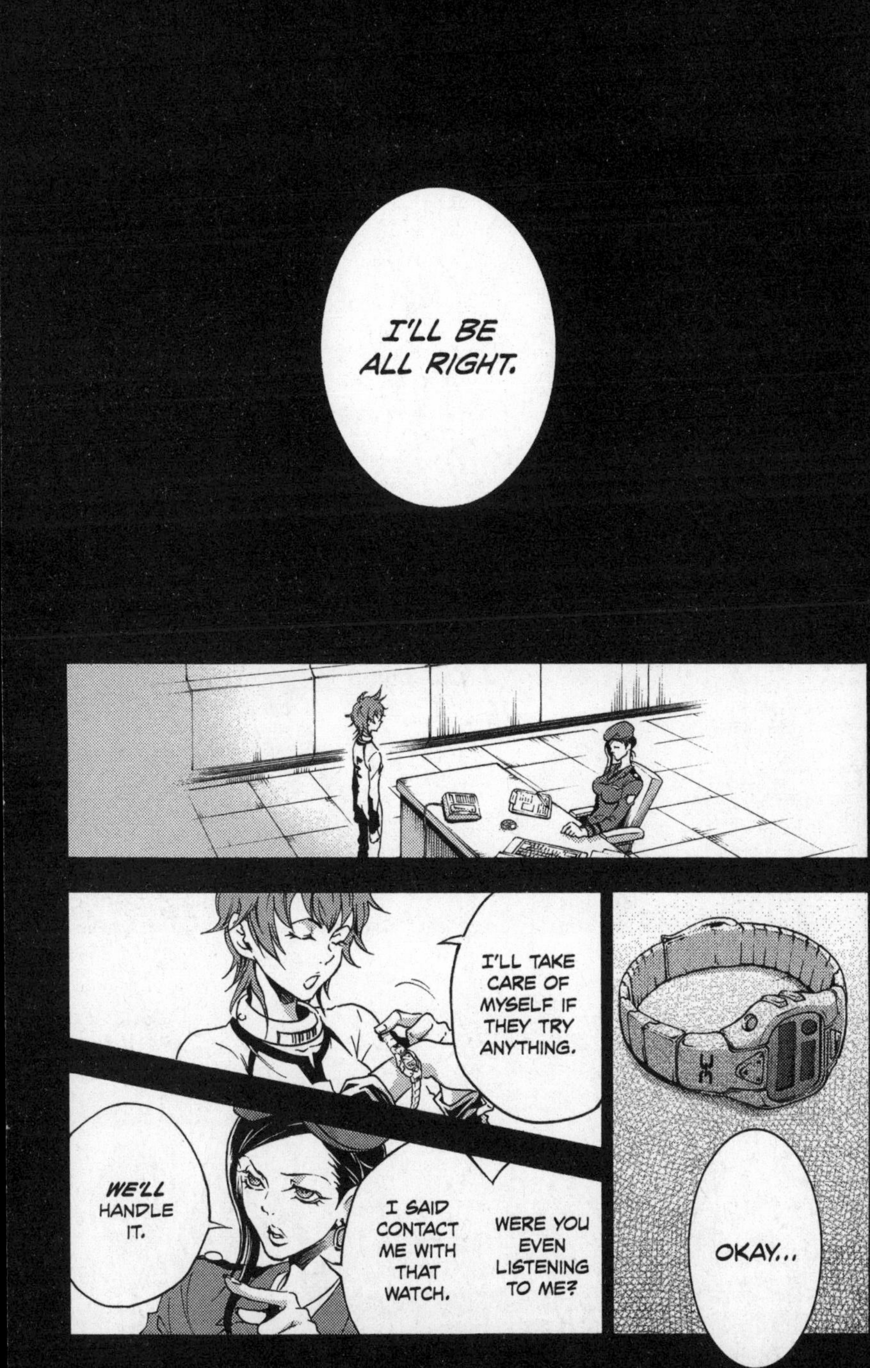
I'LL BE ALL RIGHT.
OKAY...
I'LL TAKE CARE OF MYSELF IF THEY TRY ANYTHING.
WERE YOU EVEN LISTENING TO ME?
I SAID CONTACT ME WITH THAT WATCH.
WE'LL HANDLE IT.

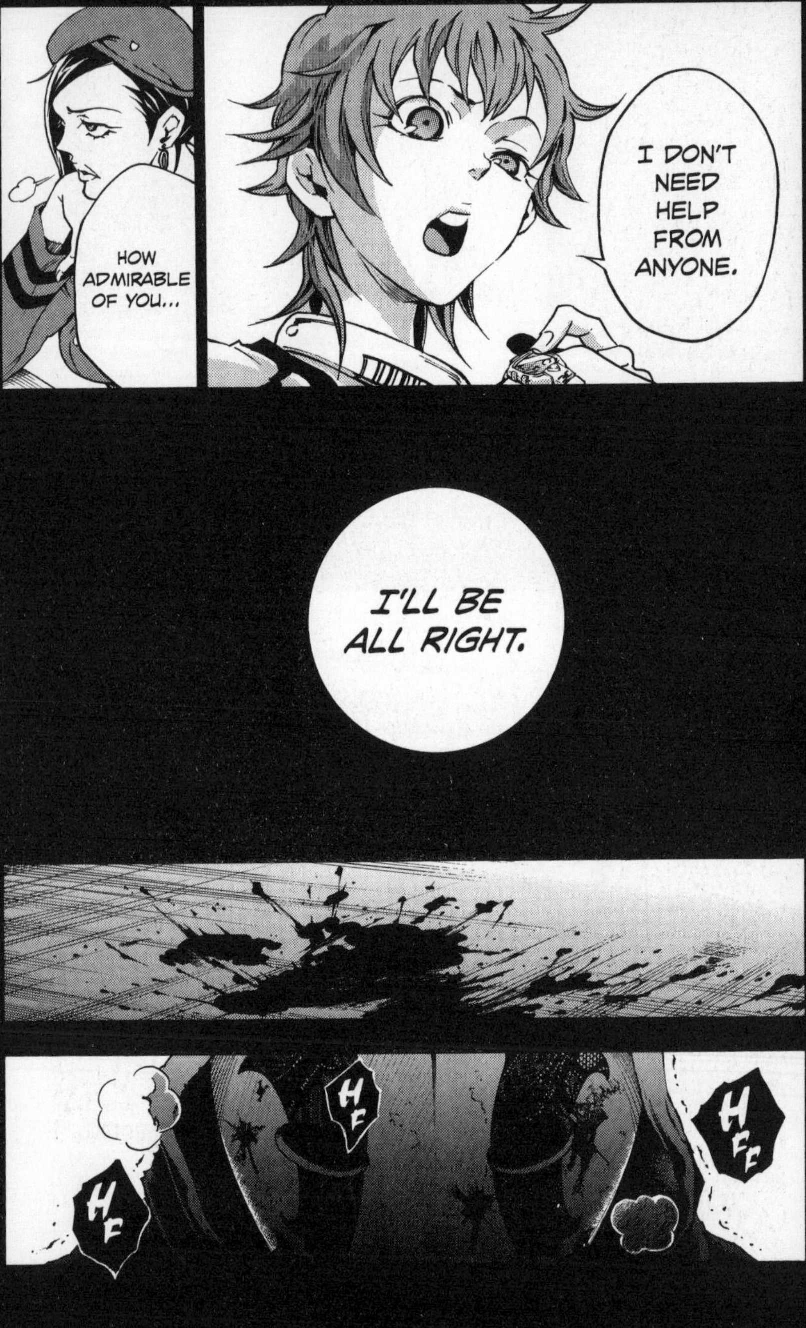
I DON'T NEED HELP FROM ANYONE.
HOW ADMIRABLE OF YOU...
I'LL BE ALL RIGHT.
HFF
HF
HF

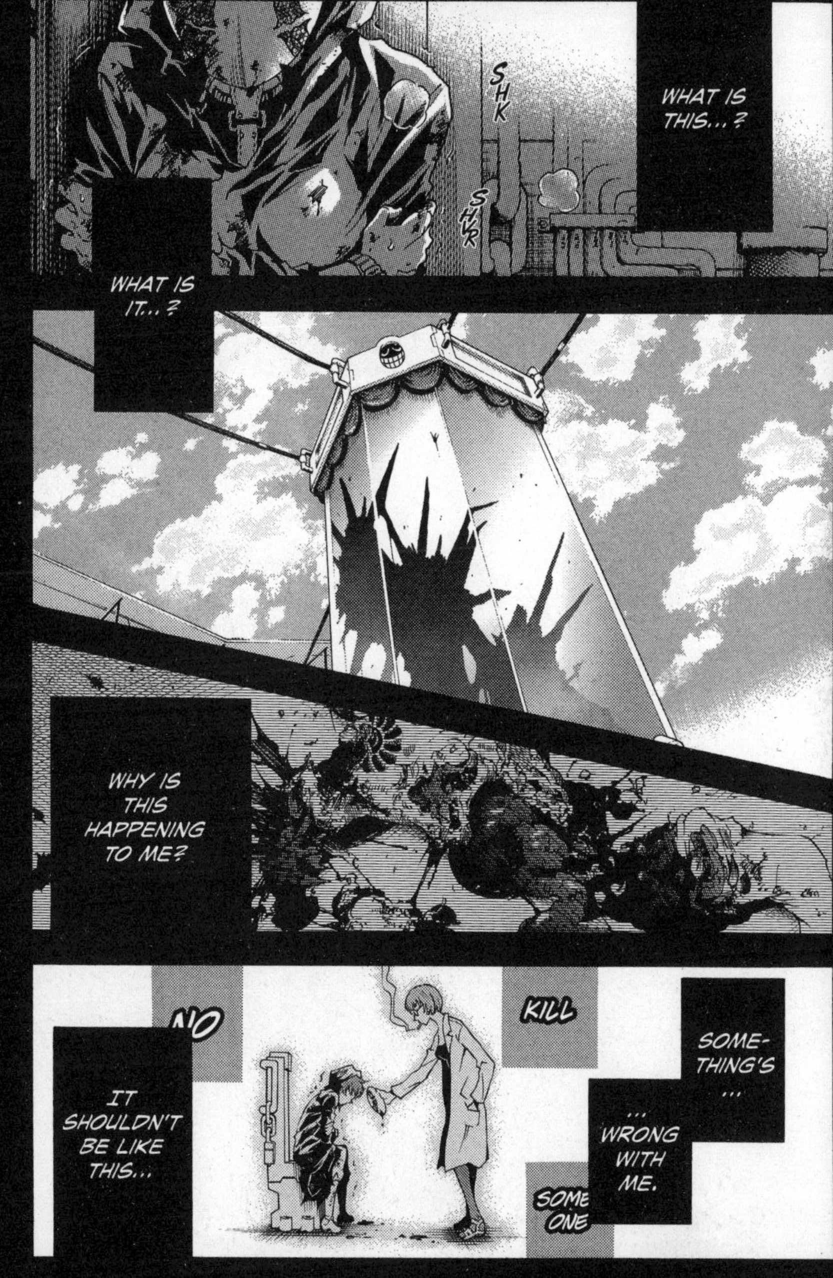
WHAT IS THIS...?
SHK
SHKR
WHAT IS IT...?
WHY IS THIS HAPPENING TO ME?
SOME-THING'S...
KILL
...WRONG WITH ME.
SOME ONE
NO
IT SHOULDN'T BE LIKE THIS...

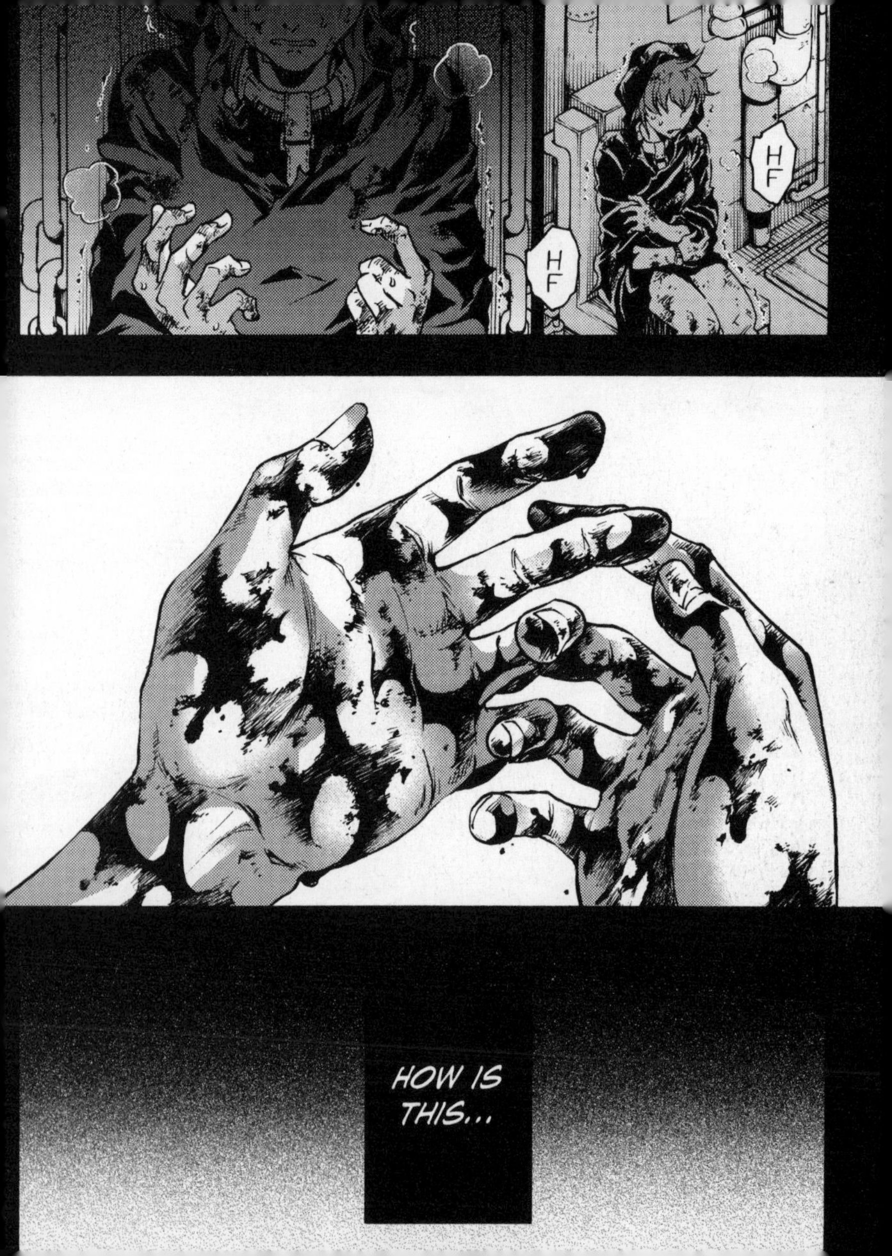
HF
HF
HOW IS THIS...

... "ALL RIGHT"?

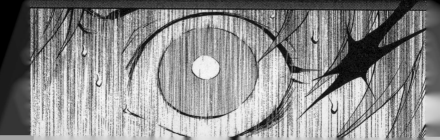

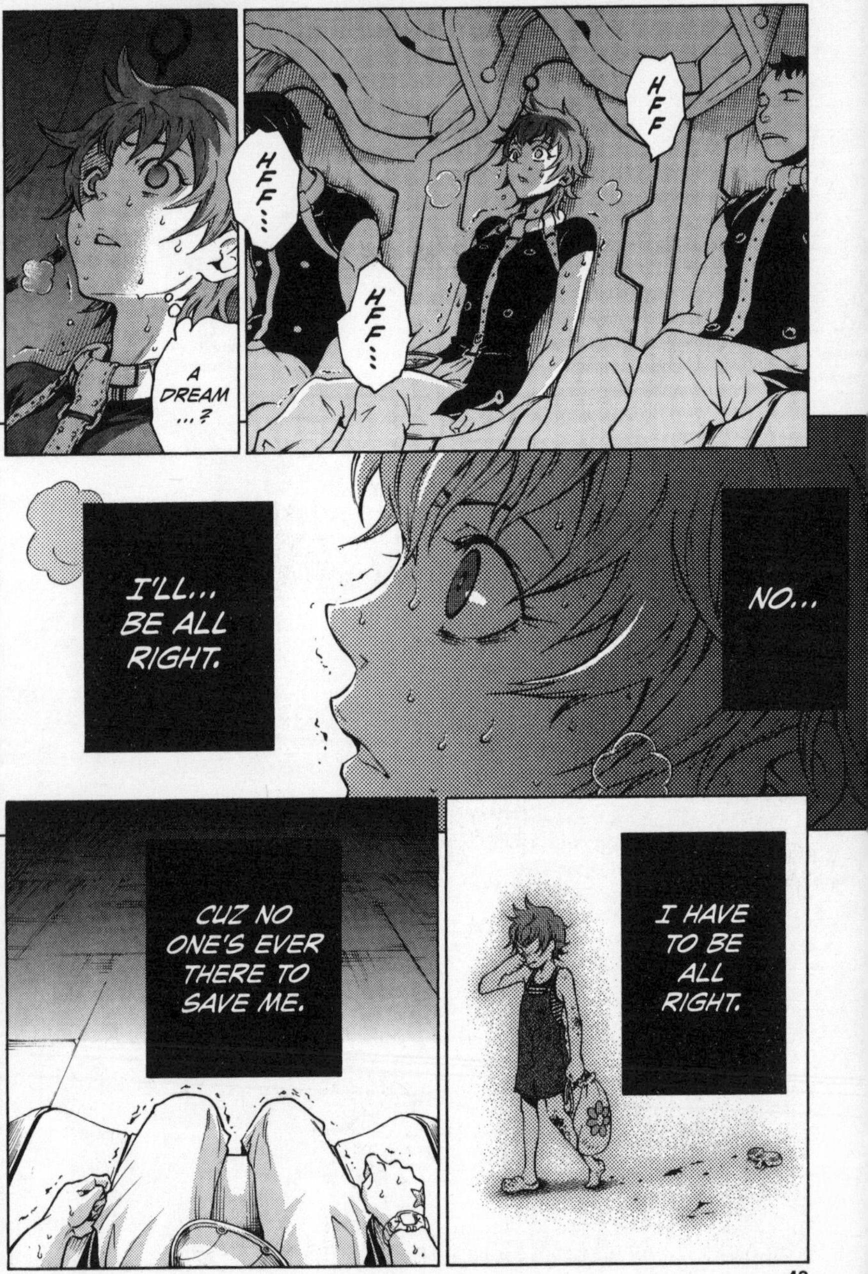
HFF
HFF...
HFF...
A DREAM ...?
NO...
I'LL... BE ALL RIGHT.
I HAVE TO BE ALL RIGHT.
CUZ NO ONE'S EVER THERE TO SAVE ME.

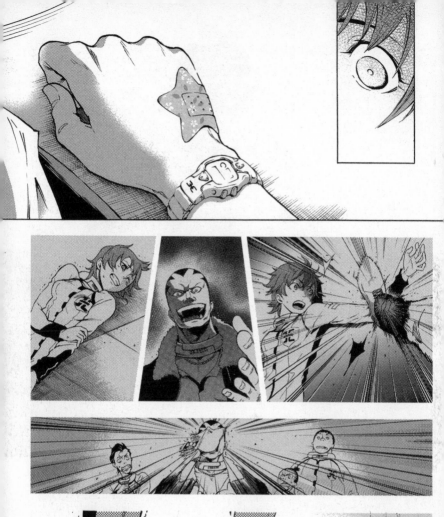
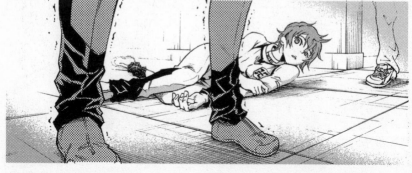

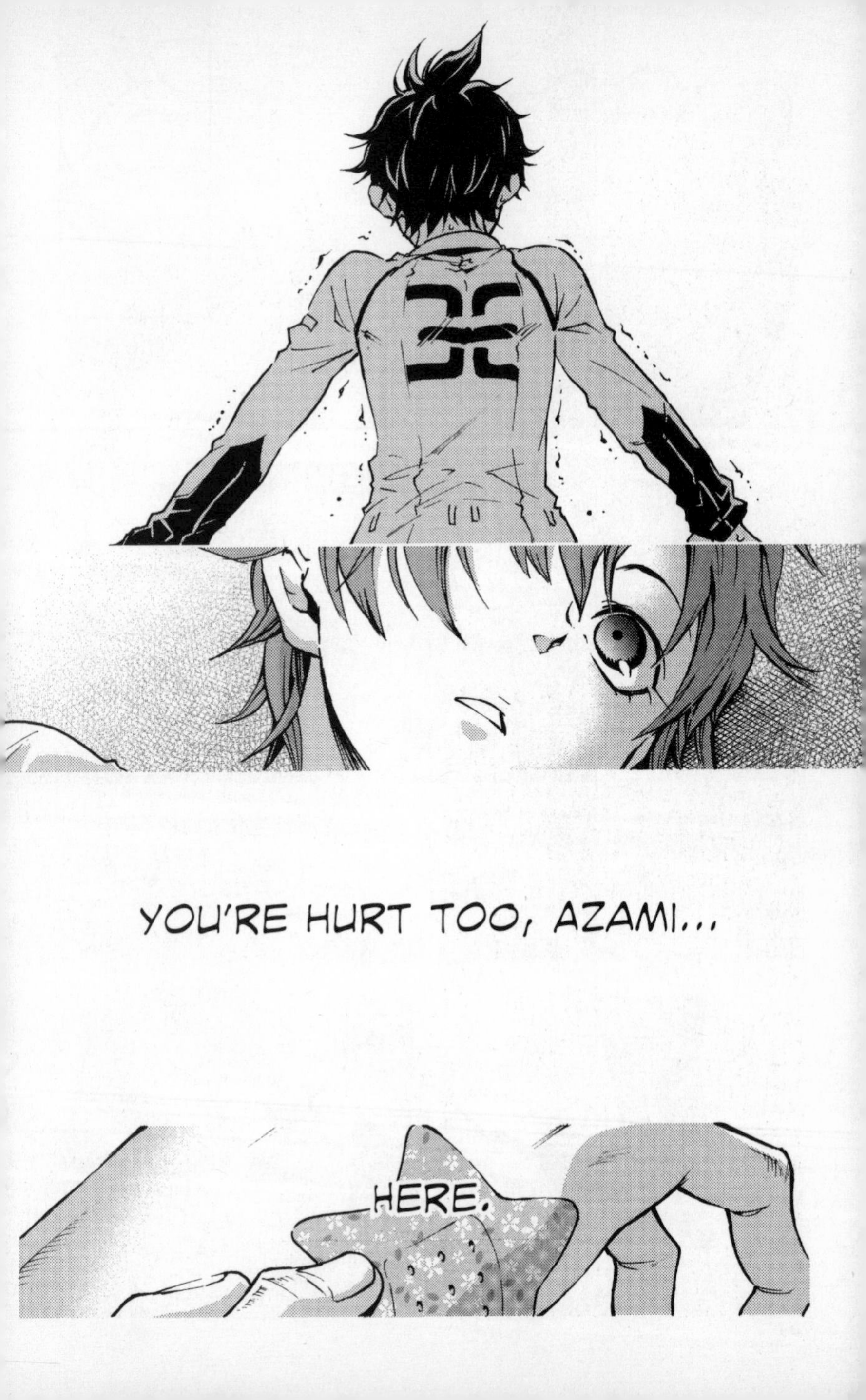
YOU'RE HURT TOO, AZAMI...
HERE.

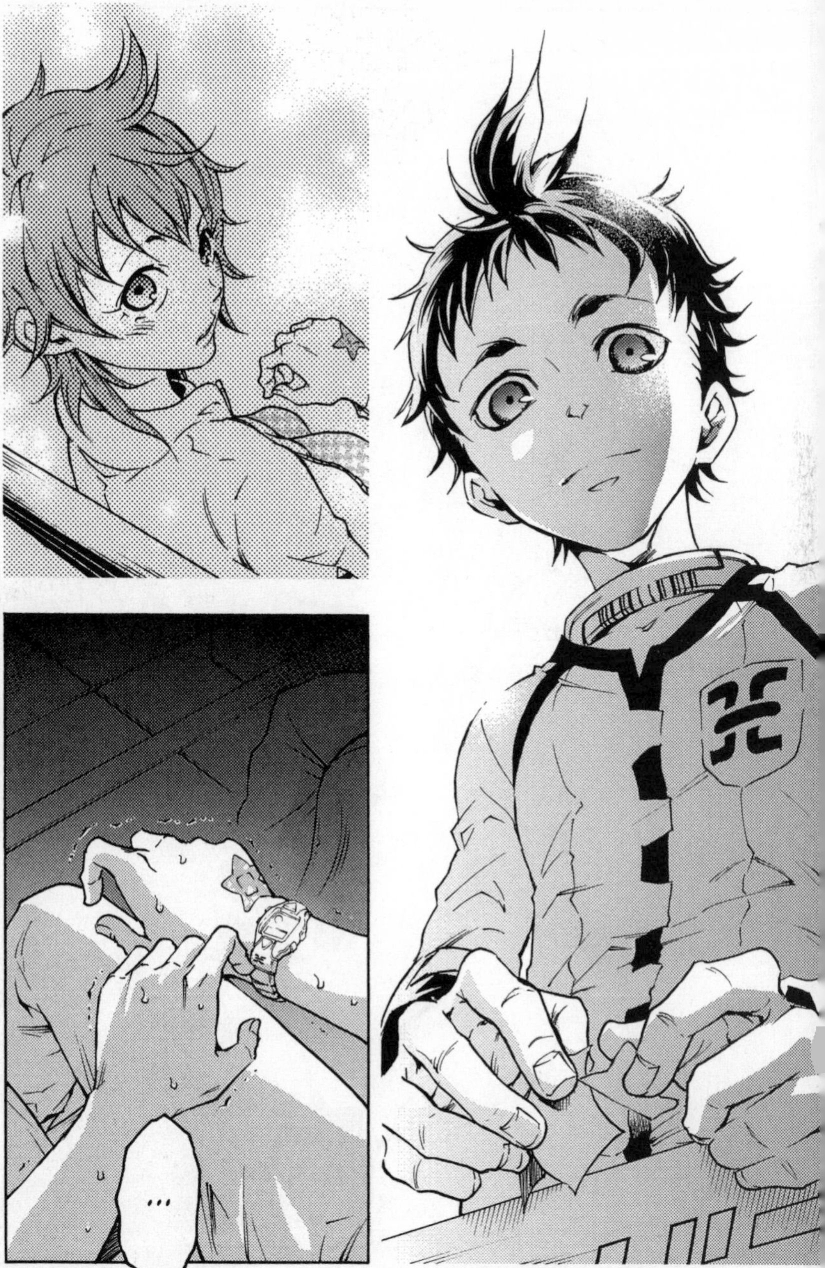
…

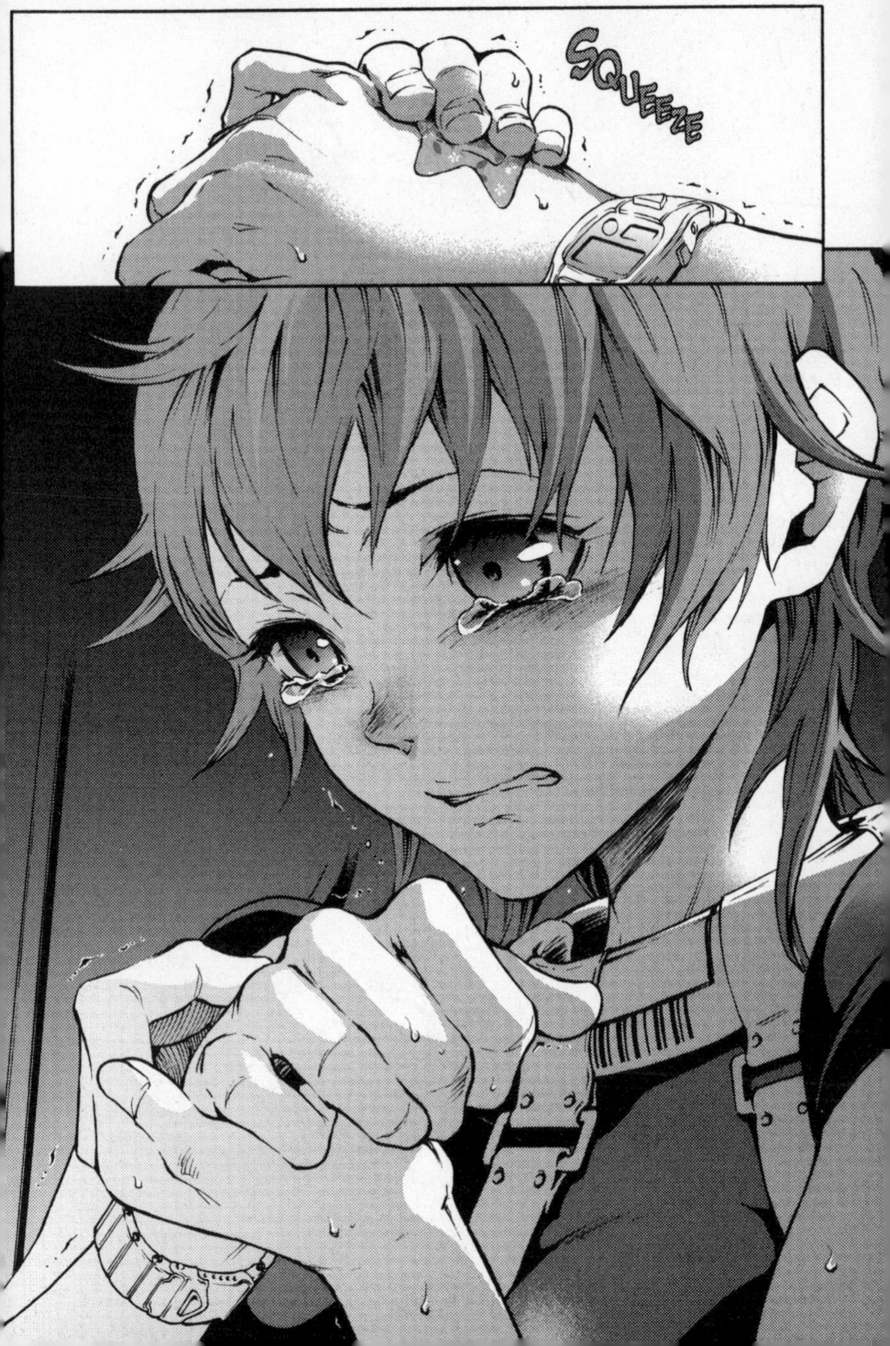
SQUEEEZE

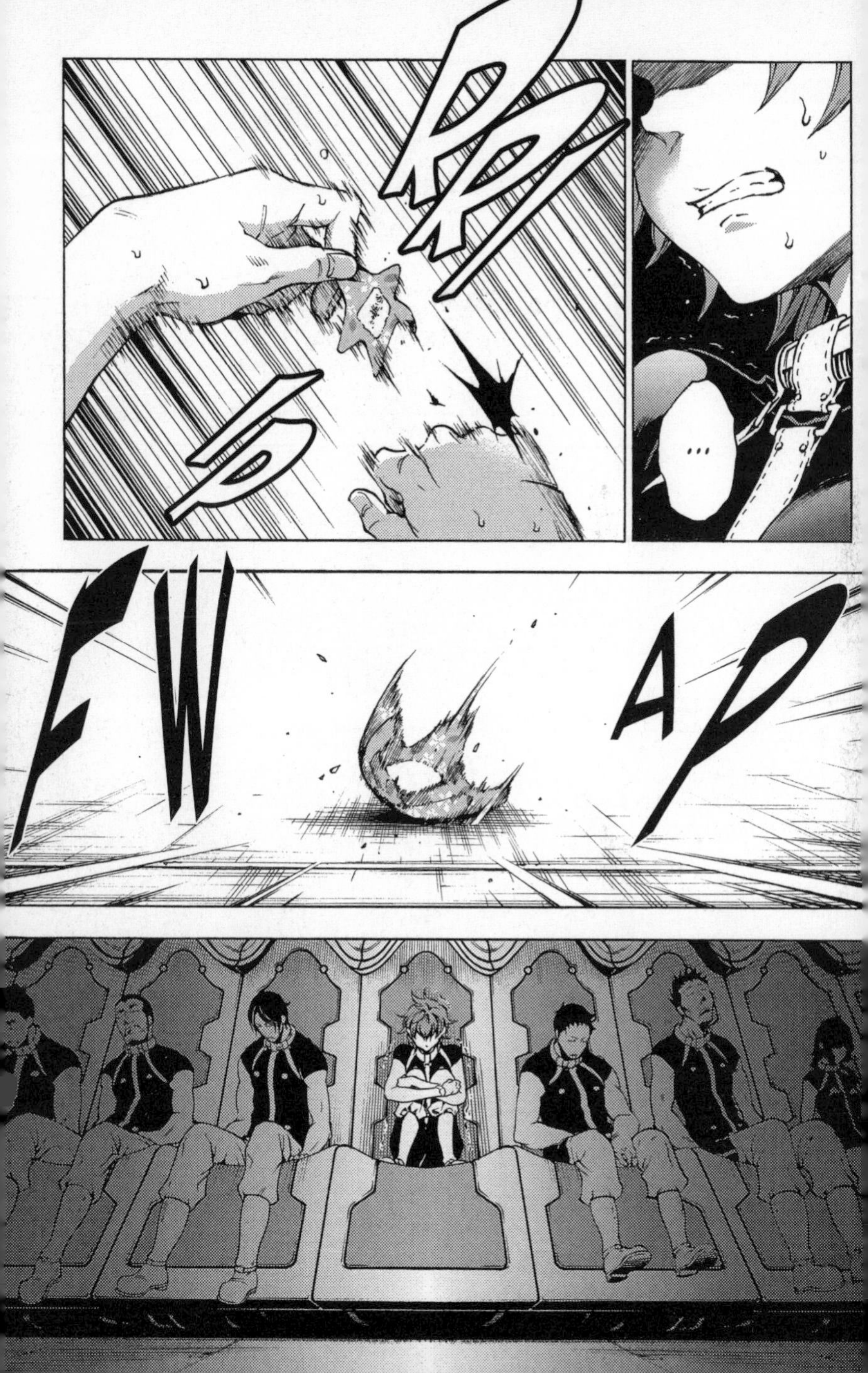
...
RRIP
FWAP

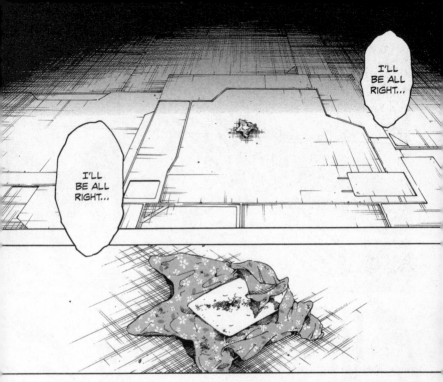

I'LL BE ALL RIGHT...

I'LL BE ALL RIGHT...

WHAT?

DOCTOR!

BREE

BREE

SECURITY

Unknown

VWRMM

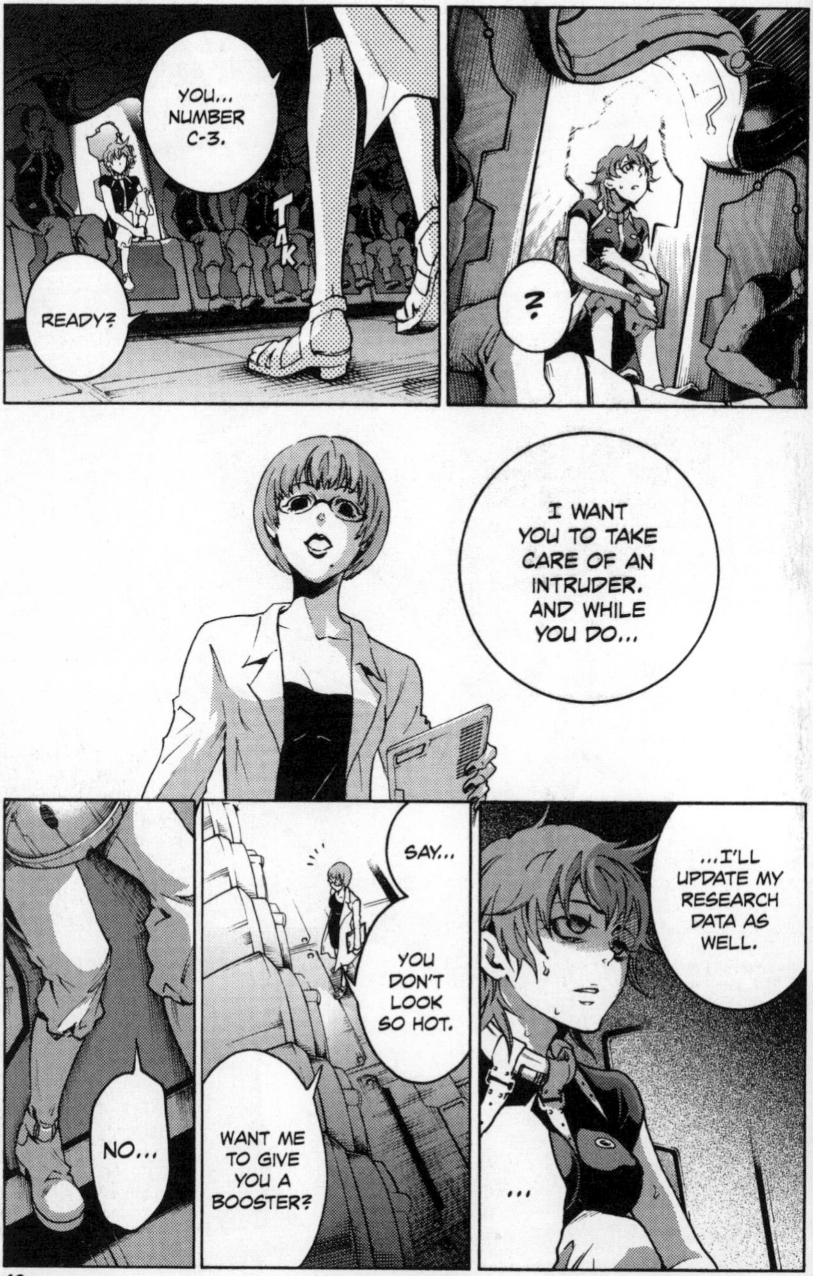
?
YOU... NUMBER C-3.
TAK
READY?
I WANT YOU TO TAKE CARE OF AN INTRUDER. AND WHILE YOU DO...
...I'LL UPDATE MY RESEARCH DATA AS WELL.
...
SAY...
YOU DON'T LOOK SO HOT.
WANT ME TO GIVE YOU A BOOSTER?
NO...

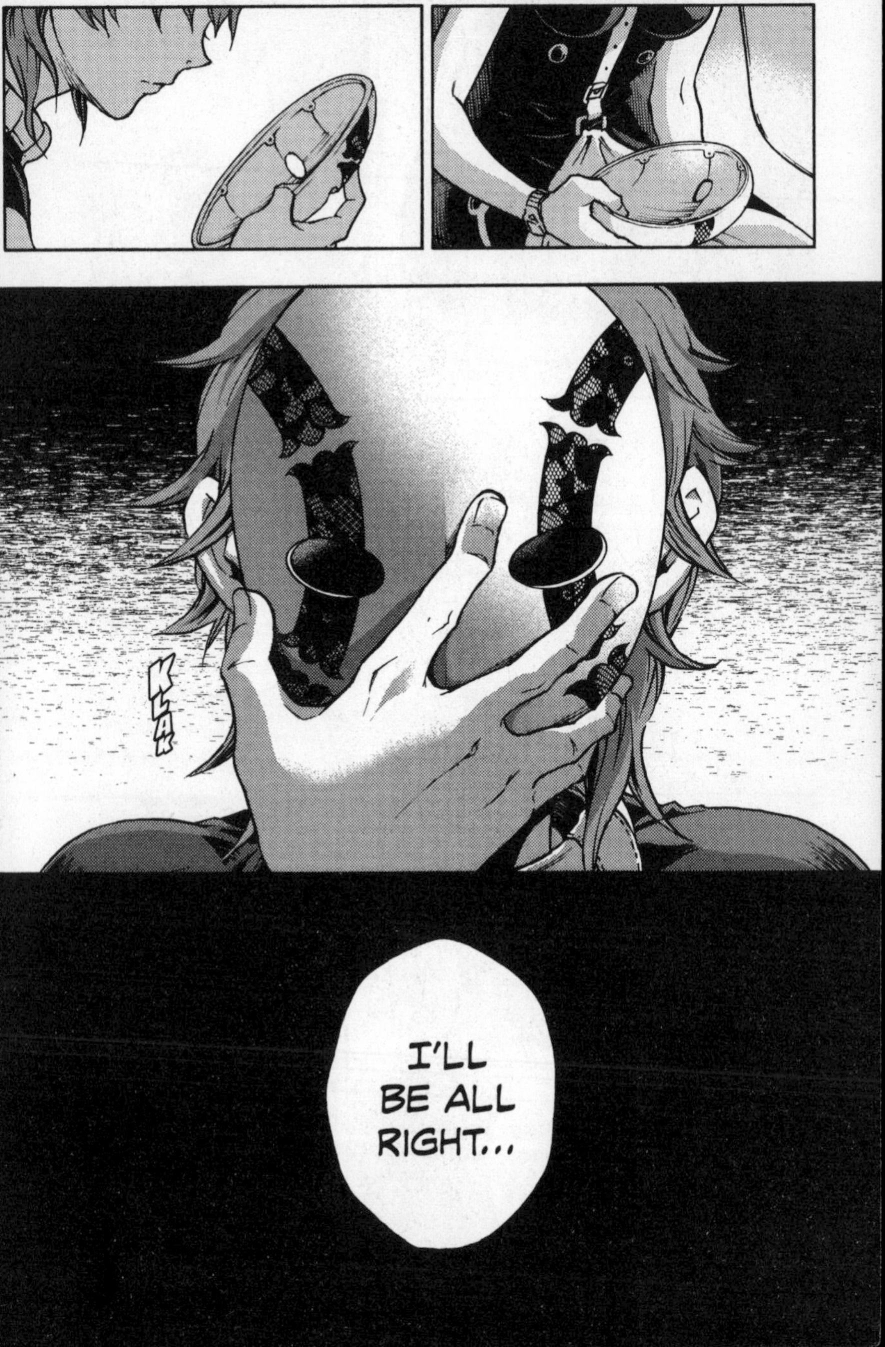
KLAK
I'LL BE ALL RIGHT...

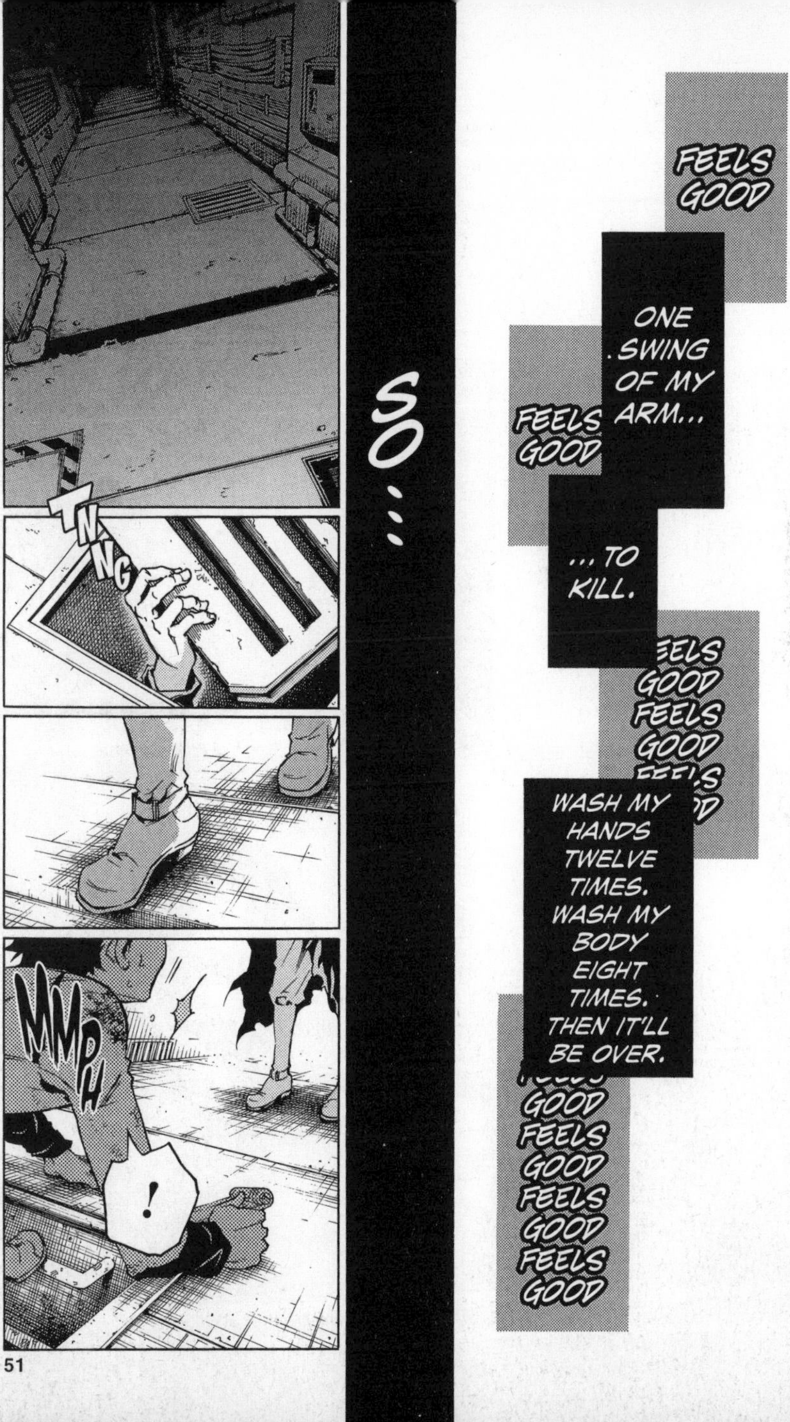
FEELS GOOD
ONE SWING OF MY ARM...
FEELS GOOD
...TO KILL.
GOOD FEELS GOOD
WASH MY HANDS TWELVE TIMES. WASH MY BODY EIGHT TIMES. THEN IT'LL BE OVER.
GOOD FEELS GOOD FEELS GOOD FEELS GOOD
SO...
TNNG
MMPH
!

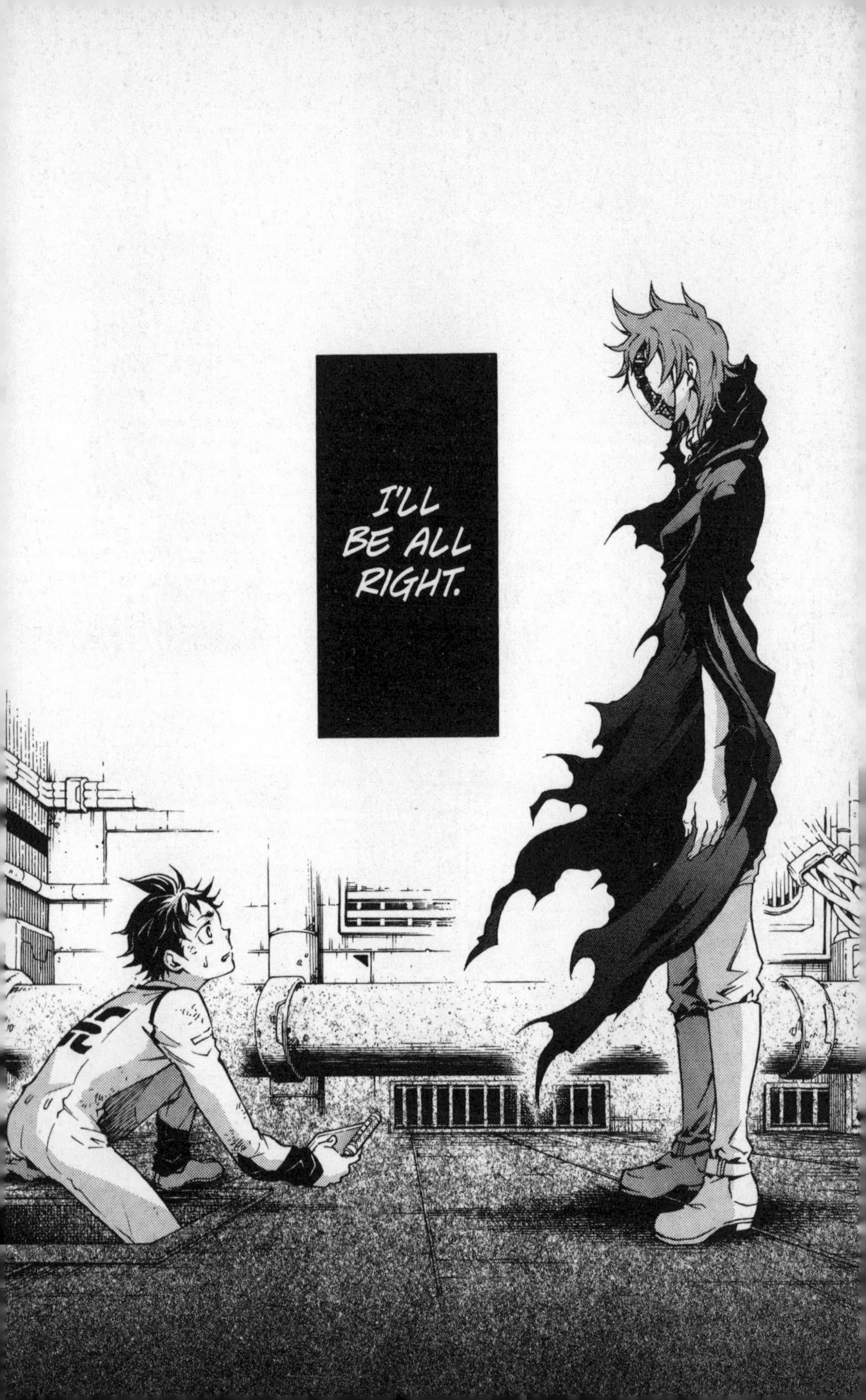
I'LL BE ALL RIGHT.

DEADMA
N WO
NDER LA
ND

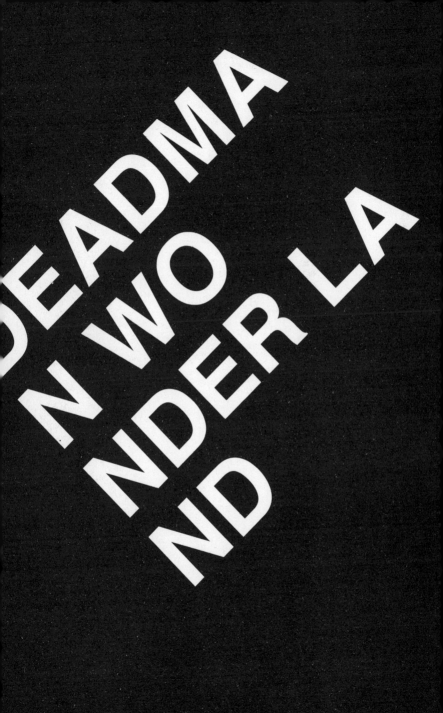

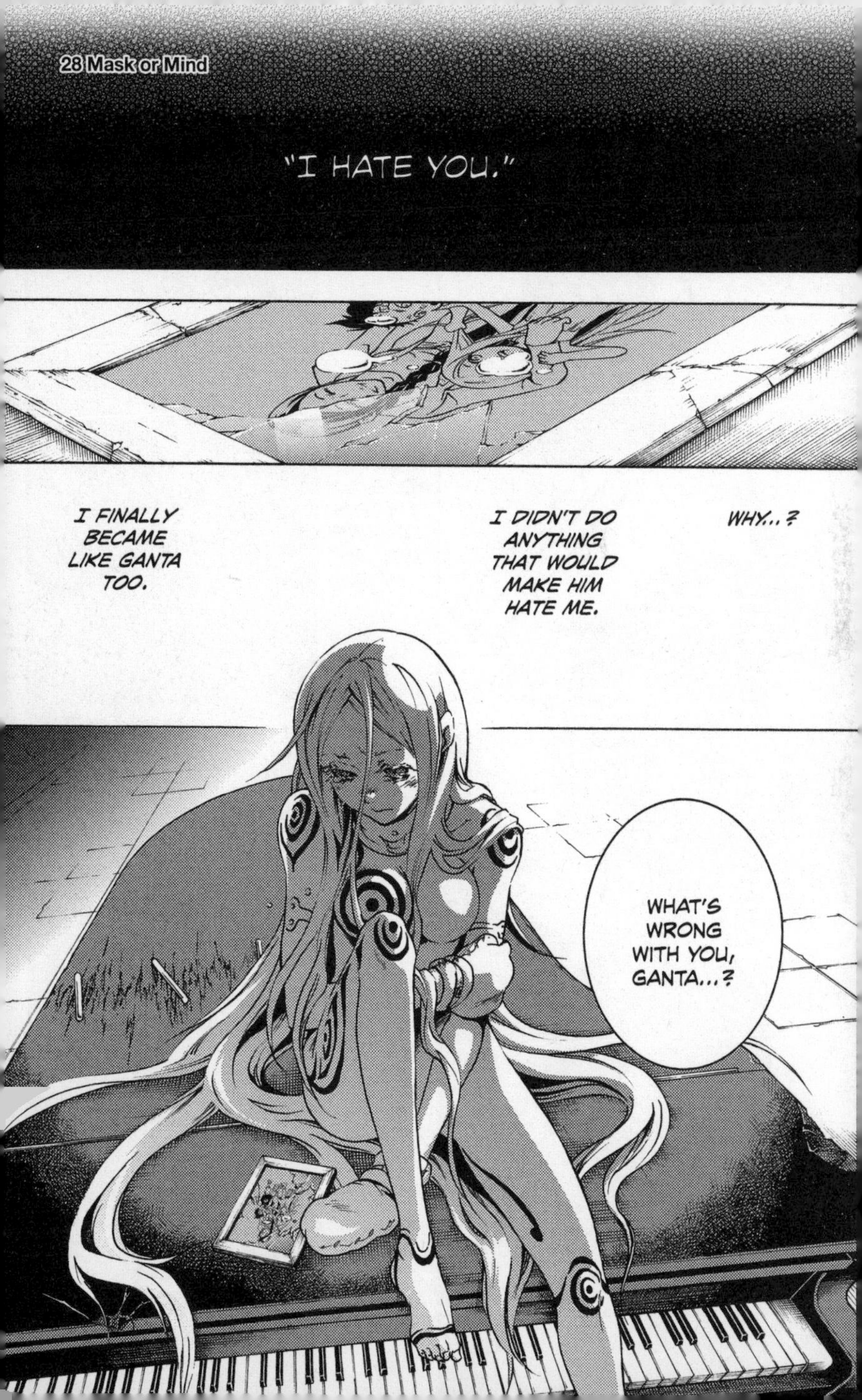
28 Mask or Mind
"I HATE YOU."
WHY...?
I DIDN'T DO ANYTHING THAT WOULD MAKE HIM HATE ME.
I FINALLY BECAME LIKE GANTA TOO.
WHAT'S WRONG WITH YOU, GANTA...?

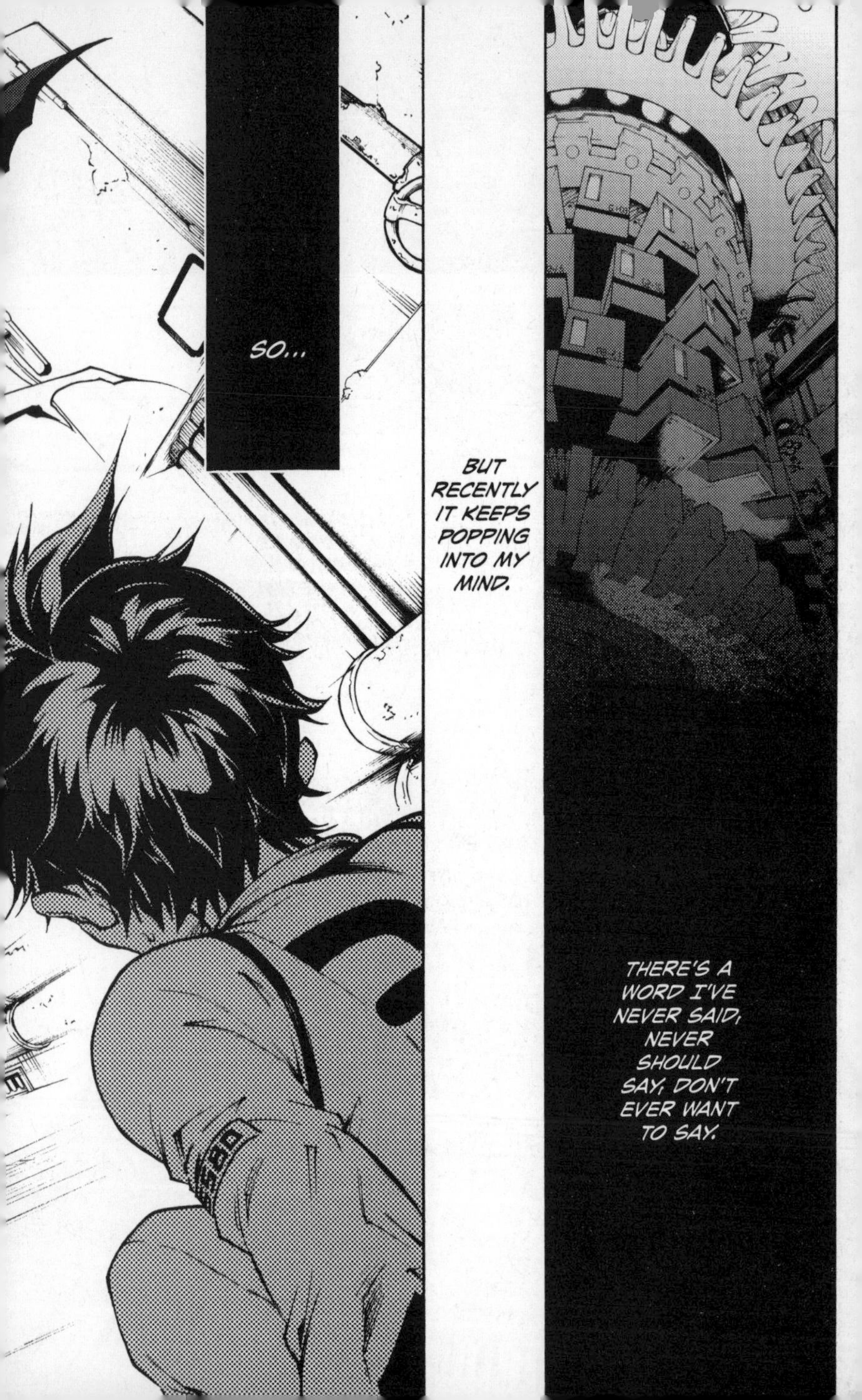

THERE'S A WORD I'VE NEVER SAID, NEVER SHOULD SAY, DON'T EVER WANT TO SAY.
BUT RECENTLY IT KEEPS POPPING INTO MY MIND.
SO...

28 Mask or Mind

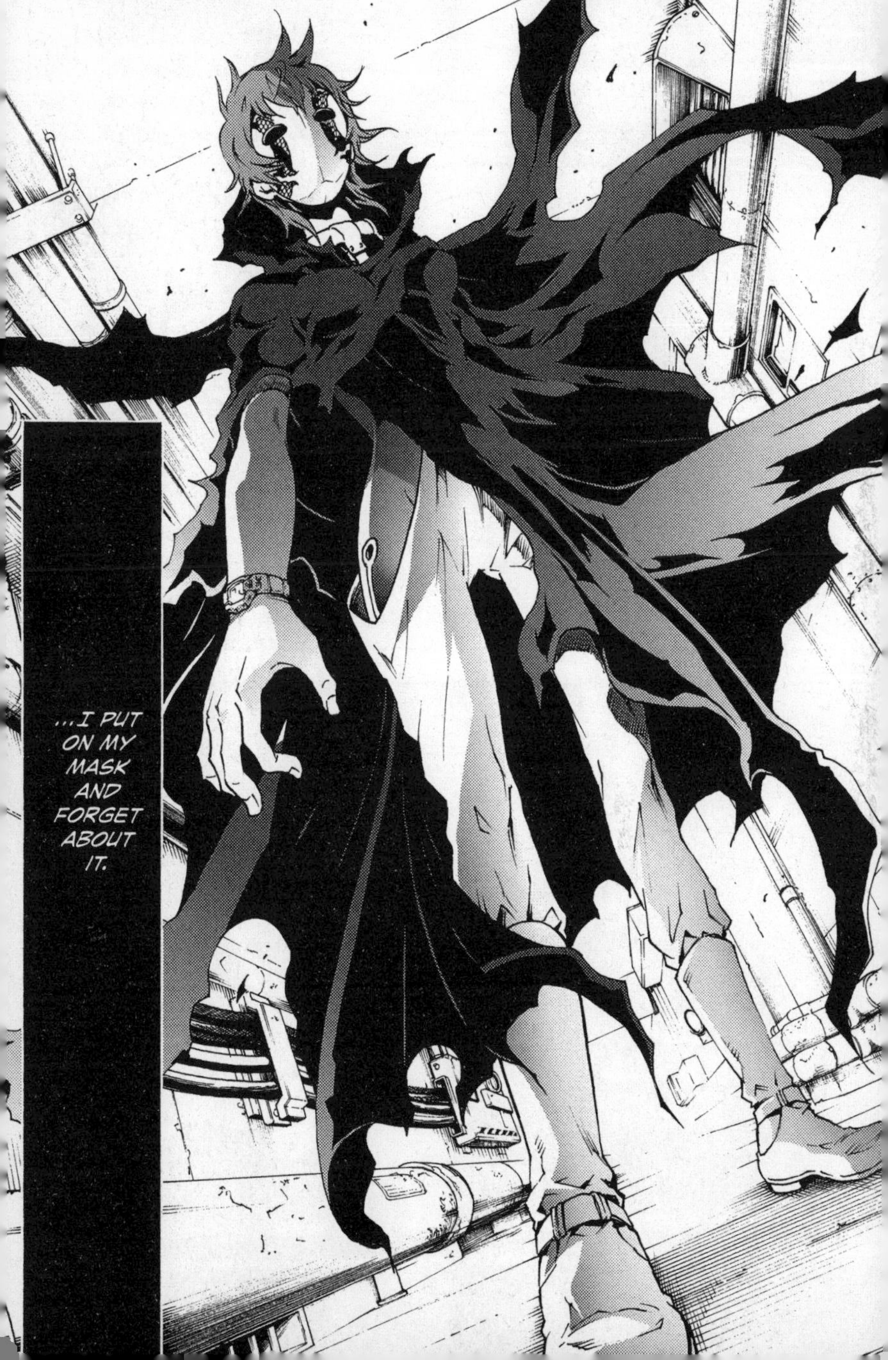
...I PUT ON MY MASK AND FORGET ABOUT IT.

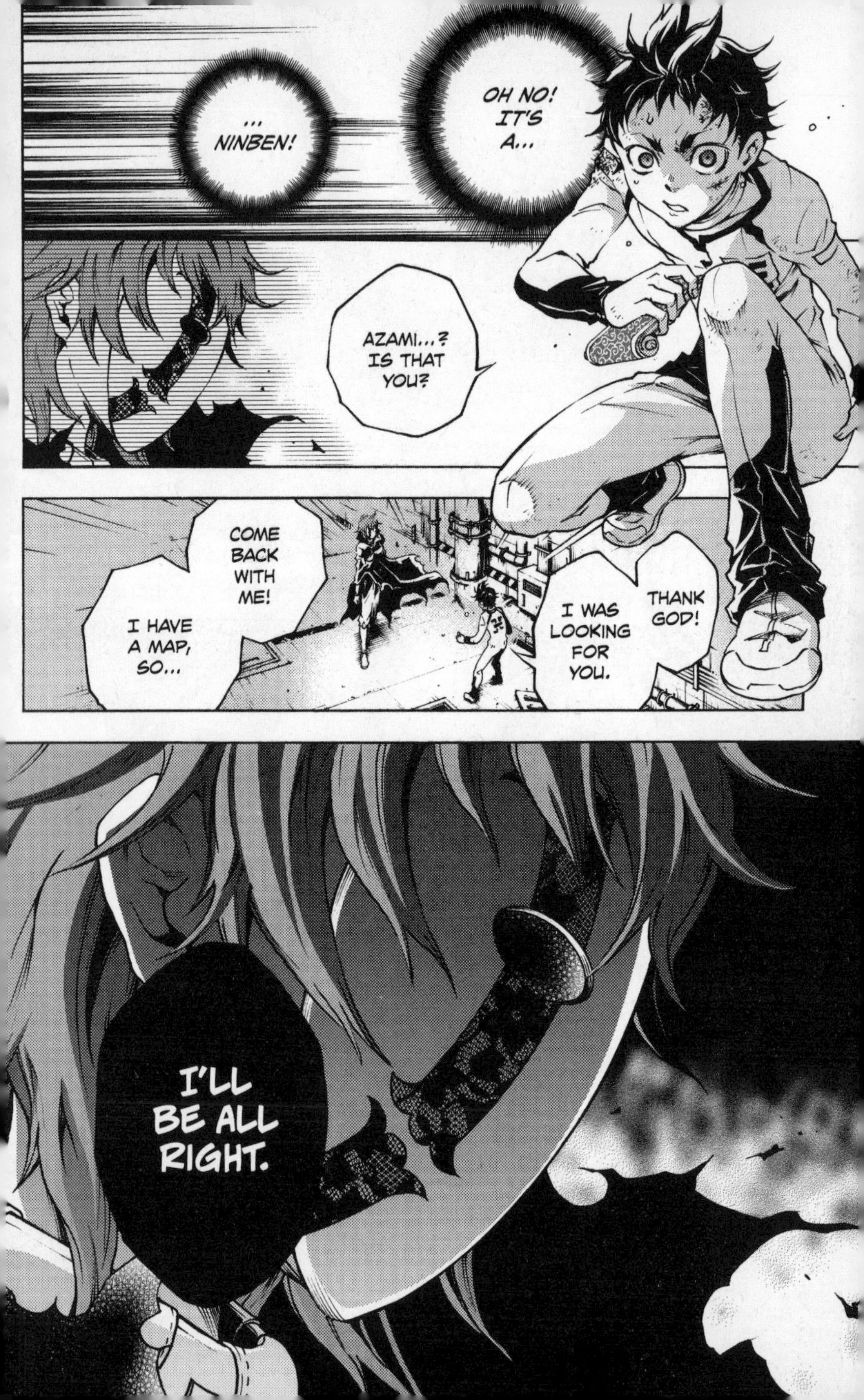
OH NO! IT'S A...
... NINBEN!
AZAMI...? IS THAT YOU?
THANK GOD!
I WAS LOOKING FOR YOU.
COME BACK WITH ME!
I HAVE A MAP, SO...
I'LL BE ALL RIGHT.

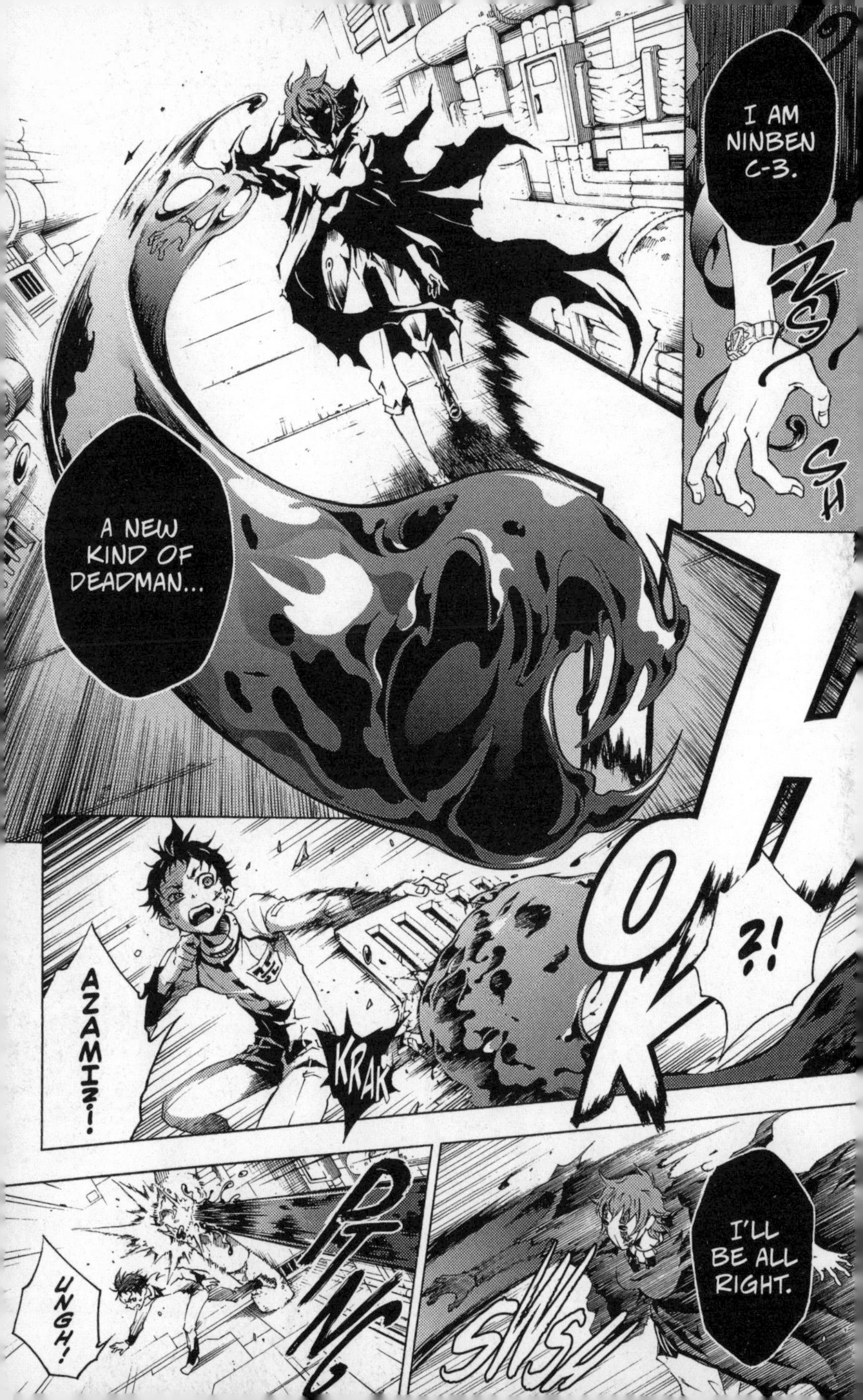
I AM NINBEN C-3.
A NEW KIND OF DEADMAN...
?!
KRAK
AZAMIZI!
I'LL BE ALL RIGHT.
UNGH!

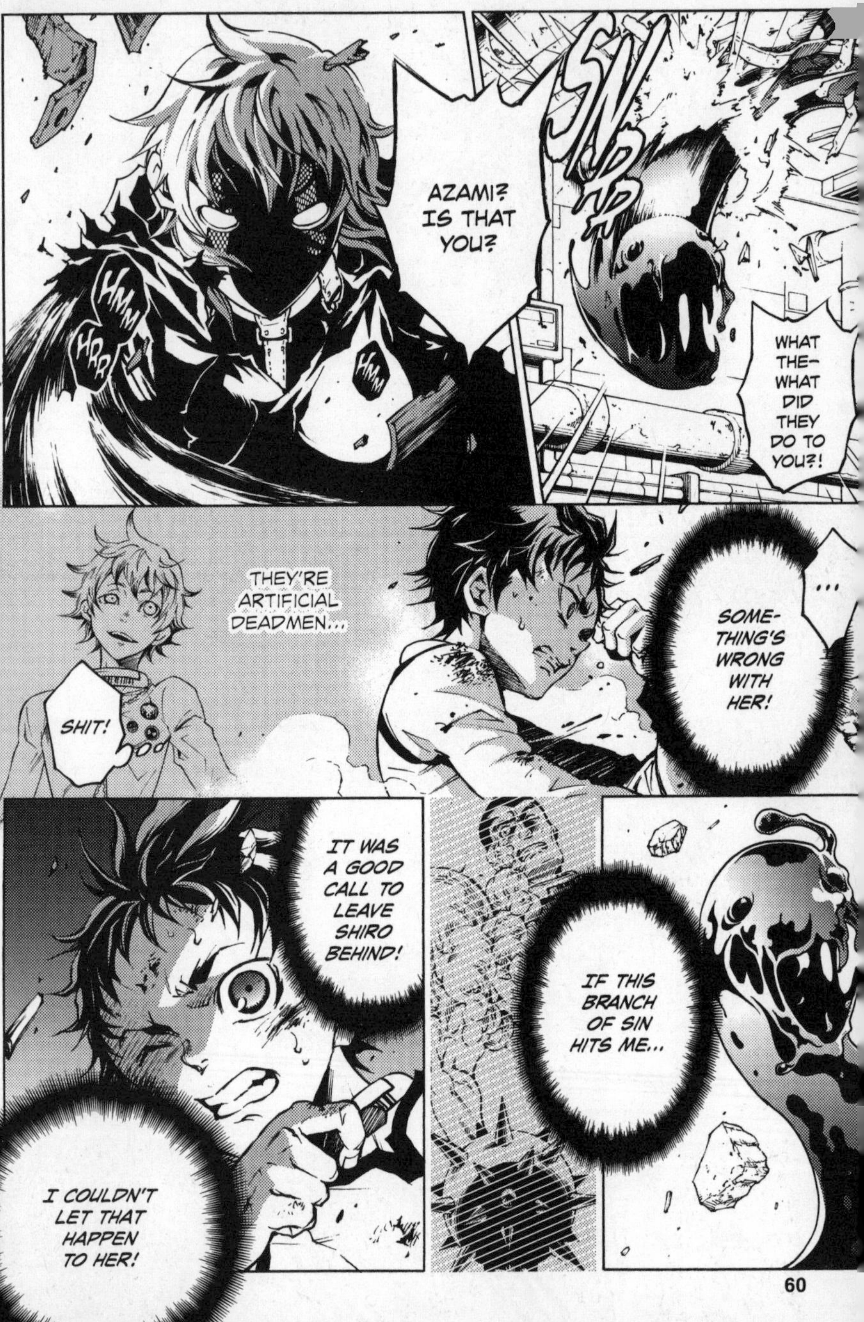
AZAMI? IS THAT YOU?
WHAT THE— WHAT DID THEY DO TO YOU?!
HMM
HRR
HMM
...
SOME-THING'S WRONG WITH HER!
THEY'RE ARTIFICIAL DEADMEN...
SHIT!
IF THIS BRANCH OF SIN HITS ME...
IT WAS A GOOD CALL TO LEAVE SHIRO BEHIND!
I COULDN'T LET THAT HAPPEN TO HER!

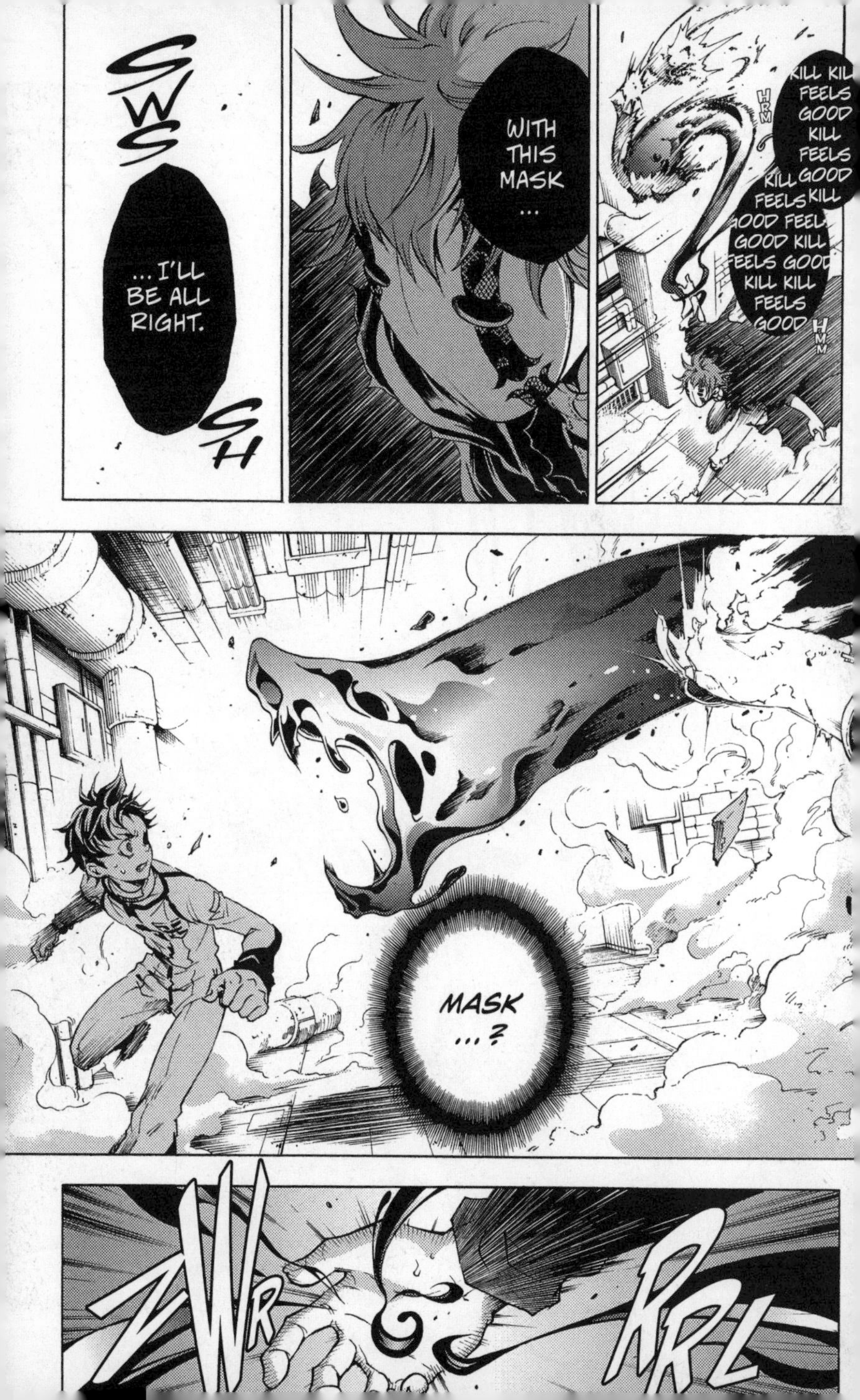
HRM
KILL KILL FEELS GOOD KILL FEELS GOOD KILL FEELS KILL GOOD FEELS GOOD FEELS GOOD KILL FEELS GOOD KILL KILL FEELS GOOD
HMM
WITH THIS MASK ...
SWS
... I'LL BE ALL RIGHT.
SH
MASK ...?
ZWR
RRL

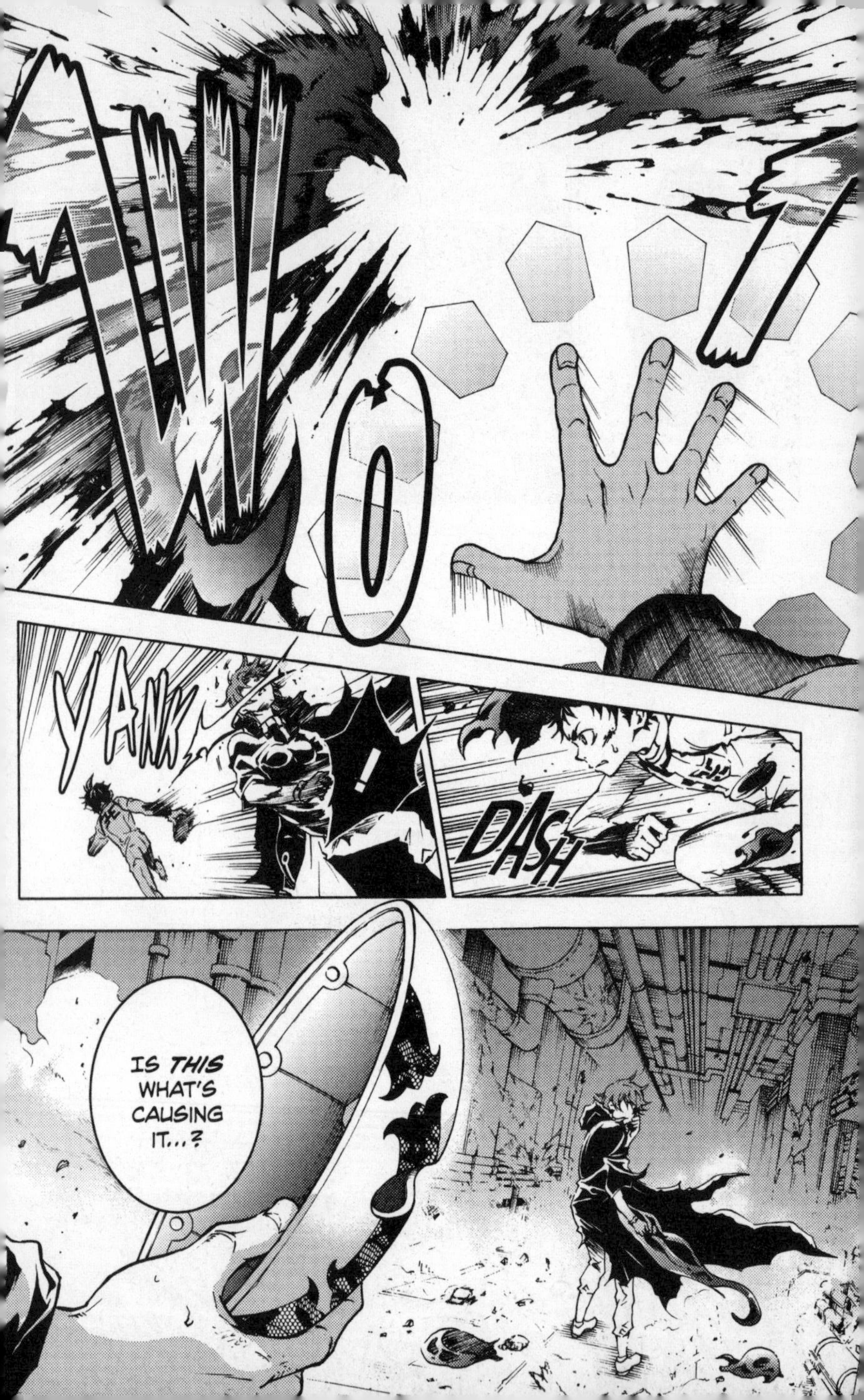
DASH
!
YANK
IS THIS WHAT'S CAUSING IT...?

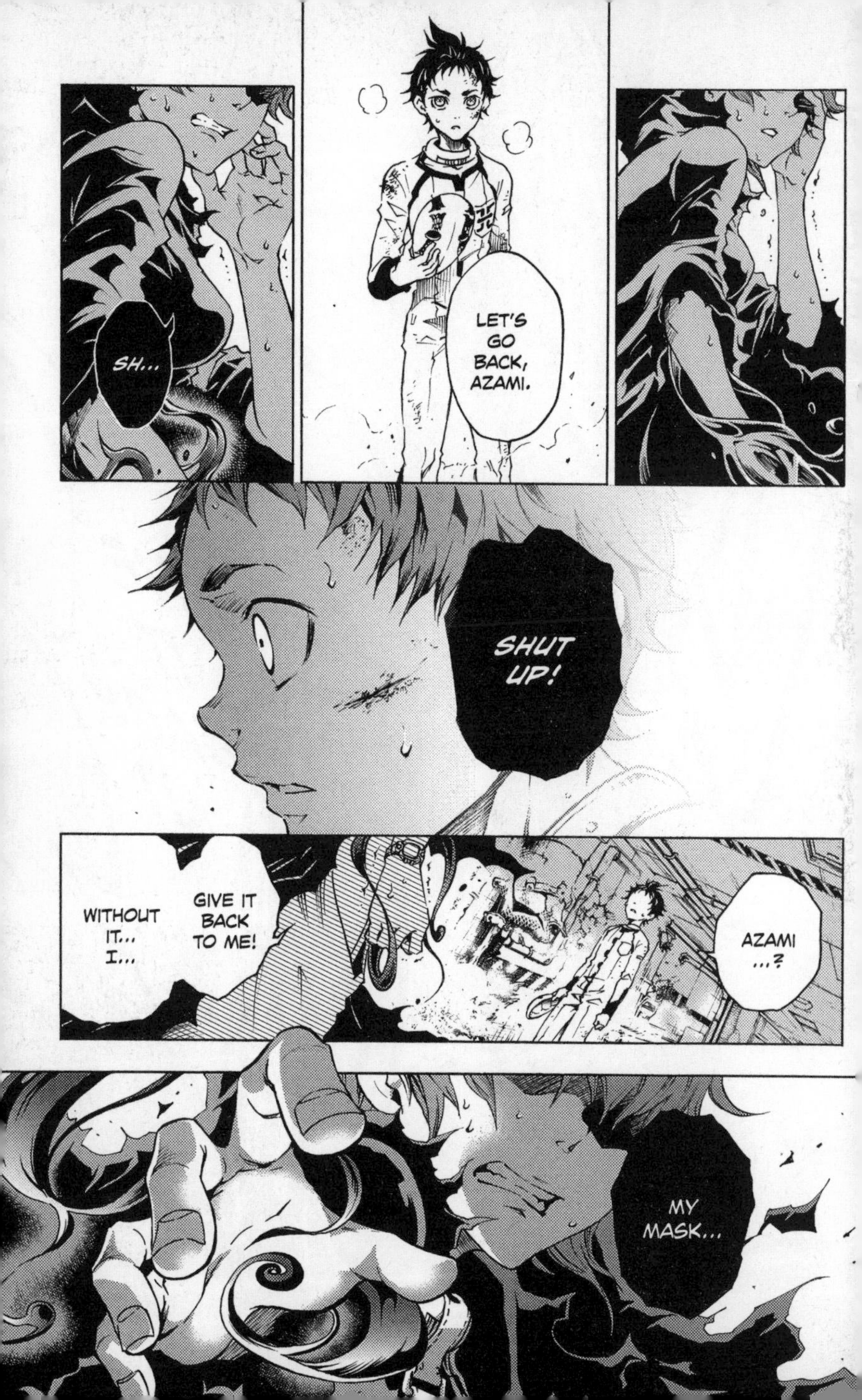
LET'S GO BACK, AZAMI.
SH...
SHUT UP!
AZAMI ...?
GIVE IT BACK TO ME!
WITHOUT IT... I...
MY MASK...

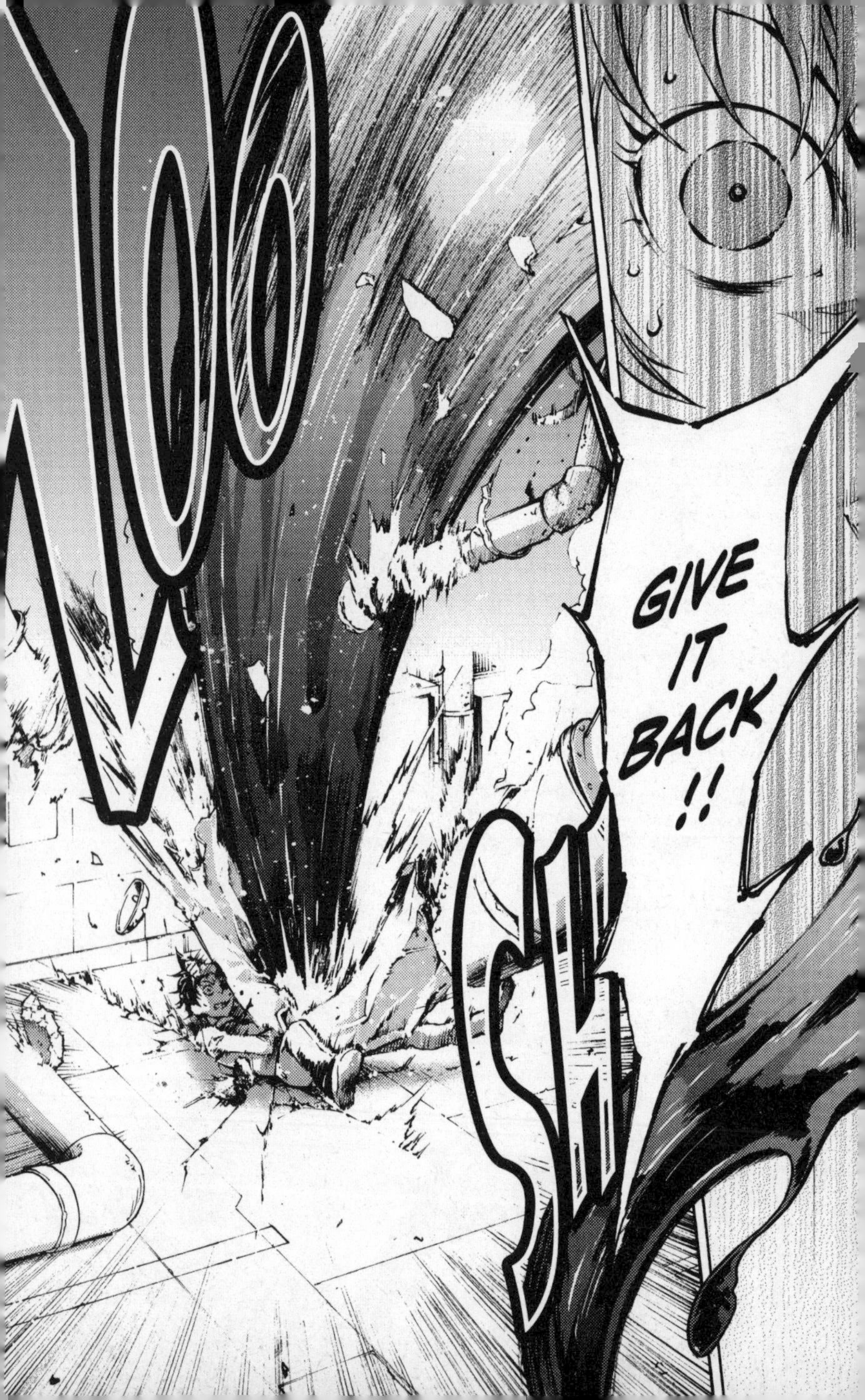
GIVE IT BACK!!

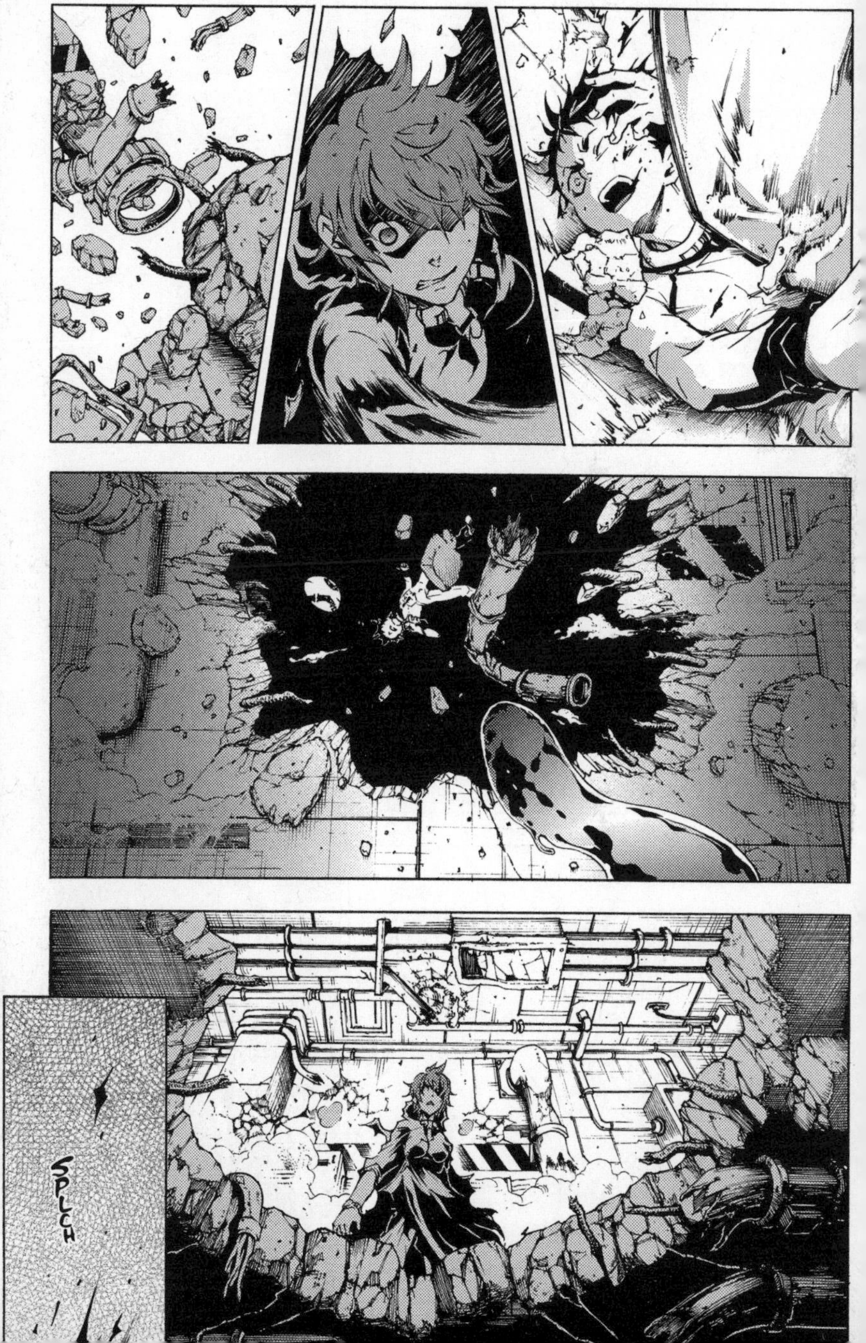
SPLCH

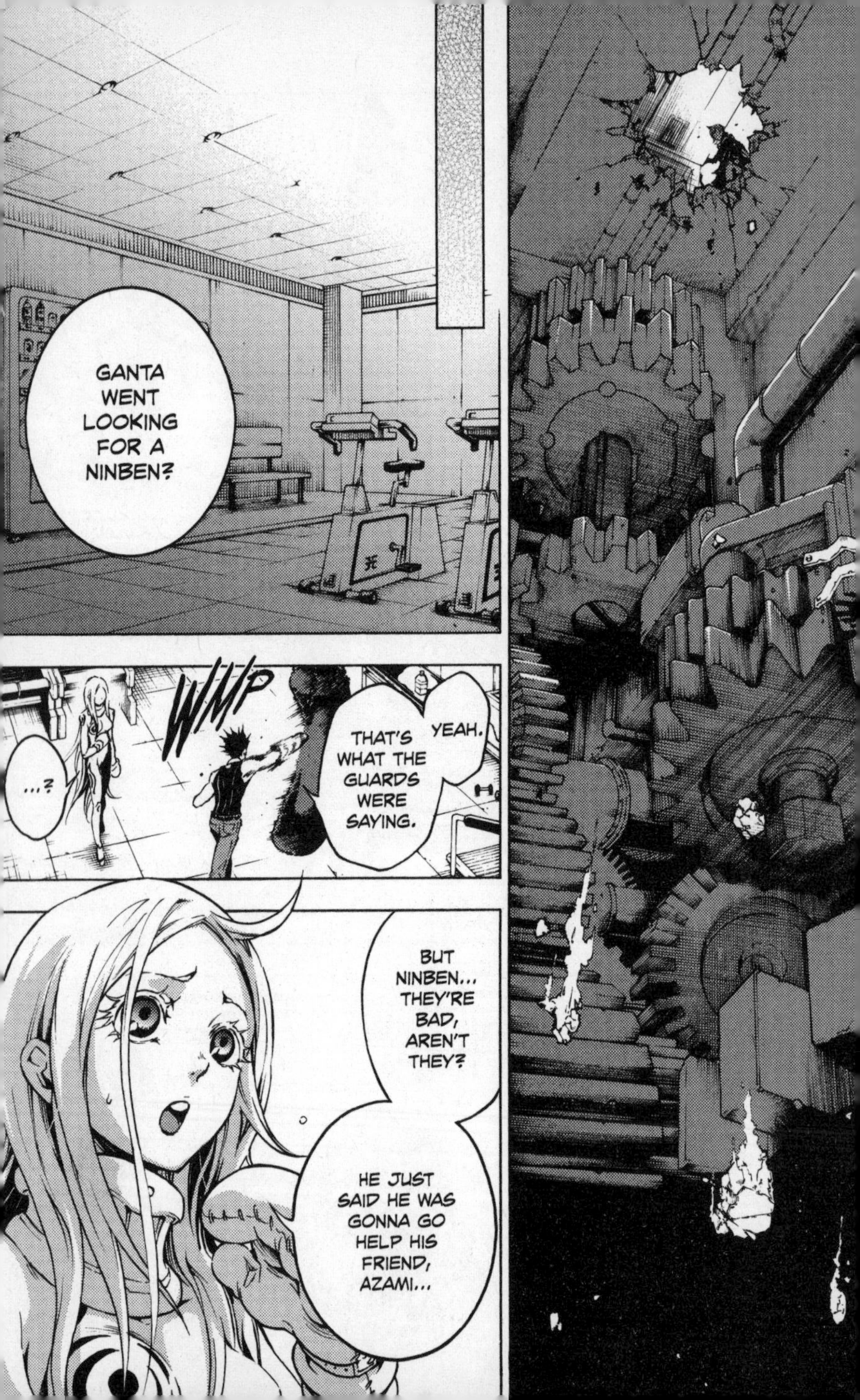
GANTA WENT LOOKING FOR A NINBEN?
YEAH.
THAT'S WHAT THE GUARDS WERE SAYING.
WMP
...?
BUT NINBEN... THEY'RE BAD, AREN'T THEY?
HE JUST SAID HE WAS GONNA GO HELP HIS FRIEND, AZAMI...

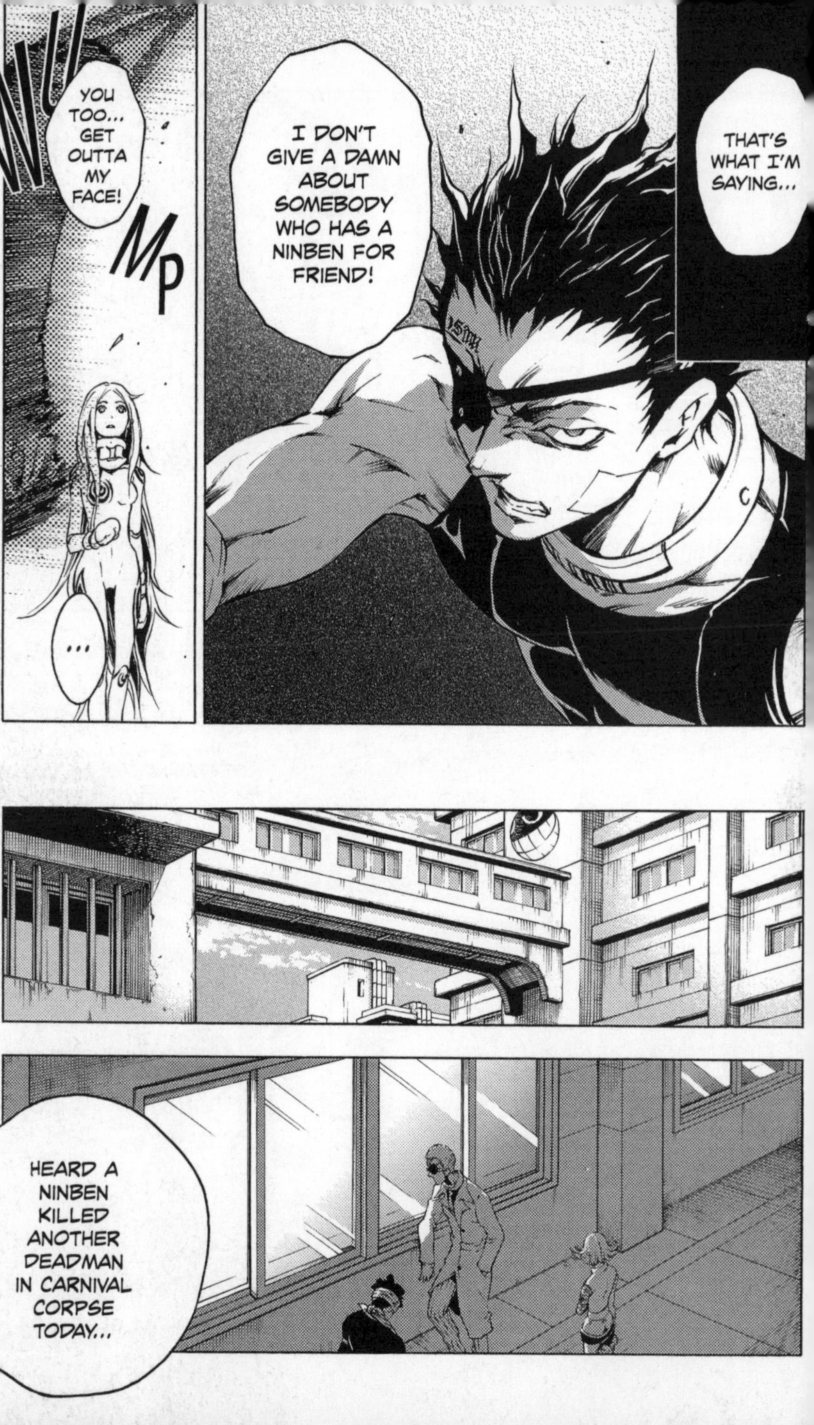
THAT'S WHAT I'M SAYING...
I DON'T GIVE A DAMN ABOUT SOMEBODY WHO HAS A NINBEN FOR FRIEND!
YOU TOO... GET OUTTA MY FACE!
WUMP
...
HEARD A NINBEN KILLED ANOTHER DEADMAN IN CARNIVAL CORPSE TODAY...

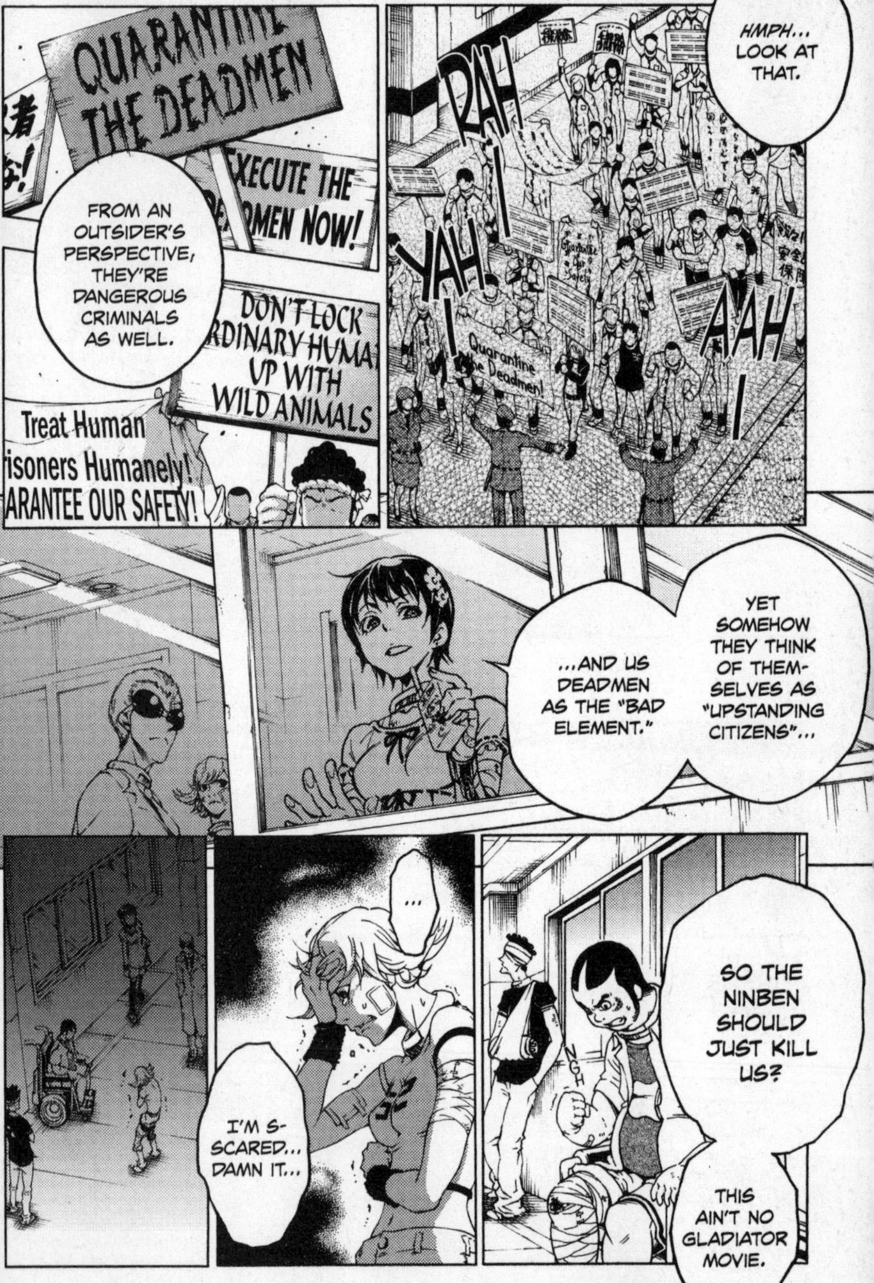
HMPH... LOOK AT THAT.
RAH!
YAH!
AAH!
Quarantine the Deadmen!
QUARANTINE THE DEADMEN
XECUTE THE
MEN NOW!
FROM AN OUTSIDER'S PERSPECTIVE, THEY'RE DANGEROUS CRIMINALS AS WELL.
DON'T LOCK
RDINARY HUMA
UP WITH WILD ANIMALS
Treat Human
risoners Humanely!
ARANTEE OUR SAFETY!
YET SOMEHOW THEY THINK OF THEMSELVES AS "UPSTANDING CITIZENS"...
...AND US DEADMEN AS THE "BAD ELEMENT."
SO THE NINBEN SHOULD JUST KILL US?
NGH
THIS AIN'T NO GLADIATOR MOVIE.
...
I'M S-SCARED... DAMN IT...

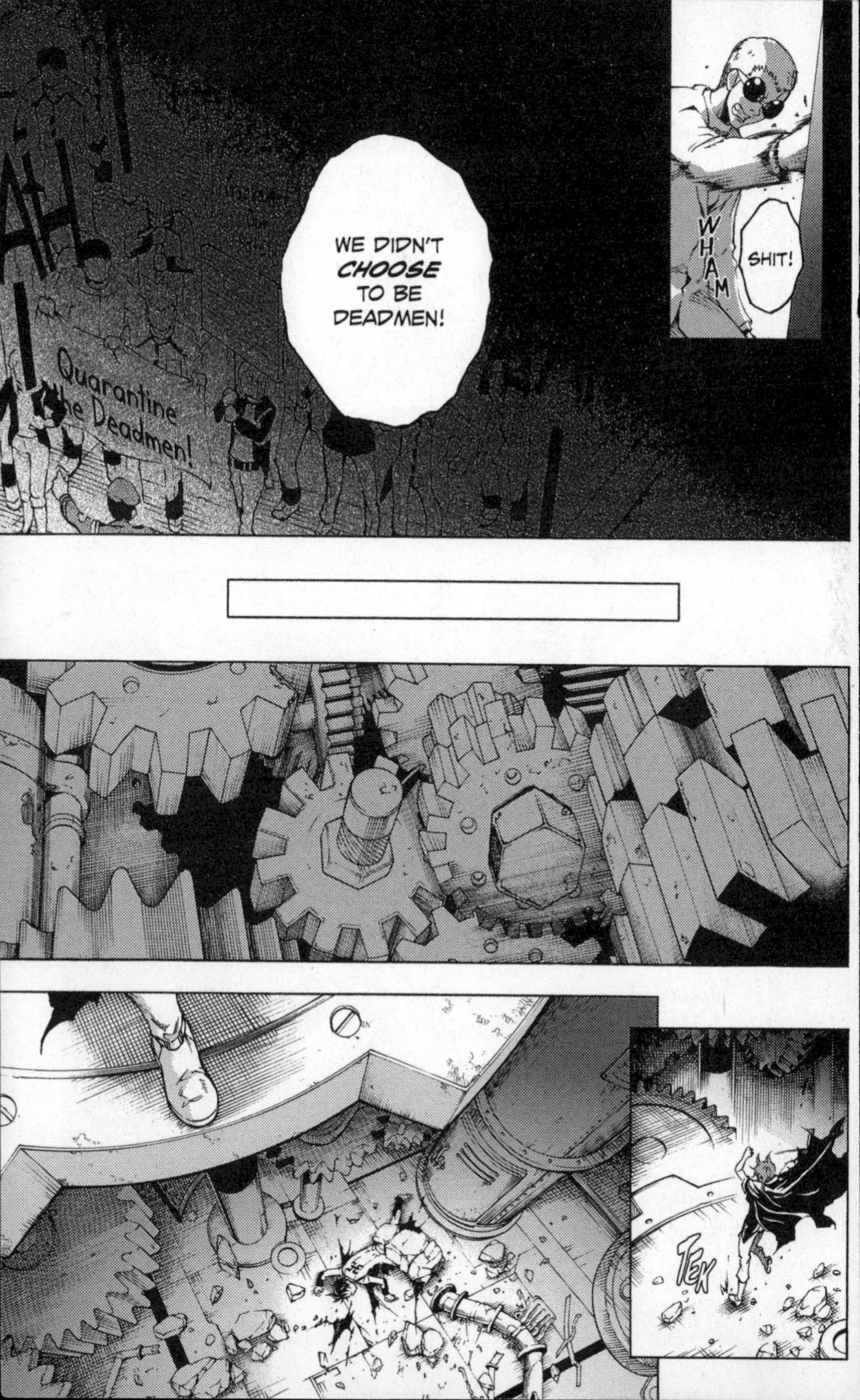
WHAM
SHIT!
WE DIDN'T *CHOOSE* TO BE DEADMEN!
Quarantine
he Deadmen!
TEK

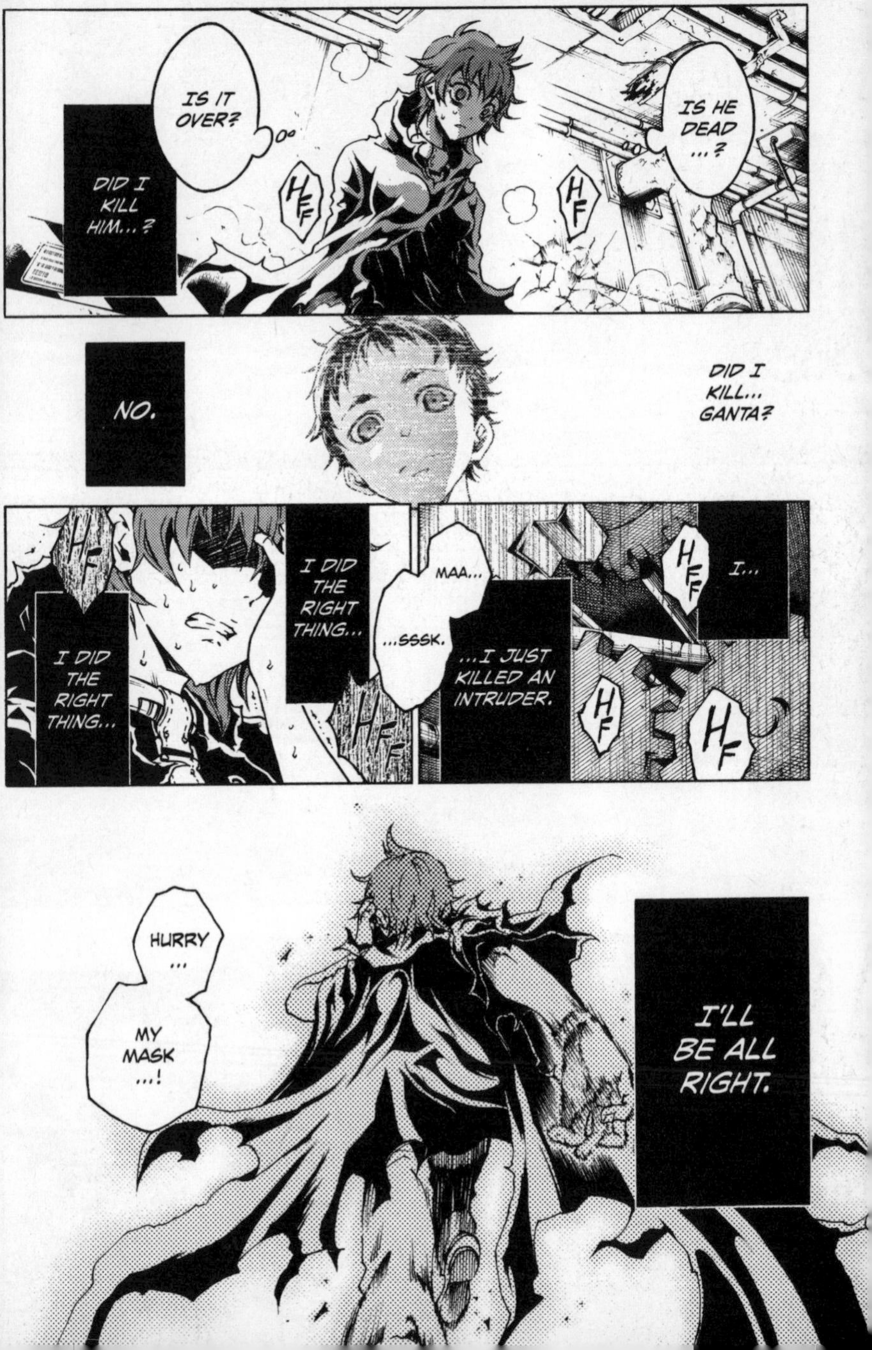
IS HE DEAD ...?
HF
IS IT OVER?
HF
DID I KILL HIM...?
DID I KILL... GANTA?
NO.
I...
HF
HF
HF
...I JUST KILLED AN INTRUDER.
MAA...
...SSSK.
I DID THE RIGHT THING...
HF
HF
I DID THE RIGHT THING...
I'LL BE ALL RIGHT.
HURRY ...
MY MASK ...!

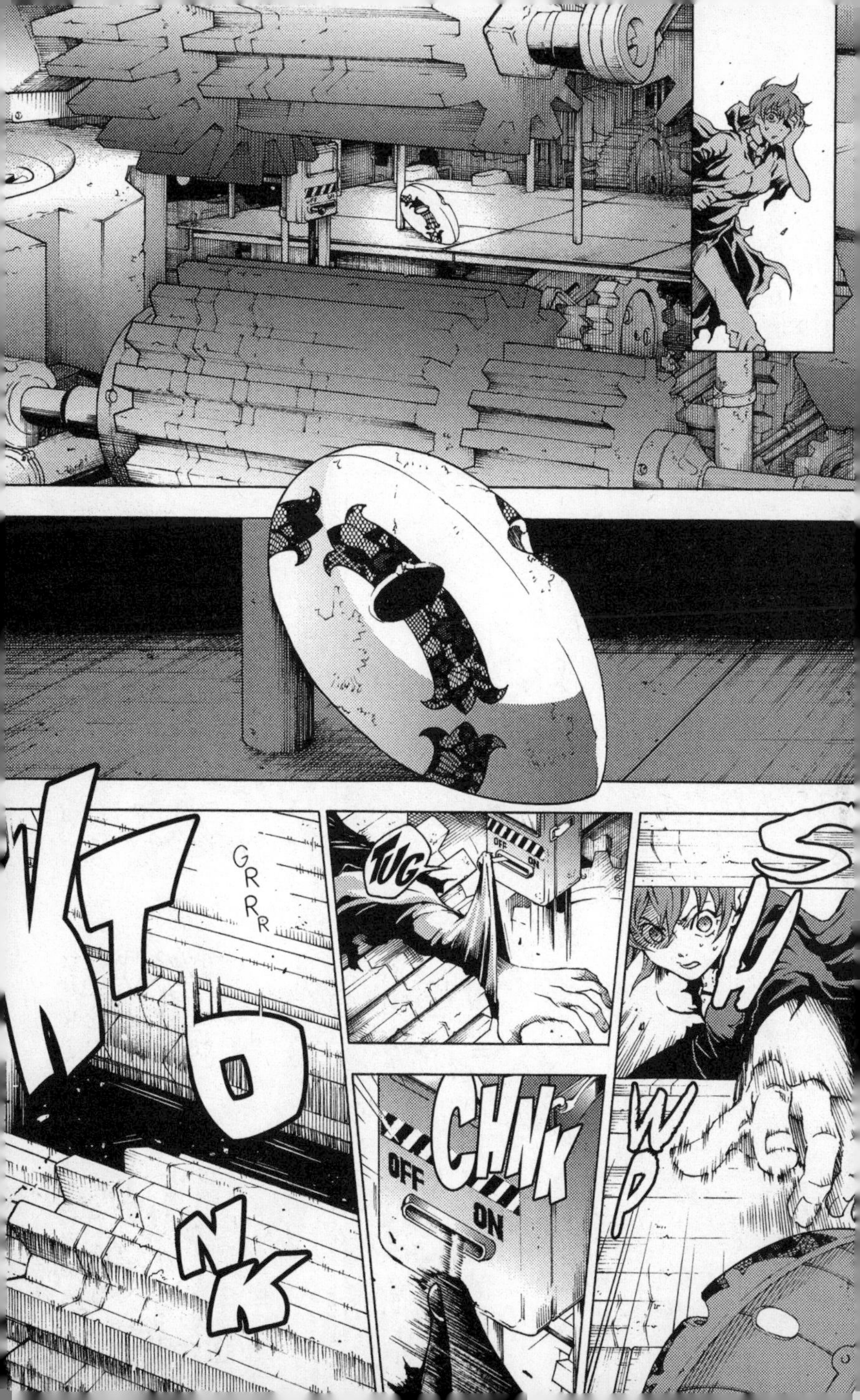
TUG
OFF ON
GRRR
CHNK
OFF
ON

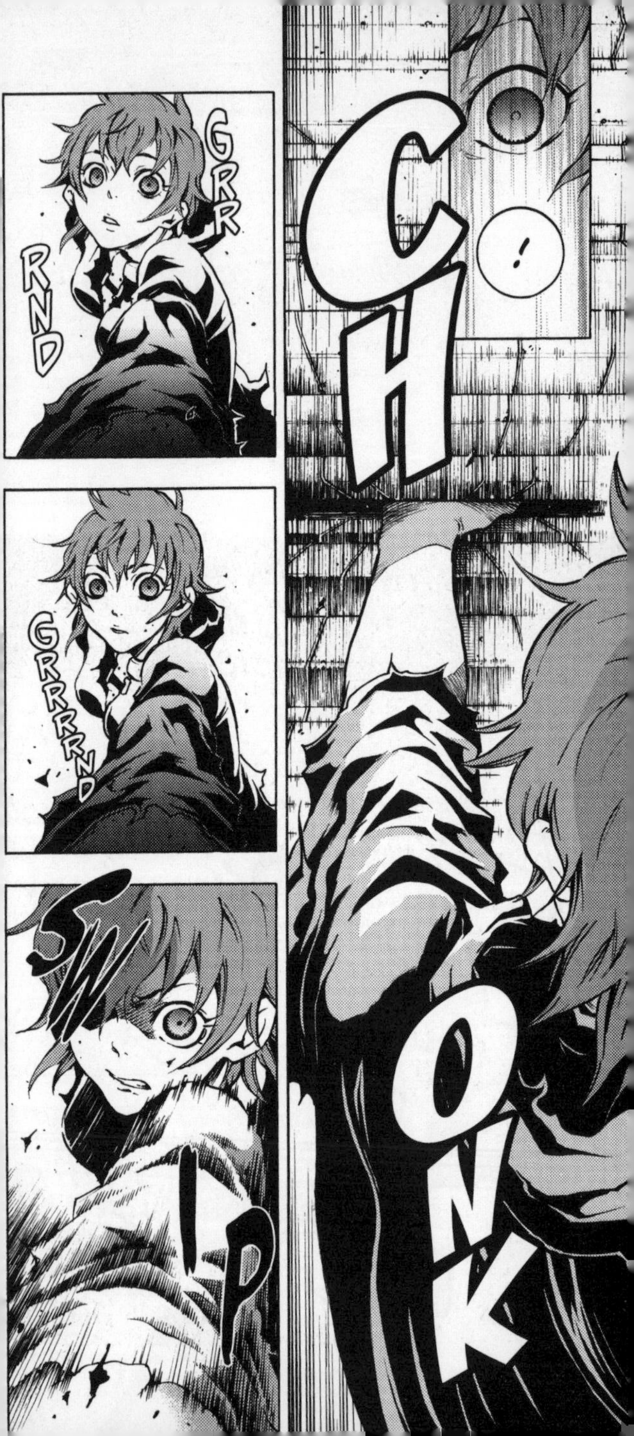
CH
!
ONK
GRRR
RND
GRRRRND
SW
IP

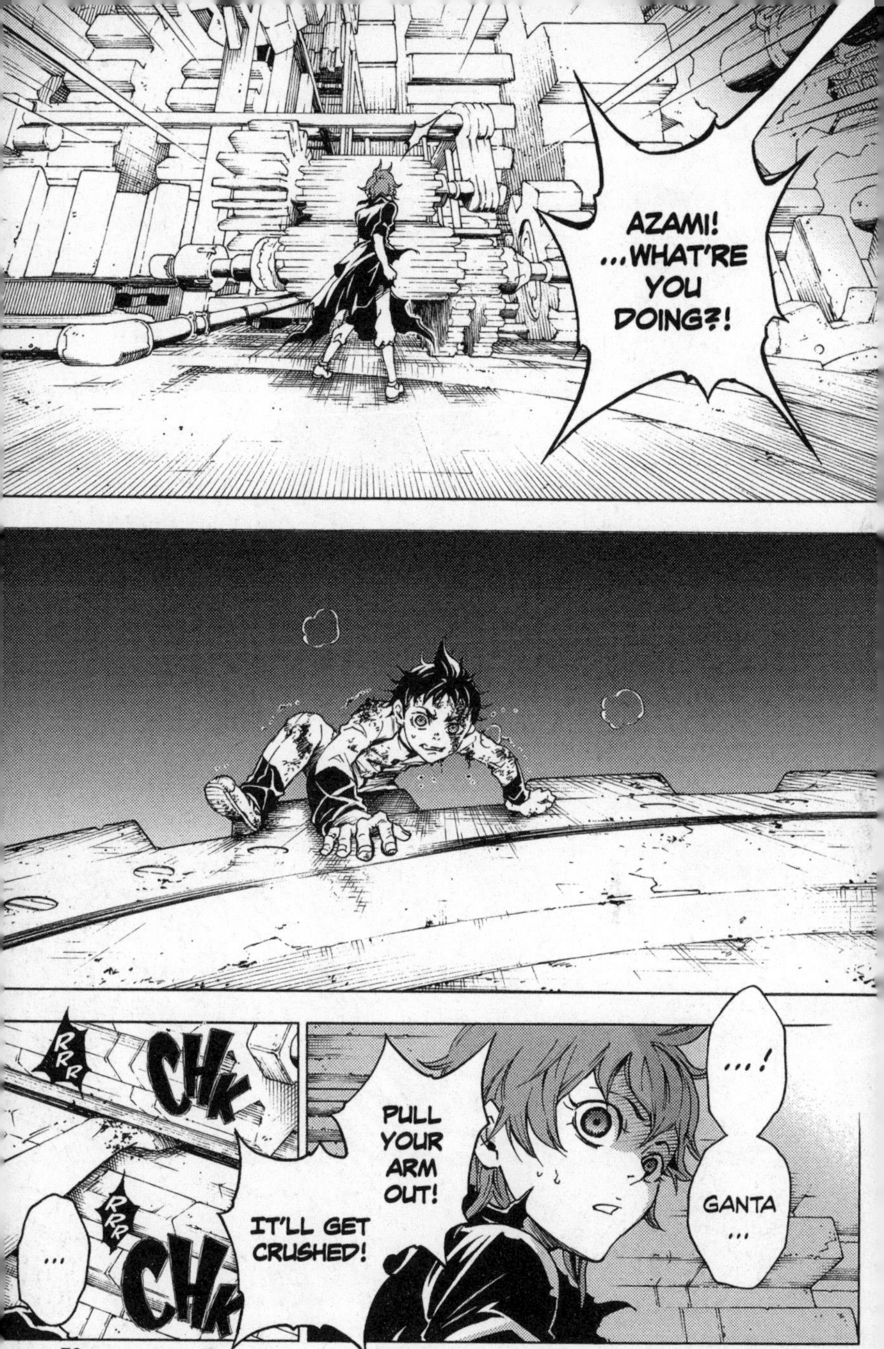
AZAMI! ...WHAT'RE YOU DOING?!
...!
GANTA ...
PULL YOUR ARM OUT!
IT'LL GET CRUSHED!
RRR
CHK
RRR
CHK
...

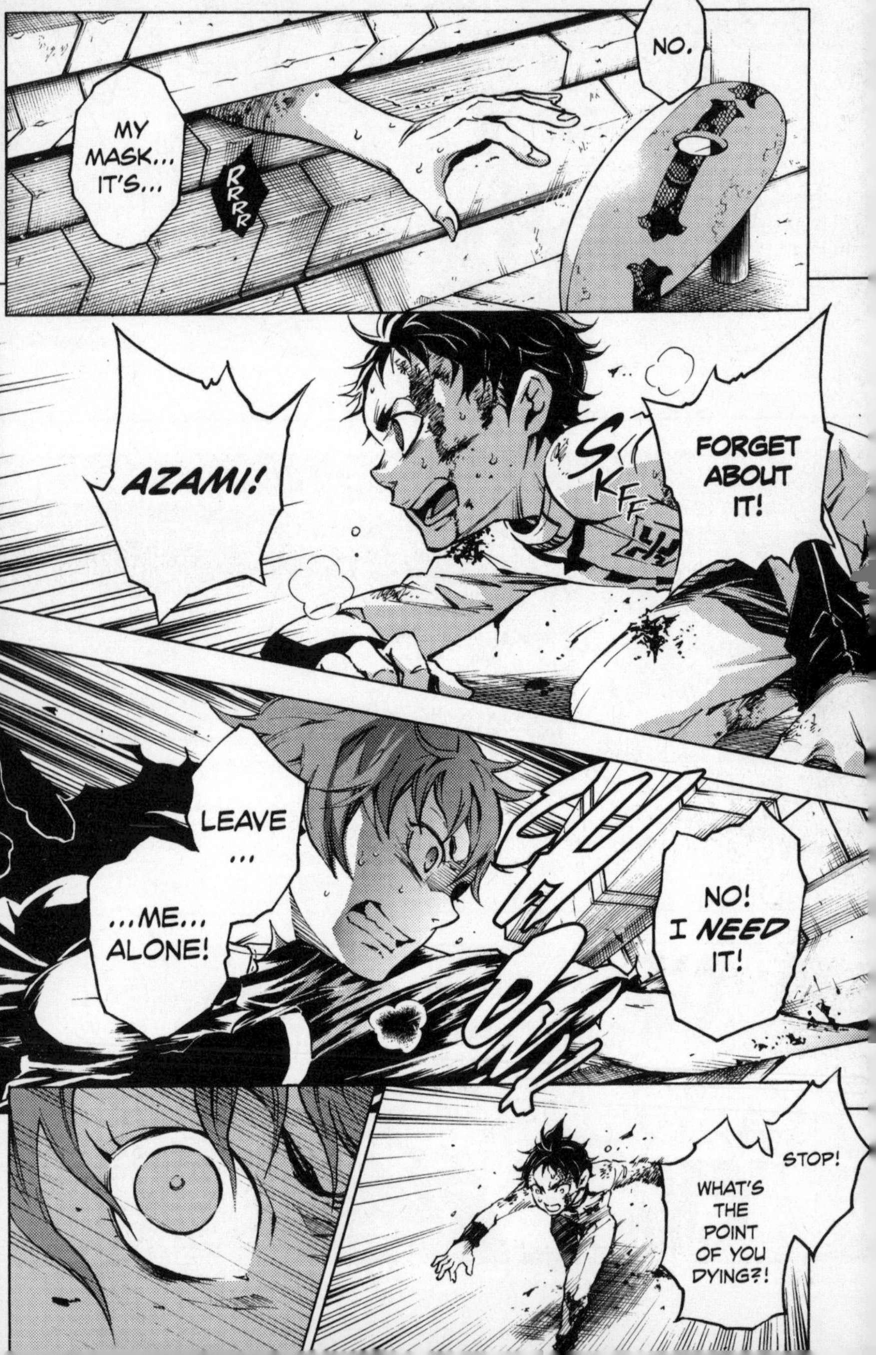
NO.
MY MASK... IT'S...
RRRR
FORGET ABOUT IT!
SKFF
AZAMI!
NO! I NEED IT!
LEAVE ...
...ME... ALONE!
STOP!
WHAT'S THE POINT OF YOU DYING?!

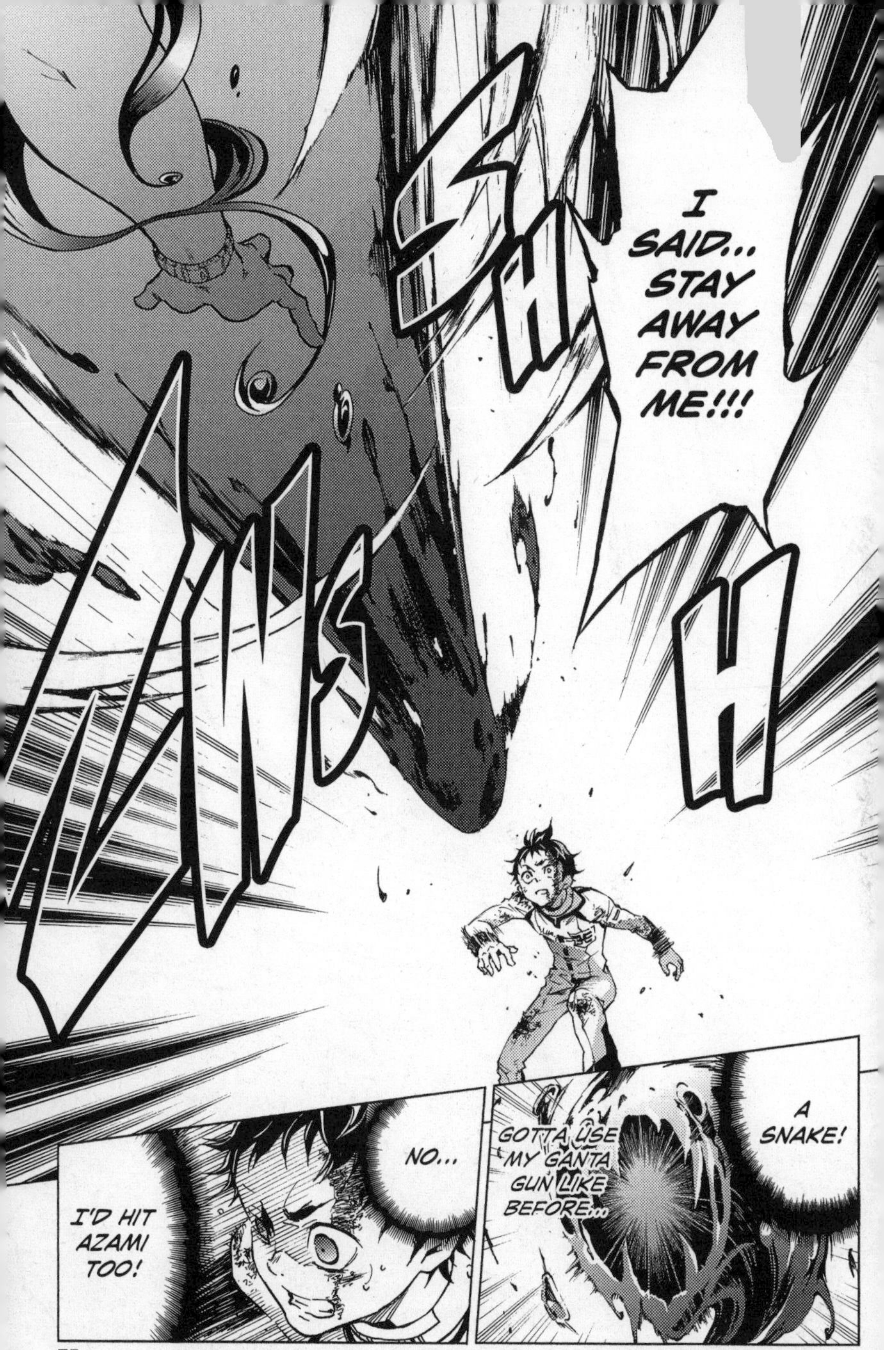
I SAID... STAY AWAY FROM ME!!!
A SNAKE!
GOTTA USE MY GANTA GUN LIKE BEFORE...
NO...
I'D HIT AZAMI TOO!

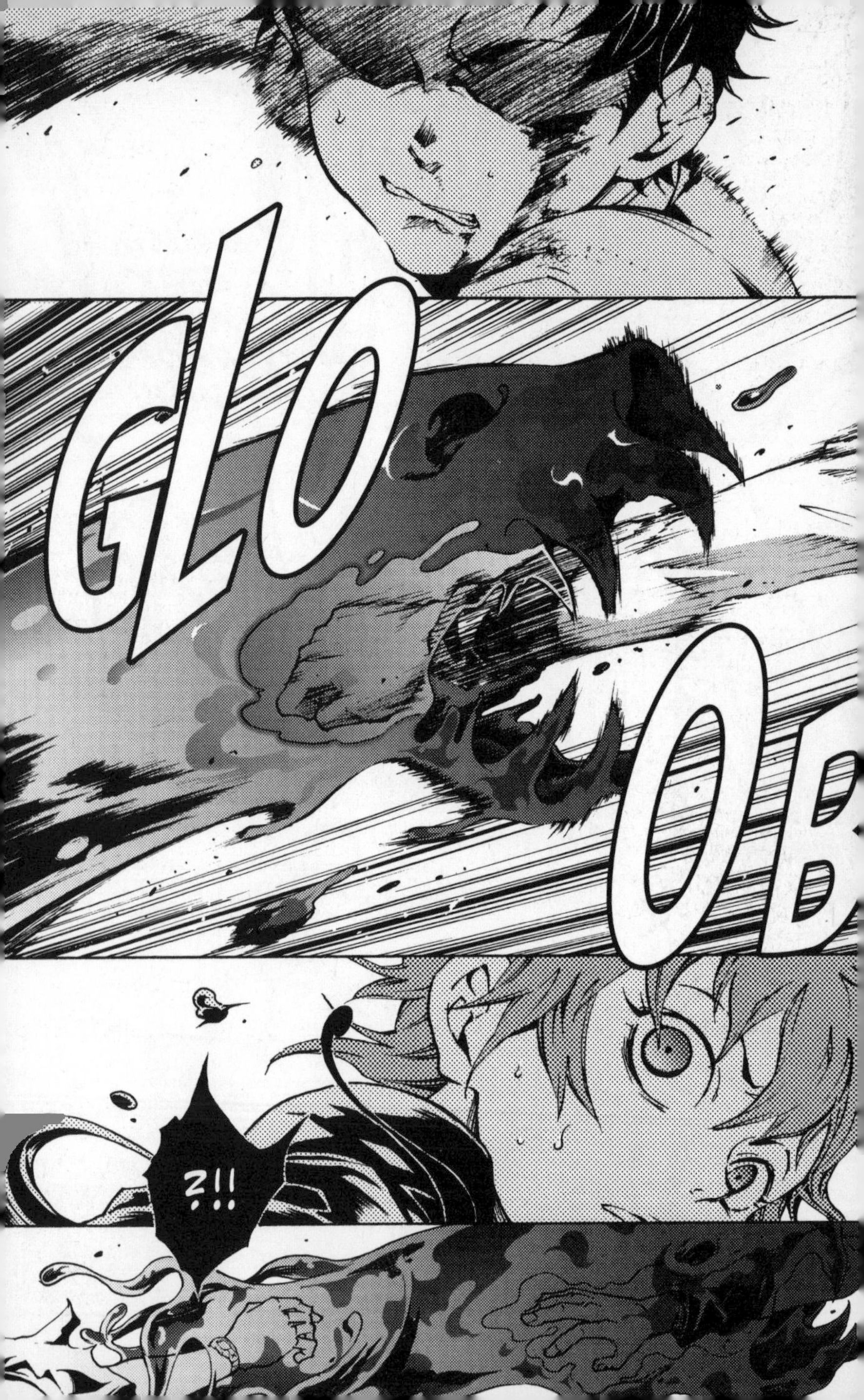
GLOOB
?!!

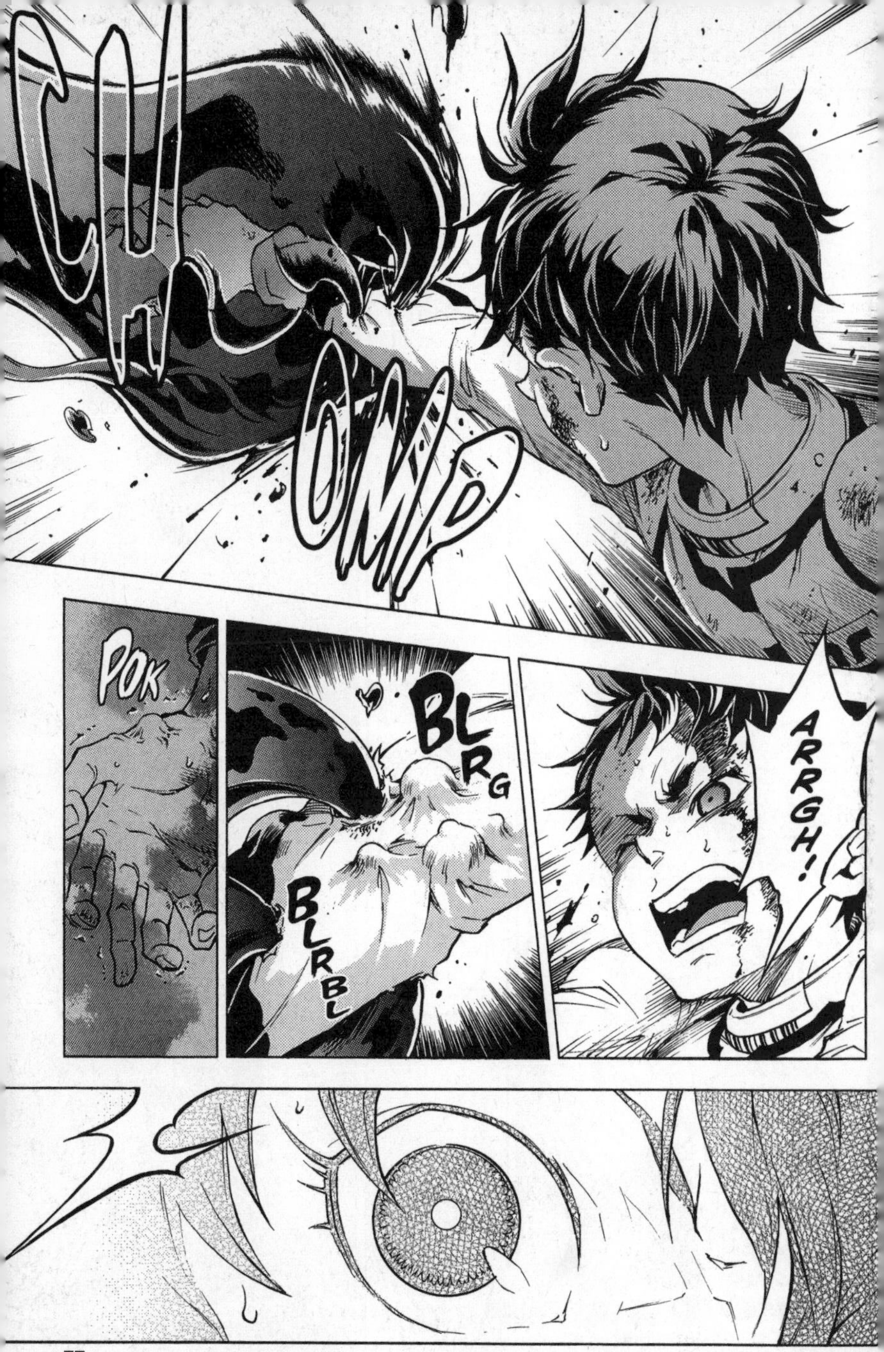
CHOMP
ARRGH!
BLRG
BLRBL
POK

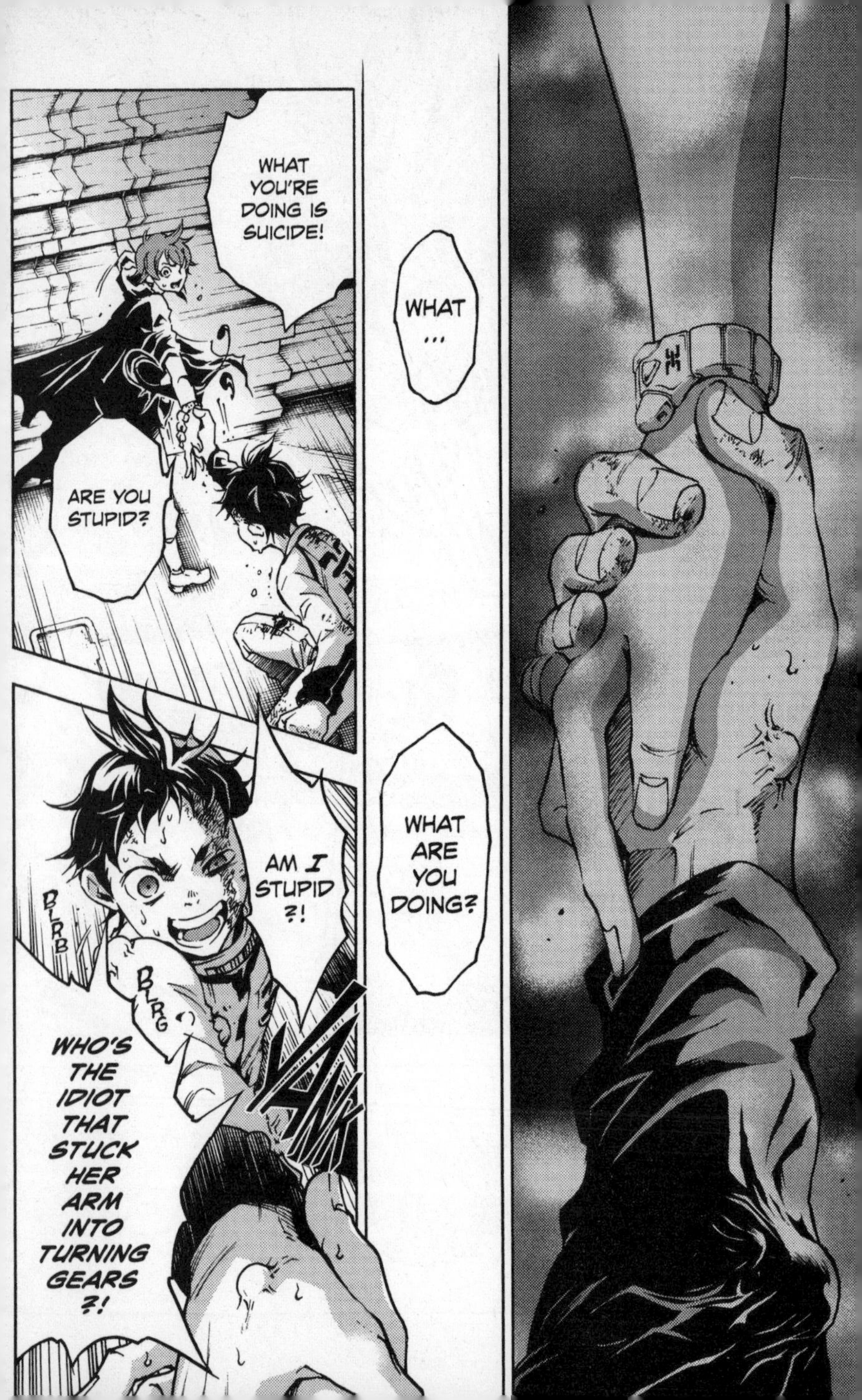
WHAT ...
WHAT ARE YOU DOING?
WHAT YOU'RE DOING IS SUICIDE!
ARE YOU STUPID?
AM I STUPID?!
BLRB
BLRG
WHO'S THE IDIOT THAT STUCK HER ARM INTO TURNING GEARS?!
YANK

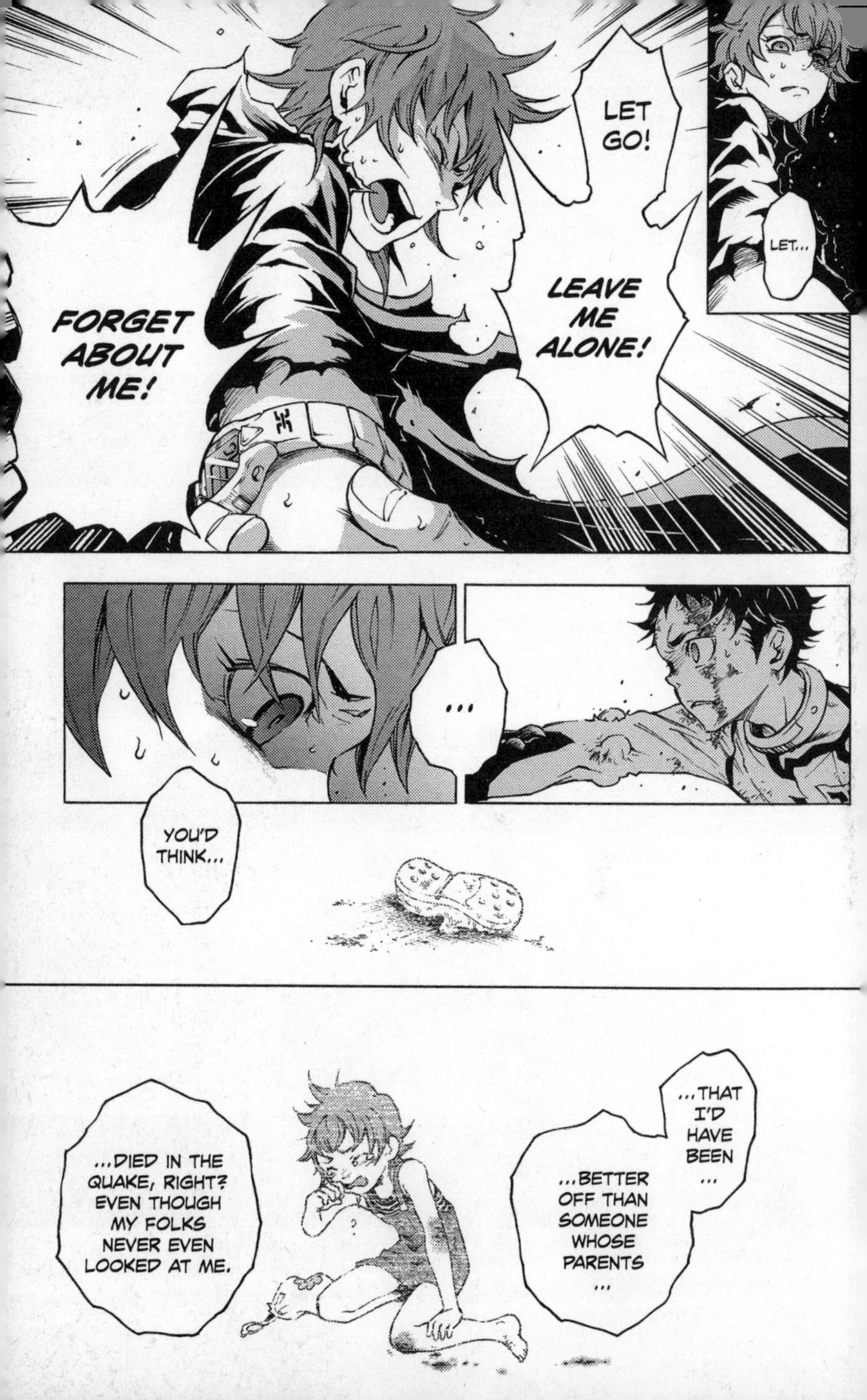
LET...
LET GO!
LEAVE ME ALONE!
FORGET ABOUT ME!
...
YOU'D THINK...
...THAT I'D HAVE BEEN ...
...BETTER OFF THAN SOMEONE WHOSE PARENTS ...
...DIED IN THE QUAKE, RIGHT? EVEN THOUGH MY FOLKS NEVER EVEN LOOKED AT ME.

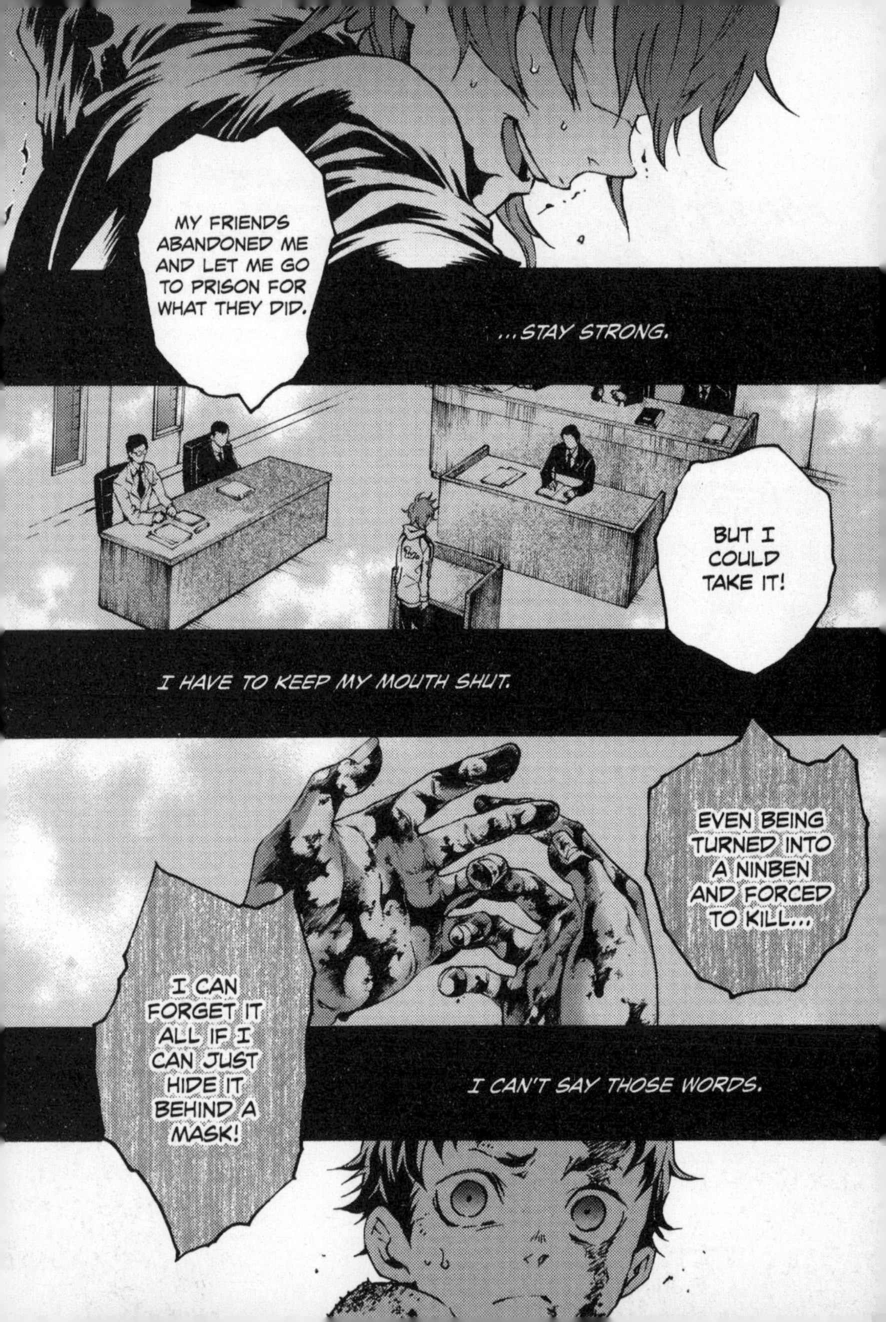
MY FRIENDS ABANDONED ME AND LET ME GO TO PRISON FOR WHAT THEY DID.
...STAY STRONG.
BUT I COULD TAKE IT!
I HAVE TO KEEP MY MOUTH SHUT.
EVEN BEING TURNED INTO A NINBEN AND FORCED TO KILL...
I CAN FORGET IT ALL IF I CAN JUST HIDE IT BEHIND A MASK!
I CAN'T SAY THOSE WORDS.

SO GO AWAY.

THAT'S WHY I...

DON'T MAKE ME ...

...ALL RIGHT!

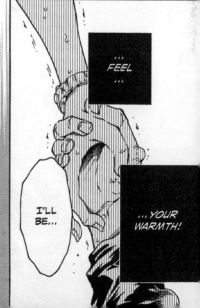

... FEEL ...

I'LL BE...

...YOUR WARMTH!

...

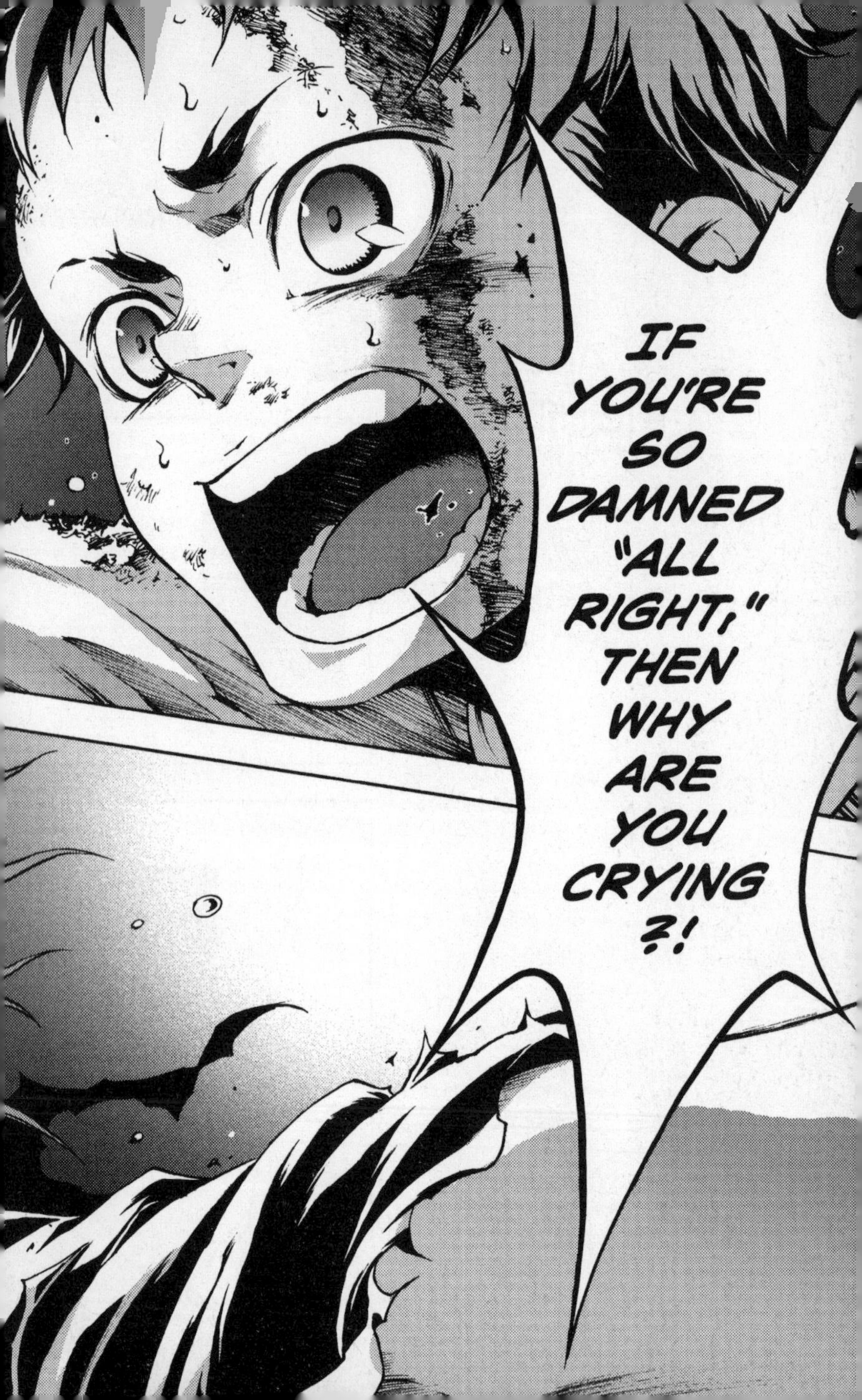
IF YOU'RE SO DAMNED "ALL RIGHT," THEN WHY ARE YOU CRYING ?!

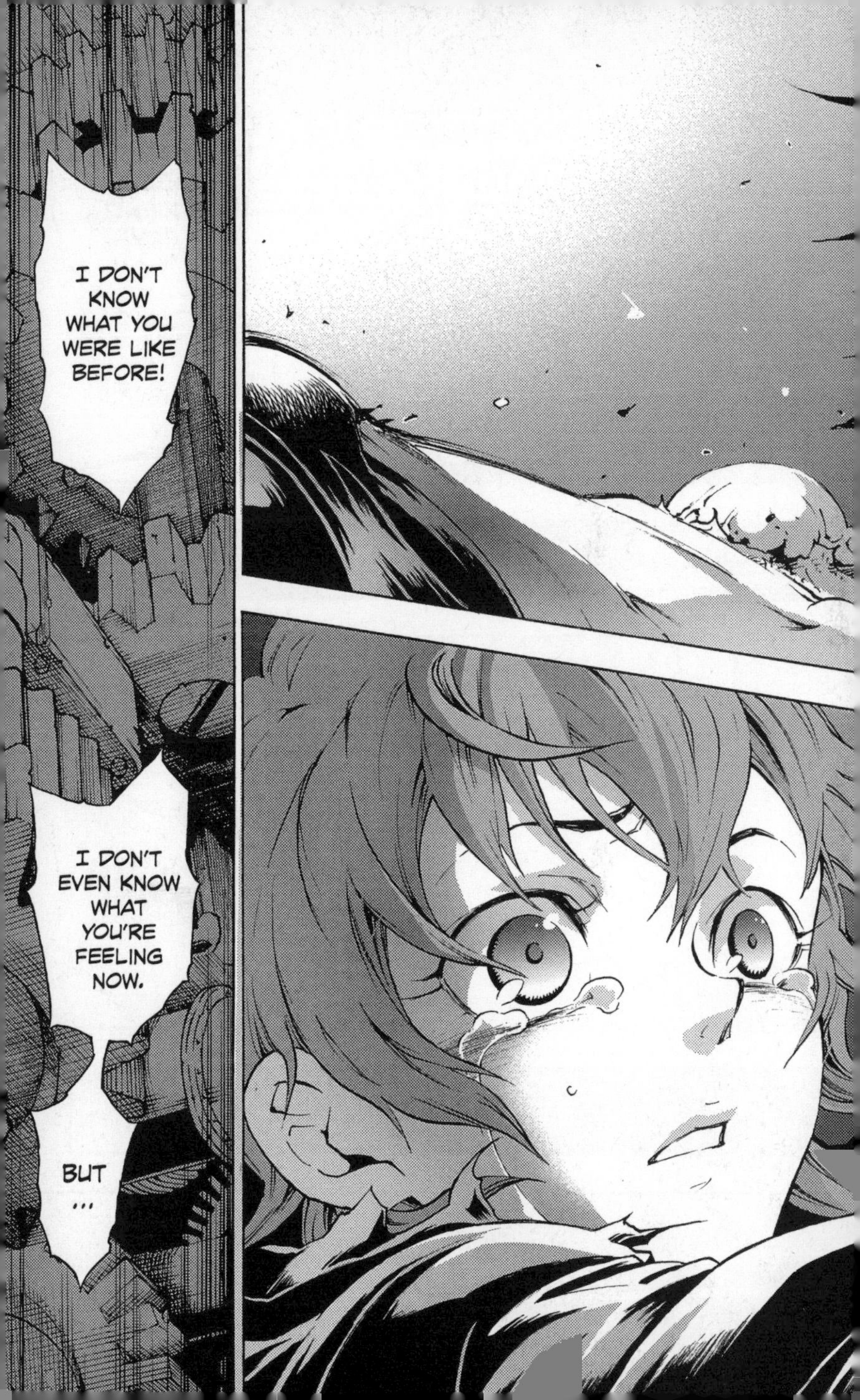
I DON'T KNOW WHAT YOU WERE LIKE BEFORE!
I DON'T EVEN KNOW WHAT YOU'RE FEELING NOW.
BUT ...

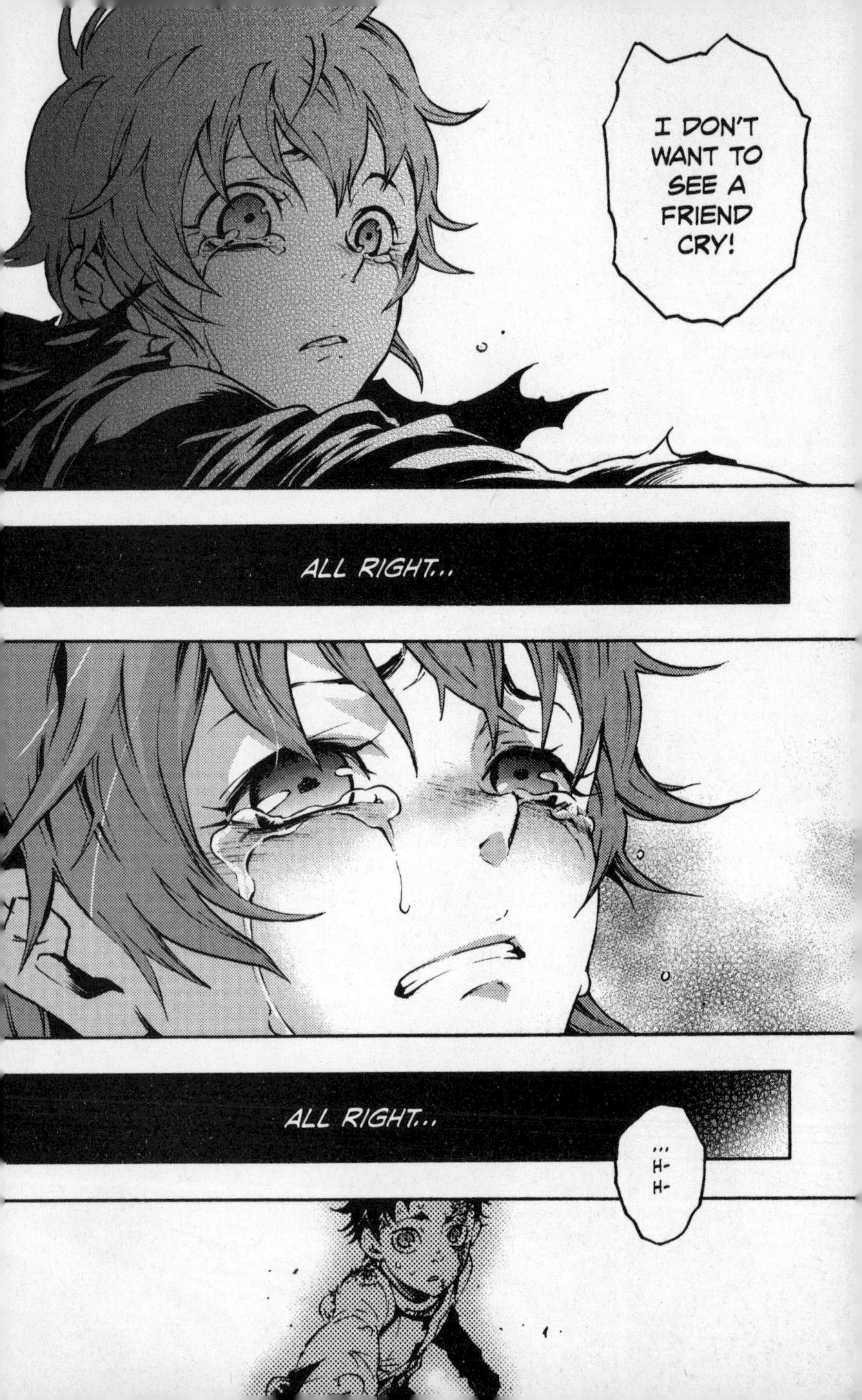
I DON'T WANT TO SEE A FRIEND CRY!
ALL RIGHT...
ALL RIGHT...
...H-H-

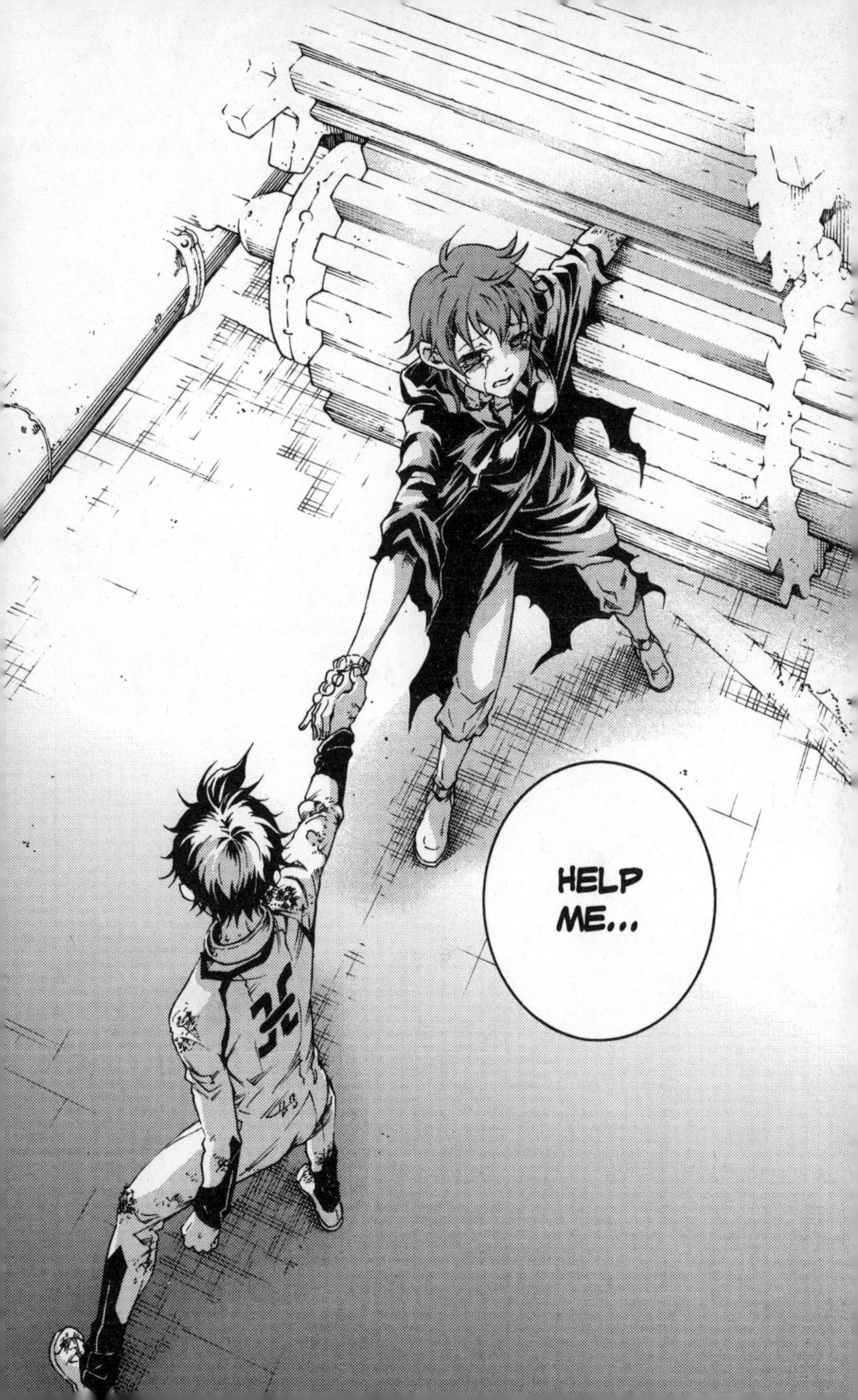
HELP ME...

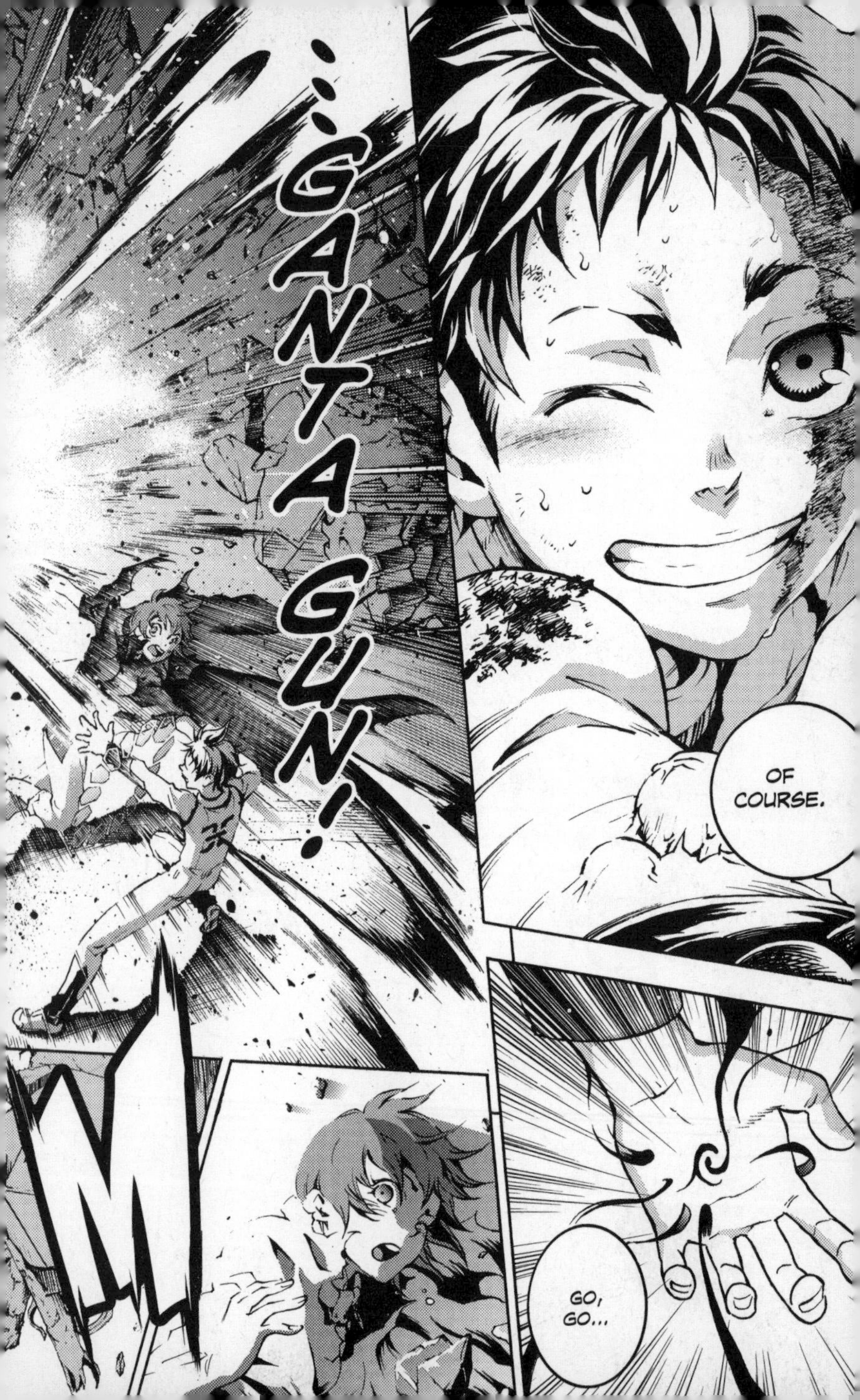
OF COURSE.
GANTAGUN!
GO, GO...
M

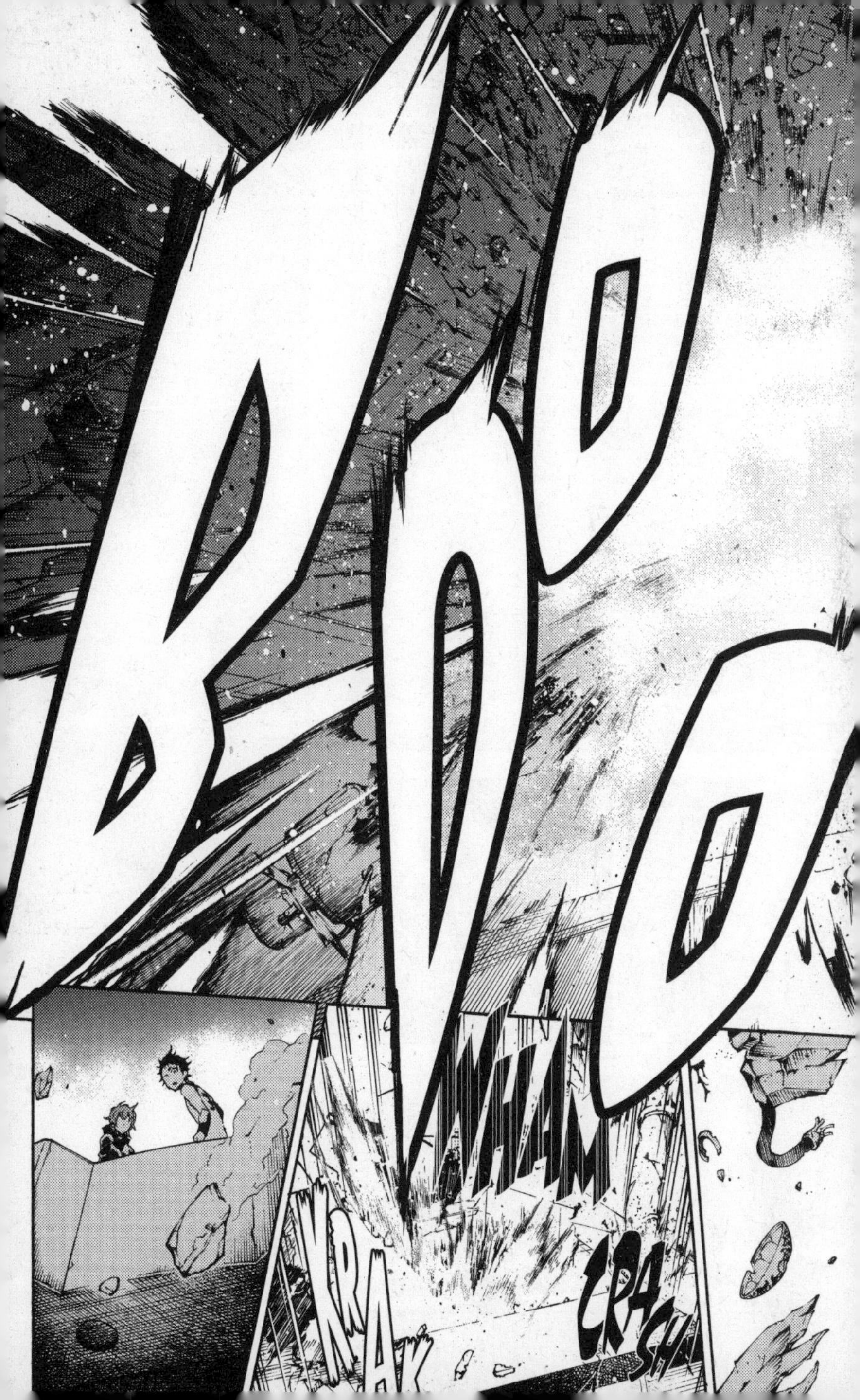
BOOO
WHAM
KRAK
CRASH

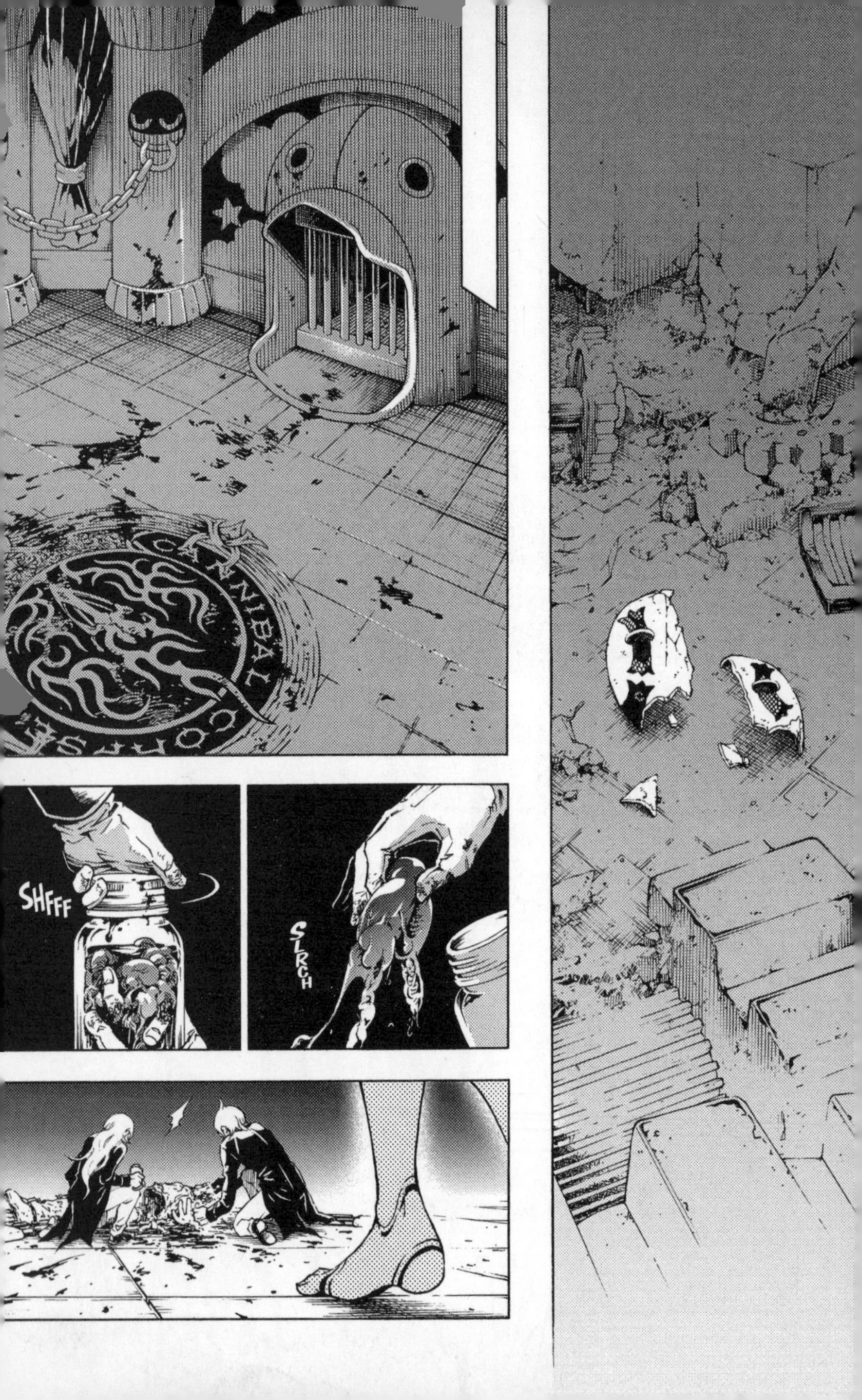
CANNIBAL CORPSE
SLRCH
SHFFFF

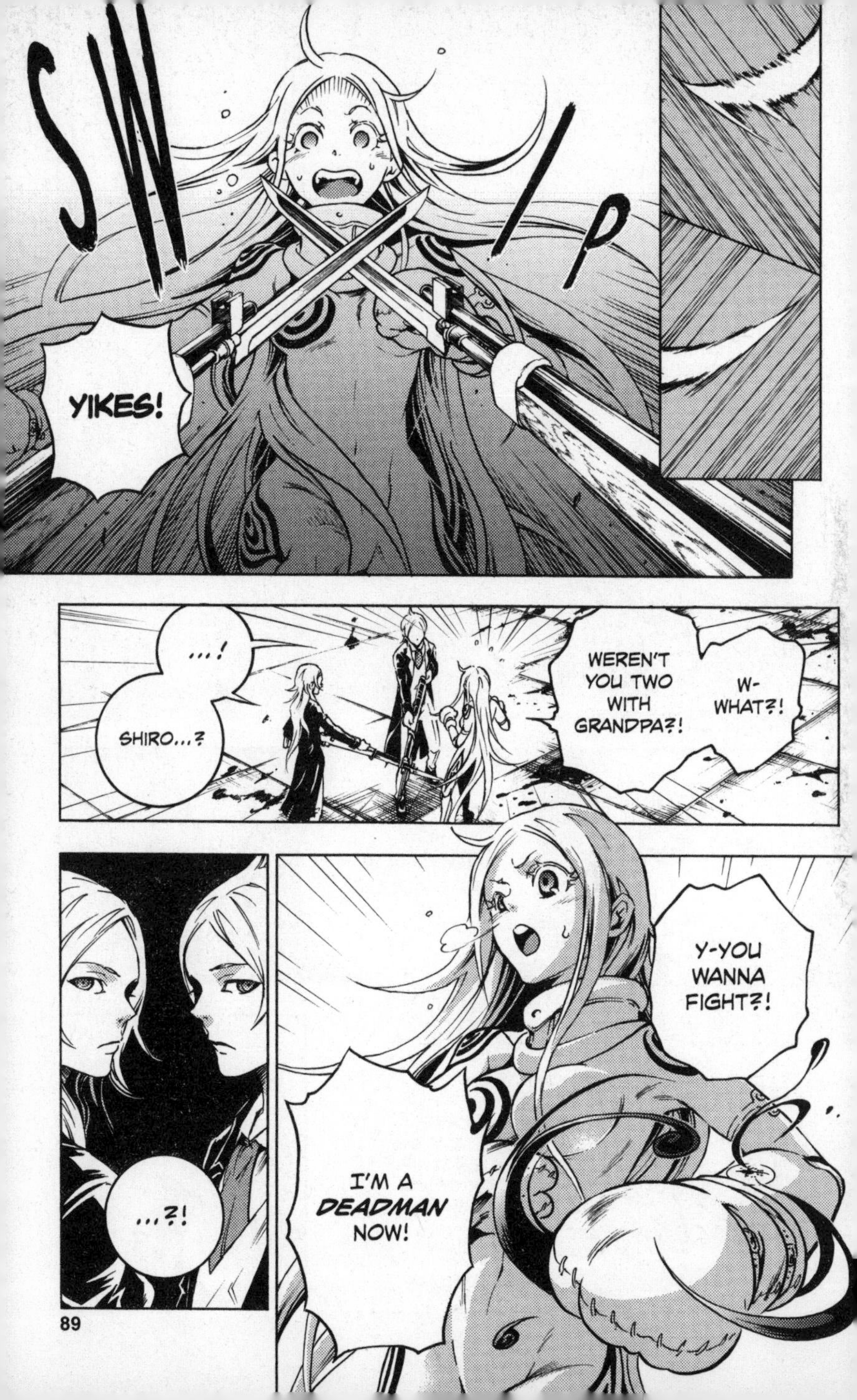
SWIP
YIKES!
W- WHAT?!
WEREN'T YOU TWO WITH GRANDPA?!
...!
SHIRO...?
Y-YOU WANNA FIGHT?!
I'M A *DEADMAN* NOW!
...?!

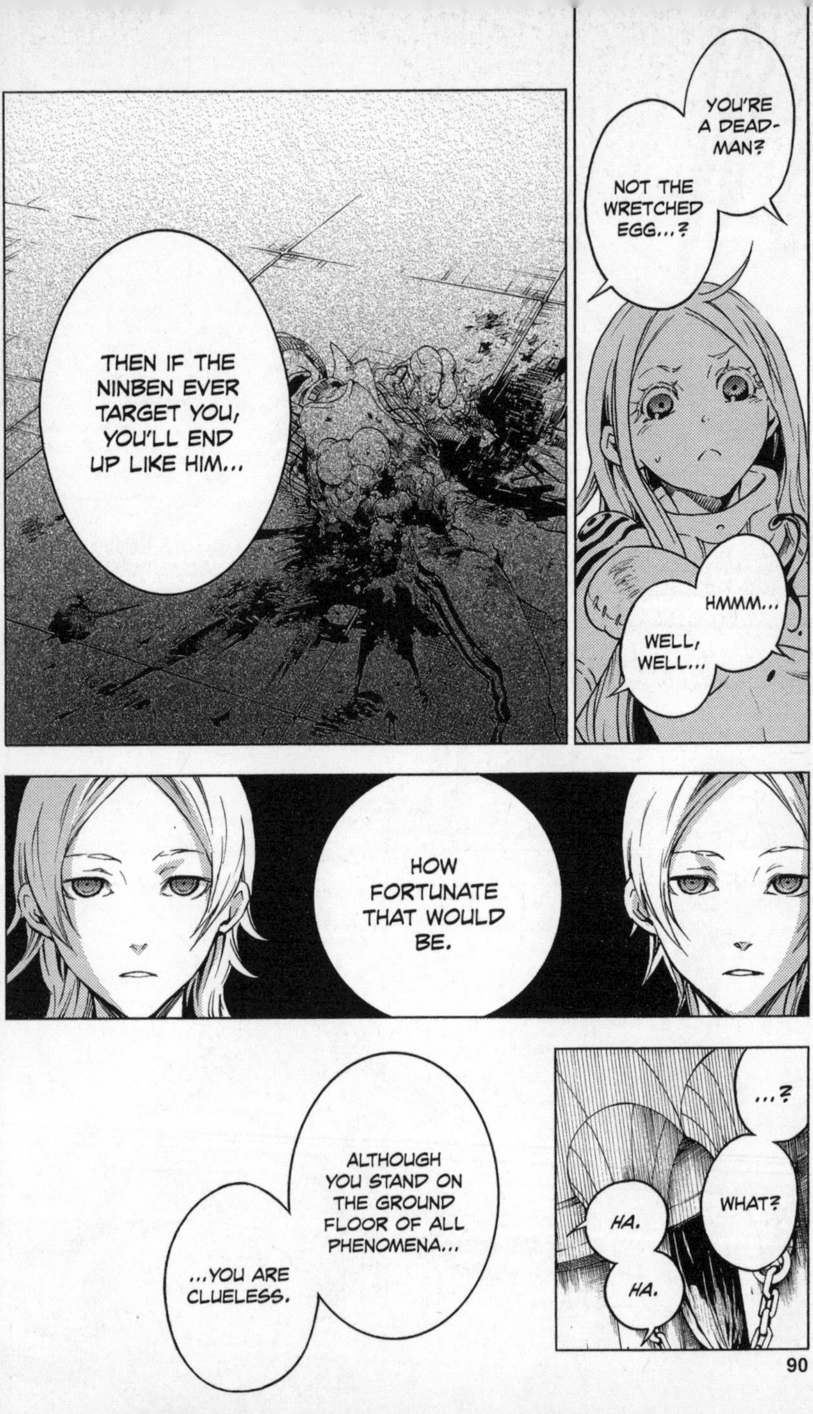
YOU'RE A DEAD-MAN?
NOT THE WRETCHED EGG...?
HMMM...
WELL, WELL...
THEN IF THE NINBEN EVER TARGET YOU, YOU'LL END UP LIKE HIM...
HOW FORTUNATE THAT WOULD BE.
...?
WHAT?
HA.
HA.
ALTHOUGH YOU STAND ON THE GROUND FLOOR OF ALL PHENOMENA...
...YOU ARE CLUELESS.

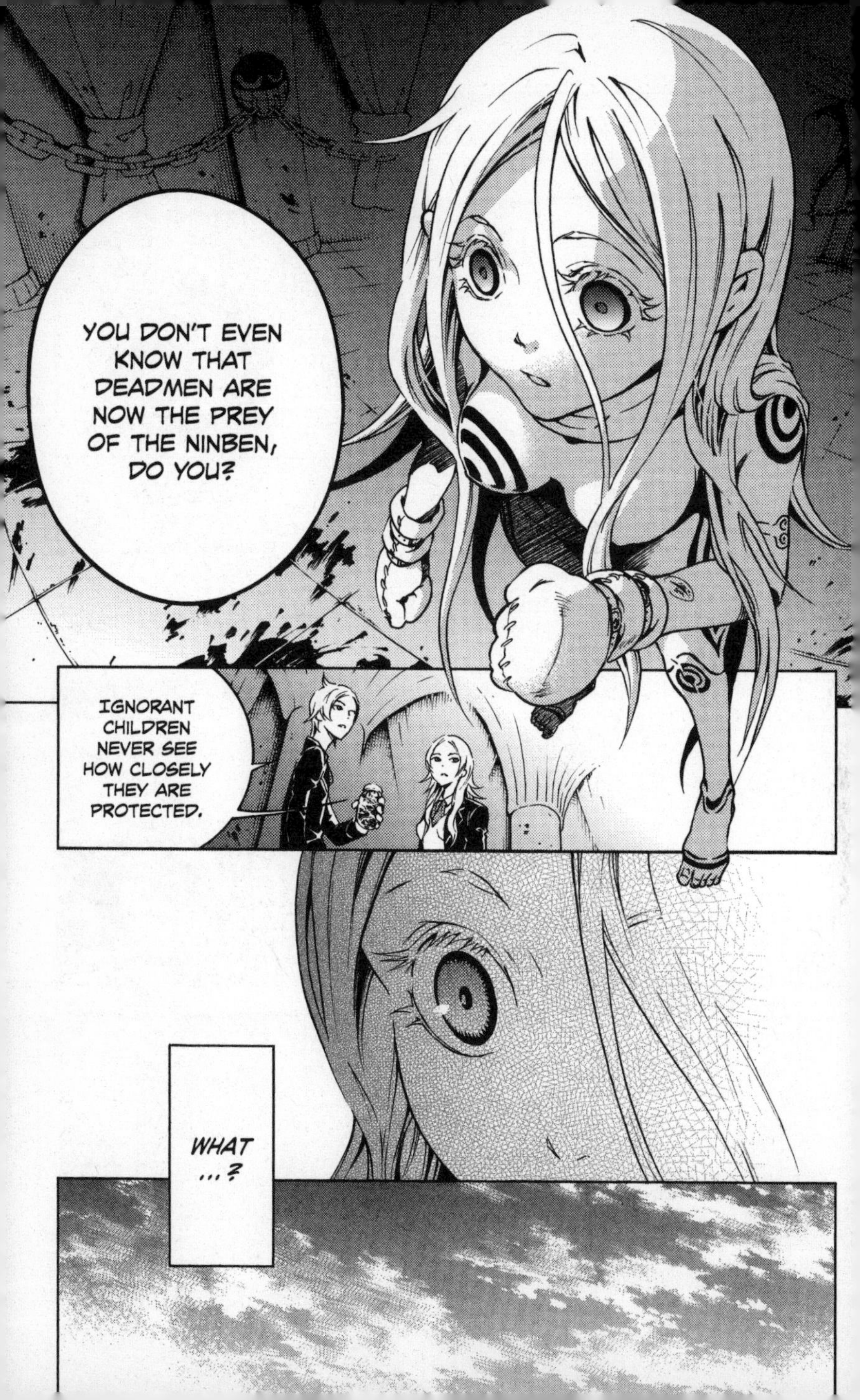
YOU DON'T EVEN KNOW THAT DEADMEN ARE NOW THE PREY OF THE NINBEN, DO YOU?
IGNORANT CHILDREN NEVER SEE HOW CLOSELY THEY ARE PROTECTED.
WHAT ...?

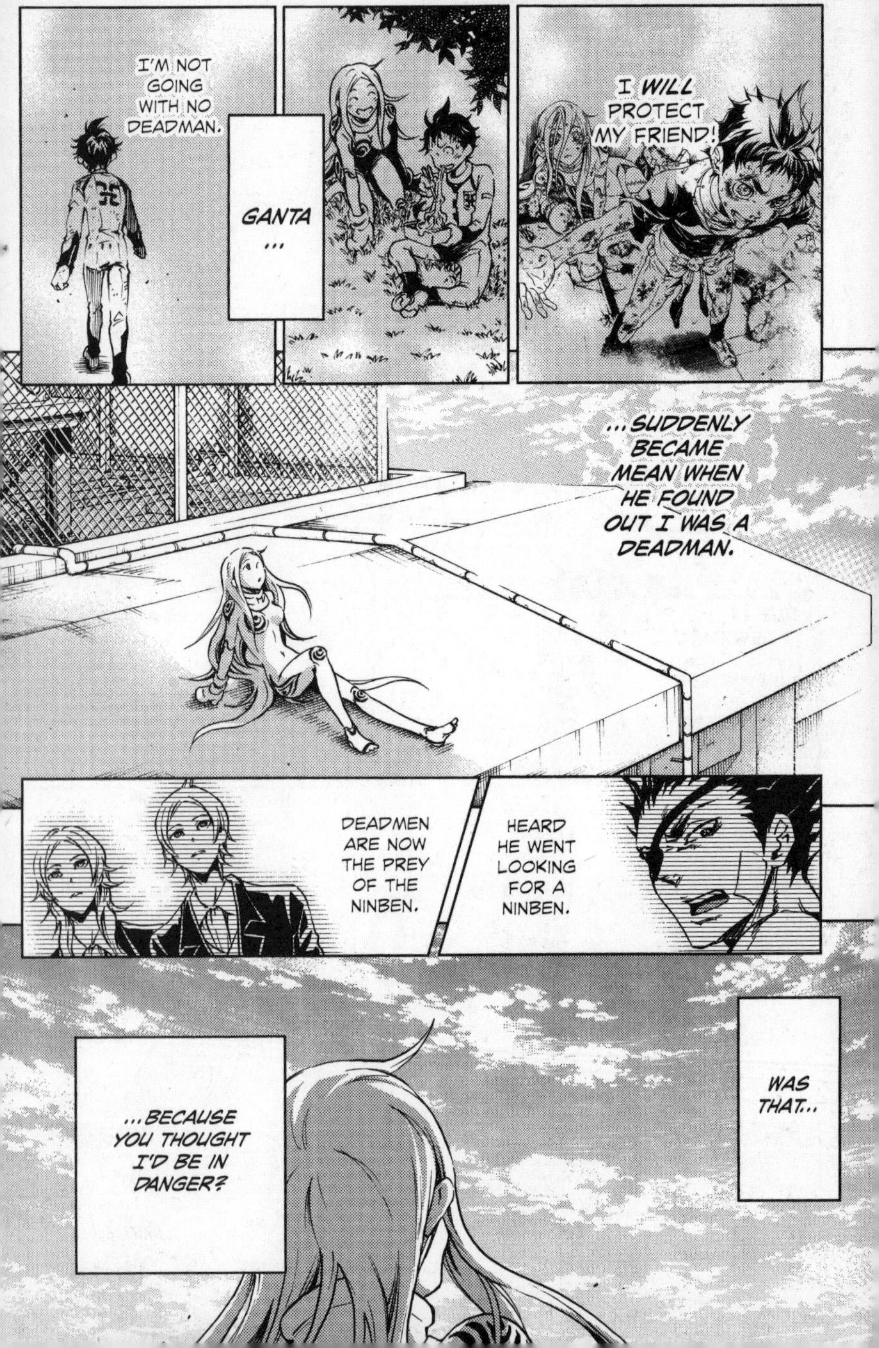
I WILL PROTECT MY FRIEND!
GANTA ...
I'M NOT GOING WITH NO DEADMAN.
...SUDDENLY BECAME MEAN WHEN HE FOUND OUT I WAS A DEADMAN.
HEARD HE WENT LOOKING FOR A NINBEN.
DEADMEN ARE NOW THE PREY OF THE NINBEN.
WAS THAT...
...BECAUSE YOU THOUGHT I'D BE IN DANGER?

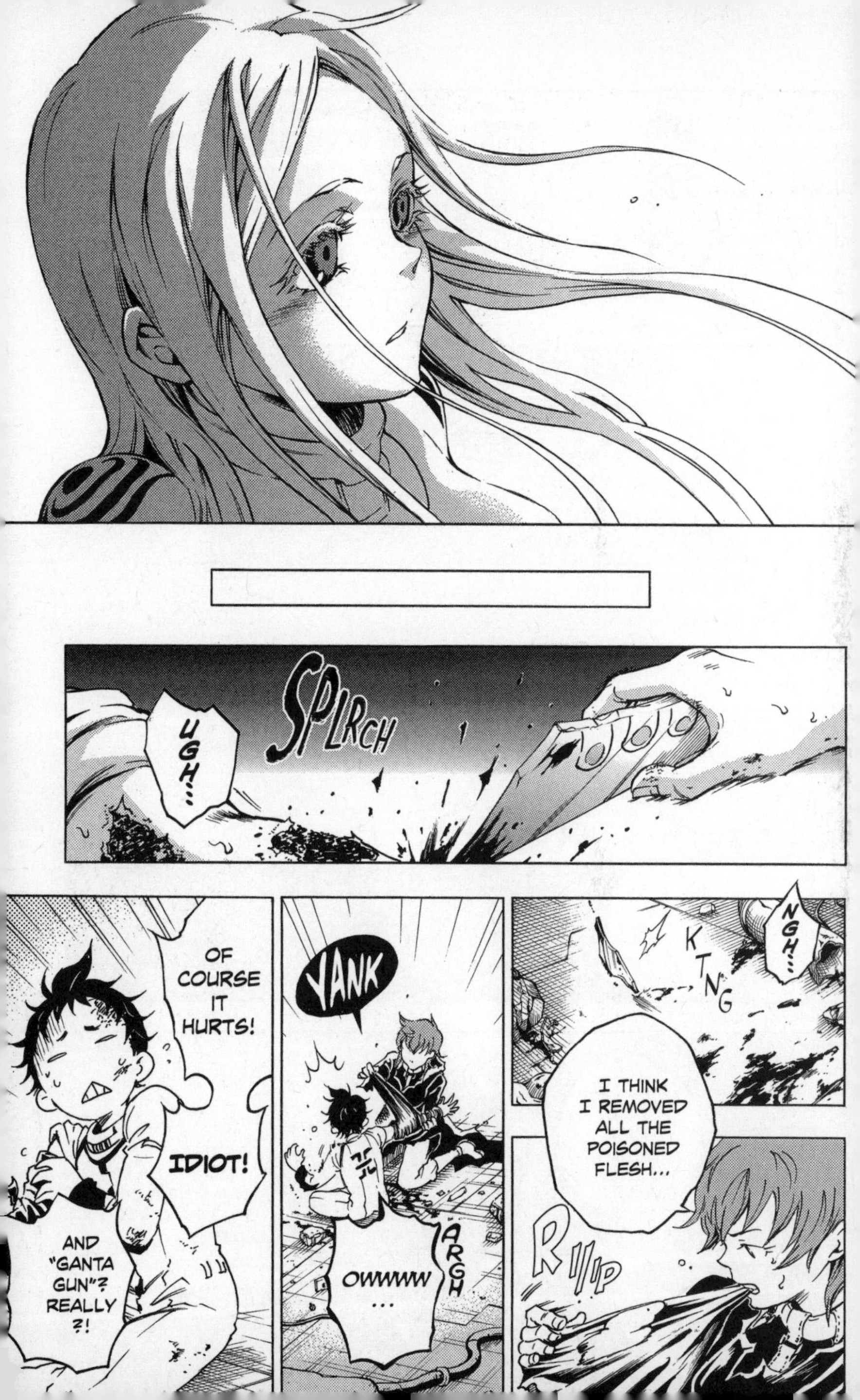
SPLRCH
UGH...
NGH...
KTNG
I THINK I REMOVED ALL THE POISONED FLESH...
RIIP
YANK
ARGH
OWWWW...
OF COURSE IT HURTS!
IDIOT!
AND "GANTA GUN"? REALLY?!

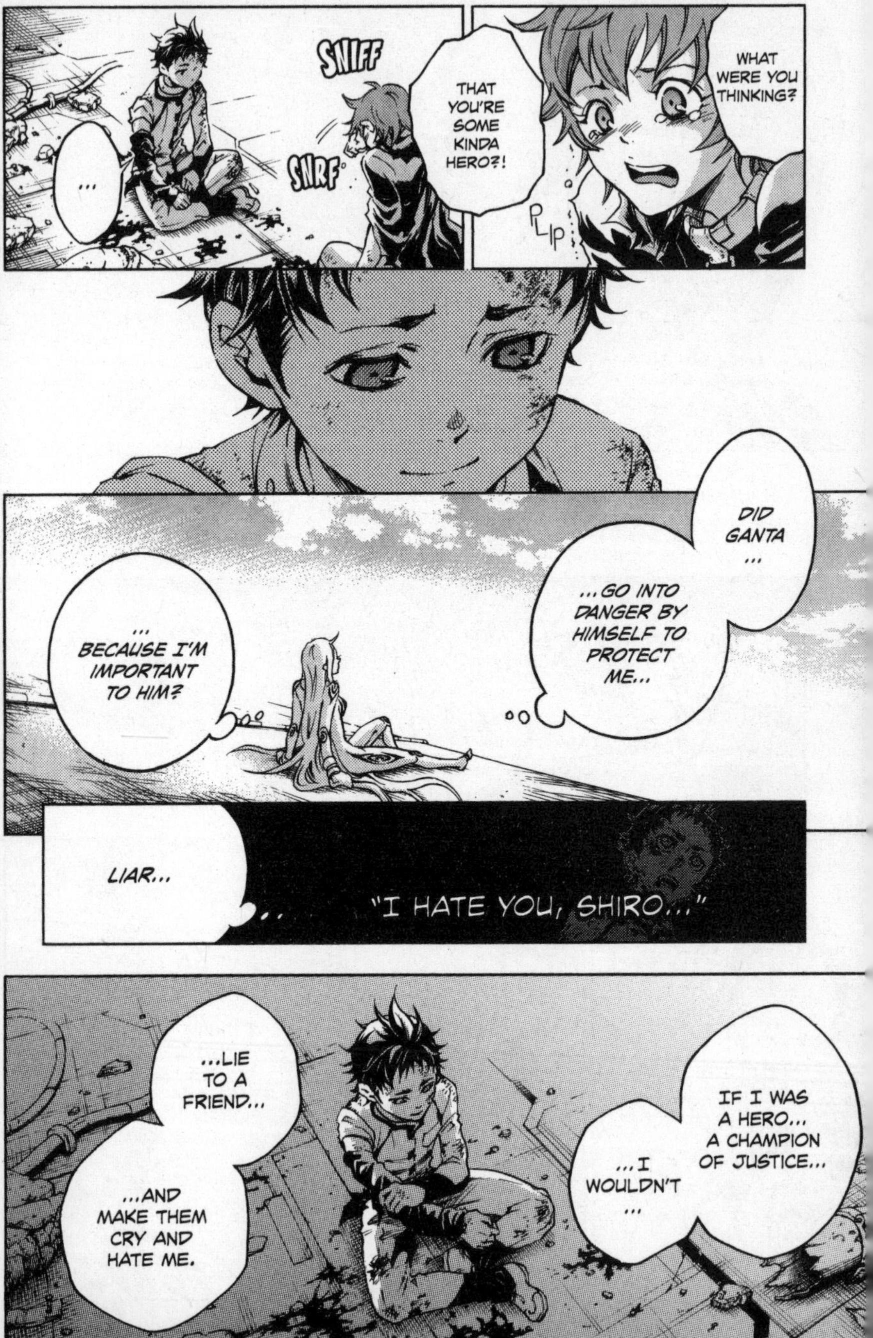
WHAT WERE YOU THINKING?
PLIP
THAT YOU'RE SOME KINDA HERO?!
SNIFF
SNRF
...
DID GANTA ...
...GO INTO DANGER BY HIMSELF TO PROTECT ME...
... BECAUSE I'M IMPORTANT TO HIM?
"I HATE YOU, SHIRO..."
LIAR...
IF I WAS A HERO... A CHAMPION OF JUSTICE...
...I WOULDN'T ...
...LIE TO A FRIEND...
...AND MAKE THEM CRY AND HATE ME.

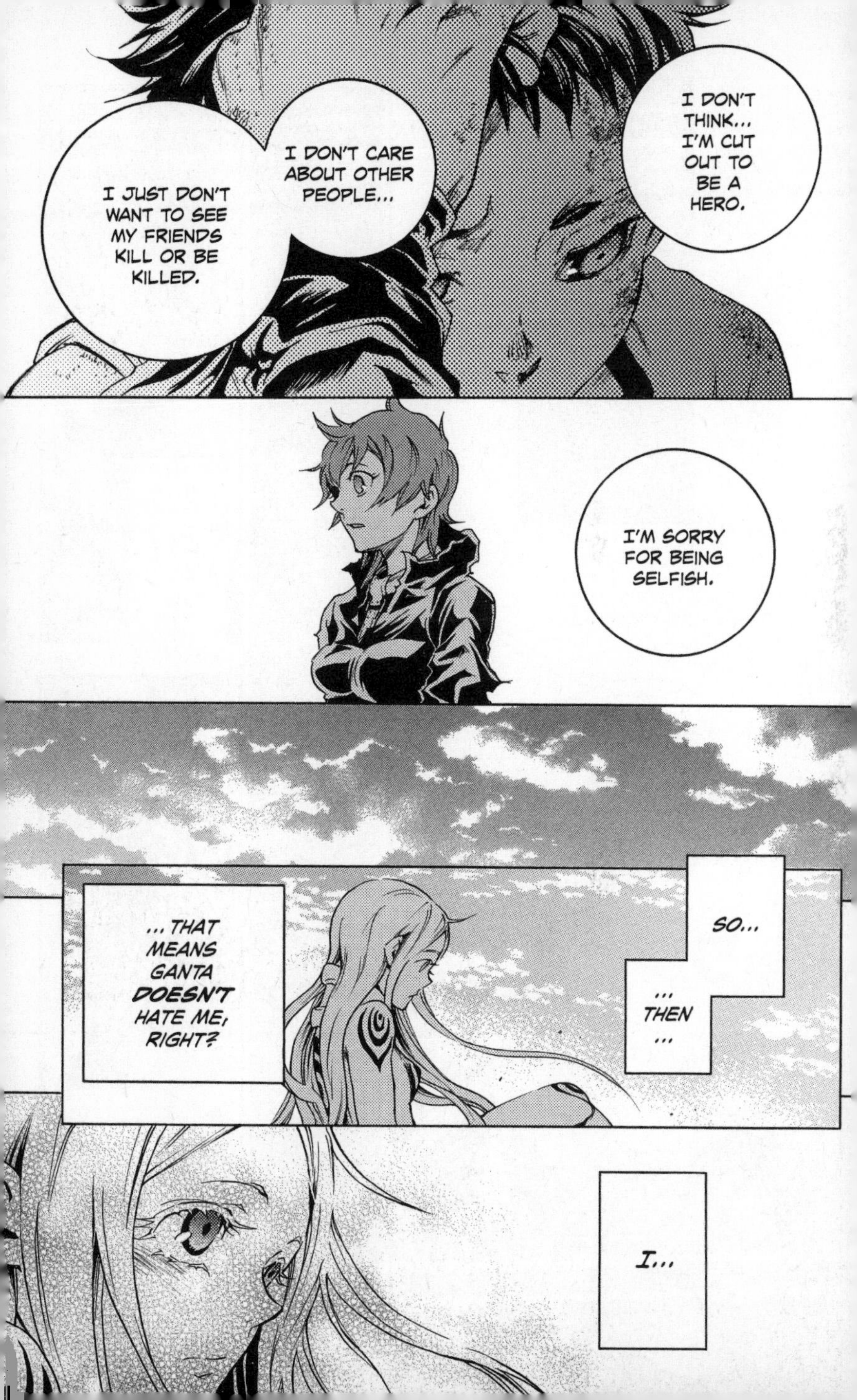
I DON'T THINK... I'M CUT OUT TO BE A HERO.
I DON'T CARE ABOUT OTHER PEOPLE...
I JUST DON'T WANT TO SEE MY FRIENDS KILL OR BE KILLED.
I'M SORRY FOR BEING SELFISH.
SO...
...THEN...
...THAT MEANS GANTA DOESN'T HATE ME, RIGHT?
I...

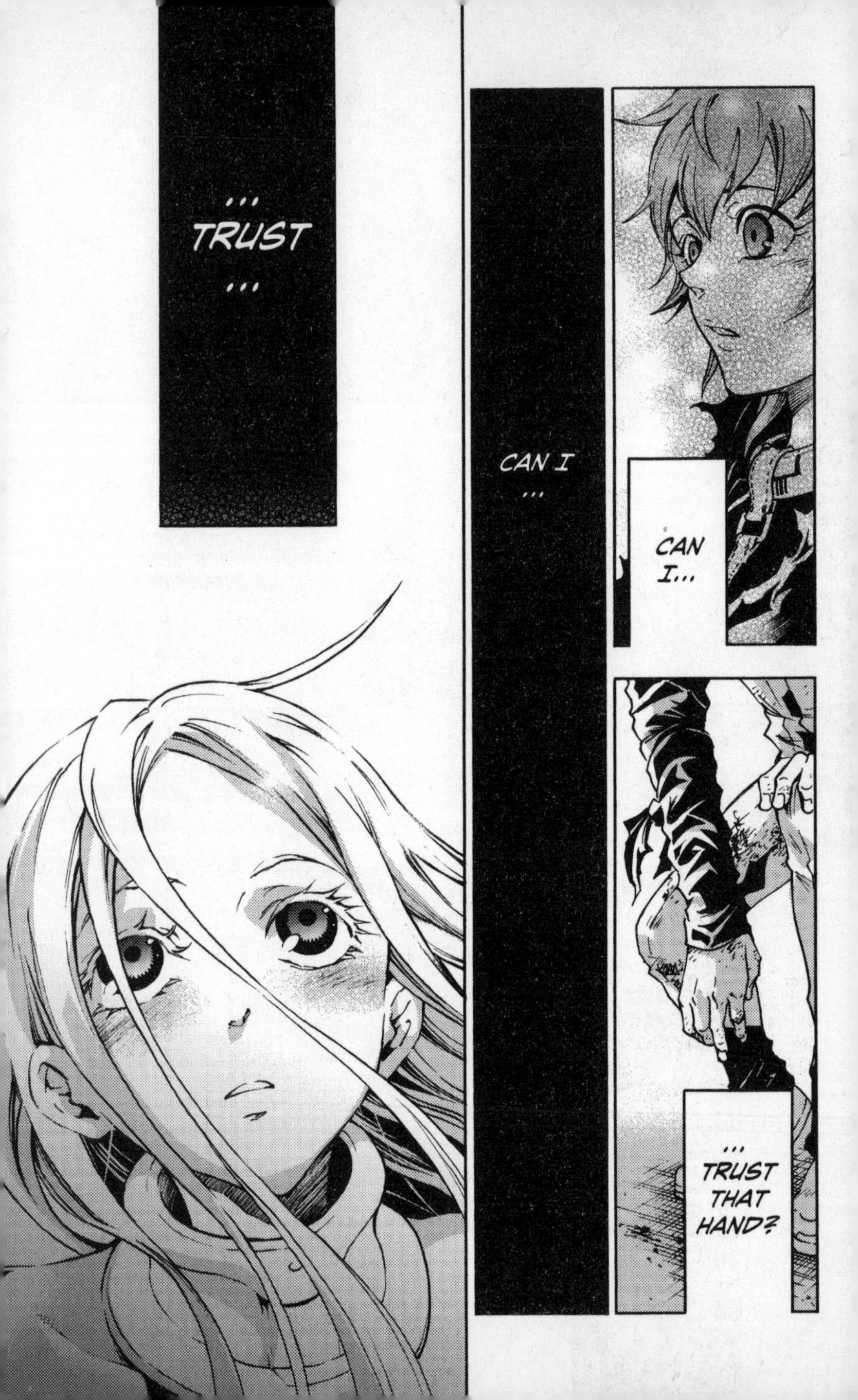
CAN I...
... TRUST THAT HAND?
CAN I ...
... TRUST ...

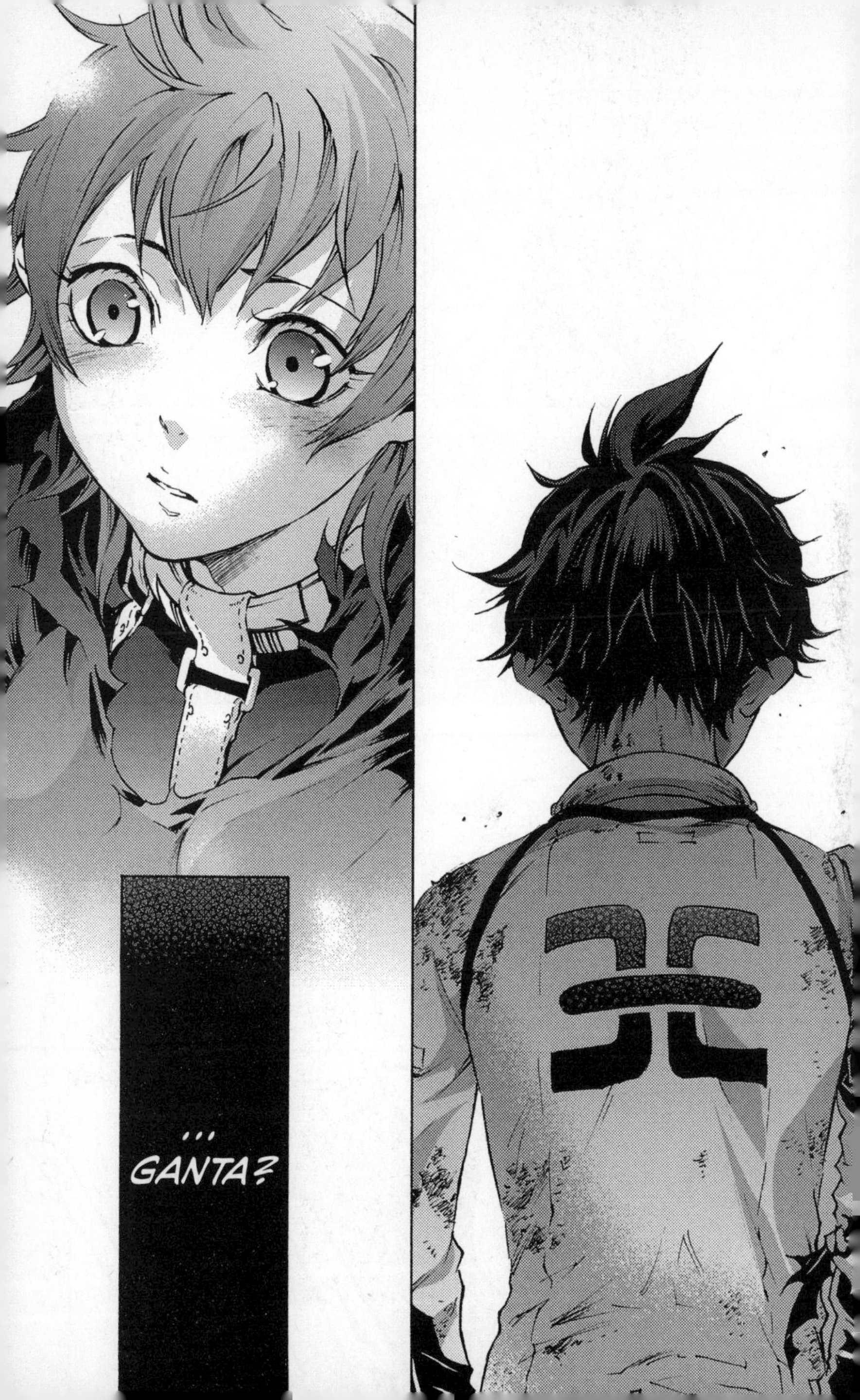

... GANTA?

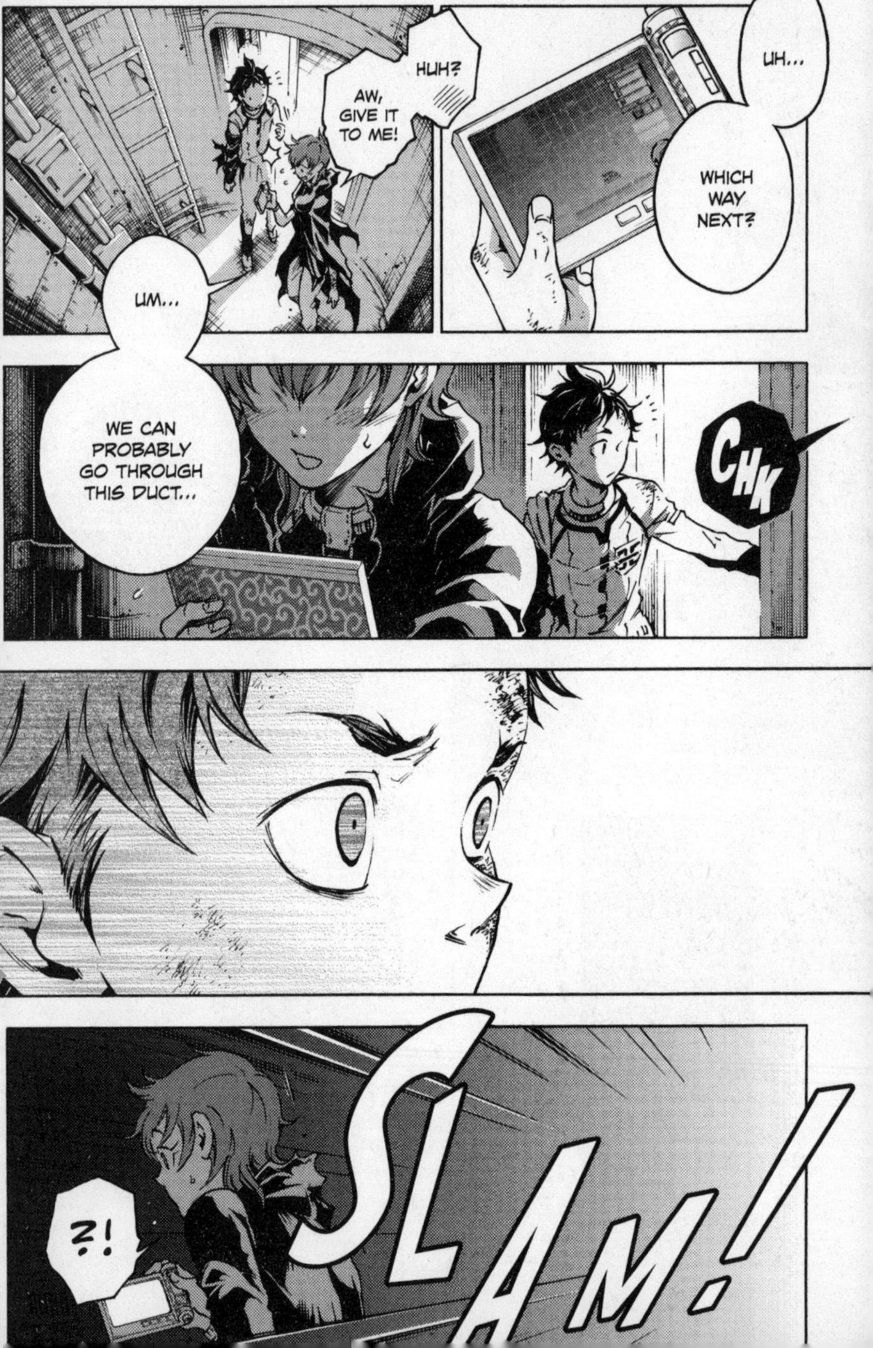
UH...
WHICH WAY NEXT?
HUH?
AW, GIVE IT TO ME!
UM...
WE CAN PROBABLY GO THROUGH THIS DUCT...
CHK
SLAM!
?!

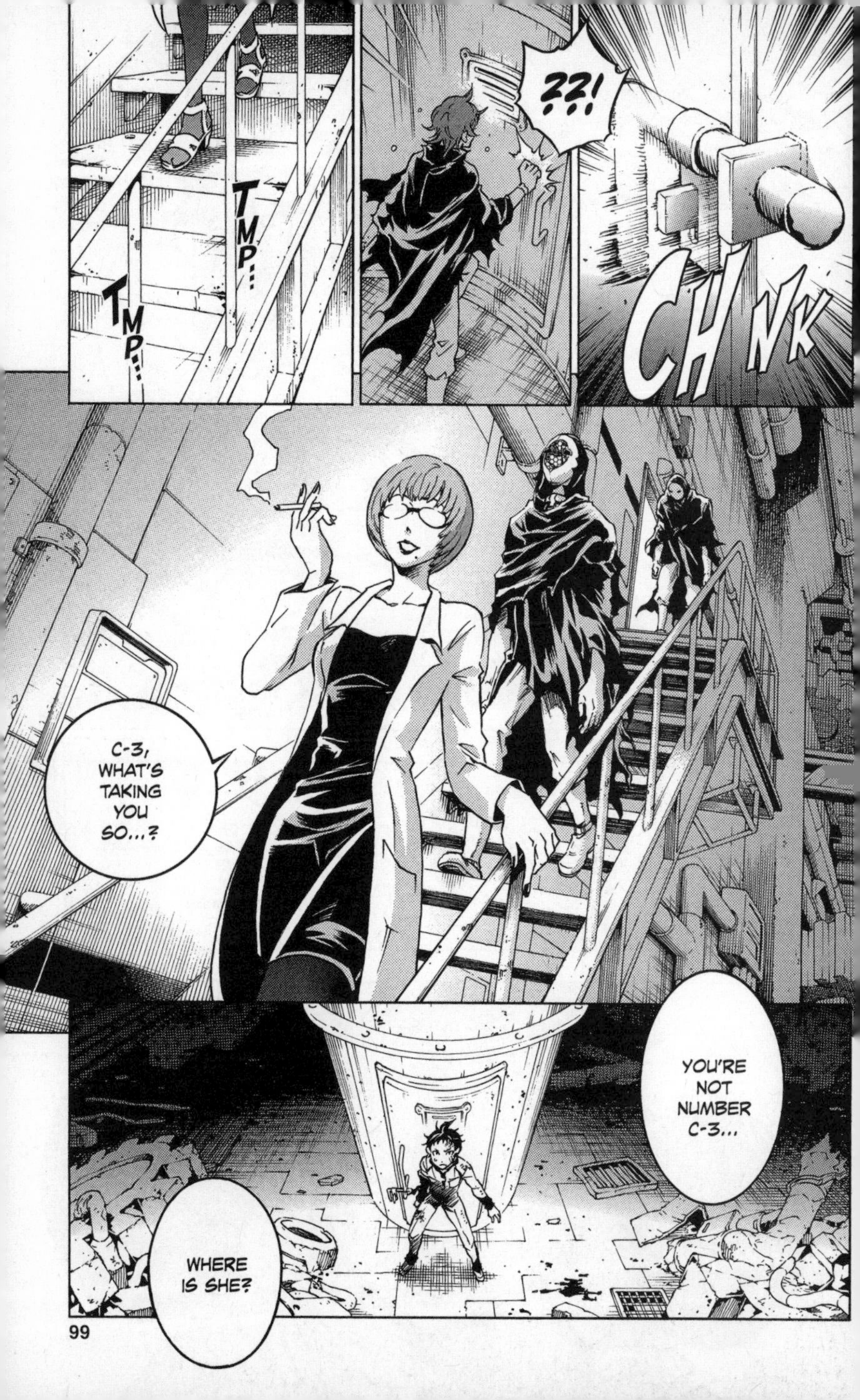
CHINK
??!
TMP...
TMP...
C-3, WHAT'S TAKING YOU SO...?
YOU'RE NOT NUMBER C-3...
WHERE IS SHE?

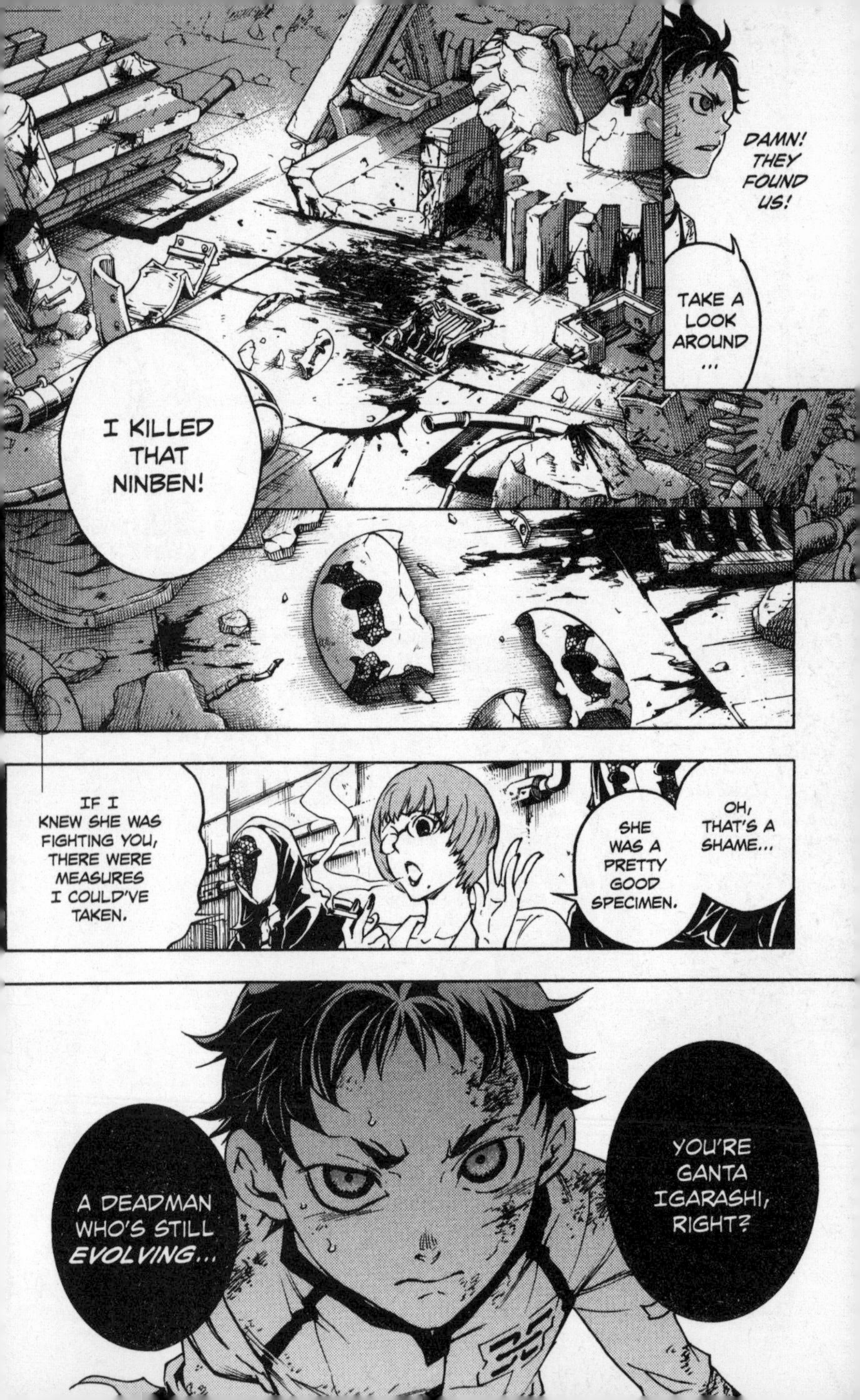
DAMN! THEY FOUND US!
TAKE A LOOK AROUND ...
I KILLED THAT NINBEN!
OH, THAT'S A SHAME...
SHE WAS A PRETTY GOOD SPECIMEN.
IF I KNEW SHE WAS FIGHTING YOU, THERE WERE MEASURES I COULD'VE TAKEN.
YOU'RE GANTA IGARASHI, RIGHT?
A DEADMAN WHO'S STILL *EVOLVING*...

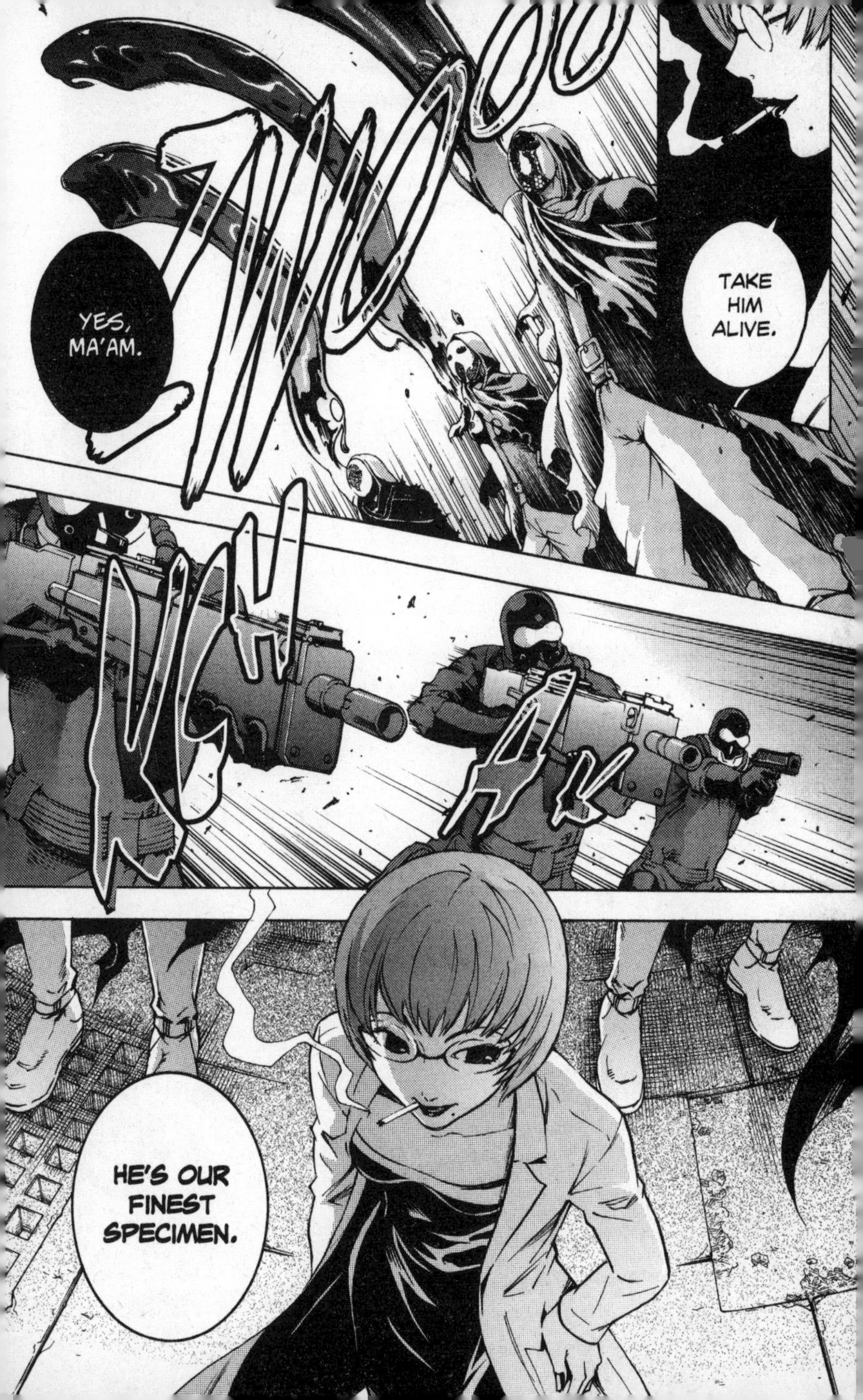
TAKE HIM ALIVE.
YES, MA'AM.
HE'S OUR FINEST SPECIMEN.

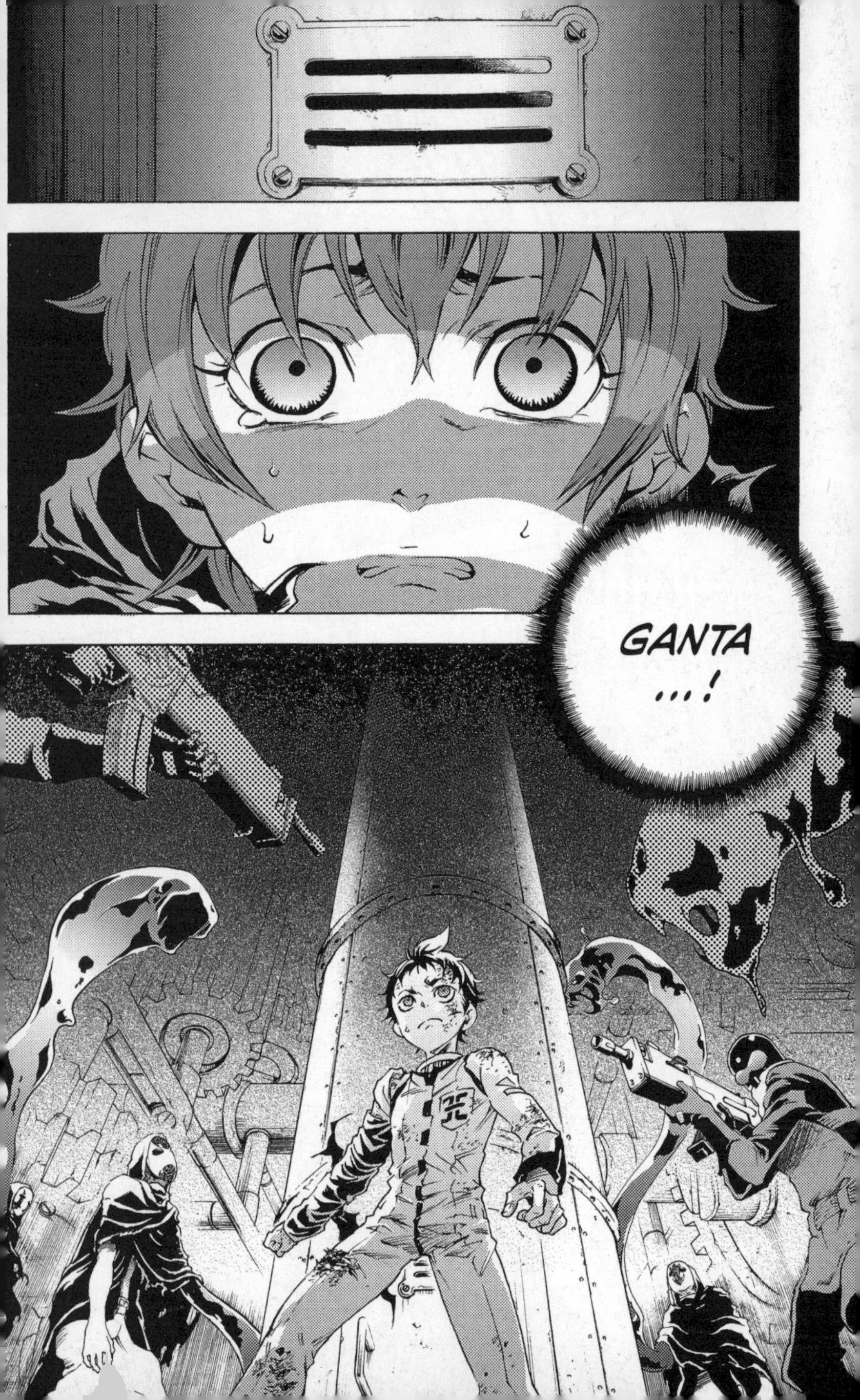
GANTA ...!

DW

DEADMAN WONDER LAND

DW DW

DEADMAN WONDER LAND

DEADMAN WONDER LAND

DW DW

DEADMAN WONDER LAND

DEADMAN WONDER LAND

DW DW

DEADMAN WONDER LAND

DEADMAN WONDER LAND

DW DW

DEADMAN WONDER LAND

DEADMAN WONDER LAND

DW DW

DEADMAN WONDER LAND

DEADMAN WONDER LAND

29 Never Say Never Again

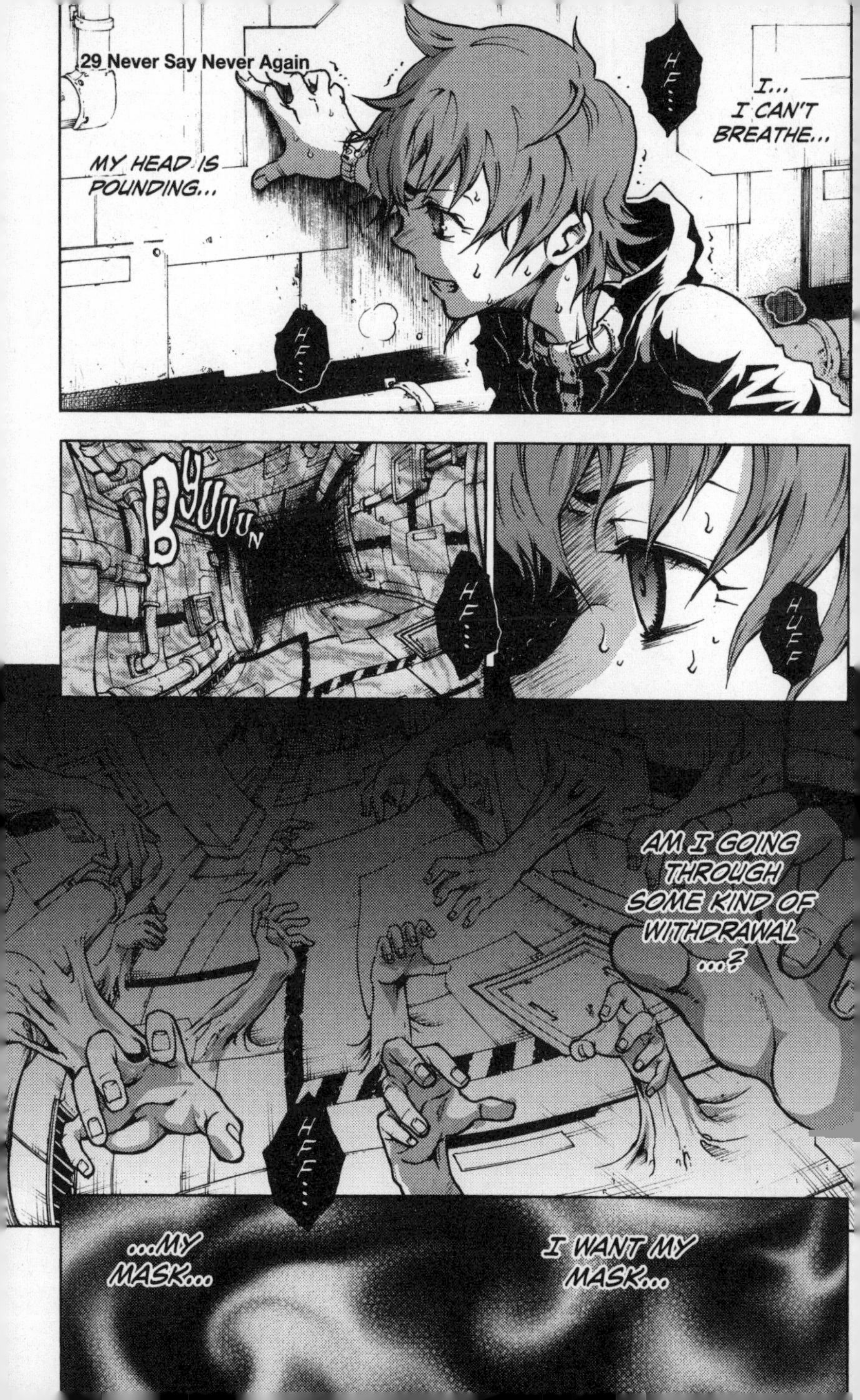
HF...
I... I CAN'T BREATHE...
MY HEAD IS POUNDING...
HF...
HUFF
HF...
BYUUUN
AM I GOING THROUGH SOME KIND OF WITHDRAWAL...?
HFF...
I WANT MY MASK...
...MY MASK...

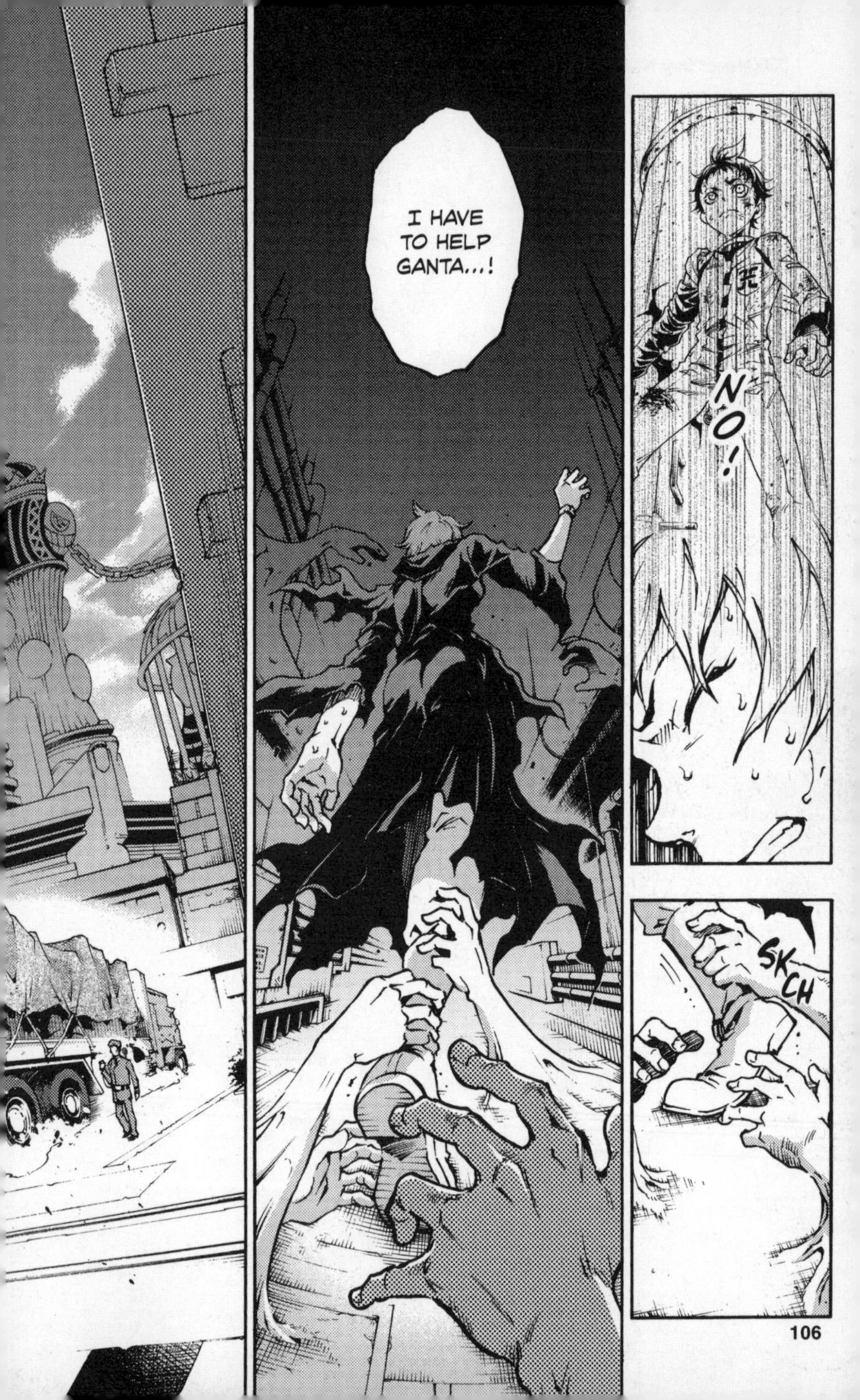
NO!
SKCH
I HAVE TO HELP GANTA...!

29 Never Say Never Again

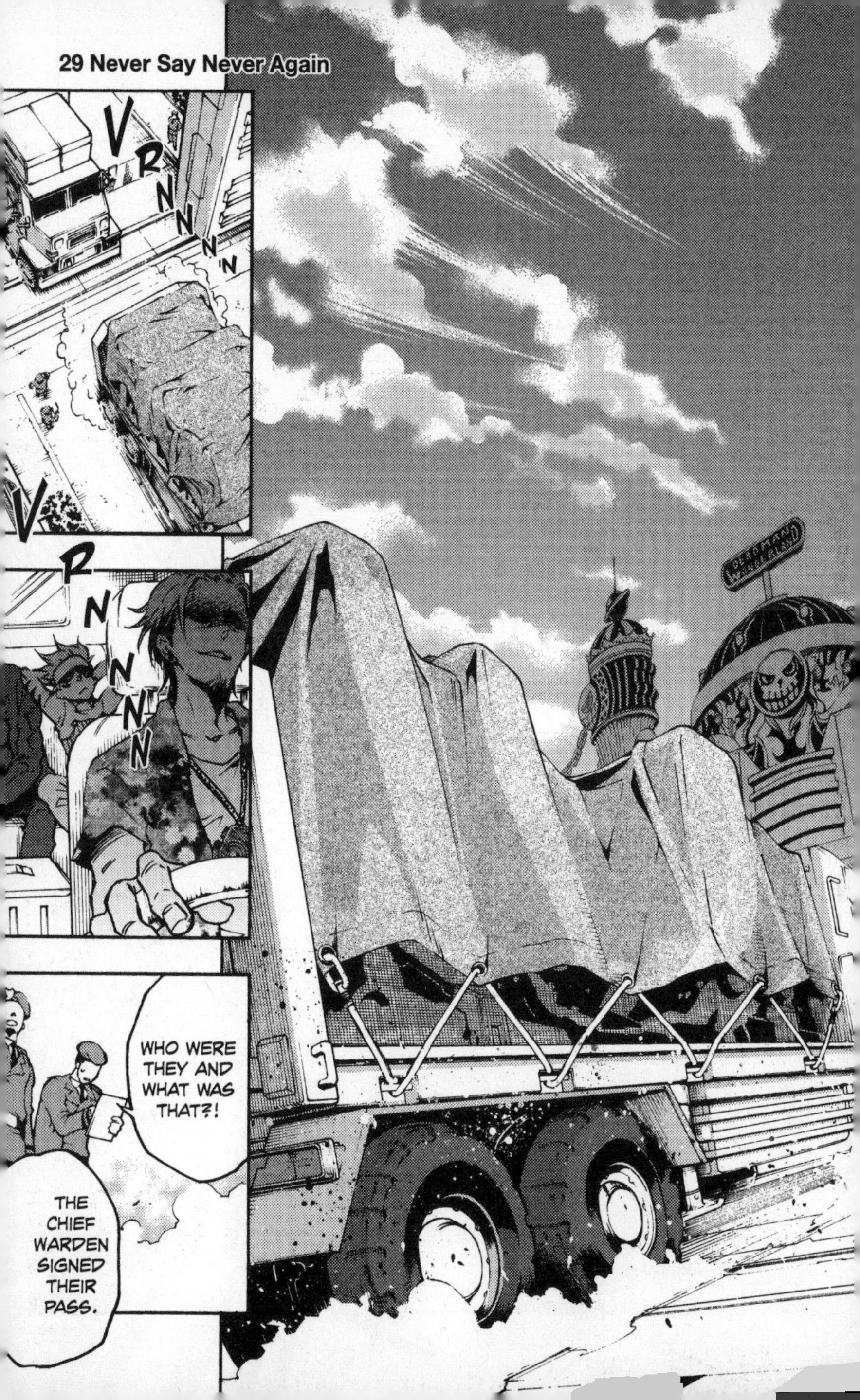
VRNNN'N
VRNNNNN
WHO WERE THEY AND WHAT WAS THAT?!
THE CHIEF WARDEN SIGNED THEIR PASS.

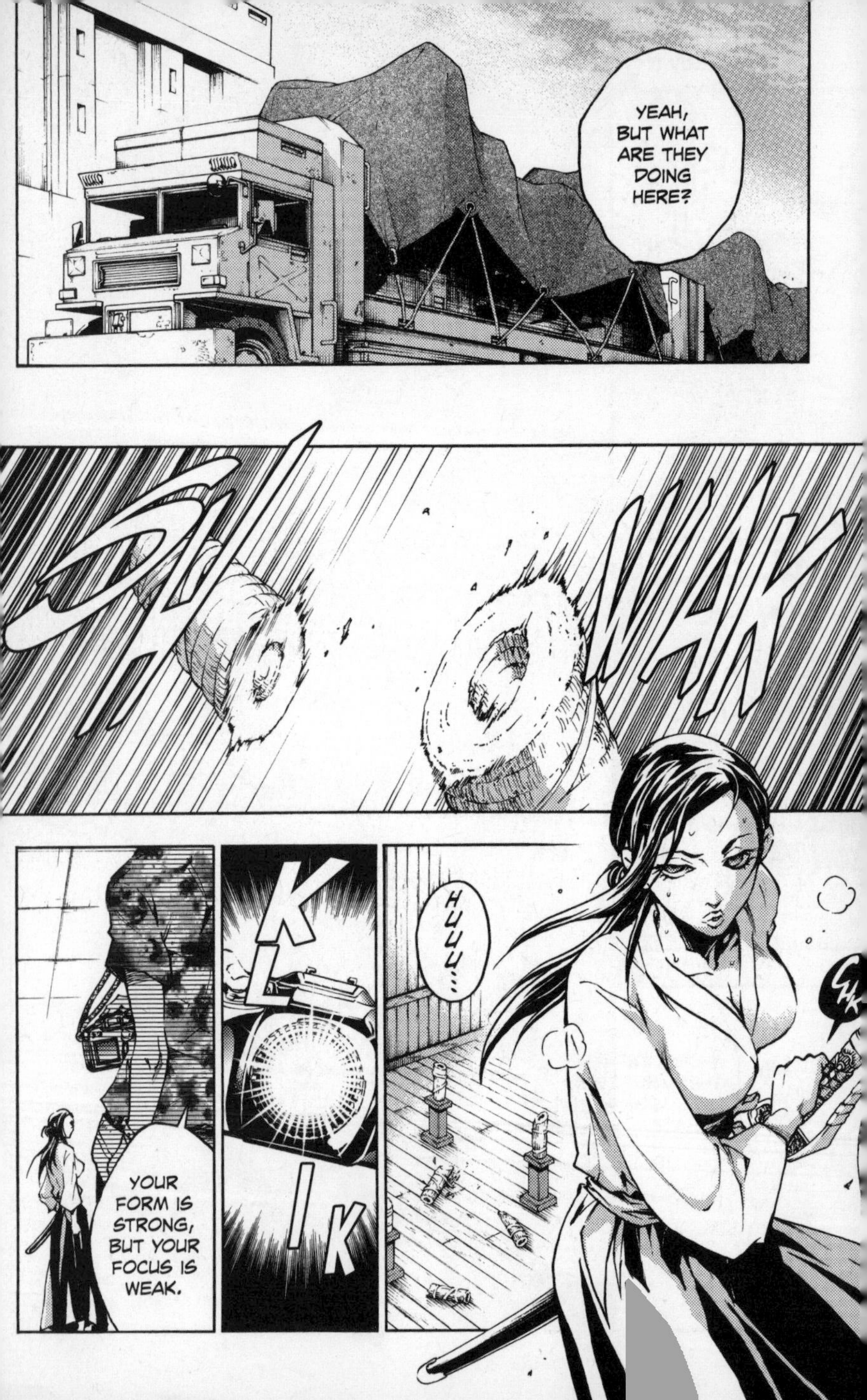
YEAH, BUT WHAT ARE THEY DOING HERE?
SHWAK
HUUU...
CHK
KLIK
YOUR FORM IS STRONG, BUT YOUR FOCUS IS WEAK.

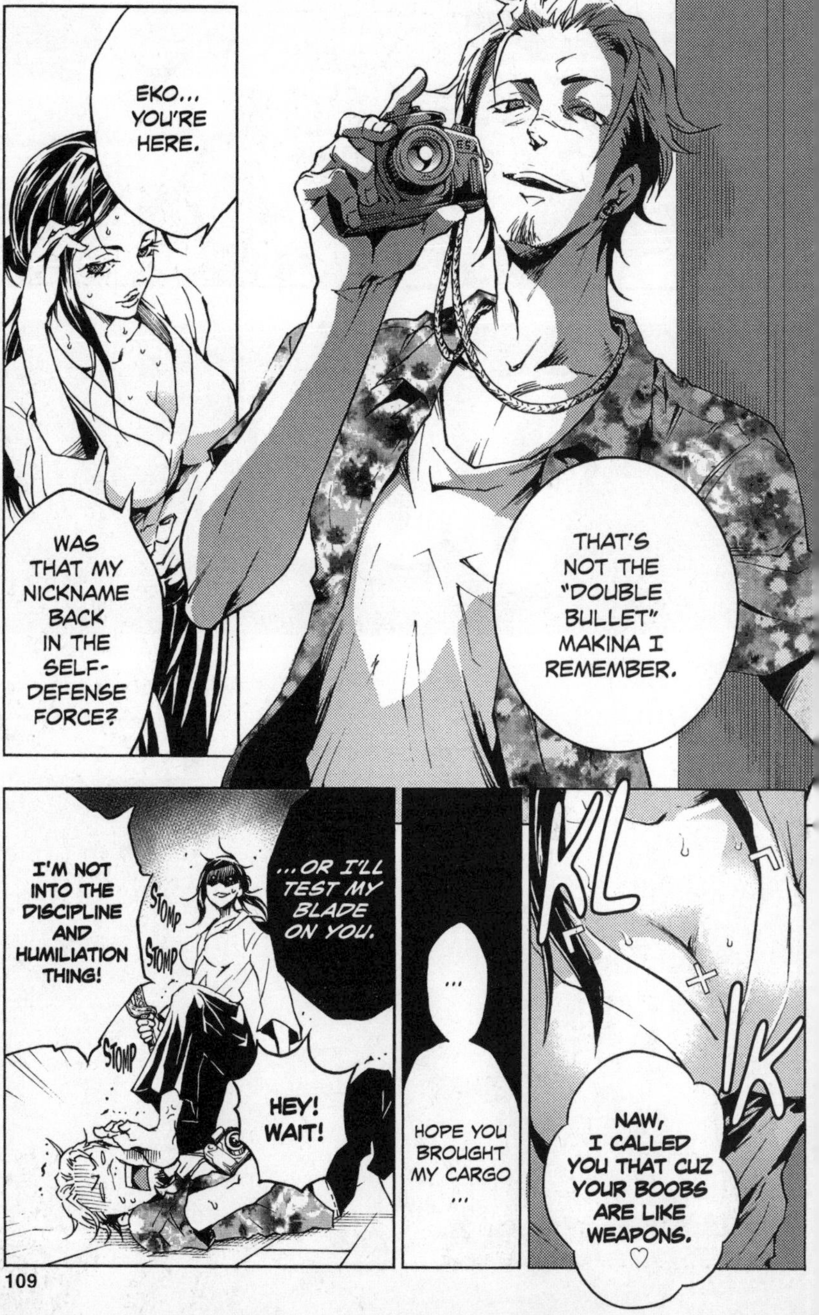
EKO... YOU'RE HERE.
THAT'S NOT THE "DOUBLE BULLET" MAKINA I REMEMBER.
WAS THAT MY NICKNAME BACK IN THE SELF-DEFENSE FORCE?
KLIK
NAW, I CALLED YOU THAT CUZ YOUR BOOBS ARE LIKE WEAPONS. ♡
...
HOPE YOU BROUGHT MY CARGO ...
...OR I'LL TEST MY BLADE ON YOU.
I'M NOT INTO THE DISCIPLINE AND HUMILIATION THING!
STOMP
STOMP
STOMP
HEY! WAIT!

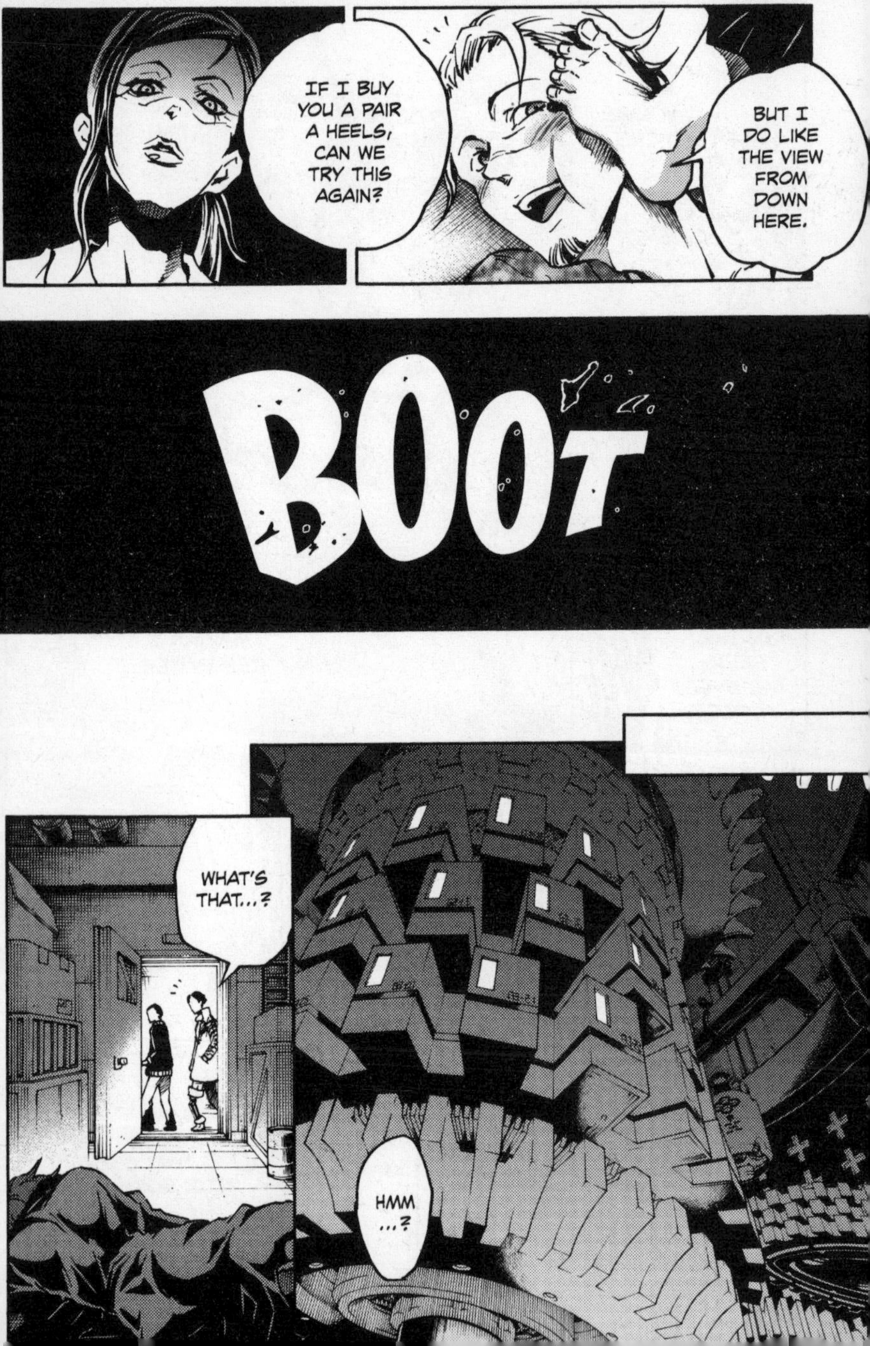
BUT I DO LIKE THE VIEW FROM DOWN HERE.
IF I BUY YOU A PAIR A HEELS, CAN WE TRY THIS AGAIN?
BOOT
HMM ...?
WHAT'S THAT...?

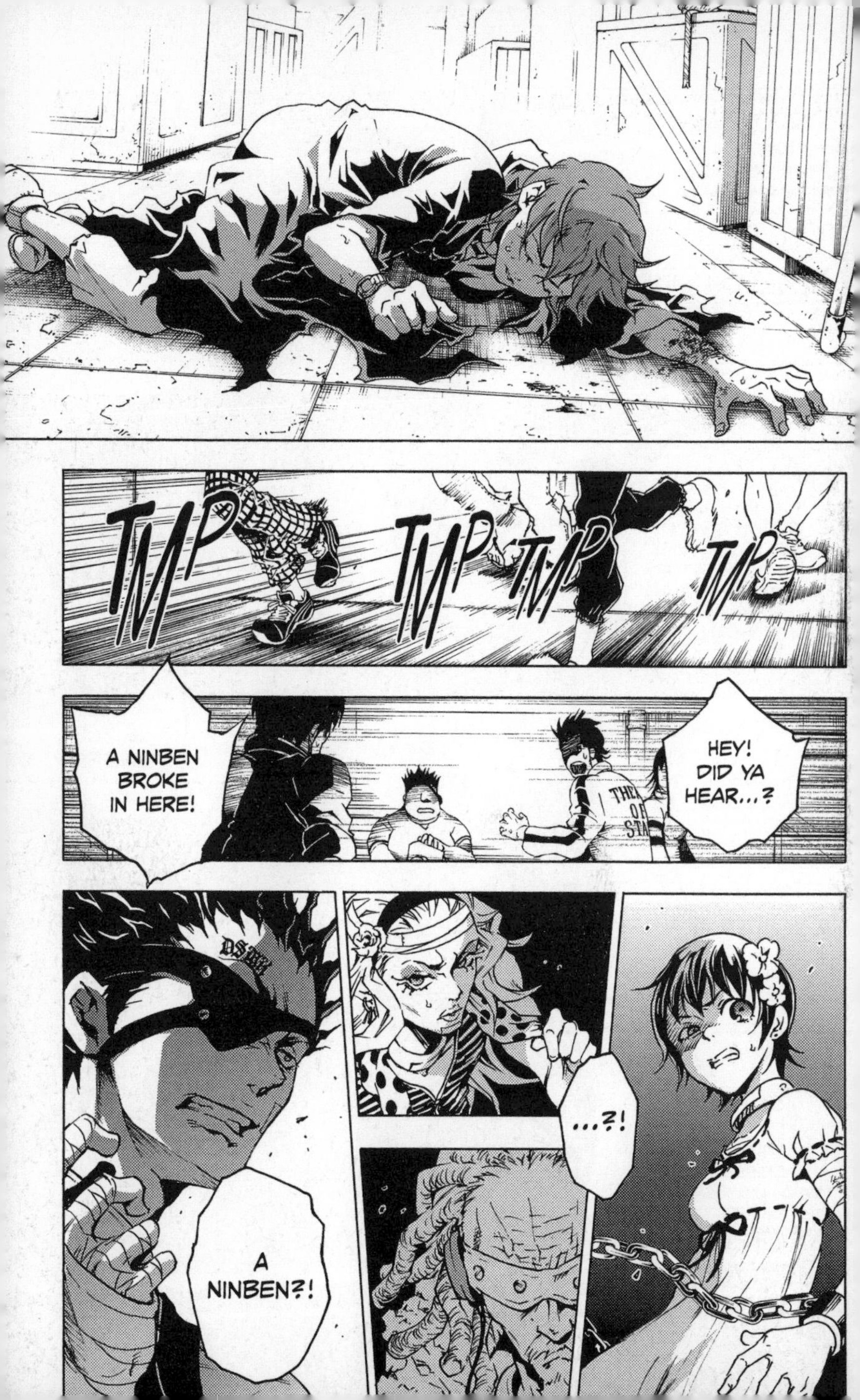
TMP TMP TMP TMP
HEY! DID YA HEAR...?
A NINBEN BROKE IN HERE!
...?!
A NINBEN?!

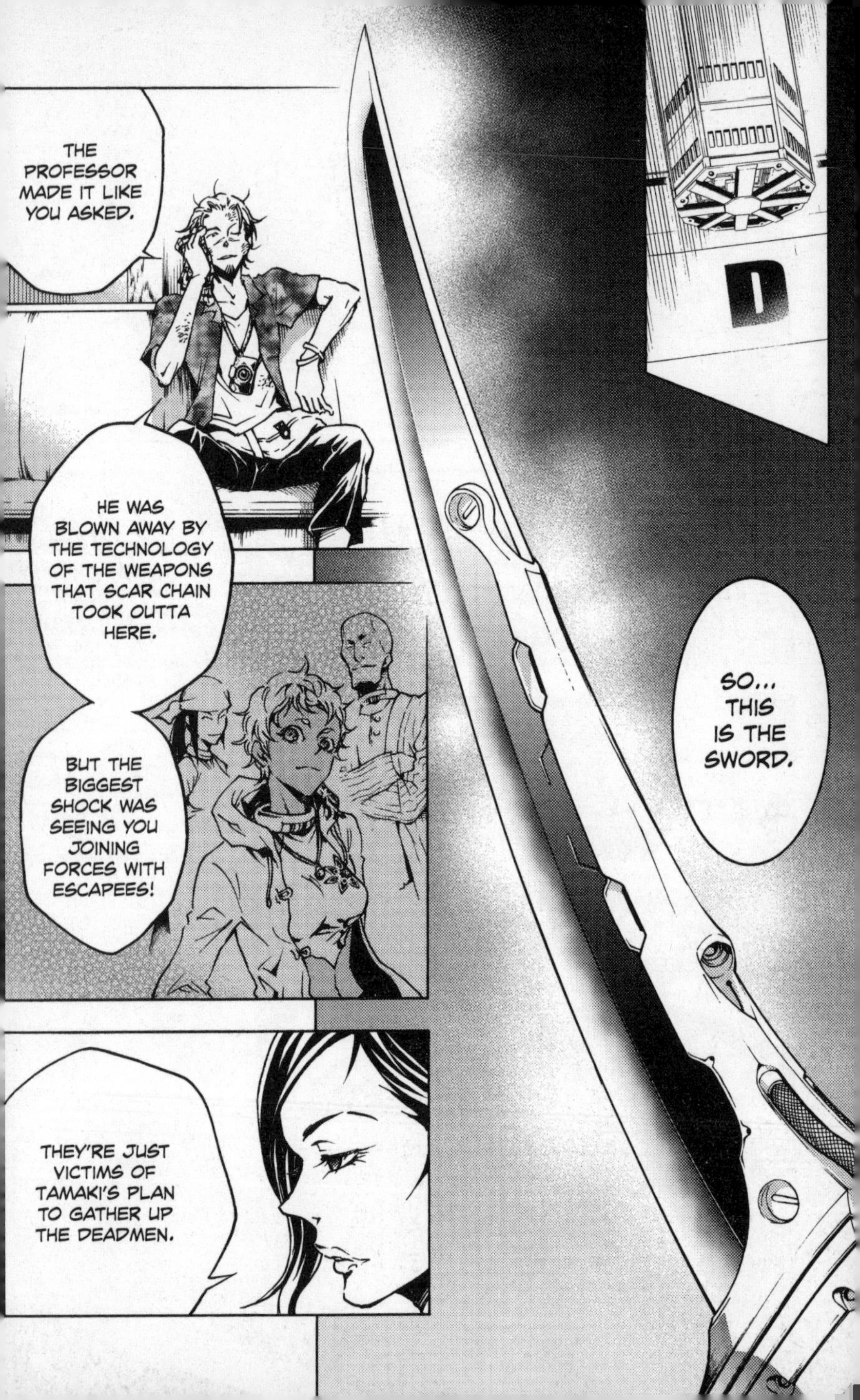
SO... THIS IS THE SWORD.
THE PROFESSOR MADE IT LIKE YOU ASKED.
HE WAS BLOWN AWAY BY THE TECHNOLOGY OF THE WEAPONS THAT SCAR CHAIN TOOK OUTTA HERE.
BUT THE BIGGEST SHOCK WAS SEEING YOU JOINING FORCES WITH ESCAPEES!
THEY'RE JUST VICTIMS OF TAMAKI'S PLAN TO GATHER UP THE DEADMEN.

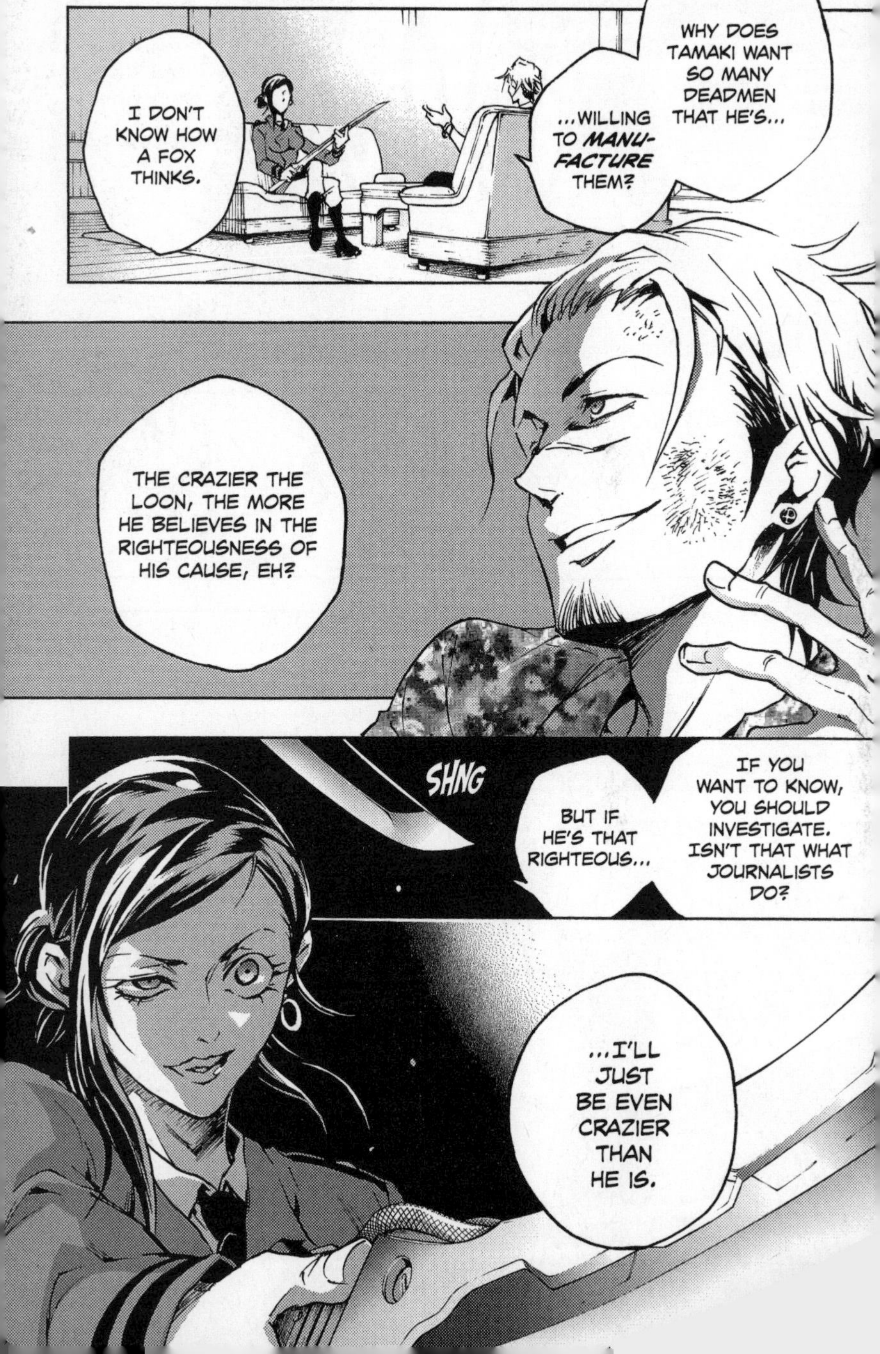
WHY DOES TAMAKI WANT SO MANY DEADMEN THAT HE'S...
...WILLING TO MANUFACTURE THEM?
I DON'T KNOW HOW A FOX THINKS.
THE CRAZIER THE LOON, THE MORE HE BELIEVES IN THE RIGHTEOUSNESS OF HIS CAUSE, EH?
IF YOU WANT TO KNOW, YOU SHOULD INVESTIGATE. ISN'T THAT WHAT JOURNALISTS DO?
BUT IF HE'S THAT RIGHTEOUS...
SHNG
...I'LL JUST BE EVEN CRAZIER THAN HE IS.

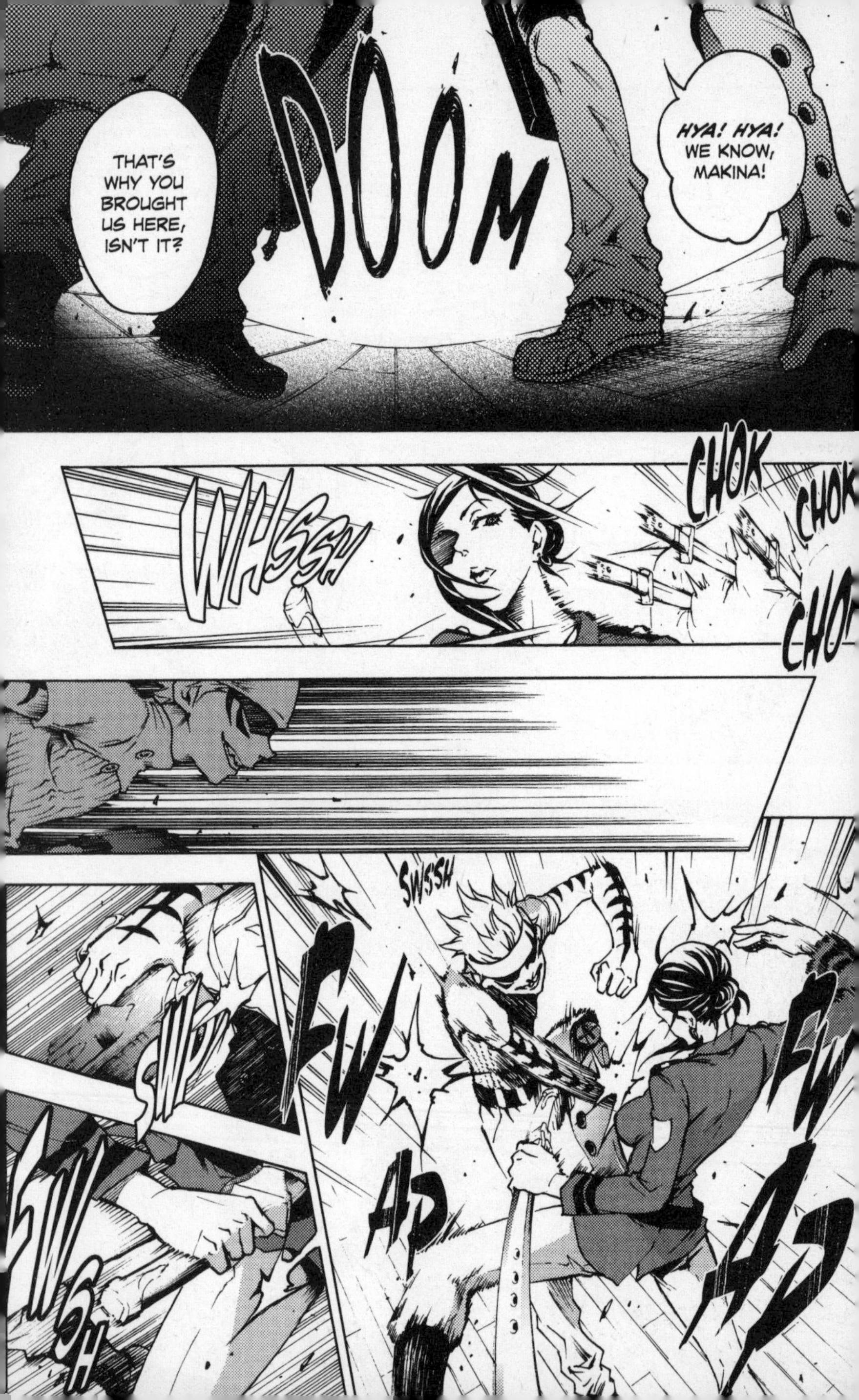
HYA! HYA! WE KNOW, MAKINA!
DOOM
THAT'S WHY YOU BROUGHT US HERE, ISN'T IT?
CHOK
CHOK
CHO
WHSSH
SWSSH
FWAP
FWAP

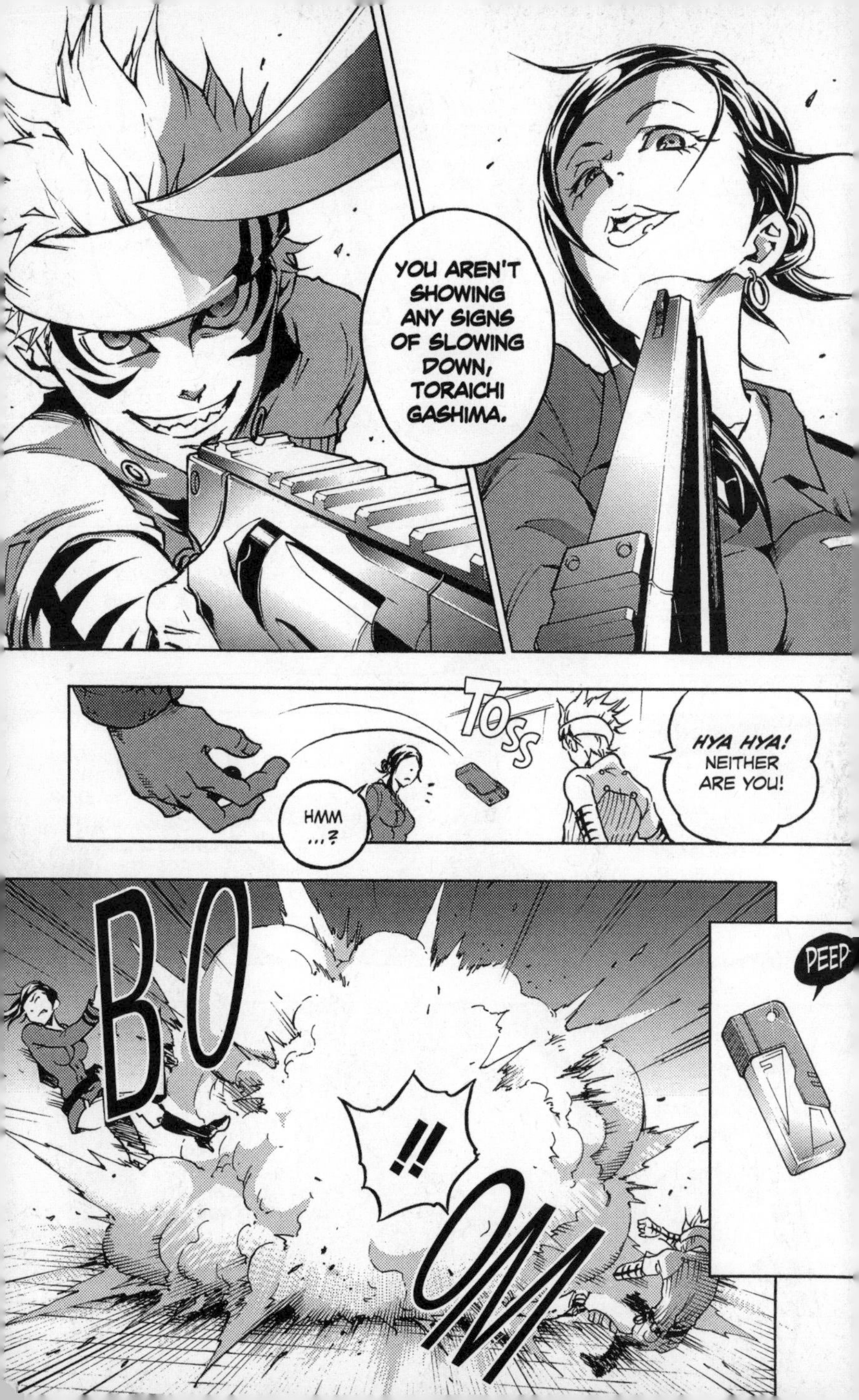
YOU AREN'T SHOWING ANY SIGNS OF SLOWING DOWN, TORAICHI GASHIMA.
HYA HYA! NEITHER ARE YOU!
TOSS
HMM ...?
PEEP
BOOM
!!

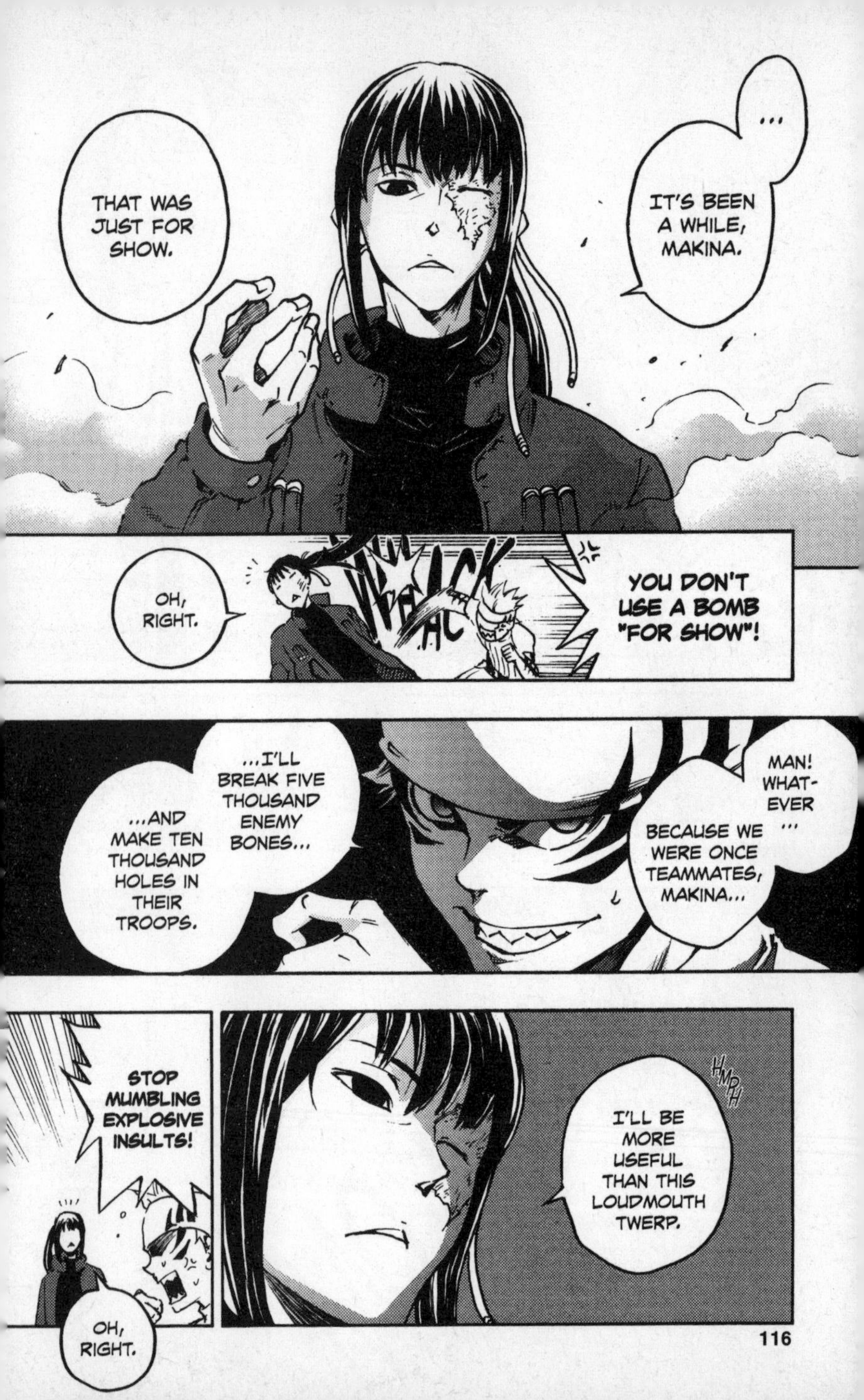
...
IT'S BEEN A WHILE, MAKINA.
THAT WAS JUST FOR SHOW.
YOU DON'T USE A BOMB "FOR SHOW"!
WHACK
OH, RIGHT.
MAN! WHATEVER...
BECAUSE WE WERE ONCE TEAMMATES, MAKINA...
...I'LL BREAK FIVE THOUSAND ENEMY BONES...
...AND MAKE TEN THOUSAND HOLES IN THEIR TROOPS.
HMPH
I'LL BE MORE USEFUL THAN THIS LOUDMOUTH TWERP.
STOP MUMBLING EXPLOSIVE INSULTS!
OH, RIGHT.

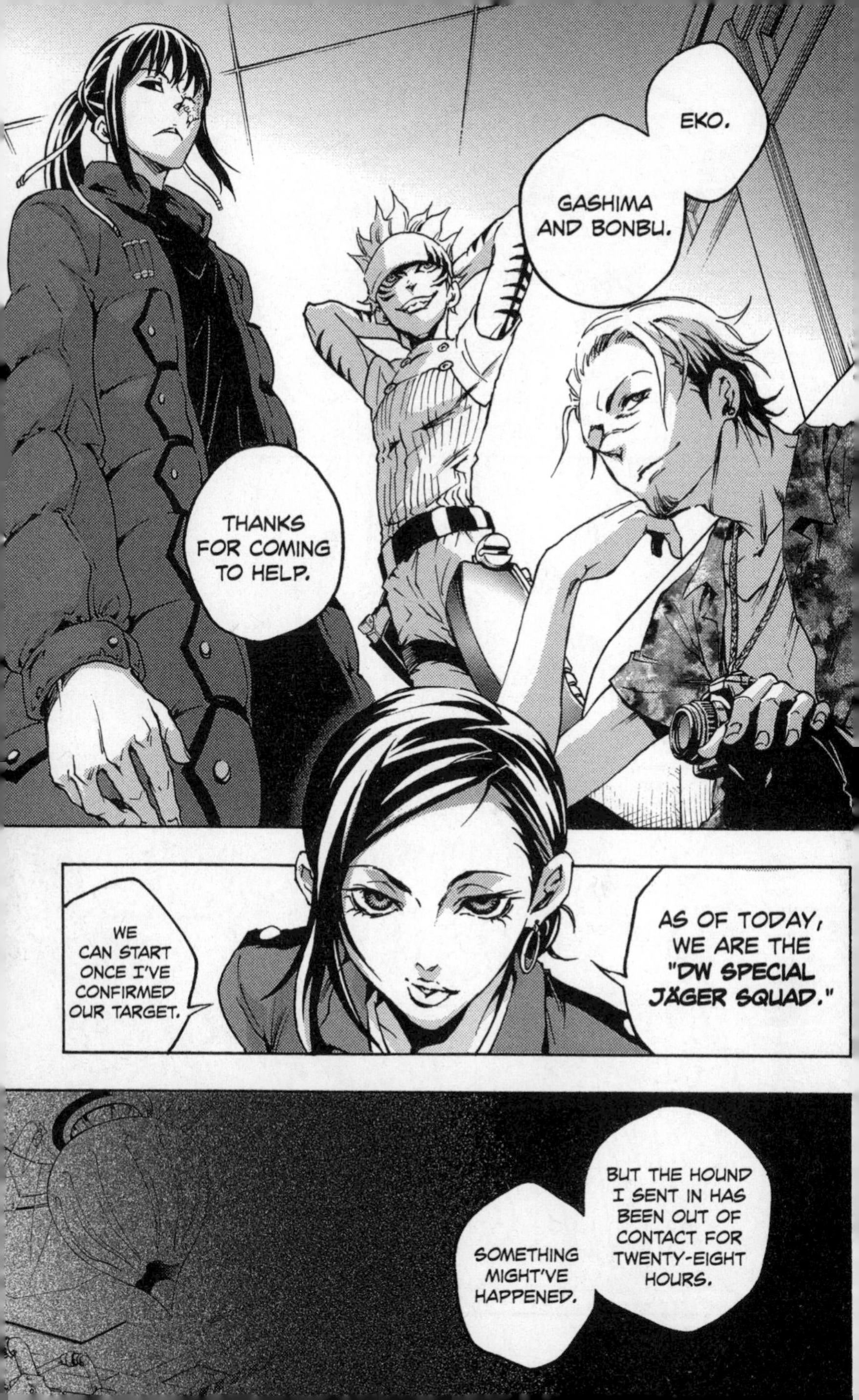
EKO.
GASHIMA AND BONBU.
THANKS FOR COMING TO HELP.
AS OF TODAY, WE ARE THE "DW SPECIAL JÄGER SQUAD."
WE CAN START ONCE I'VE CONFIRMED OUR TARGET.
BUT THE HOUND I SENT IN HAS BEEN OUT OF CONTACT FOR TWENTY-EIGHT HOURS.
SOMETHING MIGHT'VE HAPPENED.

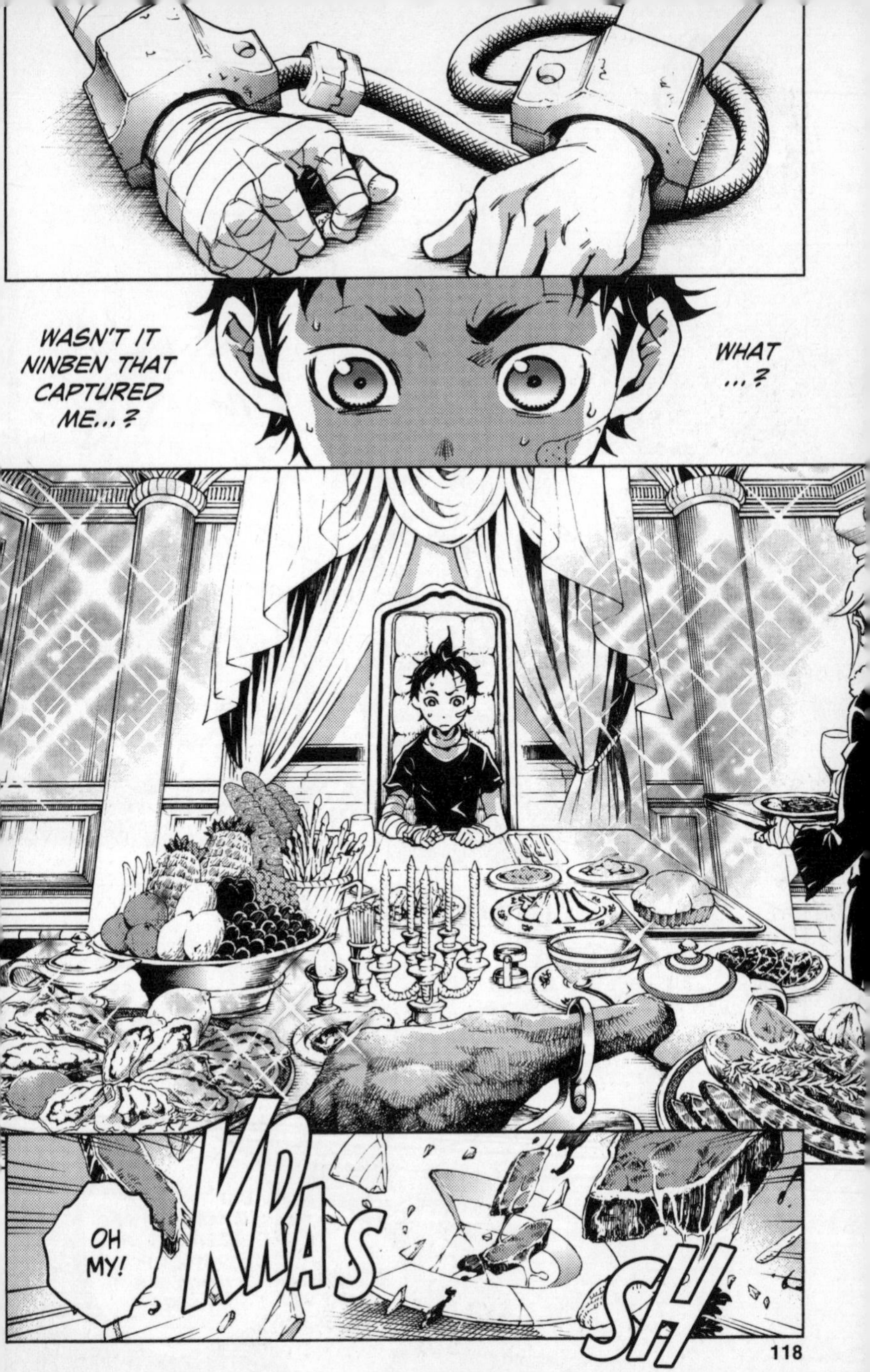
WHAT ...?
WASN'T IT NINBEN THAT CAPTURED ME...?
KRASSH
OH MY!

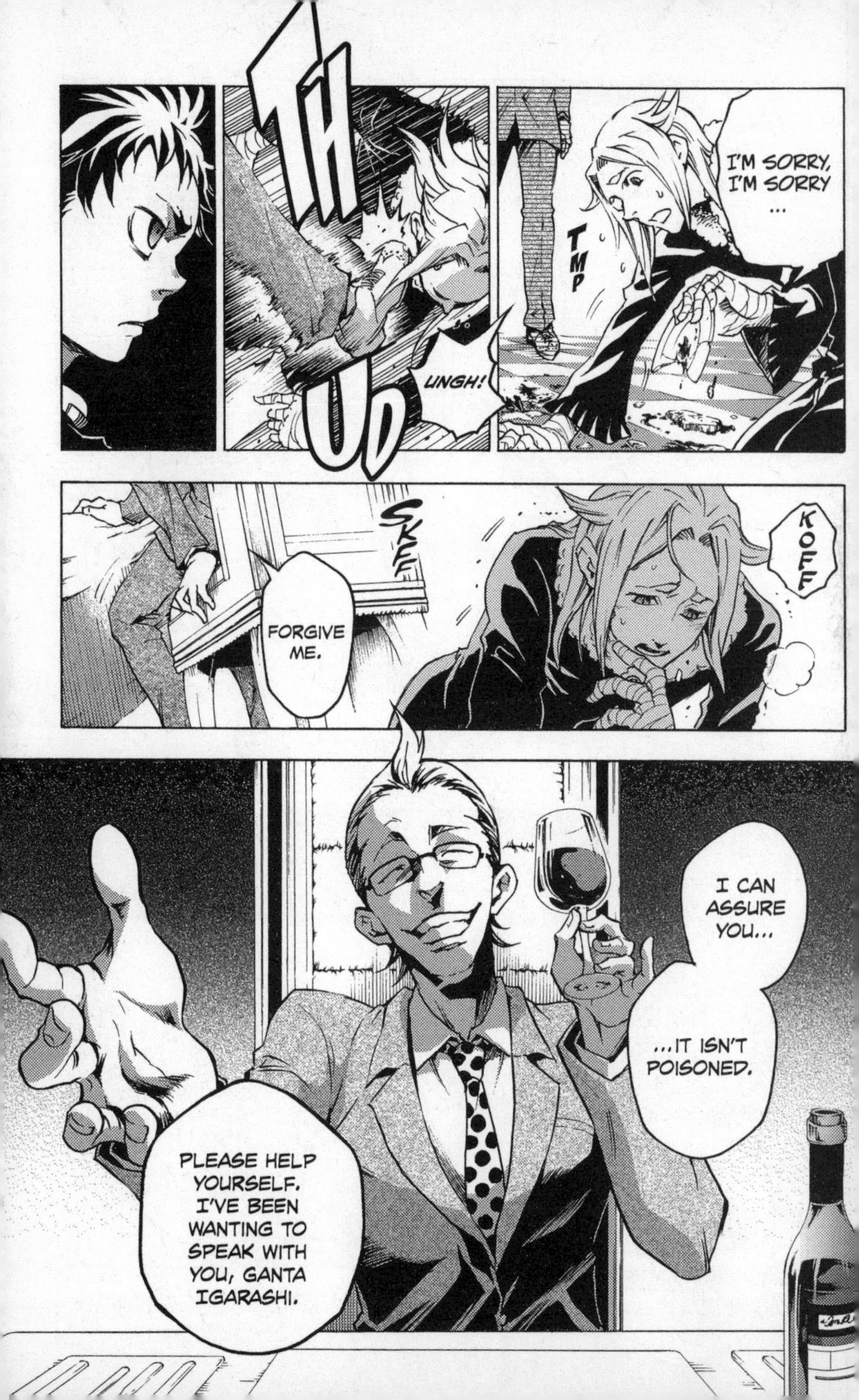
I'M SORRY, I'M SORRY ...
TMP
THUD
UNGH!
KOFF
SKFF
FORGIVE ME.
I CAN ASSURE YOU...
...IT ISN'T POISONED.
PLEASE HELP YOURSELF. I'VE BEEN WANTING TO SPEAK WITH YOU, GANTA IGARASHI.

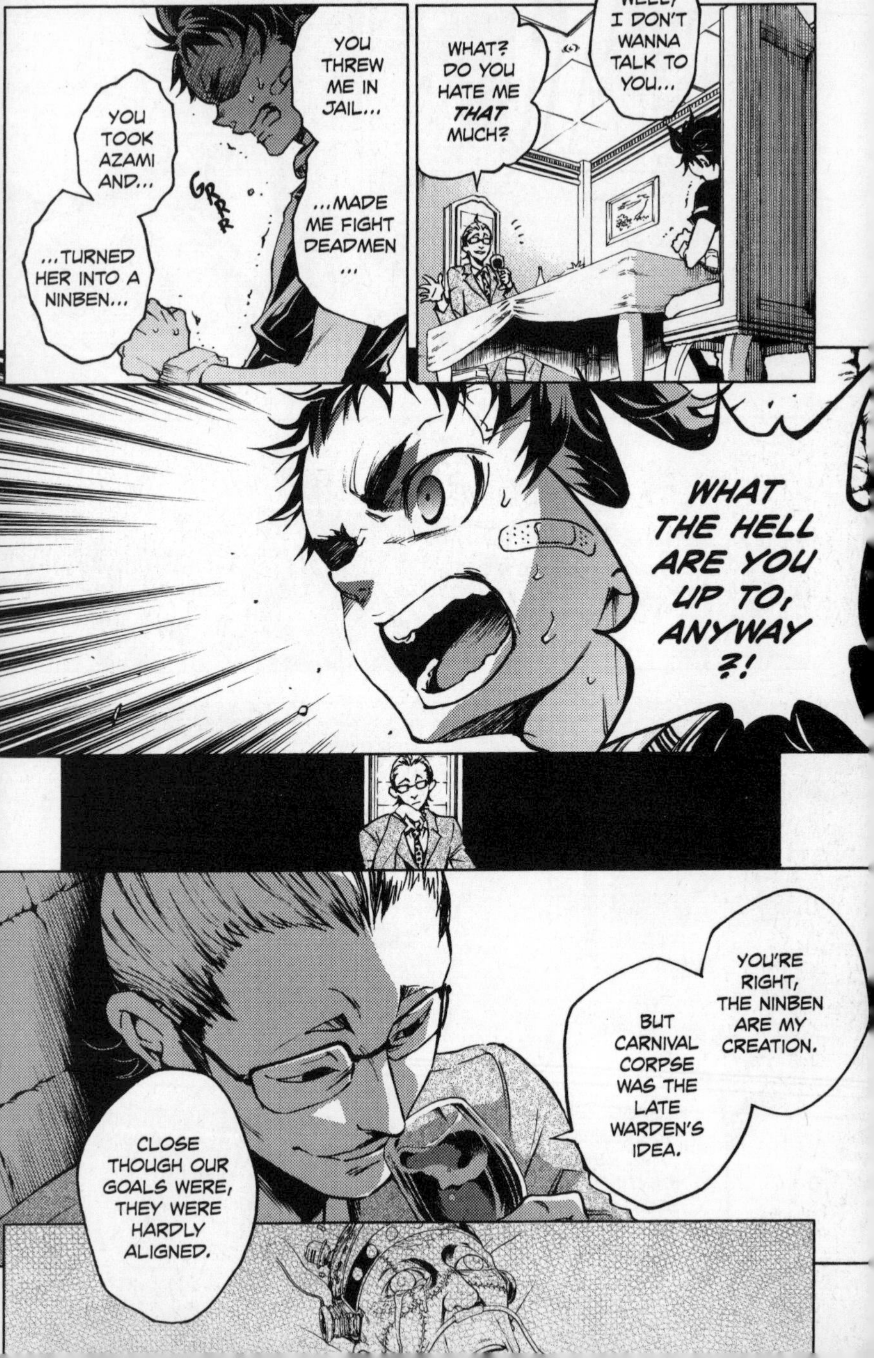
WELL, I DON'T WANNA TALK TO YOU...
WHAT? DO YOU HATE ME *THAT* MUCH?
YOU THREW ME IN JAIL...
...MADE ME FIGHT DEADMEN ...
YOU TOOK AZAMI AND...
GRRR
...TURNED HER INTO A NINBEN...
WHAT THE HELL ARE YOU UP TO, ANYWAY ?!
YOU'RE RIGHT, THE NINBEN ARE MY CREATION.
BUT CARNIVAL CORPSE WAS THE LATE WARDEN'S IDEA.
CLOSE THOUGH OUR GOALS WERE, THEY WERE HARDLY ALIGNED.

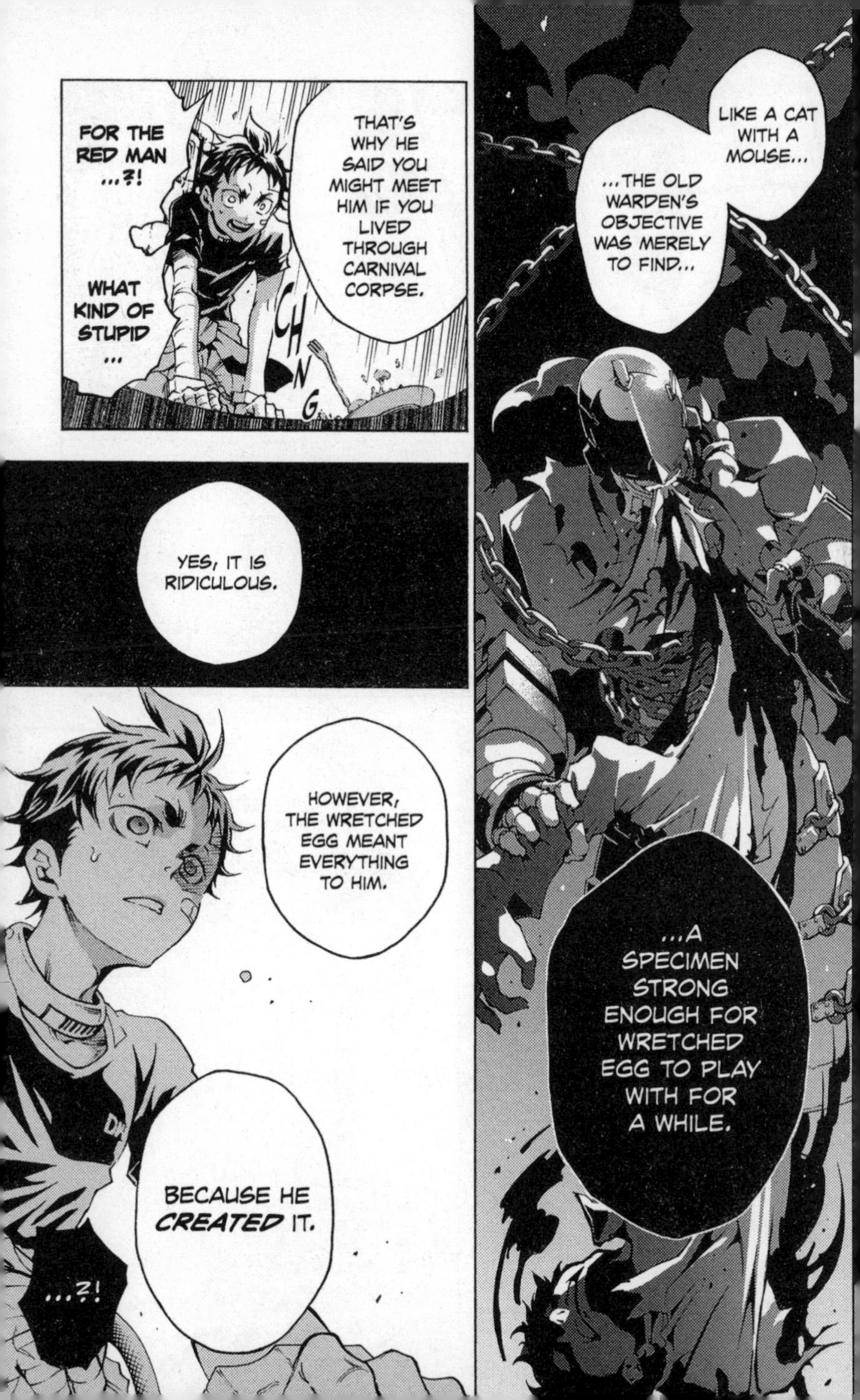
LIKE A CAT WITH A MOUSE...
...THE OLD WARDEN'S OBJECTIVE WAS MERELY TO FIND...
...A SPECIMEN STRONG ENOUGH FOR WRETCHED EGG TO PLAY WITH FOR A WHILE.
THAT'S WHY HE SAID YOU MIGHT MEET HIM IF YOU LIVED THROUGH CARNIVAL CORPSE.
FOR THE RED MAN ...?!
CHING
WHAT KIND OF STUPID ...
YES, IT IS RIDICULOUS.
HOWEVER, THE WRETCHED EGG MEANT EVERYTHING TO HIM.
BECAUSE HE *CREATED* IT.
...?!

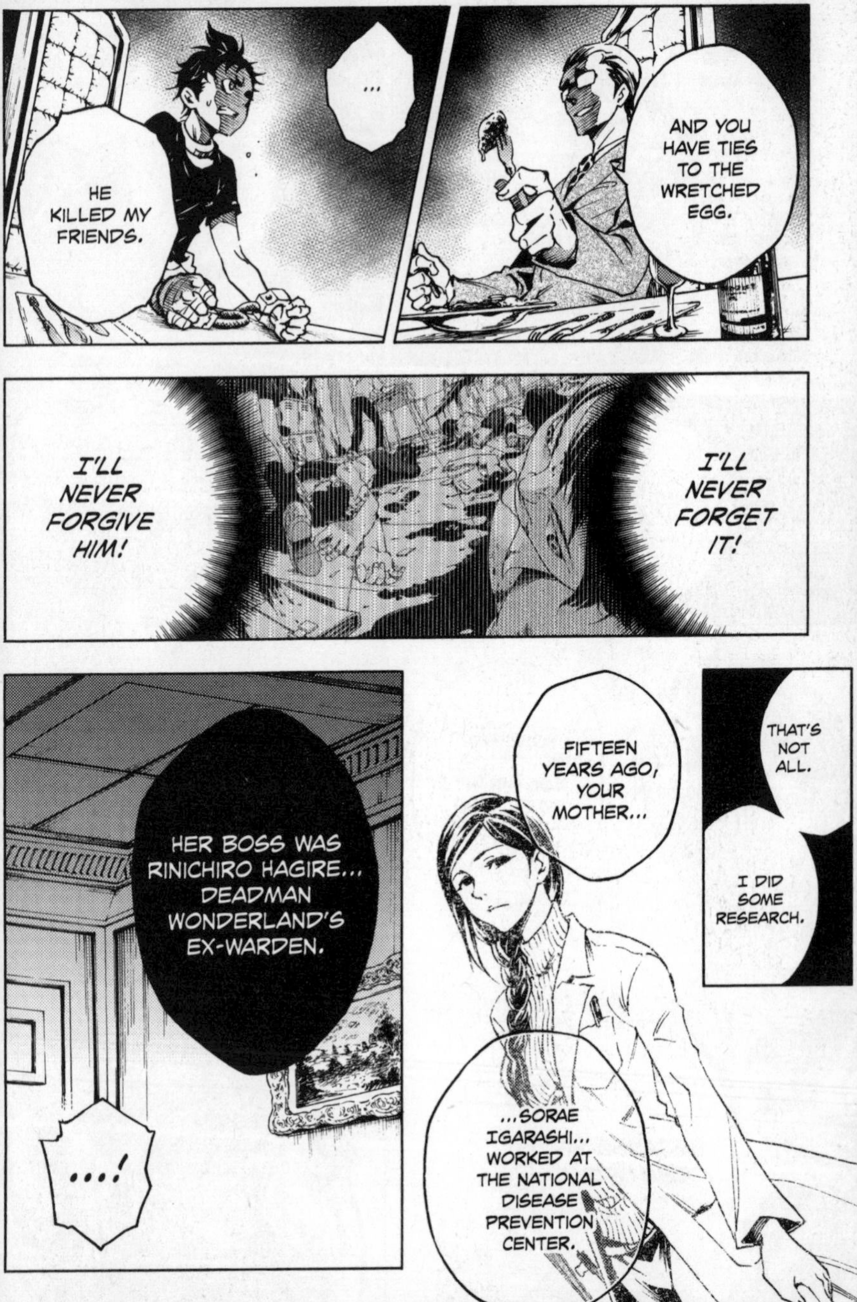
AND YOU HAVE TIES TO THE WRETCHED EGG.
...
HE KILLED MY FRIENDS.
I'LL NEVER FORGET IT!
I'LL NEVER FORGIVE HIM!
THAT'S NOT ALL.
I DID SOME RESEARCH.
FIFTEEN YEARS AGO, YOUR MOTHER...
...SORAE IGARASHI... WORKED AT THE NATIONAL DISEASE PREVENTION CENTER.
HER BOSS WAS RINICHIRO HAGIRE... DEADMAN WONDERLAND'S EX-WARDEN.
...!

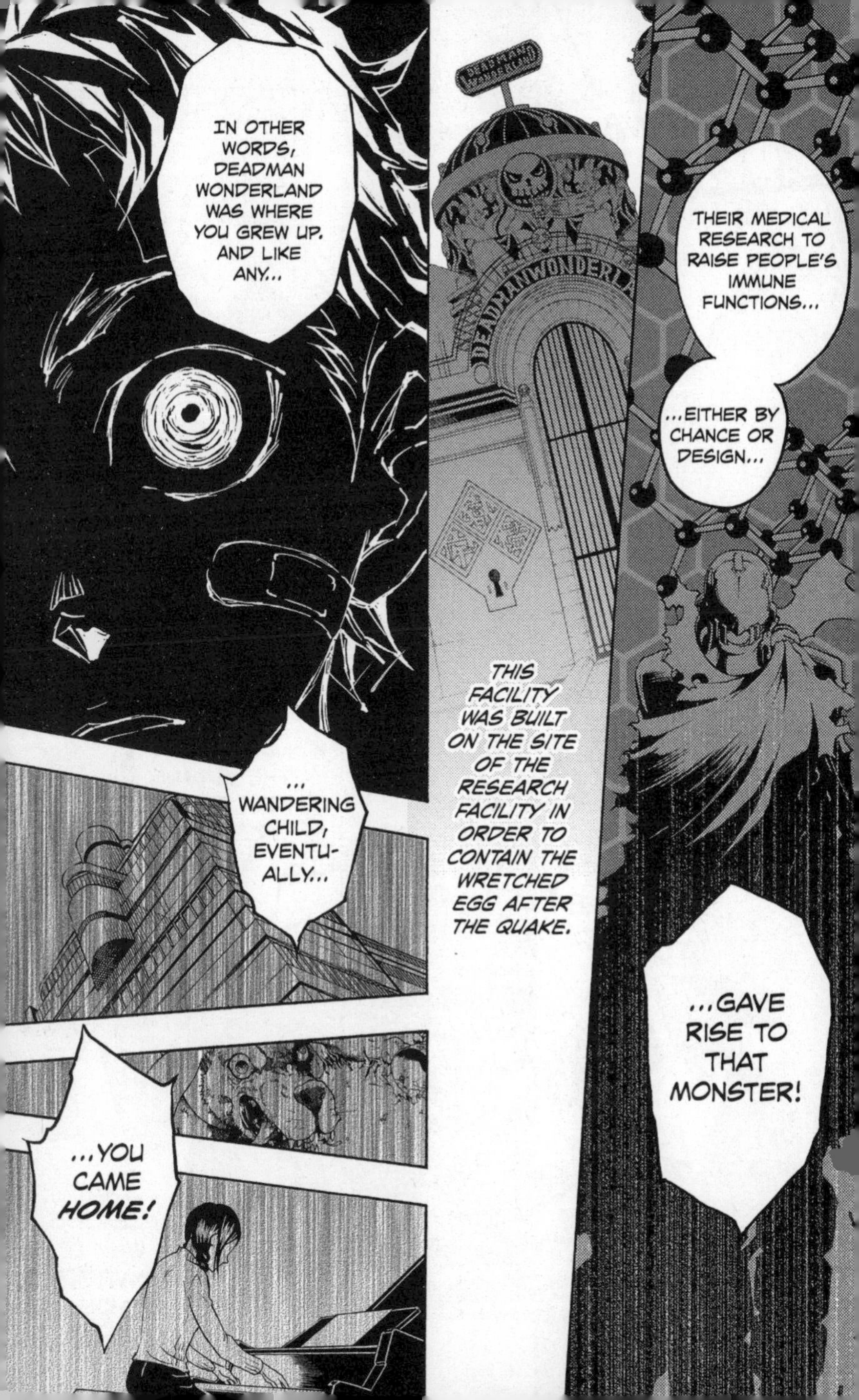
THEIR MEDICAL RESEARCH TO RAISE PEOPLE'S IMMUNE FUNCTIONS...
...EITHER BY CHANCE OR DESIGN...
...GAVE RISE TO THAT MONSTER!
THIS FACILITY WAS BUILT ON THE SITE OF THE RESEARCH FACILITY IN ORDER TO CONTAIN THE WRETCHED EGG AFTER THE QUAKE.
IN OTHER WORDS, DEADMAN WONDERLAND WAS WHERE YOU GREW UP. AND LIKE ANY...
...WANDERING CHILD, EVENTU-ALLY...
...YOU CAME *HOME!*

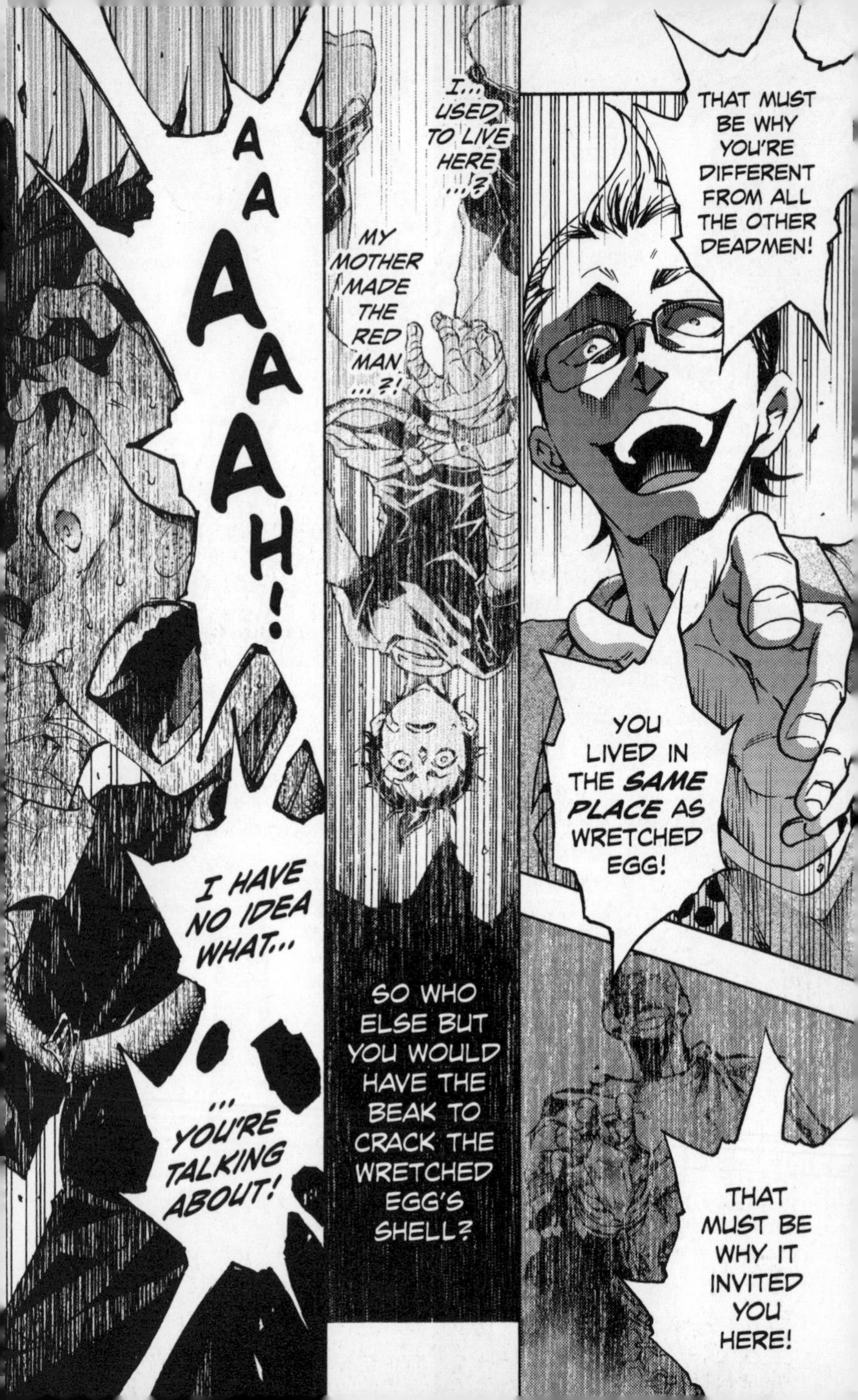
THAT MUST BE WHY YOU'RE DIFFERENT FROM ALL THE OTHER DEADMEN!
YOU LIVED IN THE ***SAME PLACE*** AS WRETCHED EGG!
THAT MUST BE WHY IT INVITED YOU HERE!
I... USED TO LIVE HERE ...!?
MY MOTHER MADE THE RED MAN ...?!
SO WHO ELSE BUT YOU WOULD HAVE THE BEAK TO CRACK THE WRETCHED EGG'S SHELL?
AAAAAAH!
I HAVE NO IDEA WHAT...
...YOU'RE TALKING ABOUT!

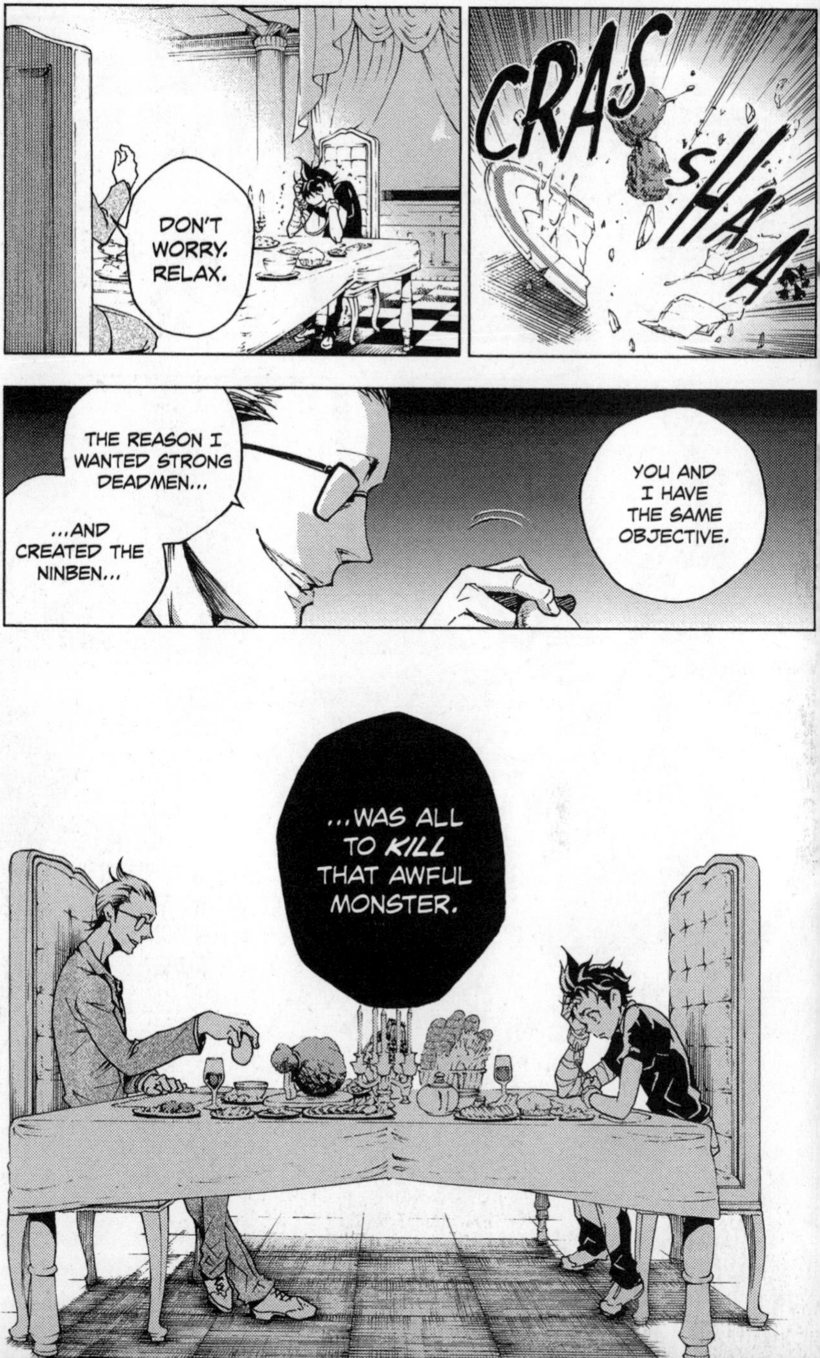
CRASSHA
DON'T WORRY. RELAX.
YOU AND I HAVE THE SAME OBJECTIVE.
THE REASON I WANTED STRONG DEADMEN...
...AND CREATED THE NINBEN...
...WAS ALL TO KILL THAT AWFUL MONSTER.

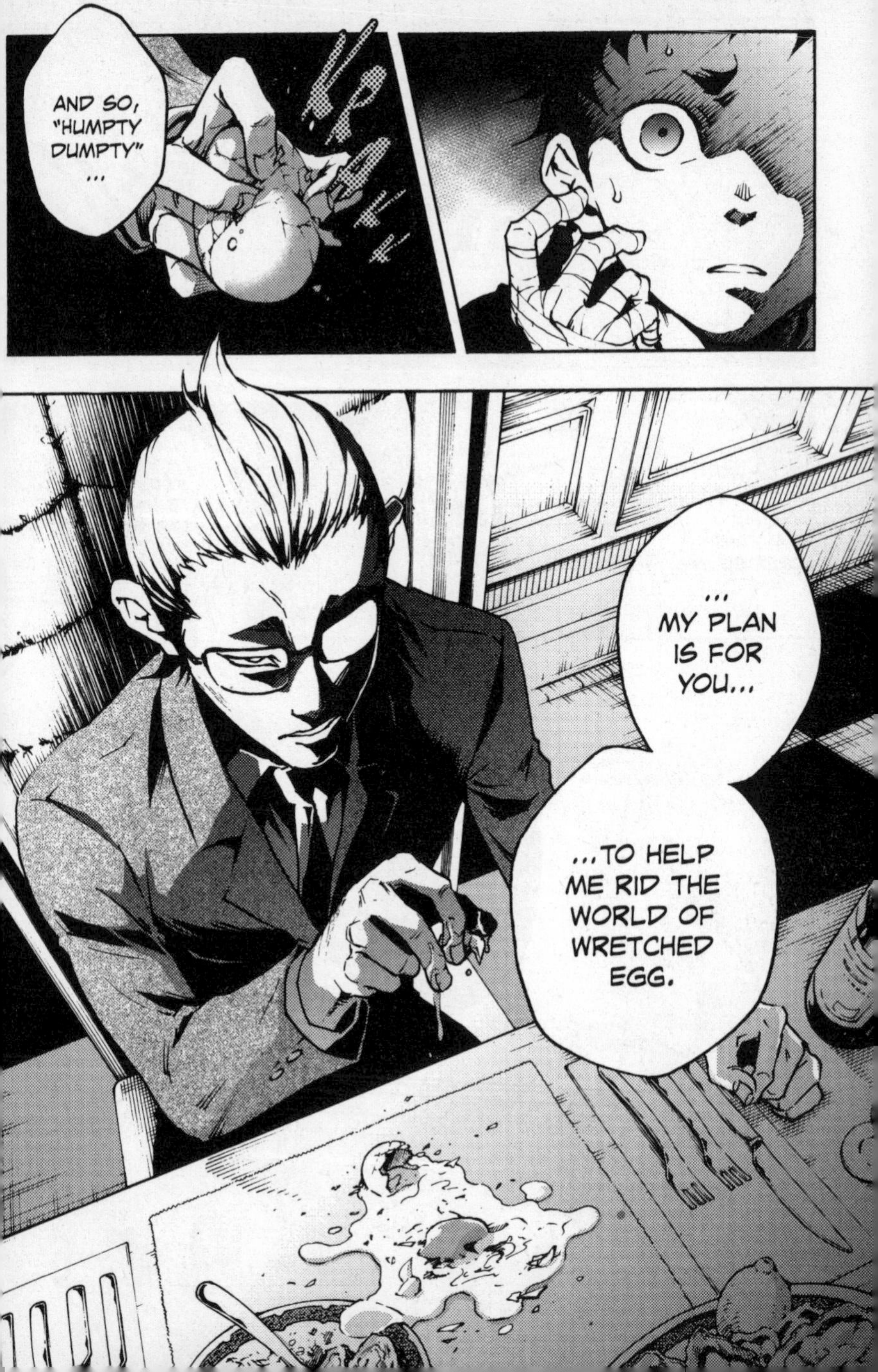
AND SO, "HUMPTY DUMPTY" ...
... MY PLAN IS FOR YOU...
...TO HELP ME RID THE WORLD OF WRETCHED EGG.

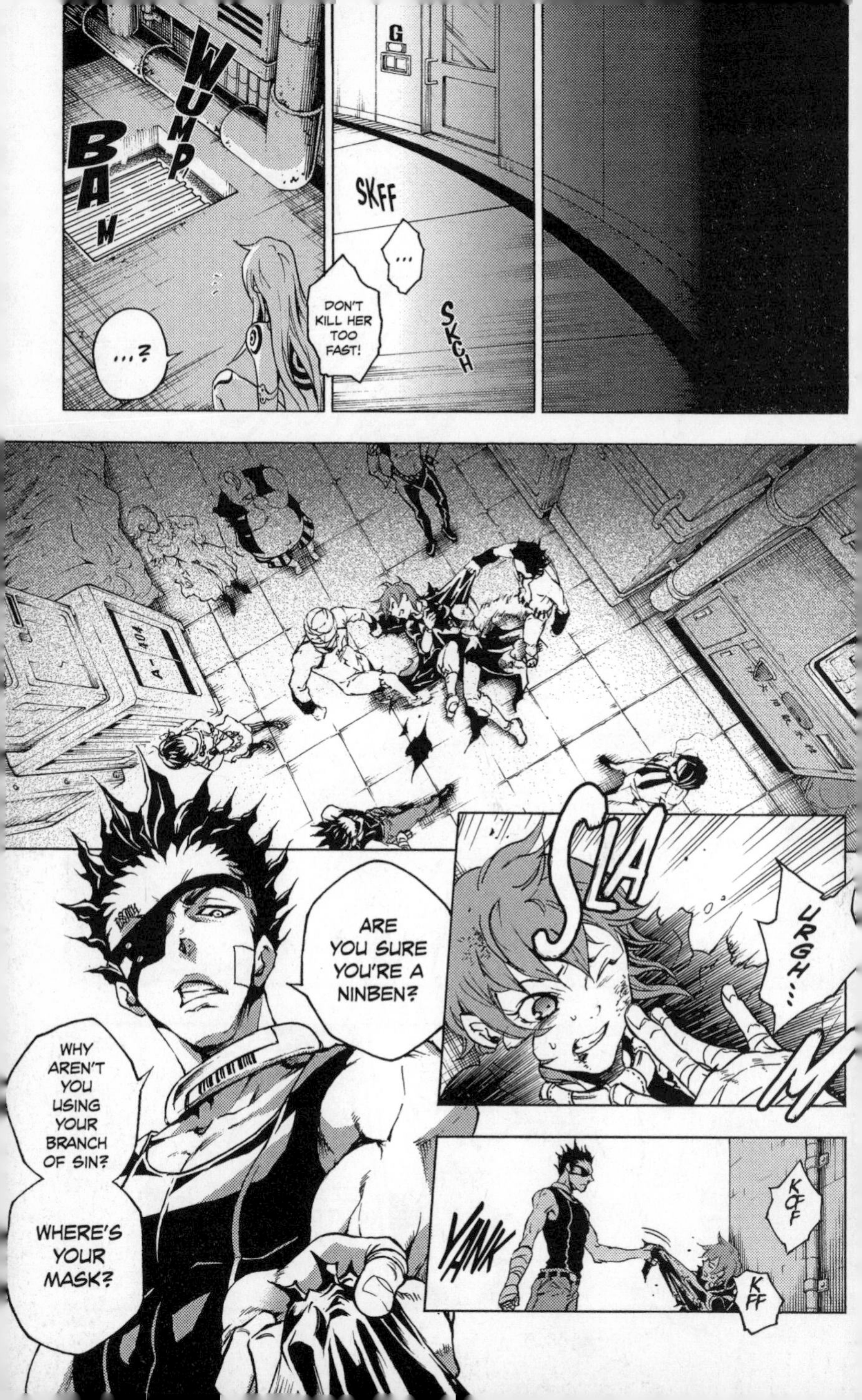
SKFF
...
DON'T KILL HER TOO FAST!
SKCH
WUMP
BAM
...?
SLAM
URGH...
KOFF
YANK
KFF
ARE YOU SURE YOU'RE A NINBEN?
WHY AREN'T YOU USING YOUR BRANCH OF SIN?
WHERE'S YOUR MASK?

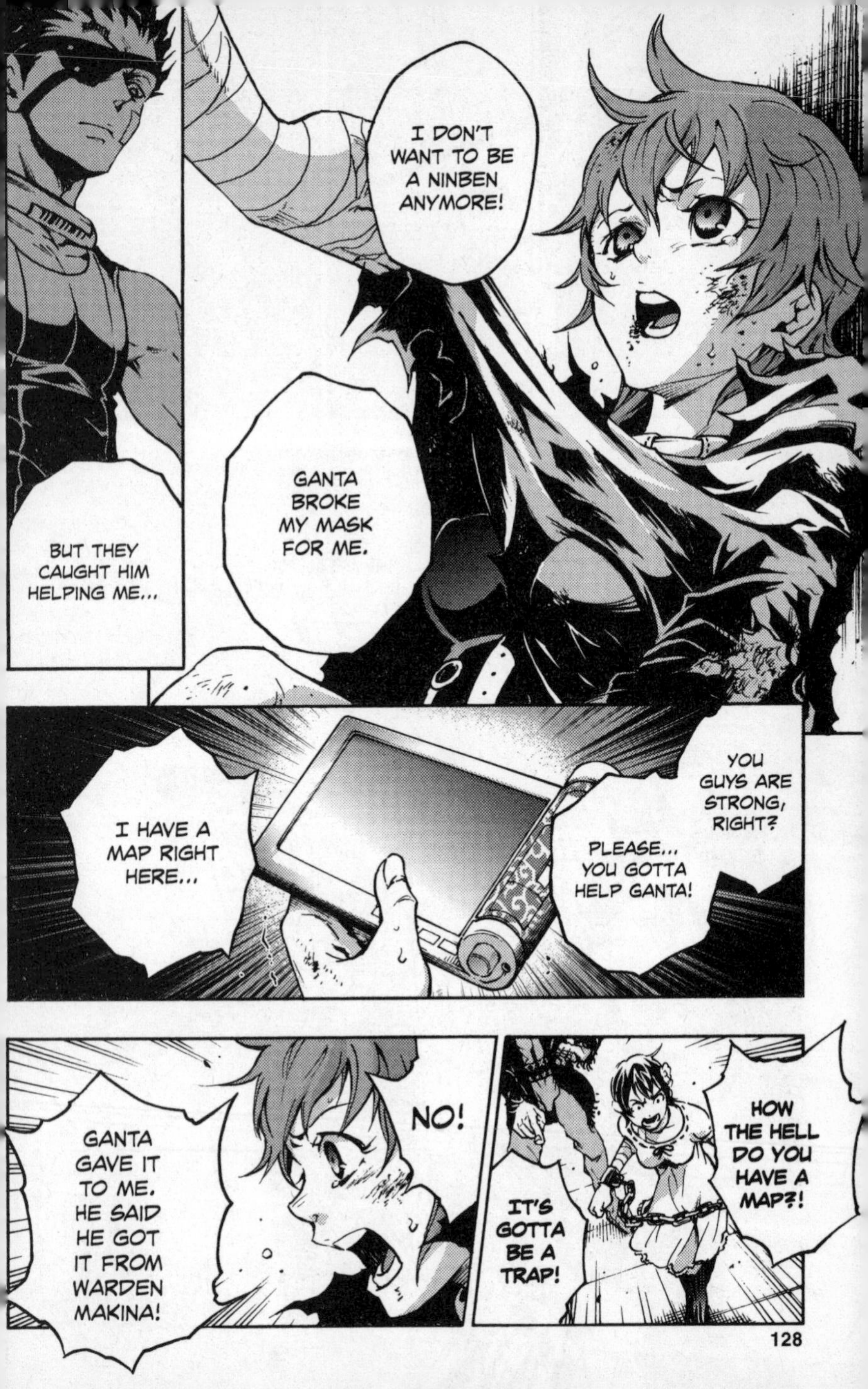

I DON'T WANT TO BE A NINBEN ANYMORE!
GANTA BROKE MY MASK FOR ME.
BUT THEY CAUGHT HIM HELPING ME...
YOU GUYS ARE STRONG, RIGHT?
PLEASE... YOU GOTTA HELP GANTA!
I HAVE A MAP RIGHT HERE...
HOW THE HELL DO YOU HAVE A MAP?!
IT'S GOTTA BE A TRAP!
NO!
GANTA GAVE IT TO ME. HE SAID HE GOT IT FROM WARDEN MAKINA!

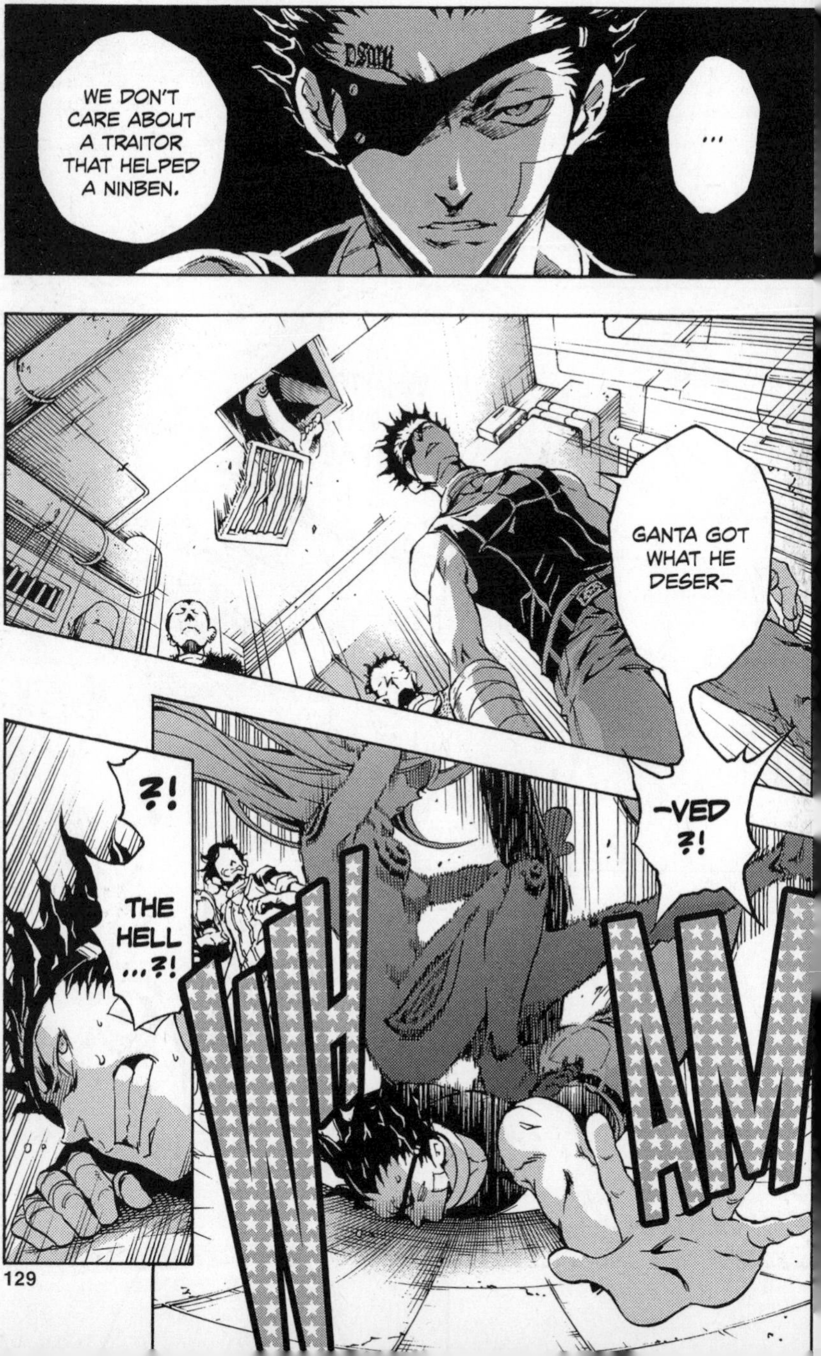
...
WE DON'T CARE ABOUT A TRAITOR THAT HELPED A NINBEN.
GANTA GOT WHAT HE DESER-
-VED ?!
?!
THE HELL ...?!

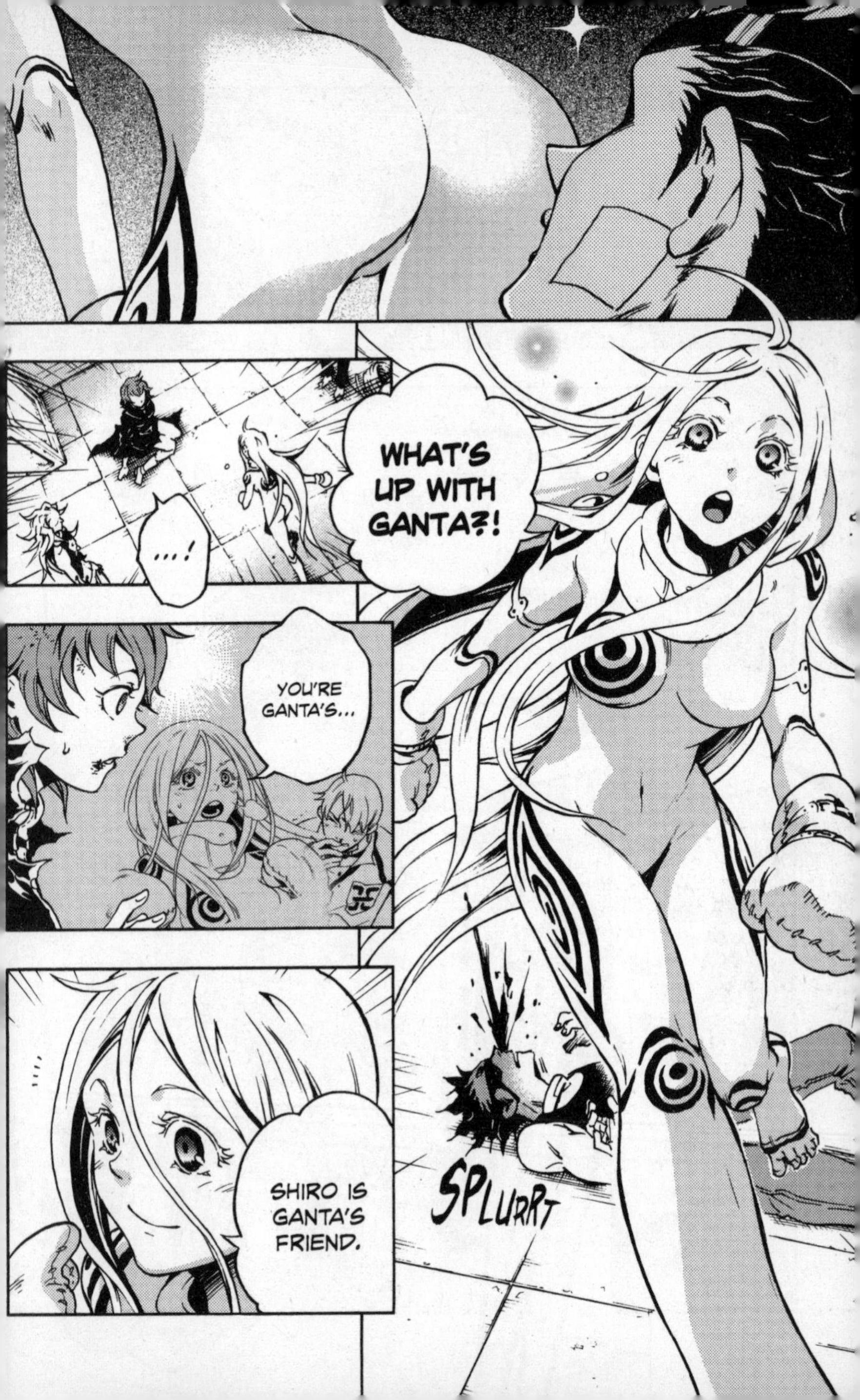

WHAT'S UP WITH GANTA?!
SPLURRT
...!
YOU'RE GANTA'S...
SHIRO IS GANTA'S FRIEND.

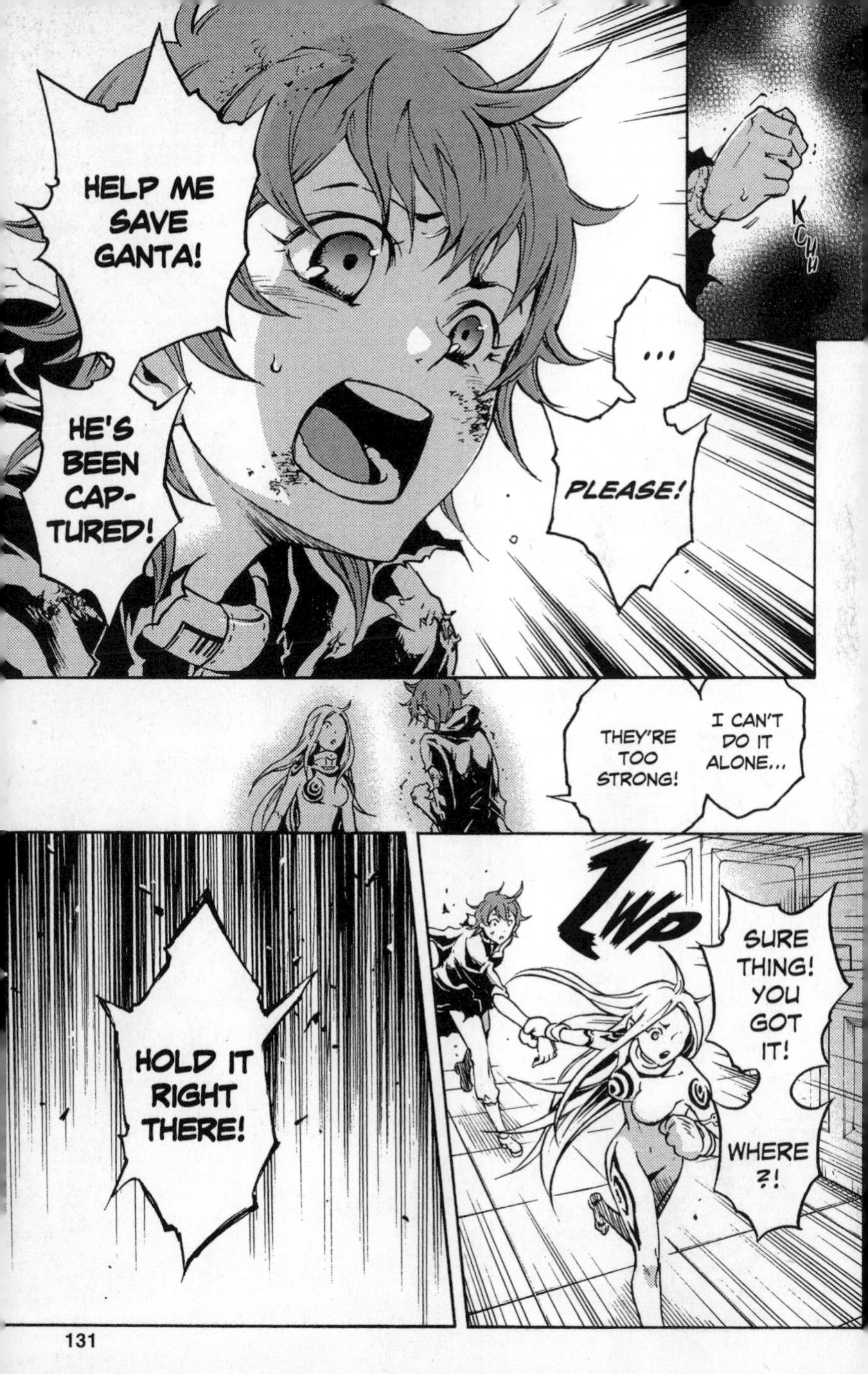
KCHH
...
HELP ME SAVE GANTA!
HE'S BEEN CAPTURED!
PLEASE!
I CAN'T DO IT ALONE...
THEY'RE TOO STRONG!
ZWIP
SURE THING! YOU GOT IT!
WHERE?!
HOLD IT RIGHT THERE!

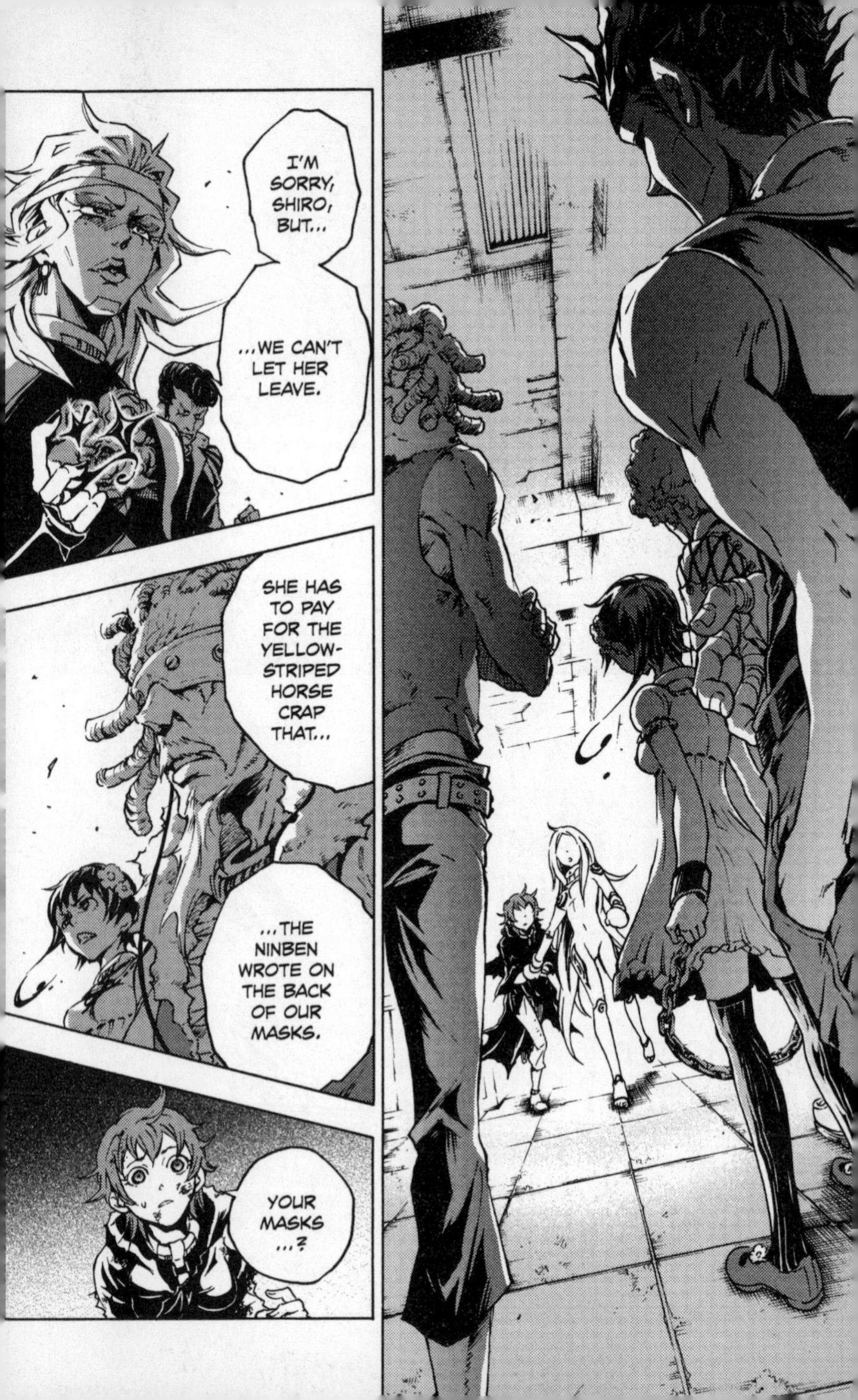
I'M SORRY, SHIRO, BUT...
...WE CAN'T LET HER LEAVE.
SHE HAS TO PAY FOR THE YELLOW-STRIPED HORSE CRAP THAT...
...THE NINBEN WROTE ON THE BACK OF OUR MASKS.
YOUR MASKS ...?

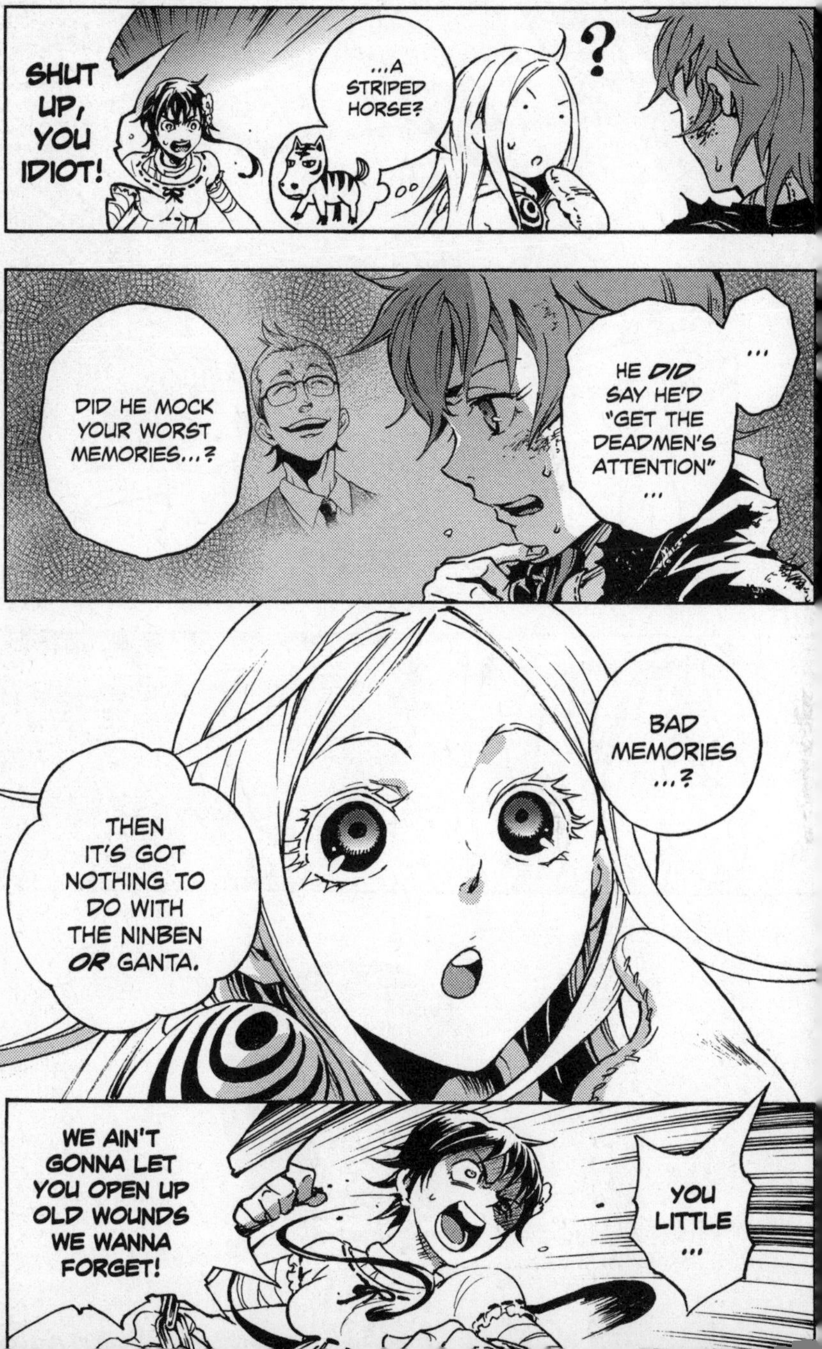
?
...A STRIPED HORSE?
SHUT UP, YOU IDIOT!
...
HE *DID* SAY HE'D "GET THE DEADMEN'S ATTENTION"...
DID HE MOCK YOUR WORST MEMORIES...?
BAD MEMORIES...?
THEN IT'S GOT NOTHING TO DO WITH THE NINBEN *OR* GANTA.
YOU LITTLE...
WE AIN'T GONNA LET YOU OPEN UP OLD WOUNDS WE WANNA FORGET!

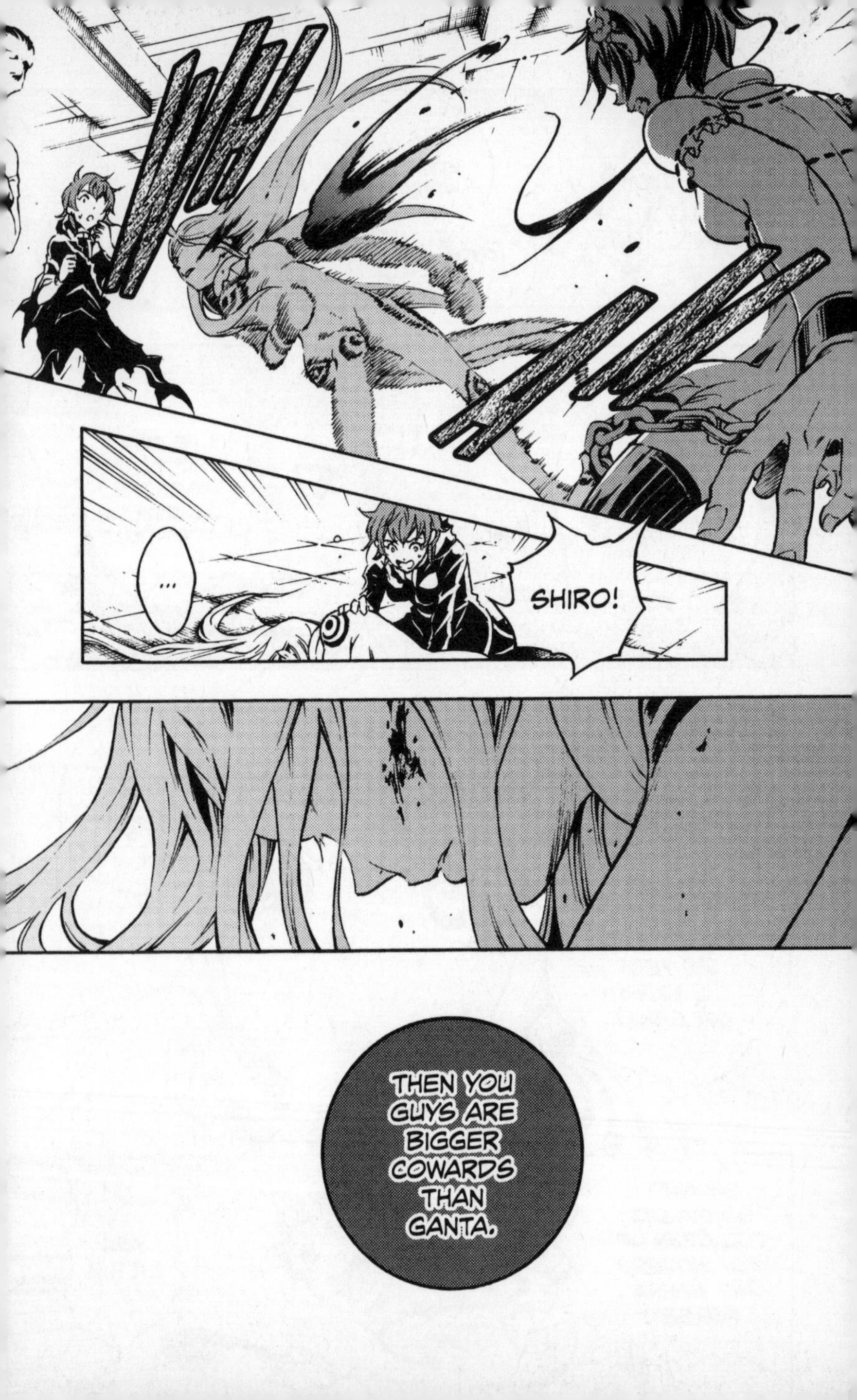
SHIRO!
...
THEN YOU GUYS ARE BIGGER COWARDS THAN GANTA.

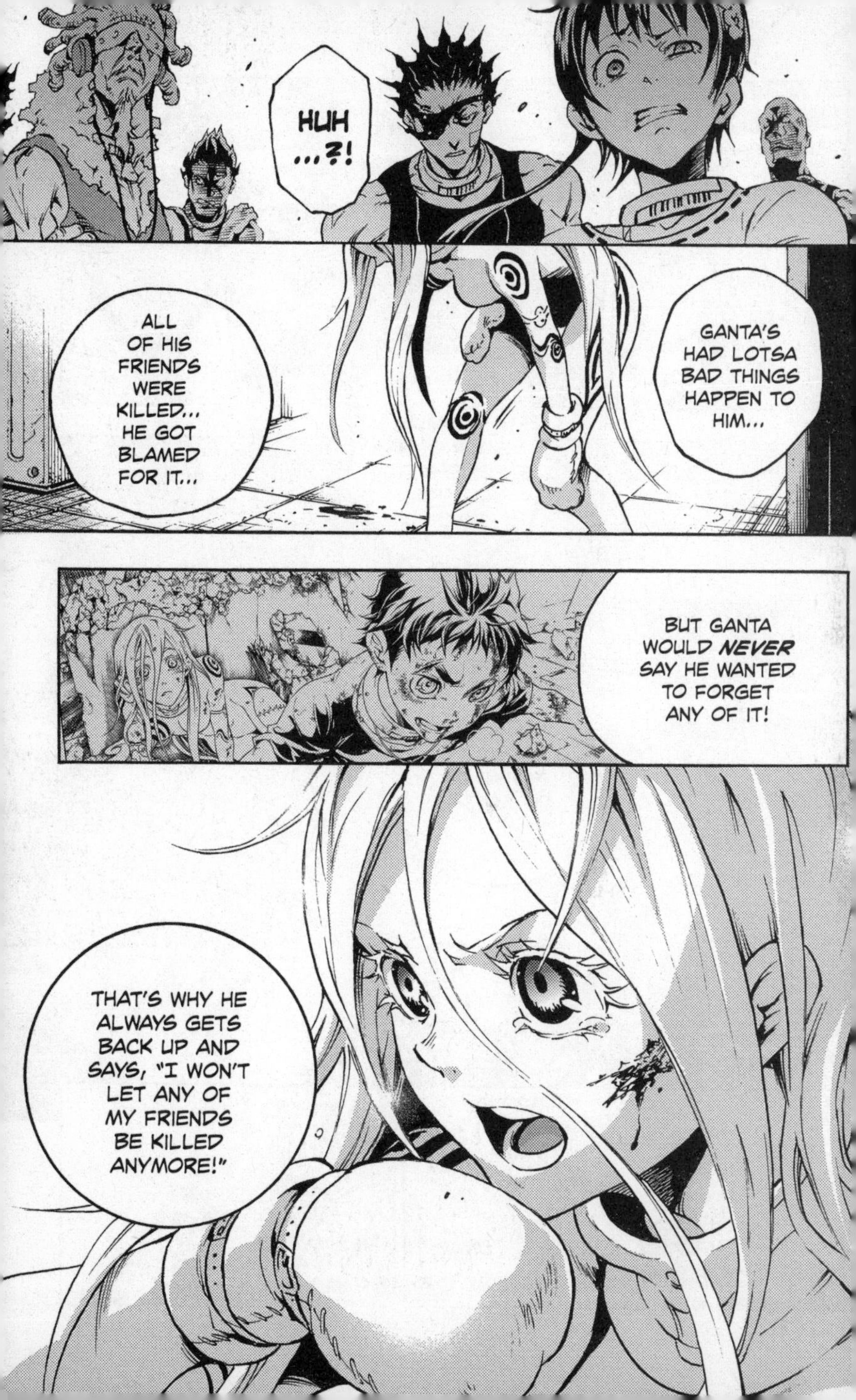
HUH ...?!
GANTA'S HAD LOTSA BAD THINGS HAPPEN TO HIM...
ALL OF HIS FRIENDS WERE KILLED... HE GOT BLAMED FOR IT...
BUT GANTA WOULD ***NEVER*** SAY HE WANTED TO FORGET ANY OF IT!
THAT'S WHY HE ALWAYS GETS BACK UP AND SAYS, "I WON'T LET ANY OF MY FRIENDS BE KILLED ANYMORE!"

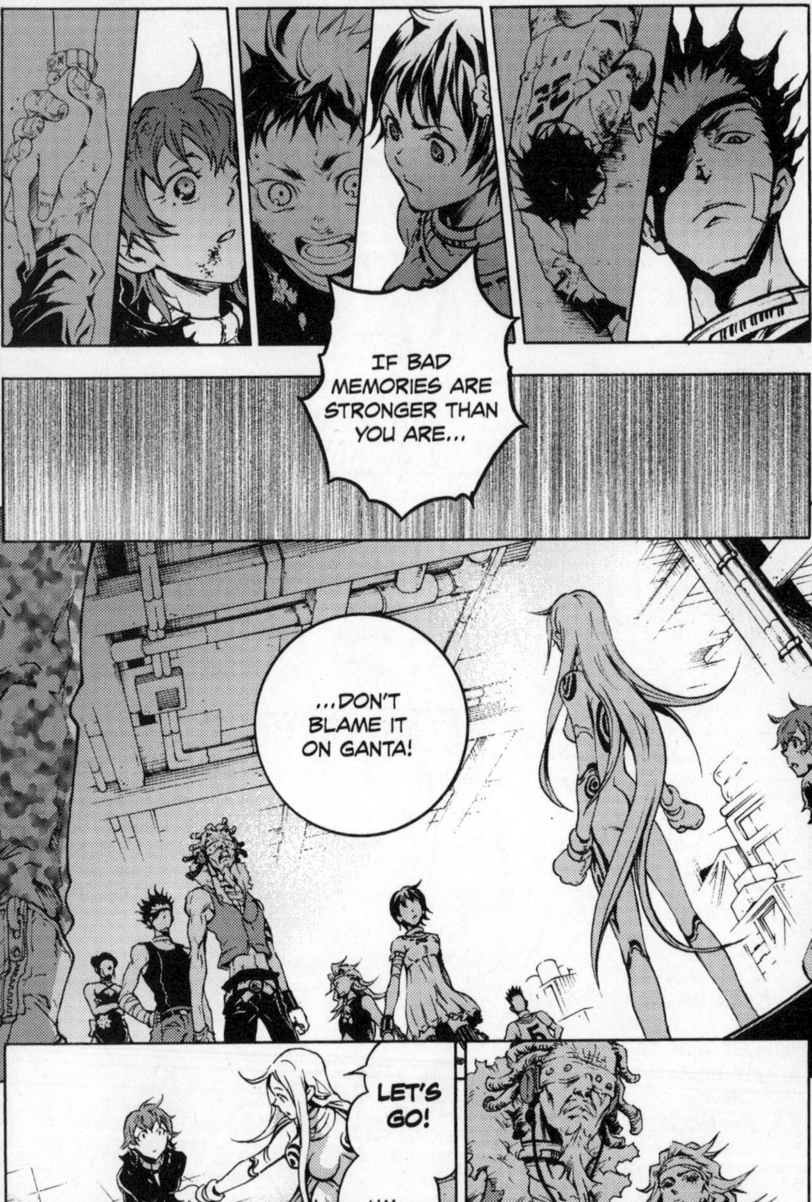
IF BAD MEMORIES ARE STRONGER THAN YOU ARE...
...DON'T BLAME IT ON GANTA!
LET'S GO!
UM...

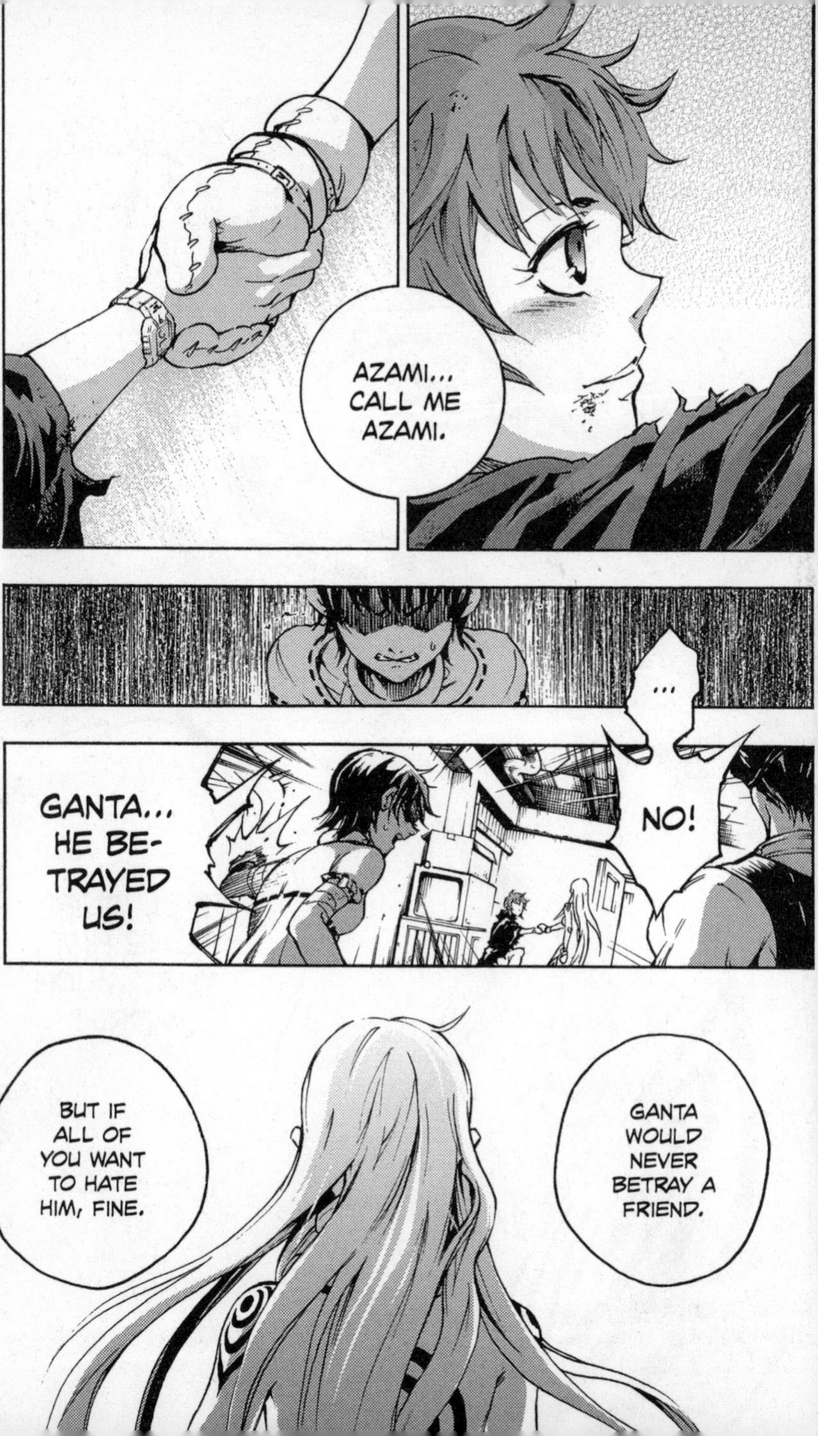
AZAMI... CALL ME AZAMI.
...
NO!
GANTA... HE BE-TRAYED US!
GANTA WOULD NEVER BETRAY A FRIEND.
BUT IF ALL OF YOU WANT TO HATE HIM, FINE.

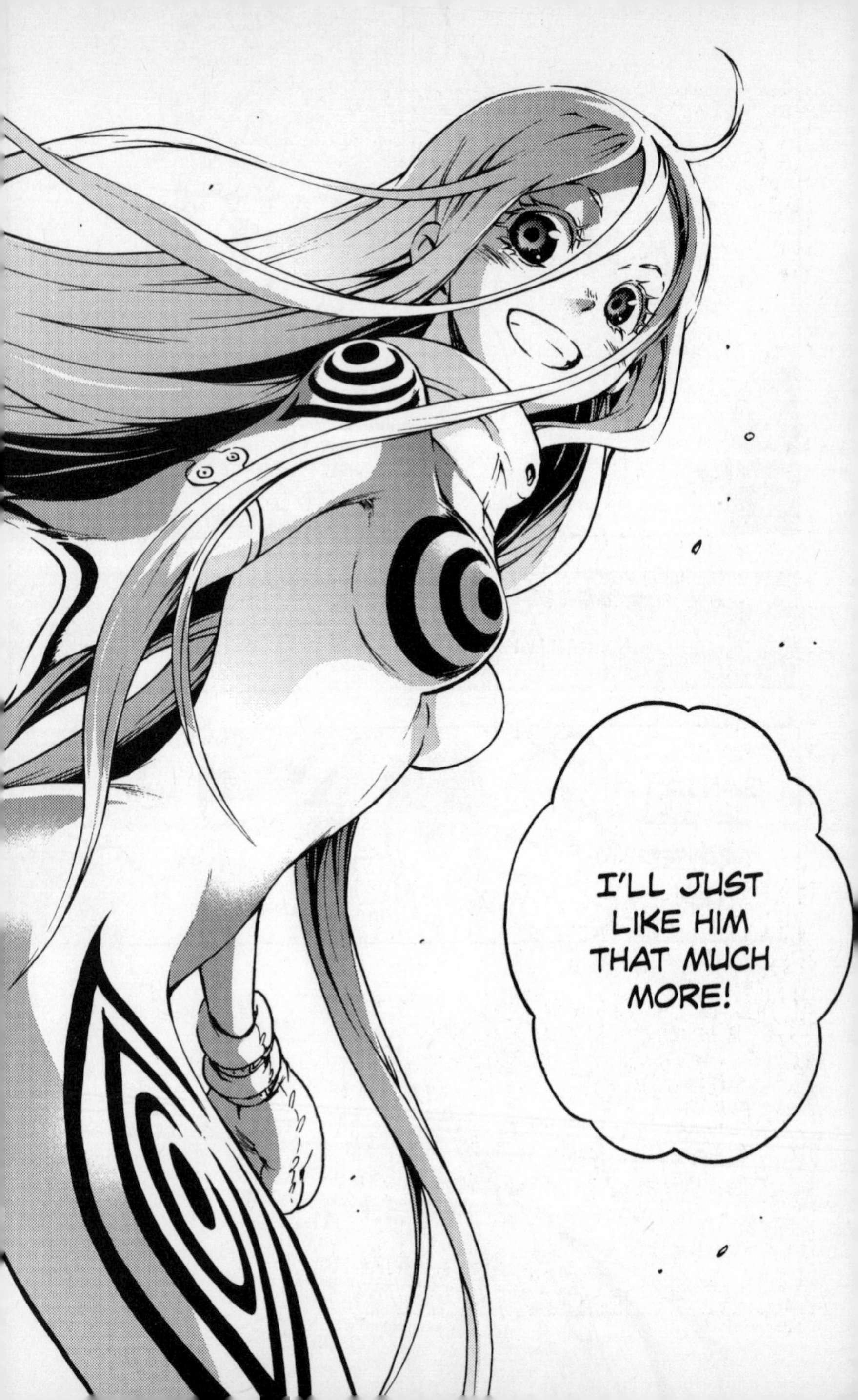
I'LL JUST LIKE HIM THAT MUCH MORE!

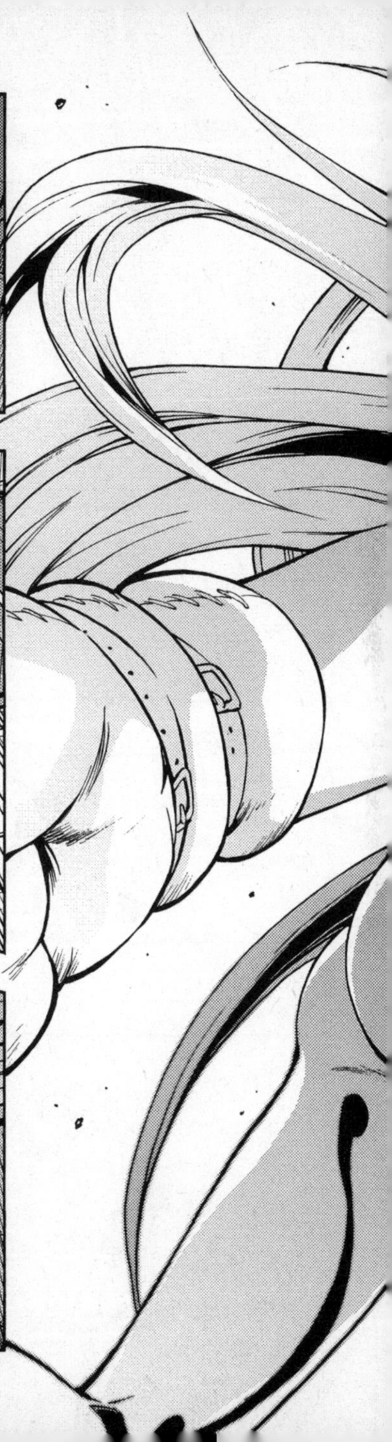

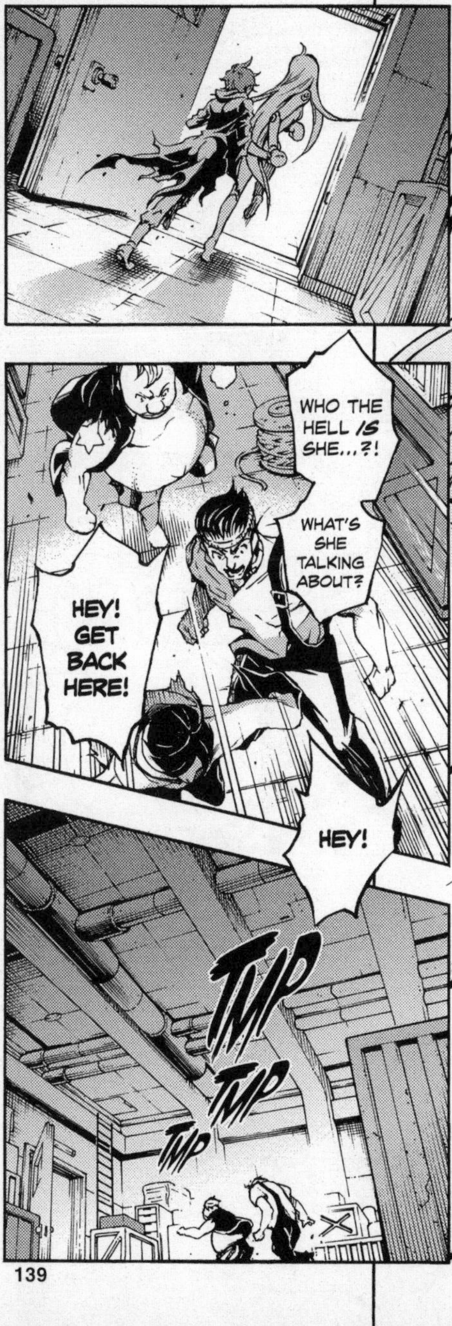
WHO THE HELL *IS* SHE...?!
WHAT'S SHE TALKING ABOUT?
HEY! GET BACK HERE!
HEY!
TMP
TMP
TMP

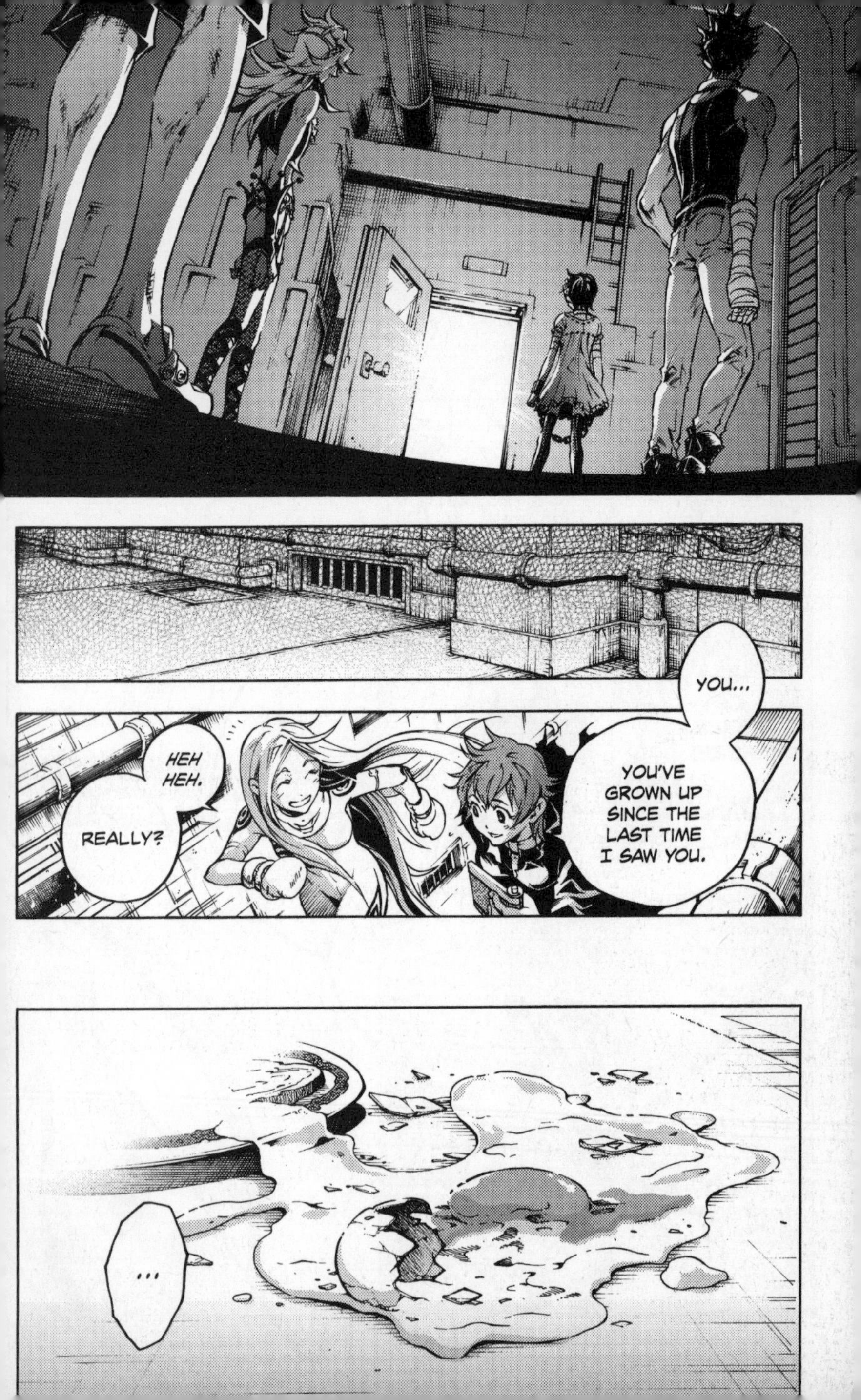
YOU...
YOU'VE GROWN UP SINCE THE LAST TIME I SAW YOU.
HEH HEH.
REALLY?
...

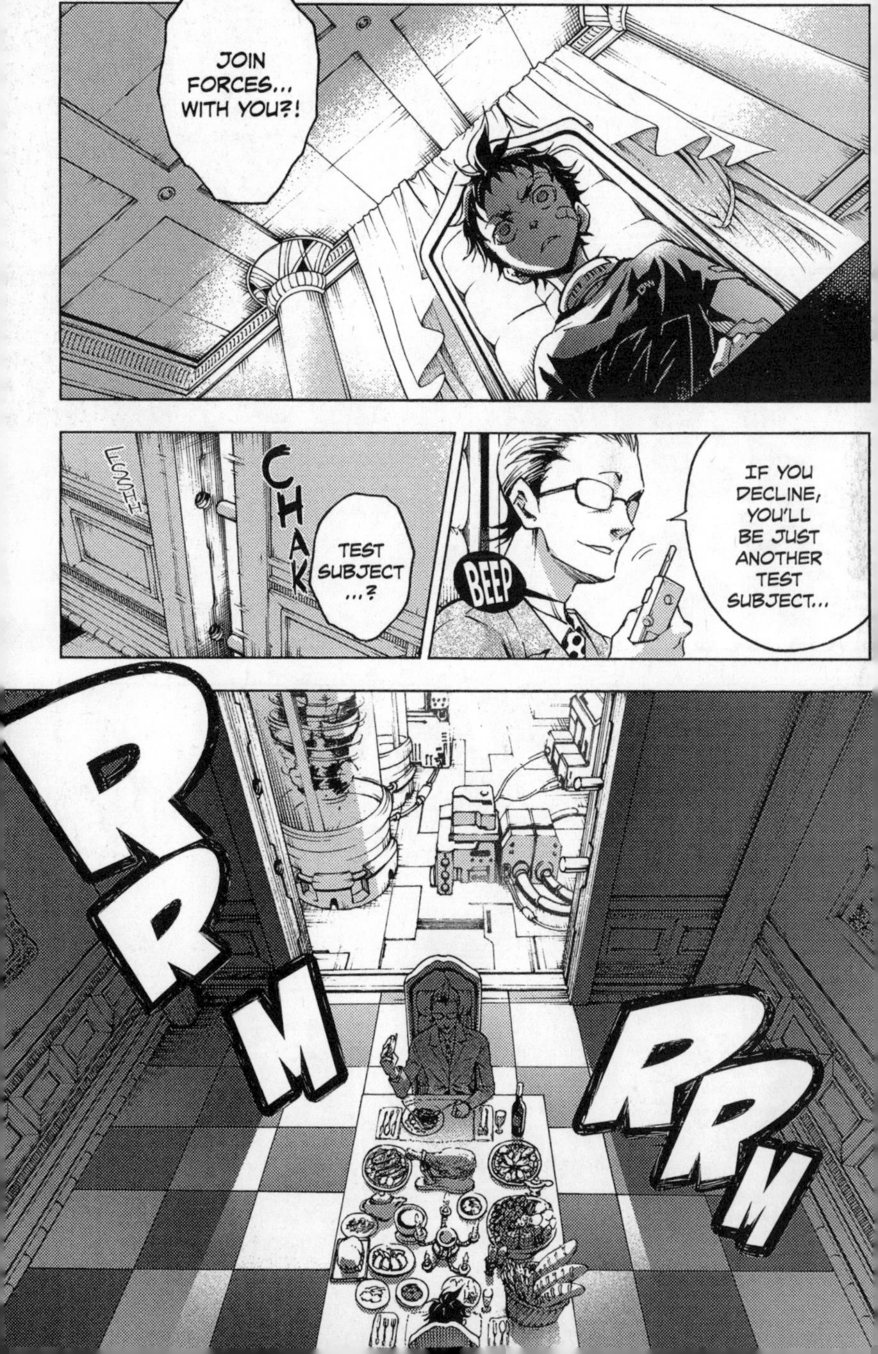
JOIN FORCES... WITH YOU?!
IF YOU DECLINE, YOU'LL BE JUST ANOTHER TEST SUBJECT...
BEEP
CHAK
TEST SUBJECT ...?
FSSHH
RRM
RRM

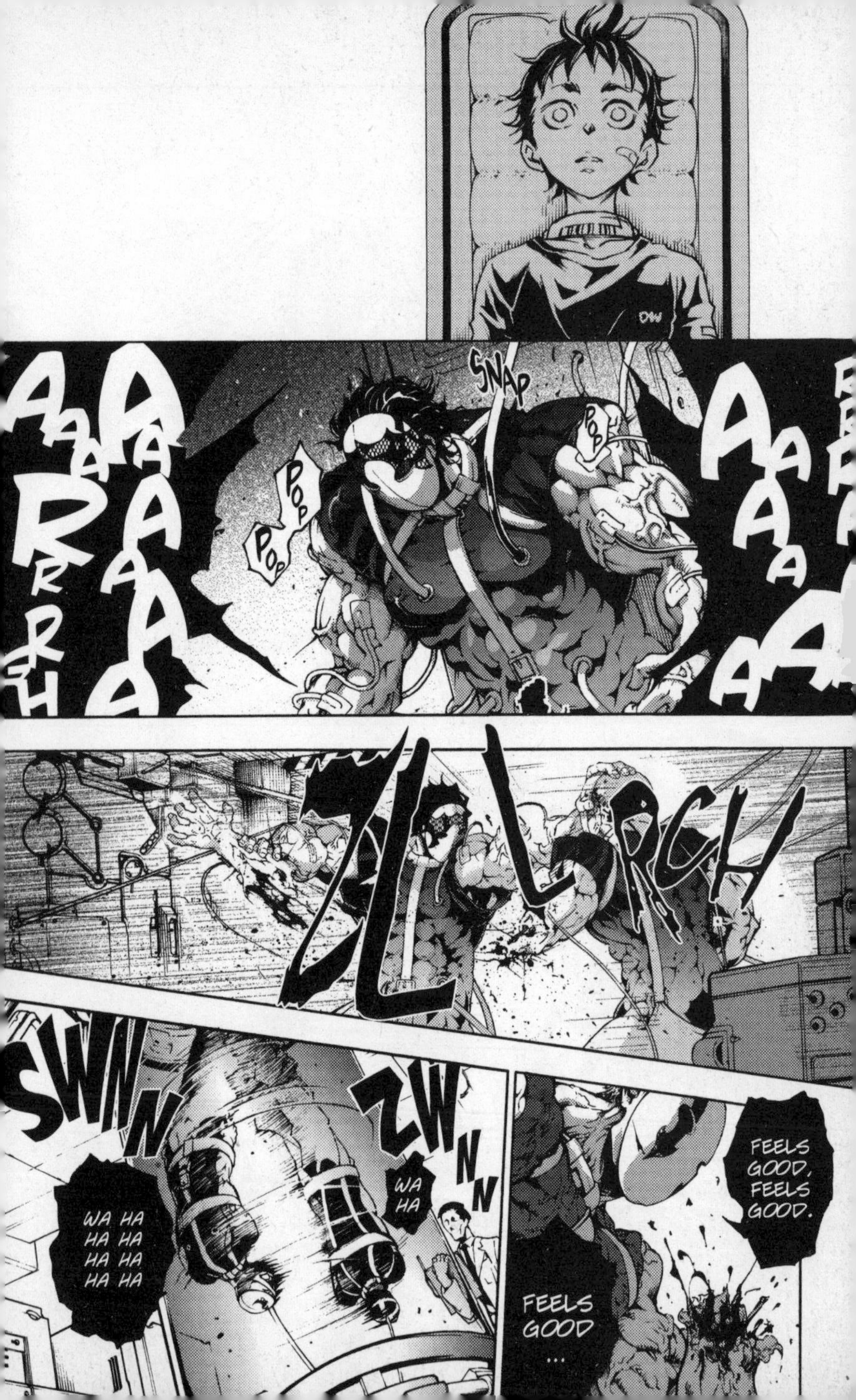

AAAAAA
SNAP
POP
POP
POP
AAAARRRGH
ZLLRCH
FEELS GOOD, FEELS GOOD.
FEELS GOOD ...
ZWNN
WA HA
SWNN
WA HA HA HA HA HA HA HA

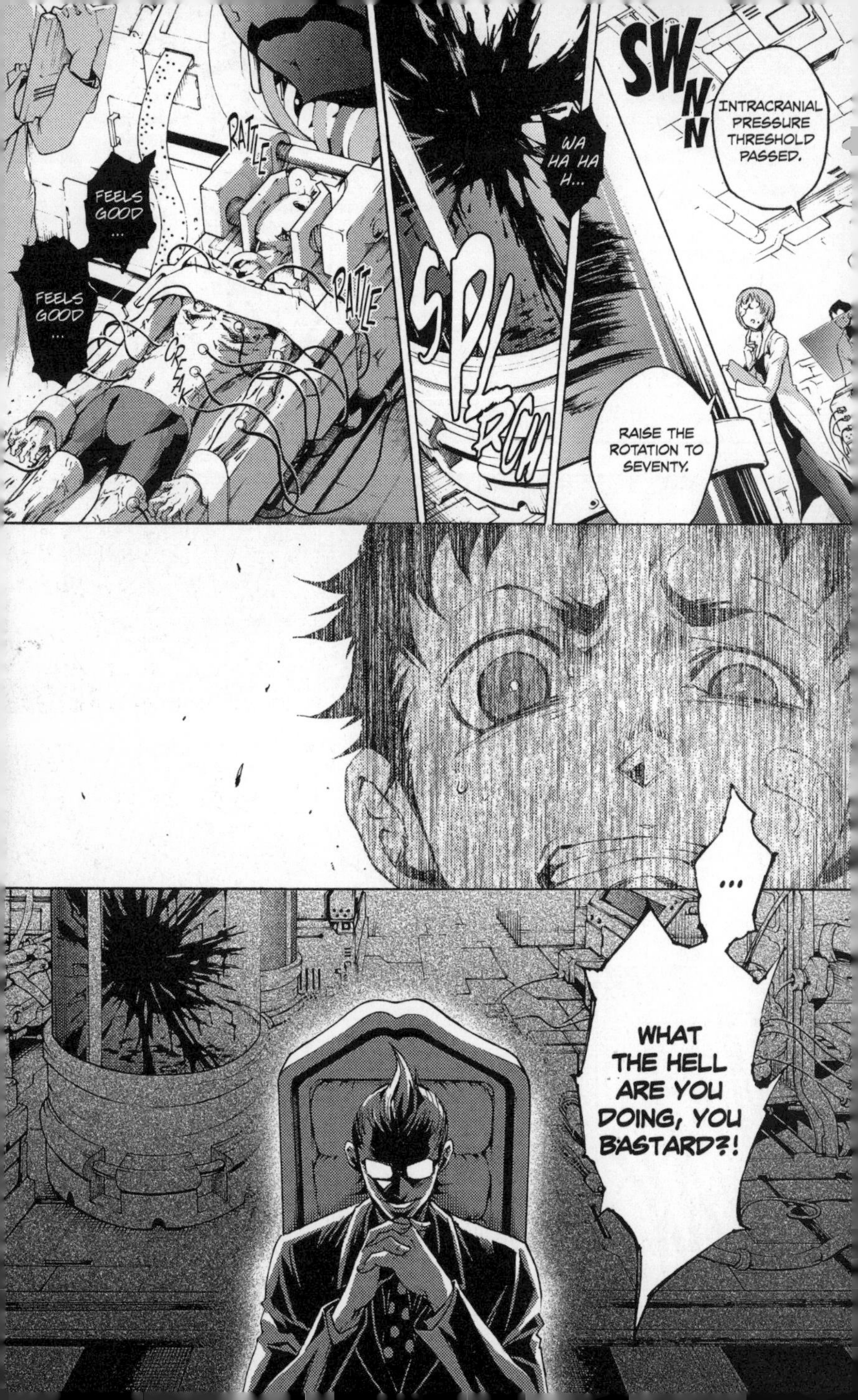
SWNN
INTRACRANIAL PRESSURE THRESHOLD PASSED.
RAISE THE ROTATION TO SEVENTY.
WA HA HA H...
SPLRCH
RATTLE
FEELS GOOD...
FEELS GOOD...
RATTLE
CREAK
...
WHAT THE HELL ARE YOU DOING, YOU BASTARD?!

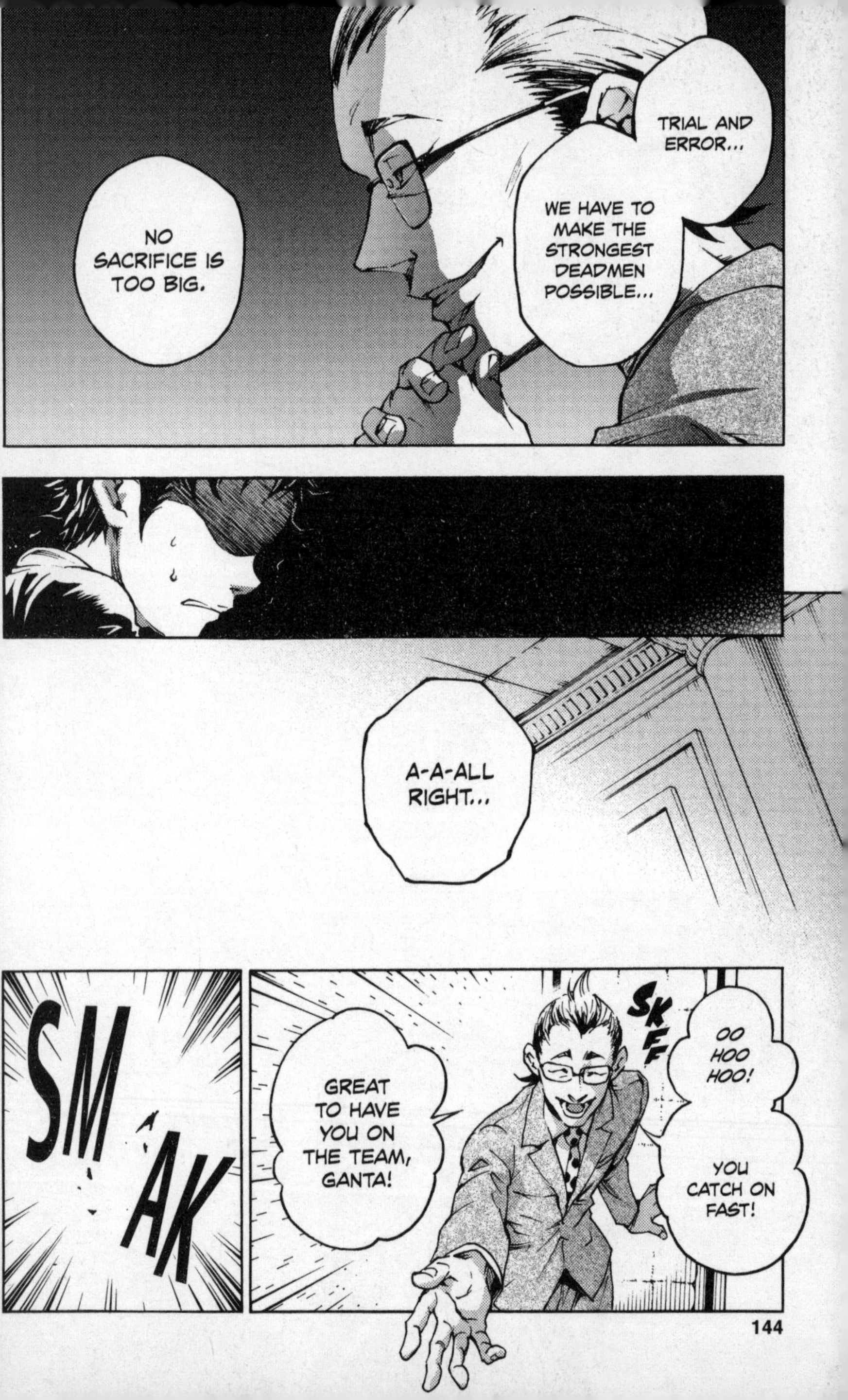
TRIAL AND ERROR...
WE HAVE TO MAKE THE STRONGEST DEADMEN POSSIBLE...
NO SACRIFICE IS TOO BIG.
A-A-ALL RIGHT...
SKFF
OO HOO HOO!
YOU CATCH ON FAST!
GREAT TO HAVE YOU ON THE TEAM, GANTA!
SMAK

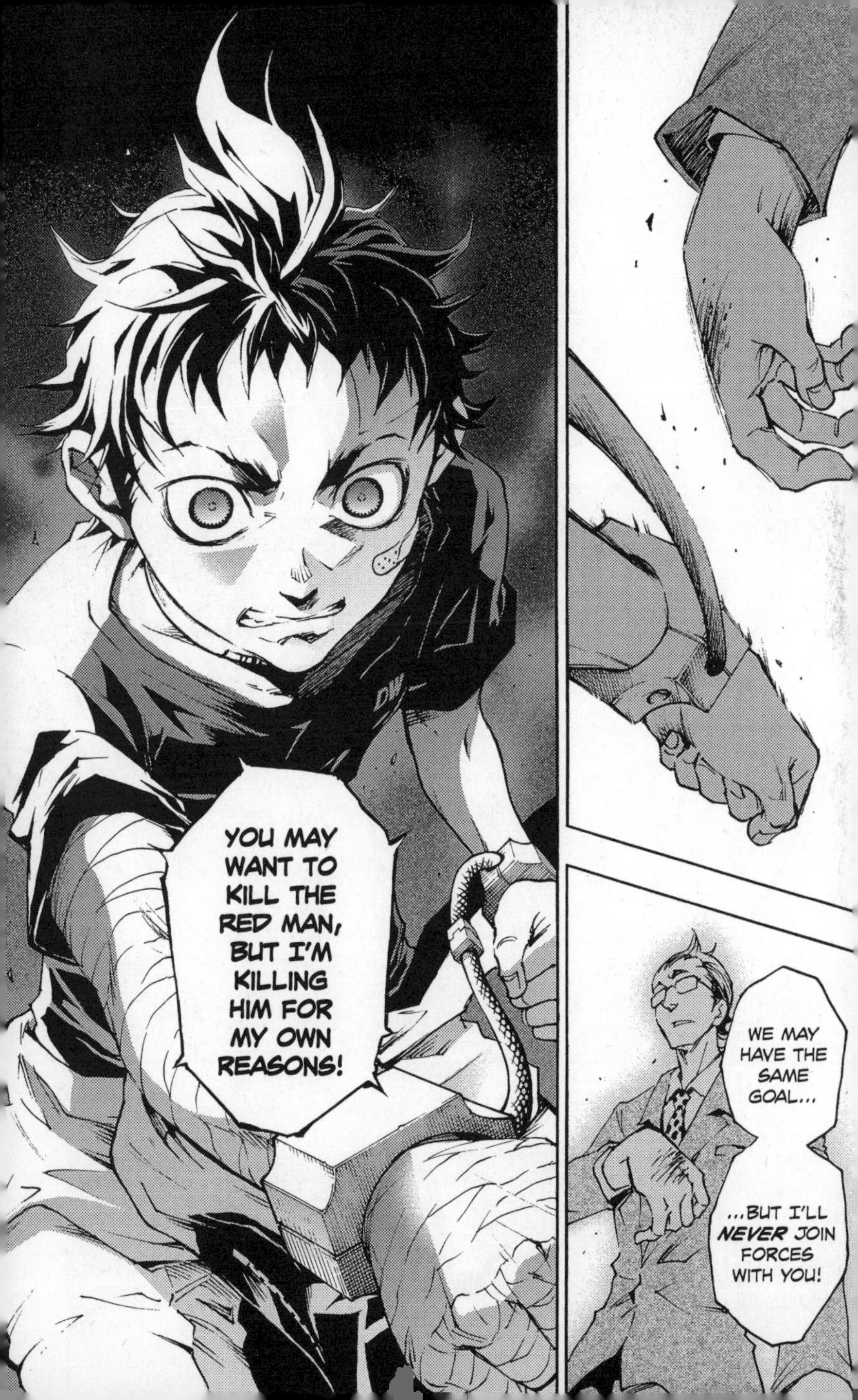
WE MAY HAVE THE SAME GOAL...
...BUT I'LL *NEVER* JOIN FORCES WITH YOU!
YOU MAY WANT TO KILL THE RED MAN, BUT I'M KILLING HIM FOR MY OWN REASONS!

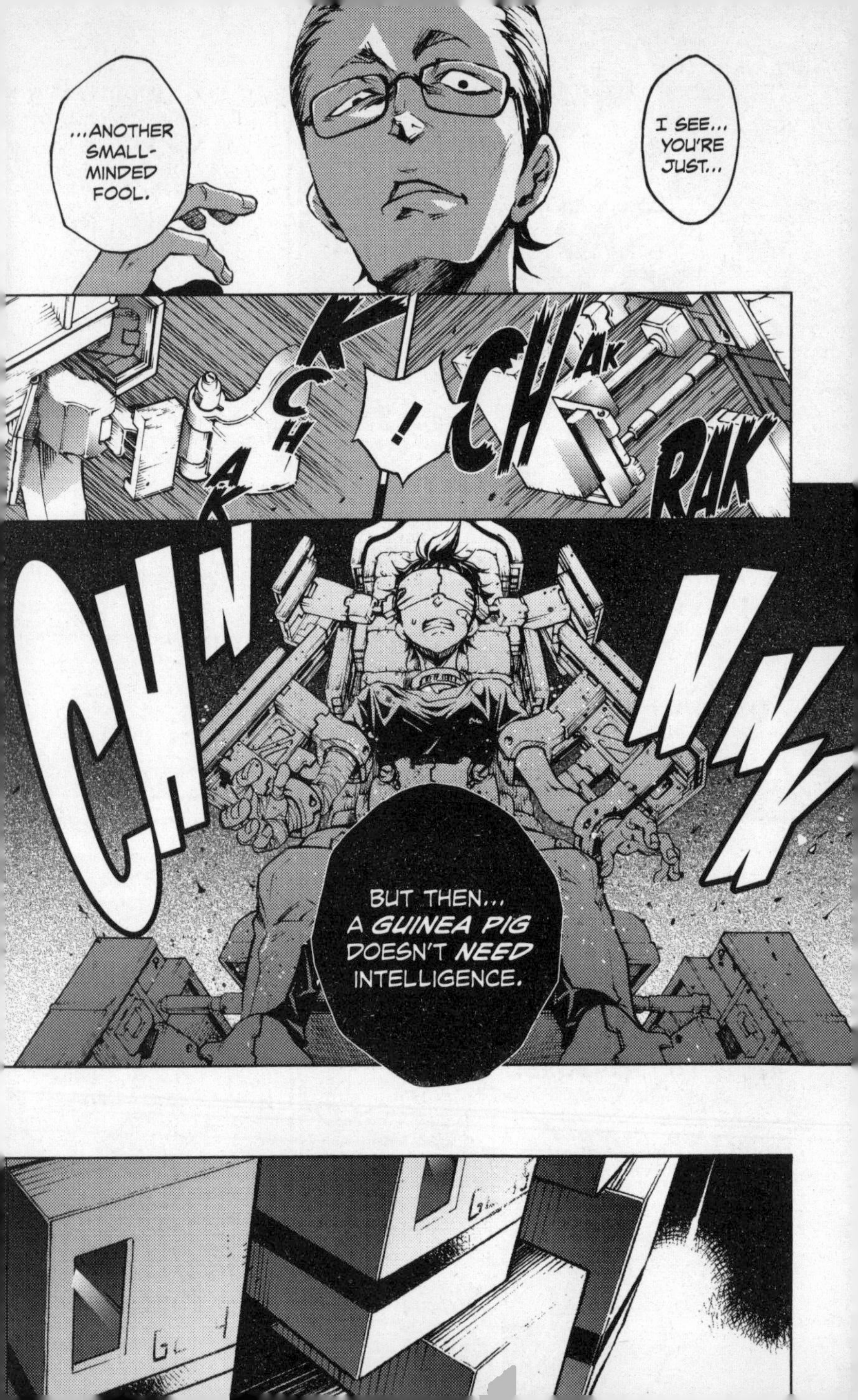
I SEE... YOU'RE JUST...
...ANOTHER SMALL-MINDED FOOL.
CHAK
RAK
!
KCHAK
NNK
CHN
BUT THEN... A *GUINEA PIG* DOESN'T *NEED* INTELLIGENCE.

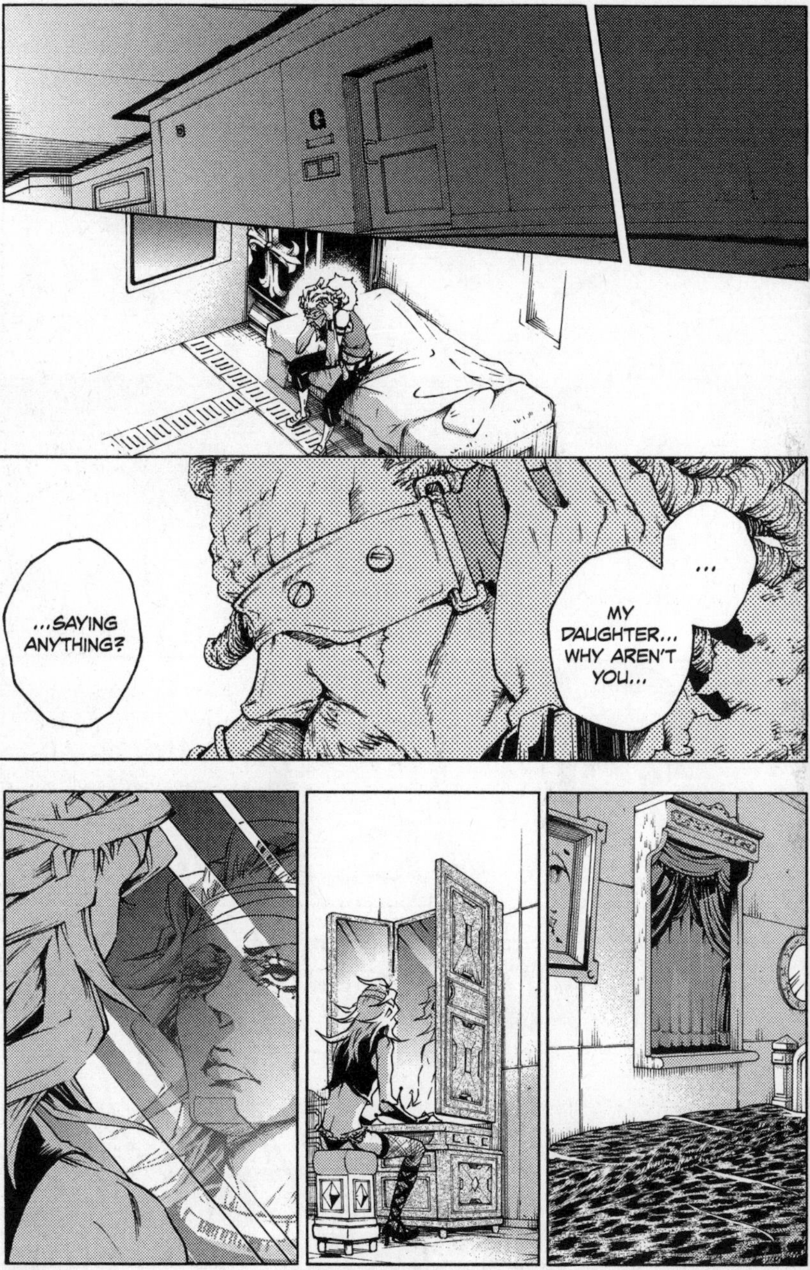
...
MY DAUGHTER... WHY AREN'T YOU...
...SAYING ANYTHING?

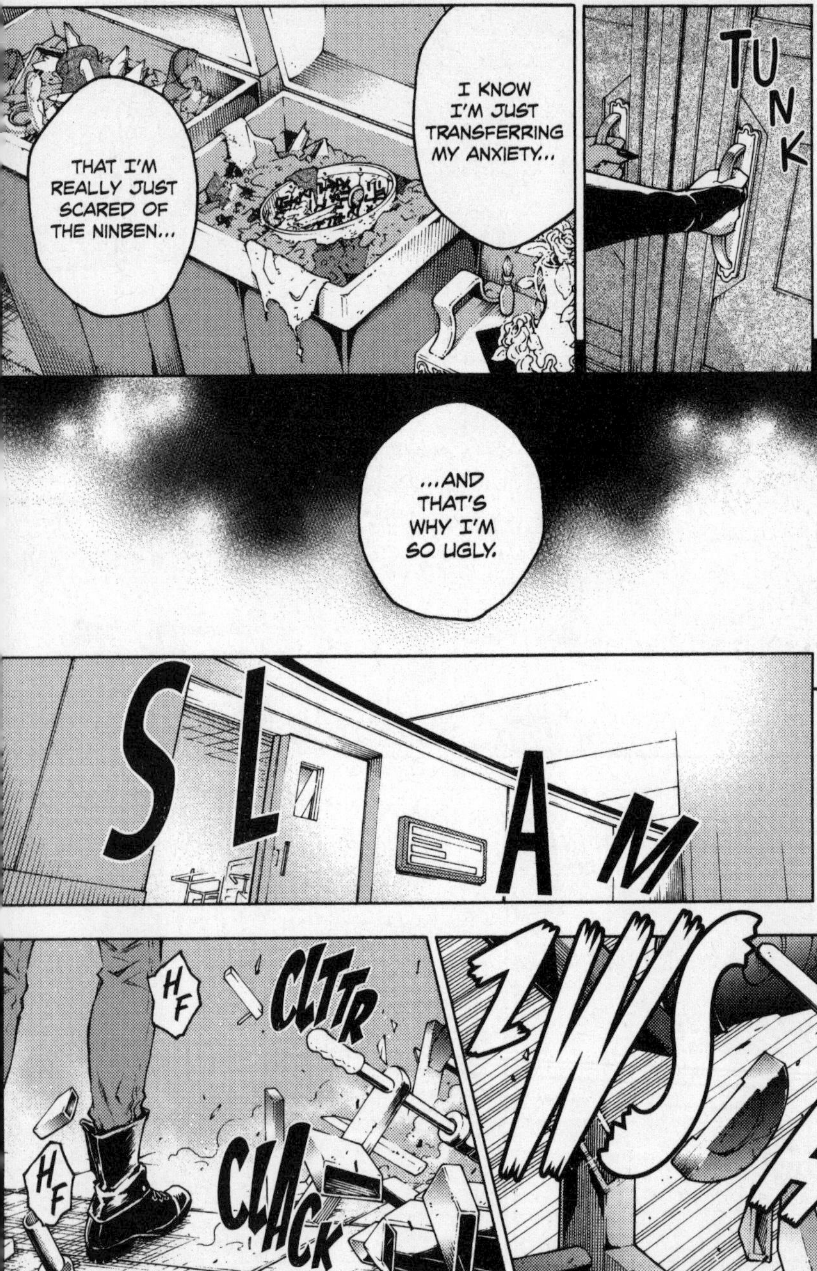
TUNK
I KNOW I'M JUST TRANSFERRING MY ANXIETY...
THAT I'M REALLY JUST SCARED OF THE NINBEN...
...AND THAT'S WHY I'M SO UGLY.
SLAM
ZWSH
CLTTR
HF
CLACK
HF

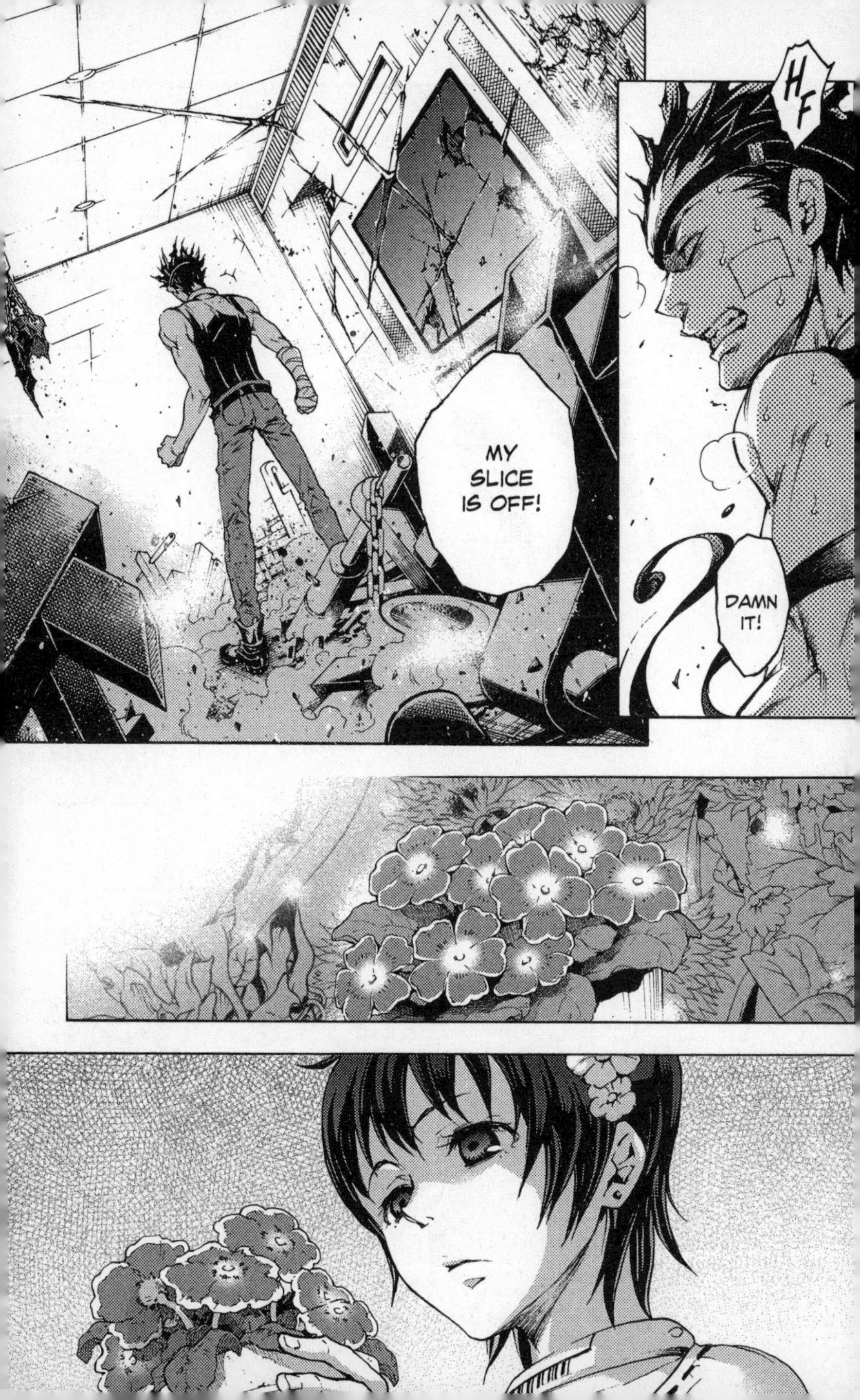
HF
DAMN IT!
MY SLICE IS OFF!

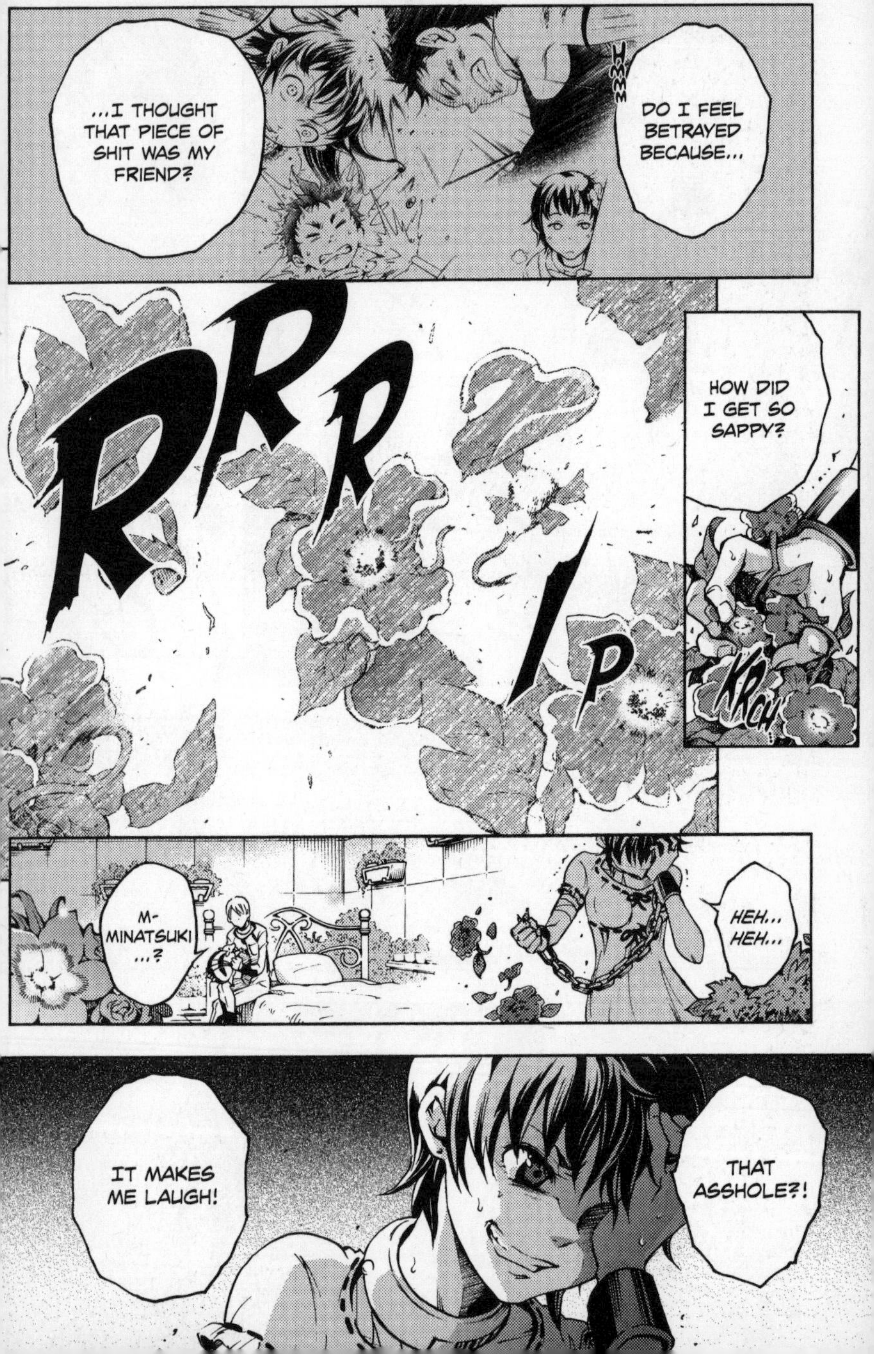
DO I FEEL BETRAYED BECAUSE...
HMMM
...I THOUGHT THAT PIECE OF SHIT WAS MY FRIEND?
HOW DID I GET SO SAPPY?
KRCH
RRRIP
HEH... HEH...
M-MINATSUKI ...?
THAT ASSHOLE?!
IT MAKES ME LAUGH!

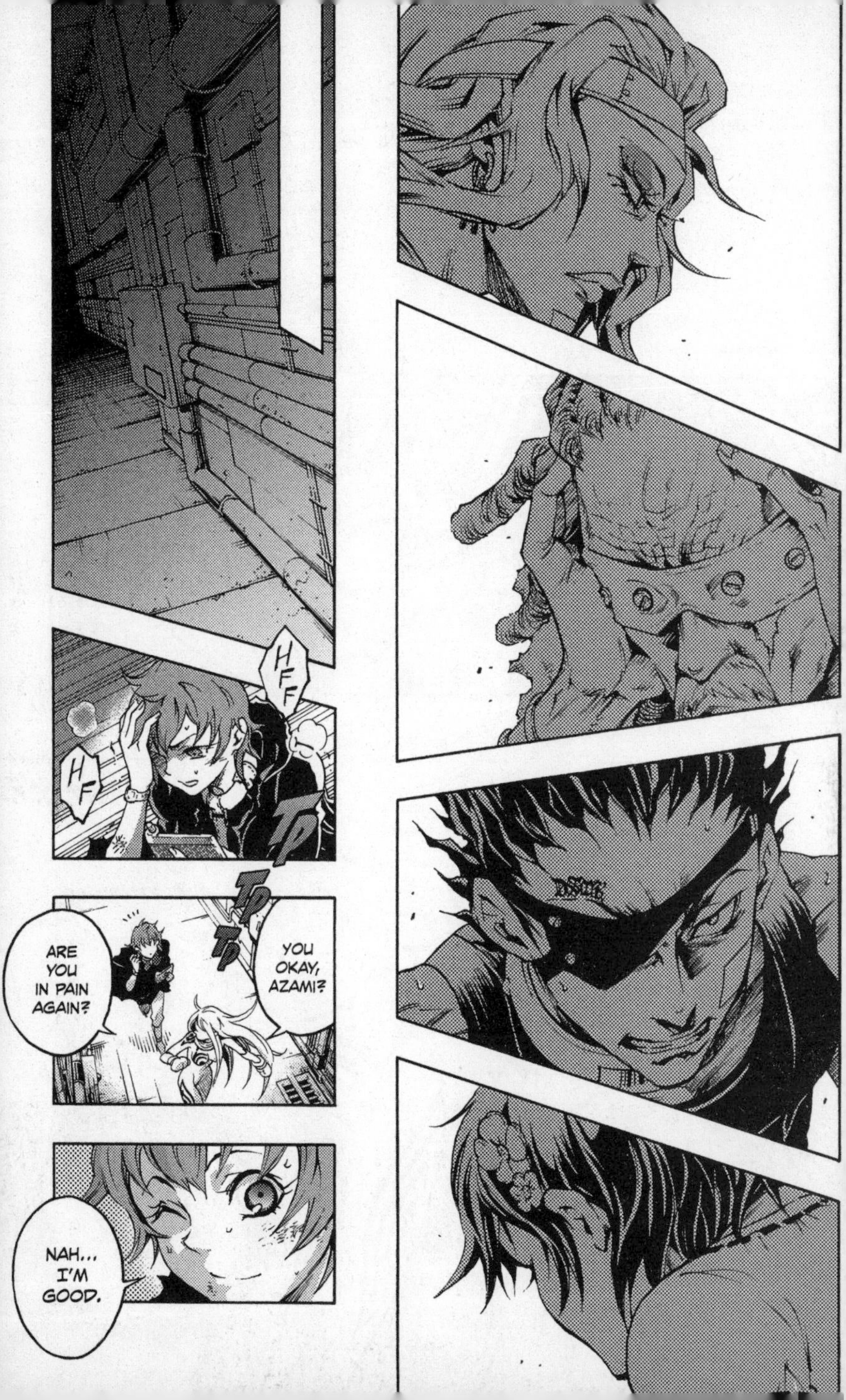
HFF
HF
TP
TP
TP
YOU OKAY, AZAMI?
ARE YOU IN PAIN AGAIN?
NAH... I'M GOOD.

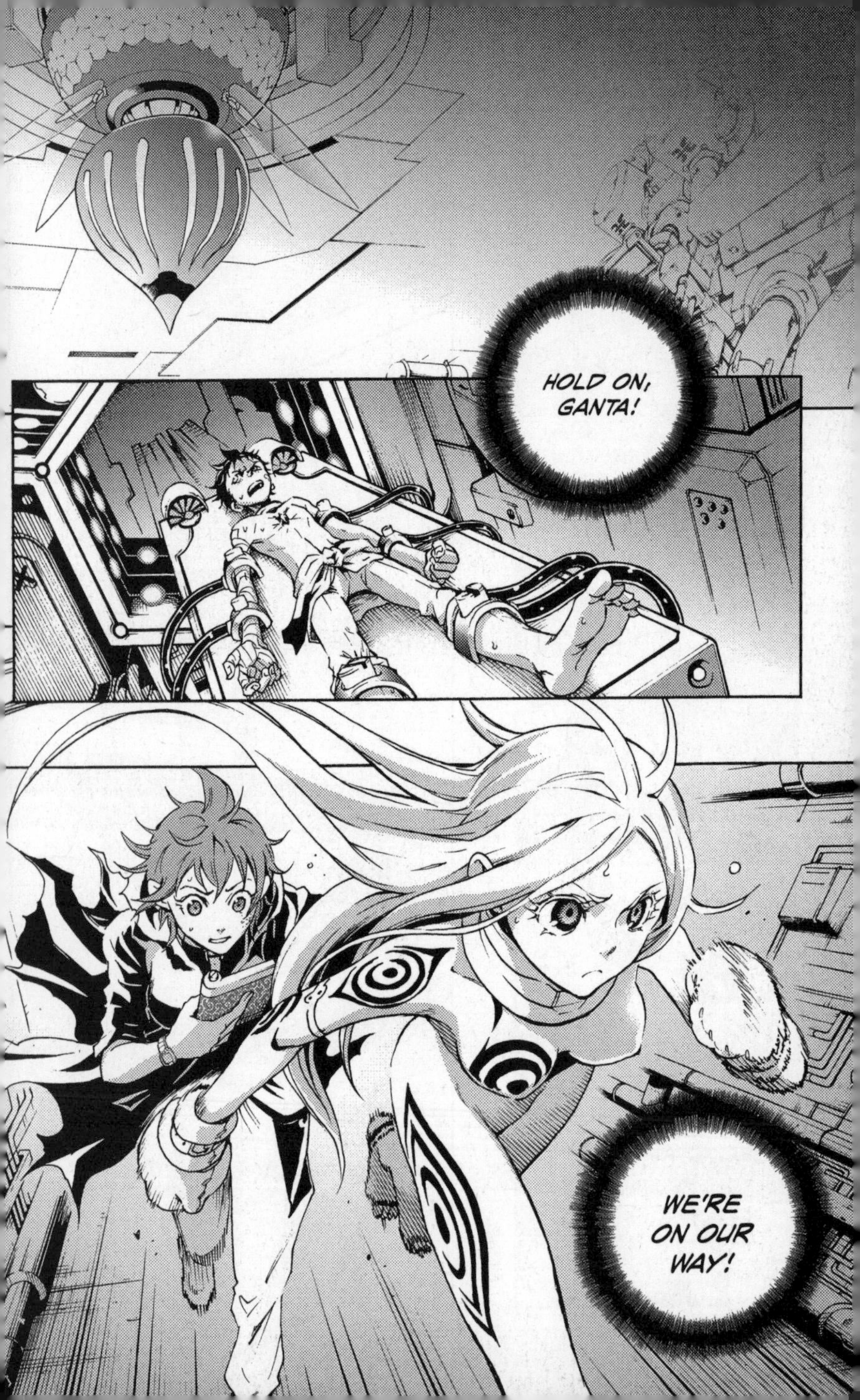
HOLD ON, GANTA!
WE'RE ON OUR WAY!

DEADMAN
WONDER
LAND
DEADMAN
WONDER
LAND
DEADMAN
WONDER
LAND

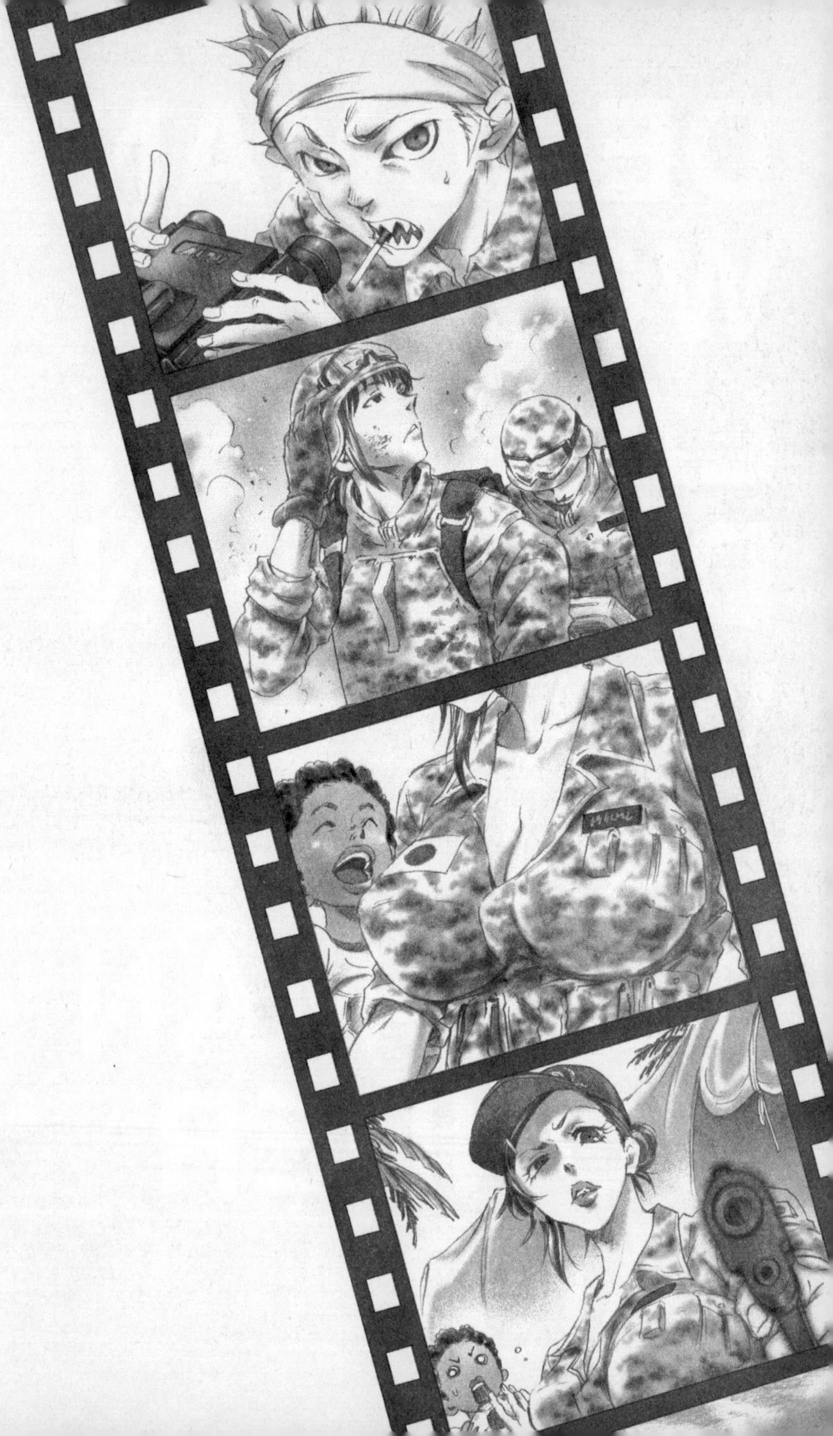

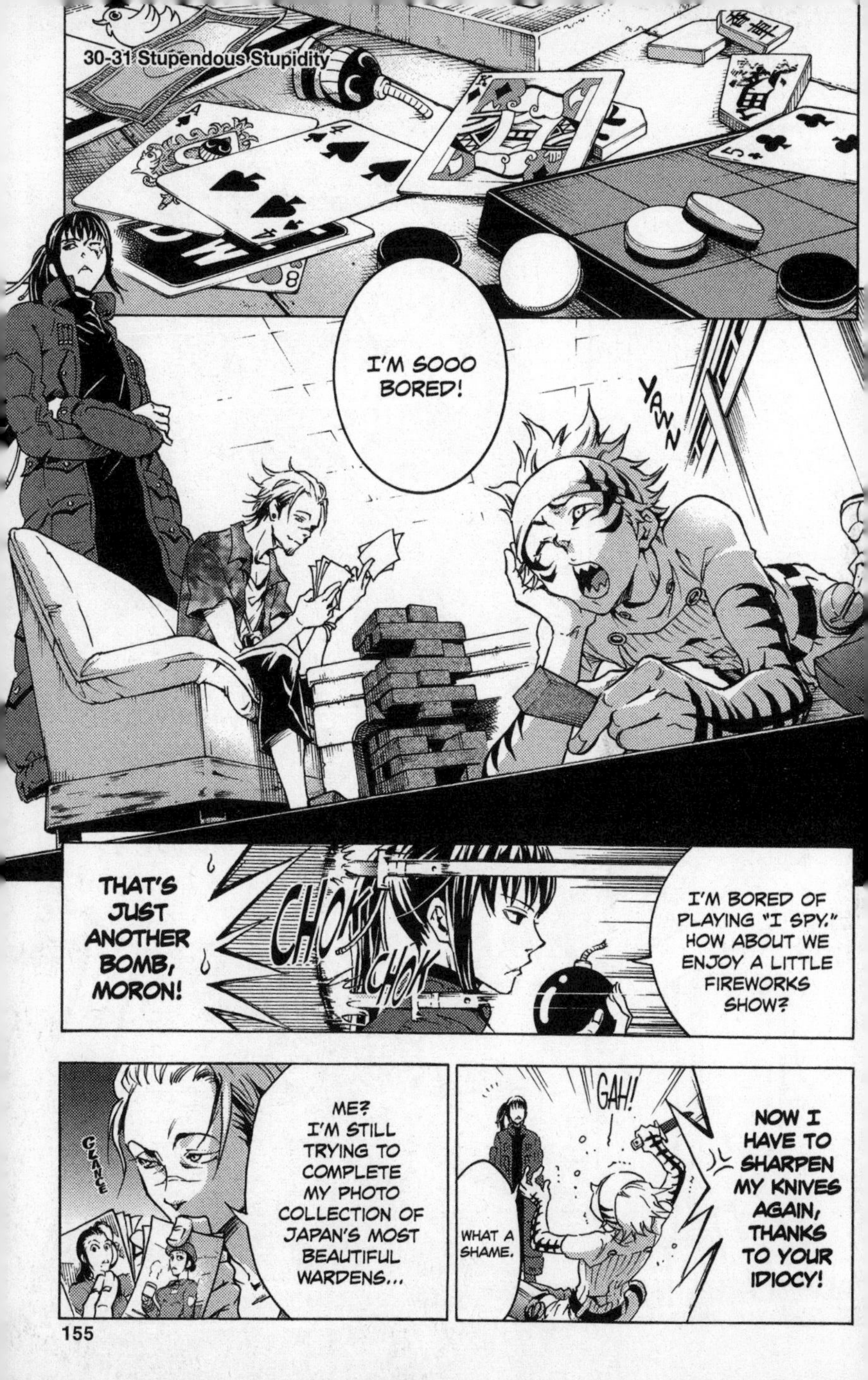
30-31 Stupendous Stupidity
I'M SOOO BORED!
YAWN
I'M BORED OF PLAYING "I SPY." HOW ABOUT WE ENJOY A LITTLE FIREWORKS SHOW?
CHOK CHOK
THAT'S JUST ANOTHER BOMB, MORON!
NOW I HAVE TO SHARPEN MY KNIVES AGAIN, THANKS TO YOUR IDIOCY!
GAH!
WHAT A SHAME.
GLANCE
ME? I'M STILL TRYING TO COMPLETE MY PHOTO COLLECTION OF JAPAN'S MOST BEAUTIFUL WARDENS...

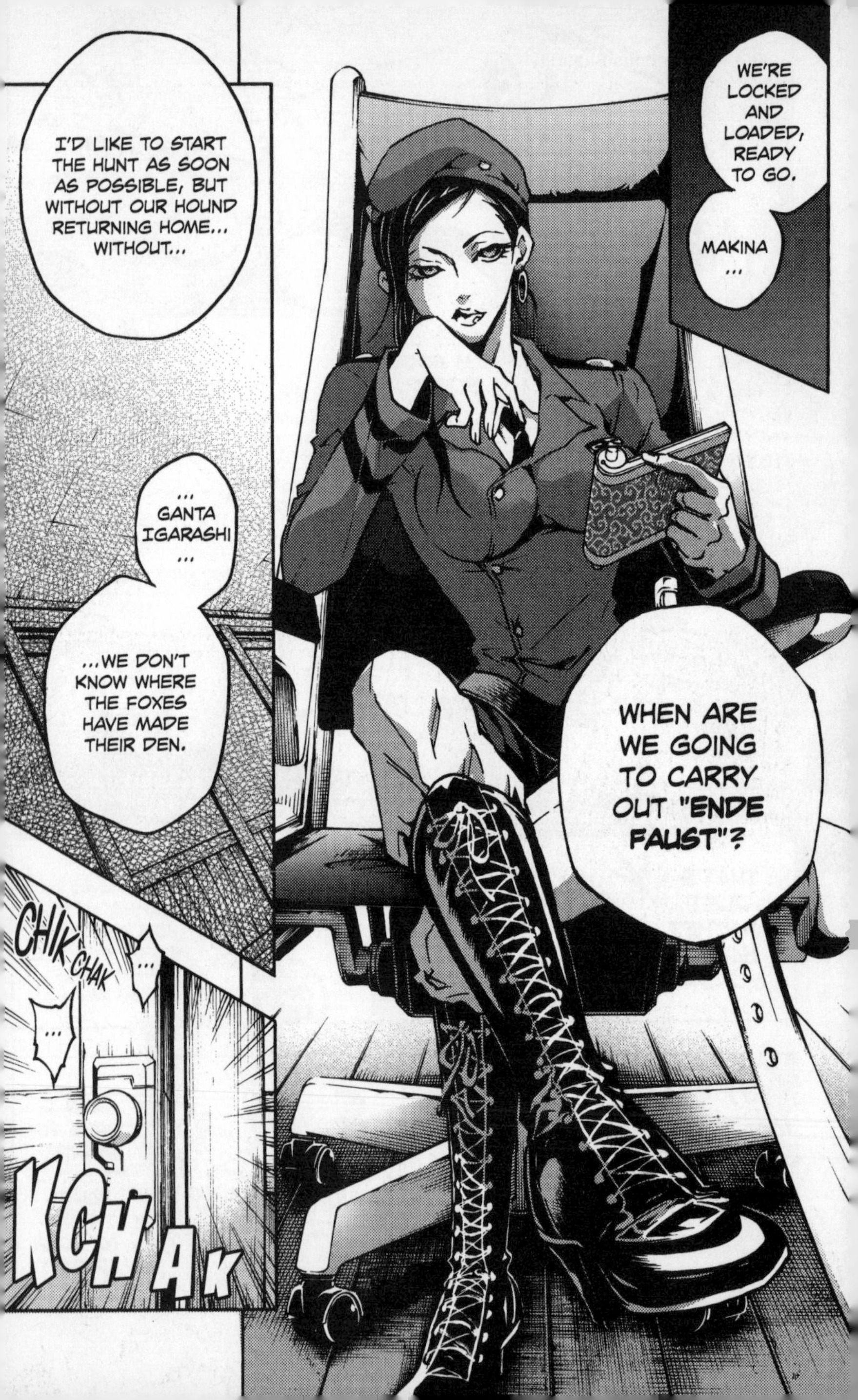
WE'RE LOCKED AND LOADED, READY TO GO.
MAKINA ...
WHEN ARE WE GOING TO CARRY OUT "ENDE FAUST"?
I'D LIKE TO START THE HUNT AS SOON AS POSSIBLE, BUT WITHOUT OUR HOUND RETURNING HOME... WITHOUT...
... GANTA IGARASHI ...
...WE DON'T KNOW WHERE THE FOXES HAVE MADE THEIR DEN.
CHIK CHAK
...
...
KCHAK

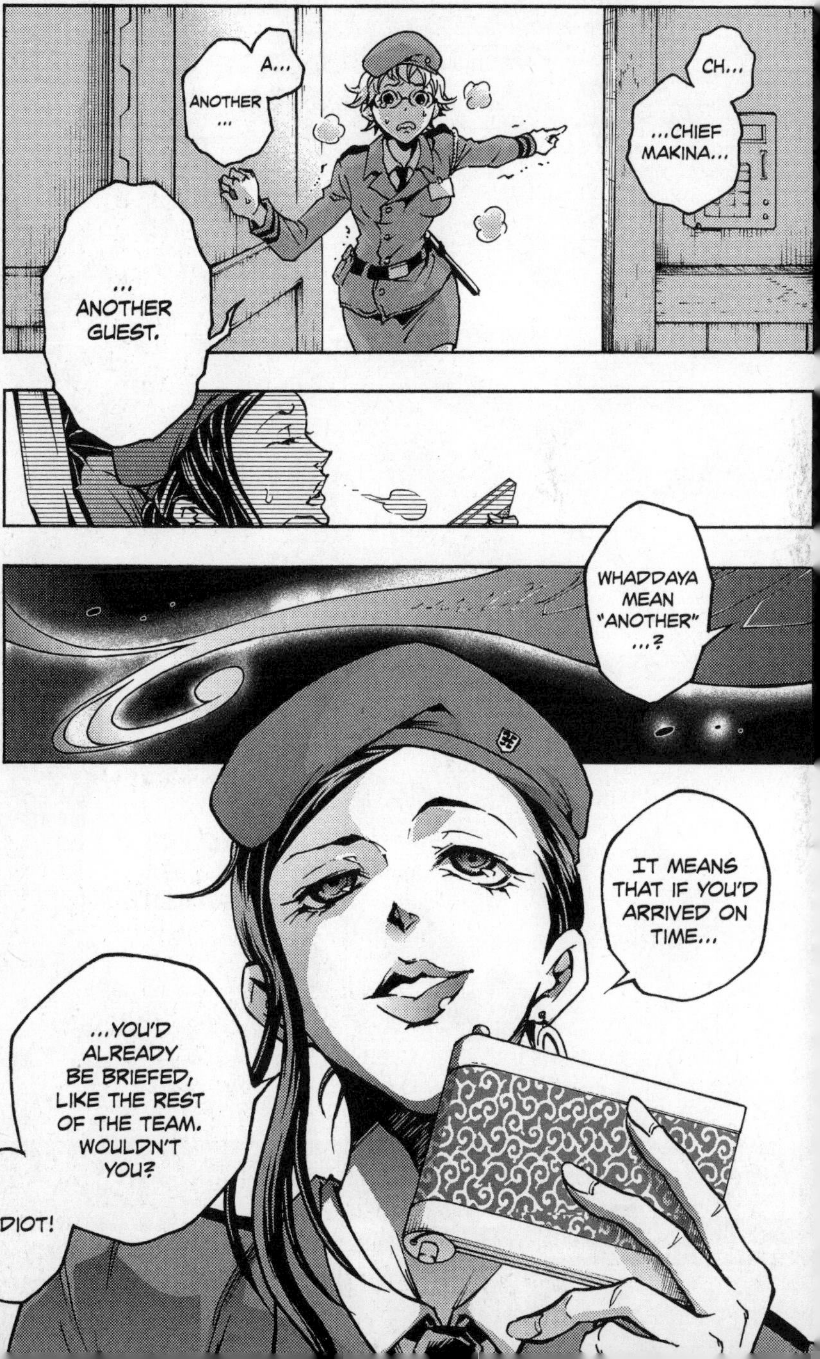
CH... ...CHIEF MAKINA...
A... ANOTHER ...
... ANOTHER GUEST.
WHADDAYA MEAN "ANOTHER" ...?
IT MEANS THAT IF YOU'D ARRIVED ON TIME...
...YOU'D ALREADY BE BRIEFED, LIKE THE REST OF THE TEAM. WOULDN'T YOU?
IDIOT!

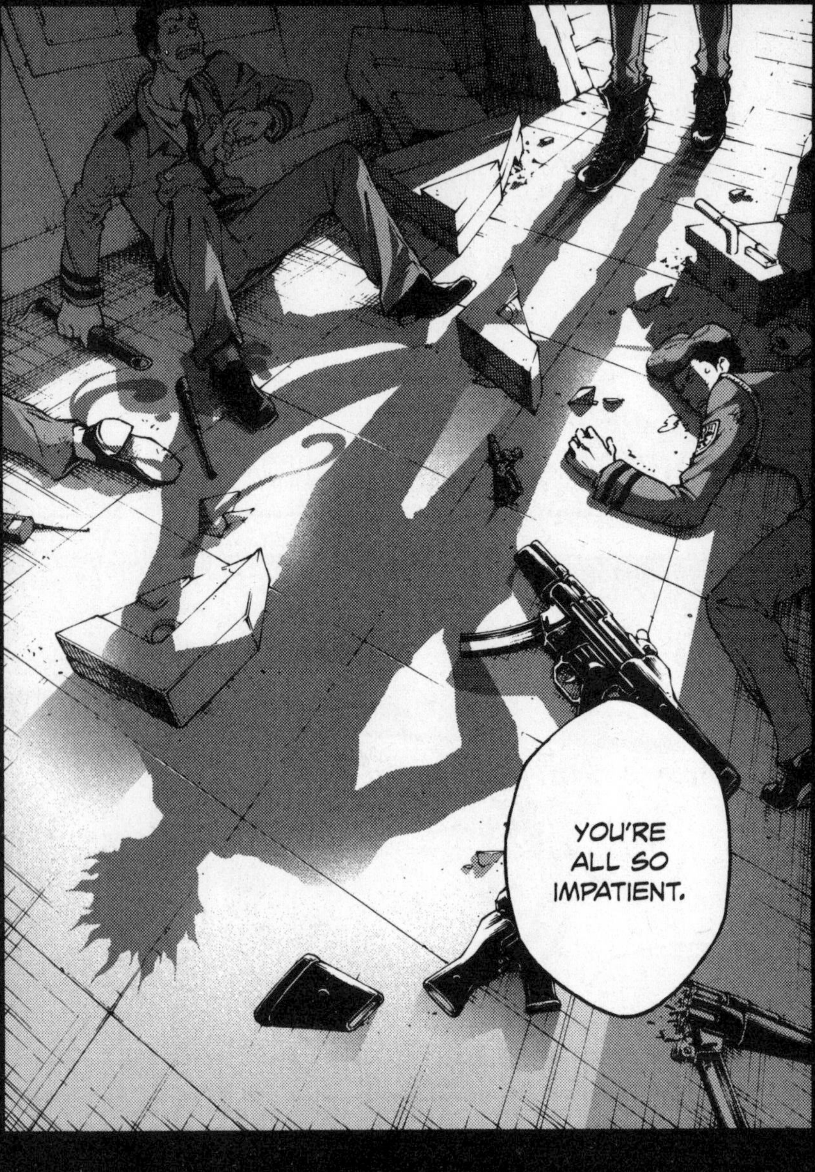
YOU'RE ALL SO IMPATIENT.

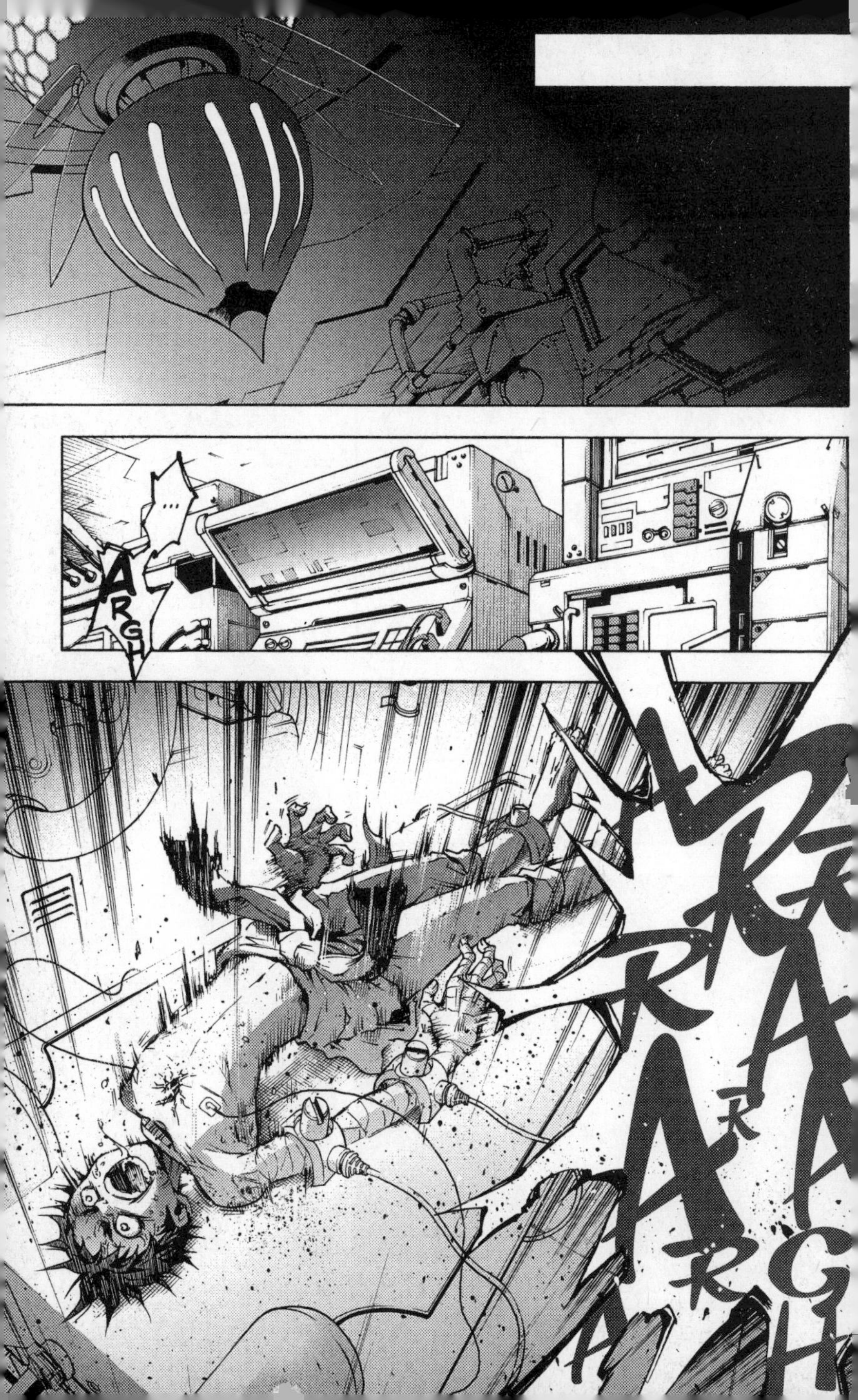
...
ARGH

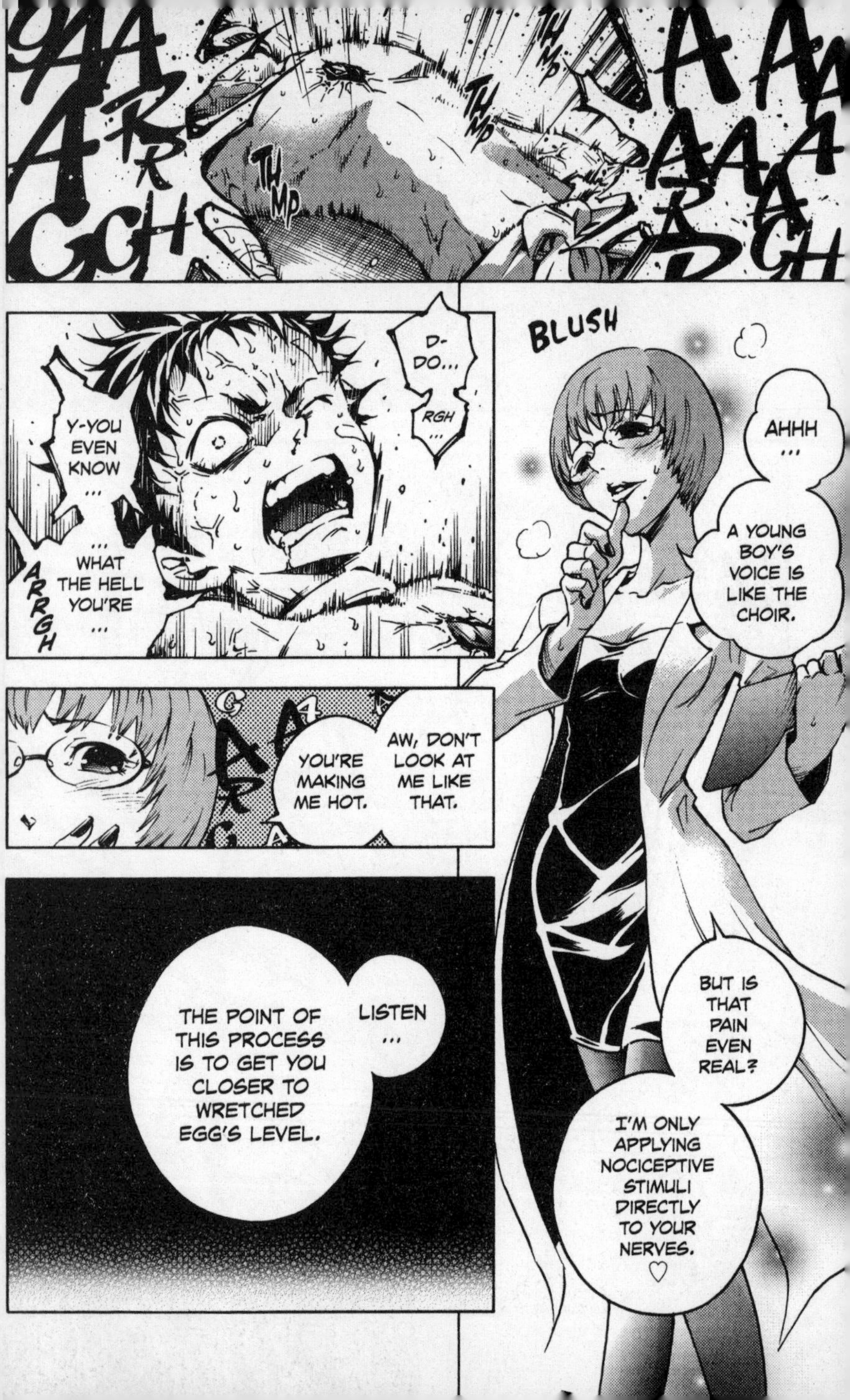
THMP
THMP
THMP
BLUSH
AHHH...
A YOUNG BOY'S VOICE IS LIKE THE CHOIR.
BUT IS THAT PAIN EVEN REAL?
I'M ONLY APPLYING NOCICEPTIVE STIMULI DIRECTLY TO YOUR NERVES. ♡
D-DO... RGH...
Y-YOU EVEN KNOW...
...WHAT THE HELL YOU'RE...
ARRGH
AW, DON'T LOOK AT ME LIKE THAT.
YOU'RE MAKING ME HOT.
LISTEN...
THE POINT OF THIS PROCESS IS TO GET YOU CLOSER TO WRETCHED EGG'S LEVEL.

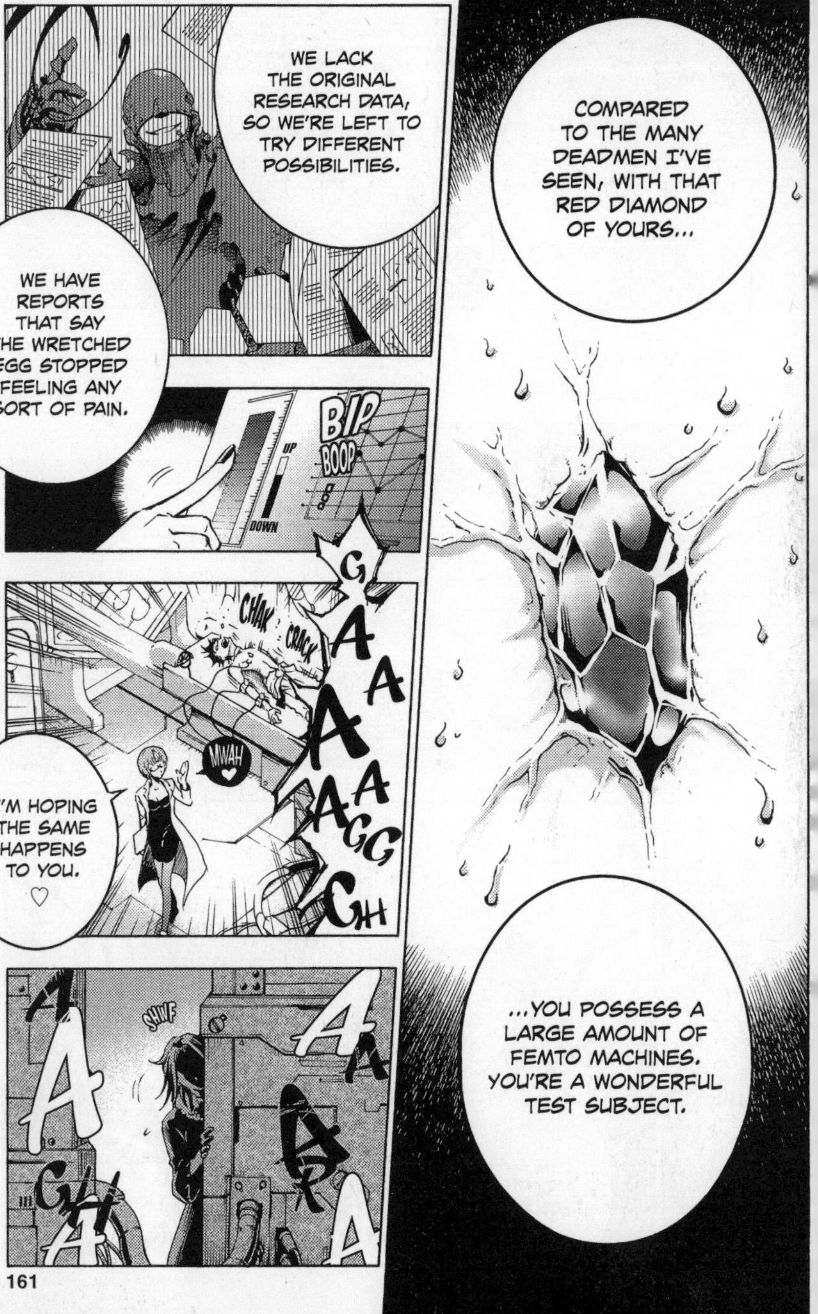
COMPARED TO THE MANY DEADMEN I'VE SEEN, WITH THAT RED DIAMOND OF YOURS...
...YOU POSSESS A LARGE AMOUNT OF FEMTO MACHINES. YOU'RE A WONDERFUL TEST SUBJECT.
WE LACK THE ORIGINAL RESEARCH DATA, SO WE'RE LEFT TO TRY DIFFERENT POSSIBILITIES.
WE HAVE REPORTS THAT SAY THE WRETCHED EGG STOPPED FEELING ANY SORT OF PAIN.
BIP
BOOP
UP
DOWN
GAAAAAAAGGCH
CHAK
CRACK
MWAH ♥
I'M HOPING THE SAME HAPPENS TO YOU. ♡
SHUF

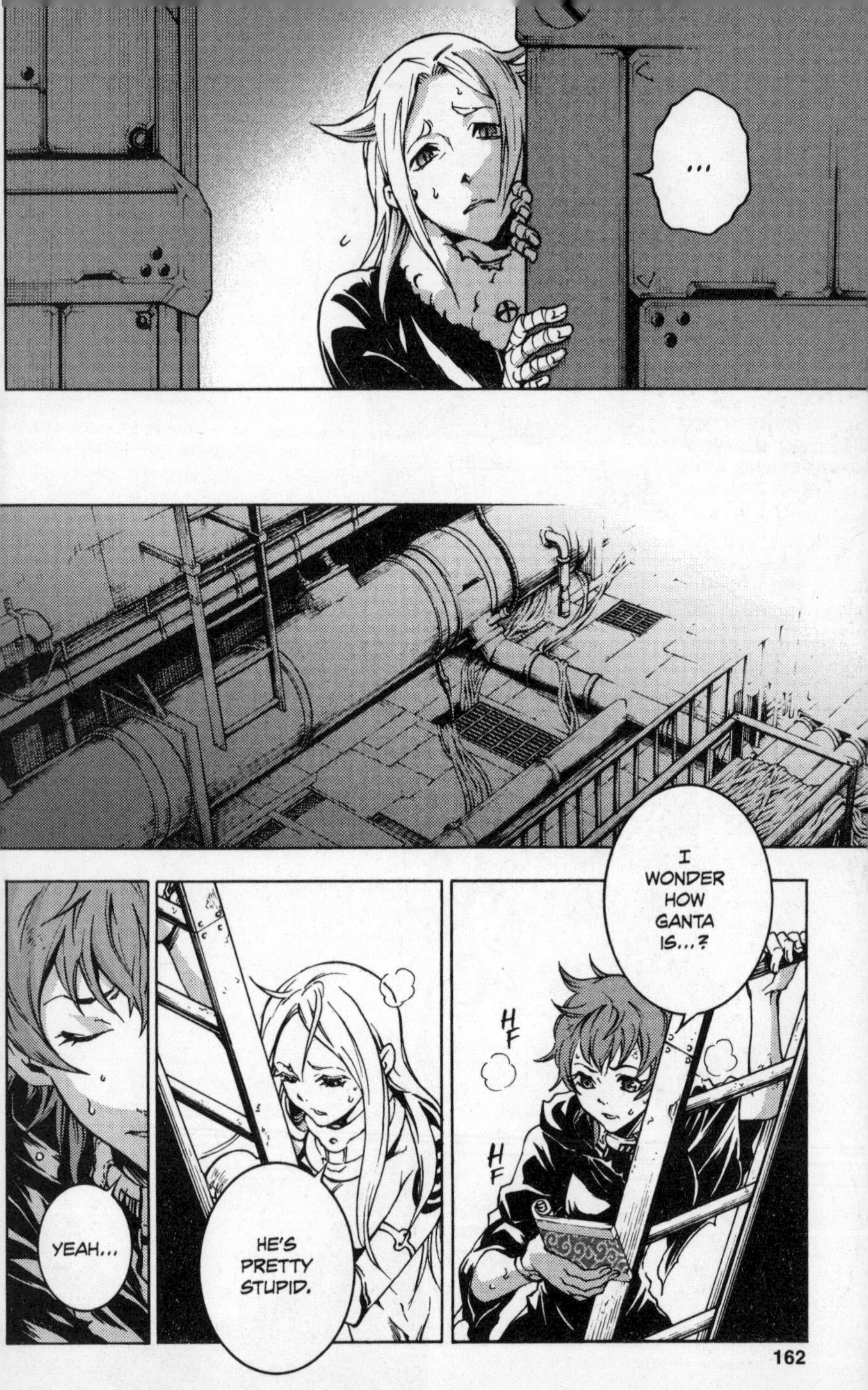
...
I WONDER HOW GANTA IS...?
HF
HF
HE'S PRETTY STUPID.
YEAH...

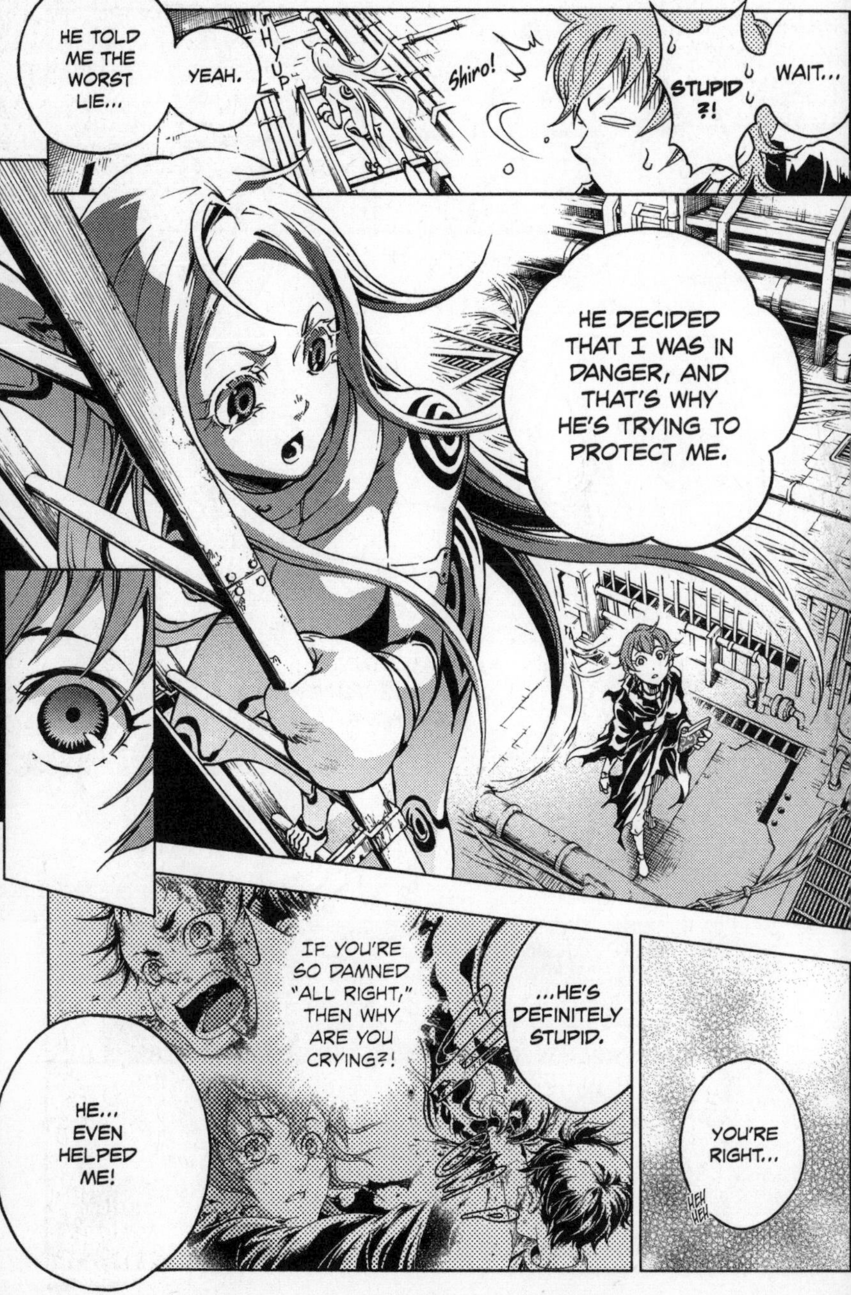
WAIT...
STUPID ?!
Shiro!
HYUP
YEAH.
HE TOLD ME THE WORST LIE...
HE DECIDED THAT I WAS IN DANGER, AND THAT'S WHY HE'S TRYING TO PROTECT ME.
YOU'RE RIGHT...
HEH HEH
...HE'S DEFINITELY STUPID.
IF YOU'RE SO DAMNED "ALL RIGHT," THEN WHY ARE YOU CRYING?!
HE... EVEN HELPED ME!

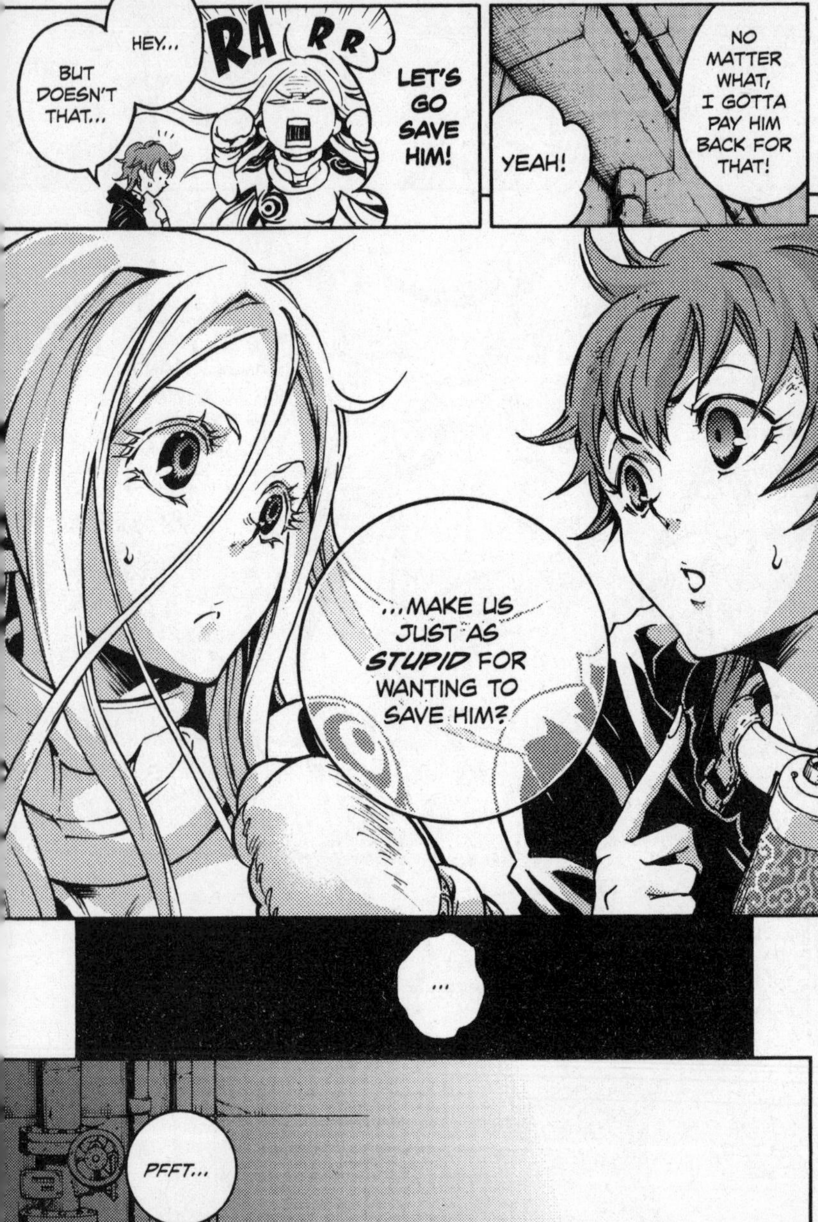
NO MATTER WHAT, I GOTTA PAY HIM BACK FOR THAT!
YEAH!
LET'S GO SAVE HIM!
RARRR
HEY...
BUT DOESN'T THAT...
...MAKE US JUST AS STUPID FOR WANTING TO SAVE HIM?
...
PFFT...

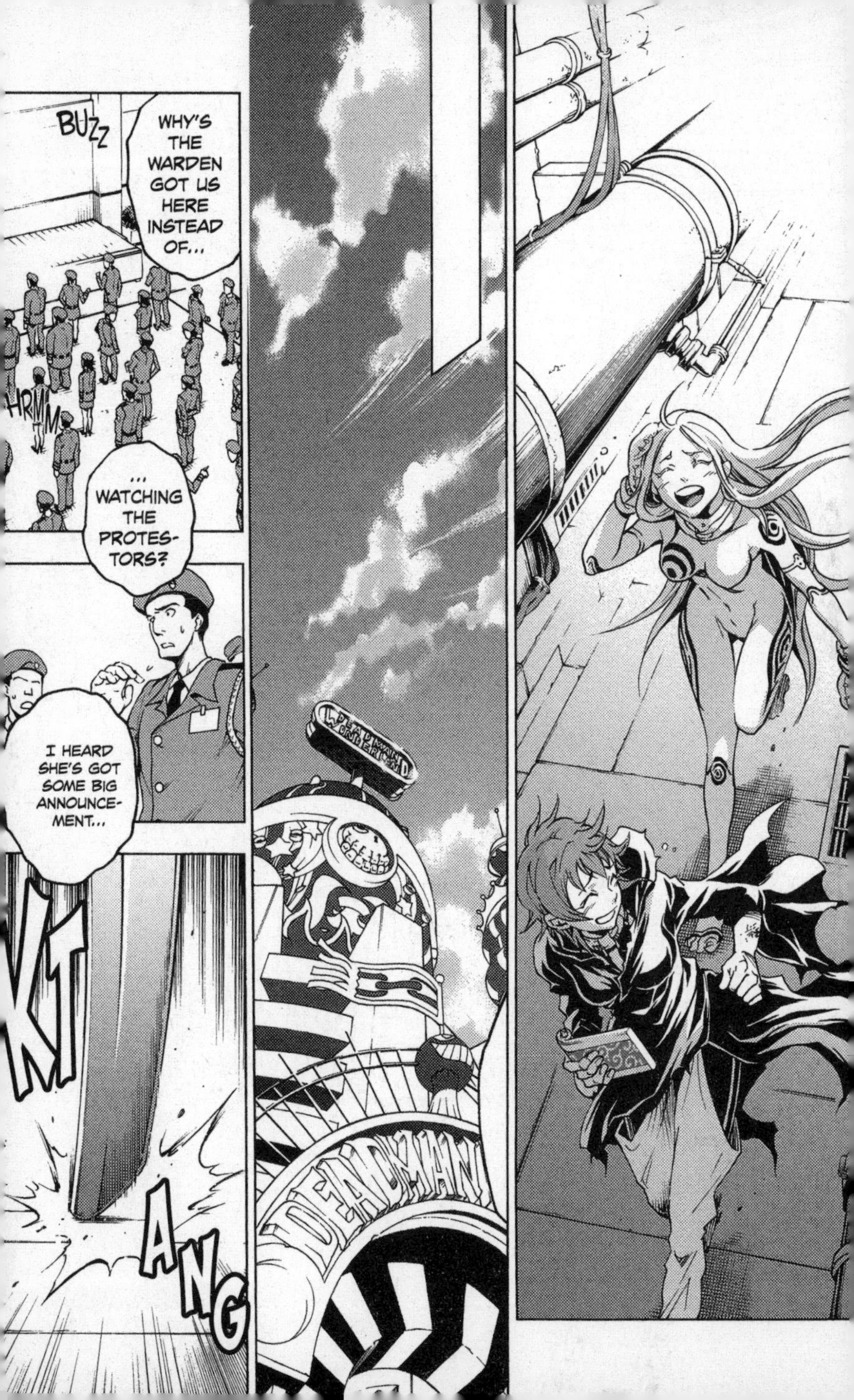
DEADMAN
BUZZ
WHY'S THE WARDEN GOT US HERE INSTEAD OF...
HRMM
...WATCHING THE PROTESTORS?
I HEARD SHE'S GOT SOME BIG ANNOUNCEMENT...
KT
ANG

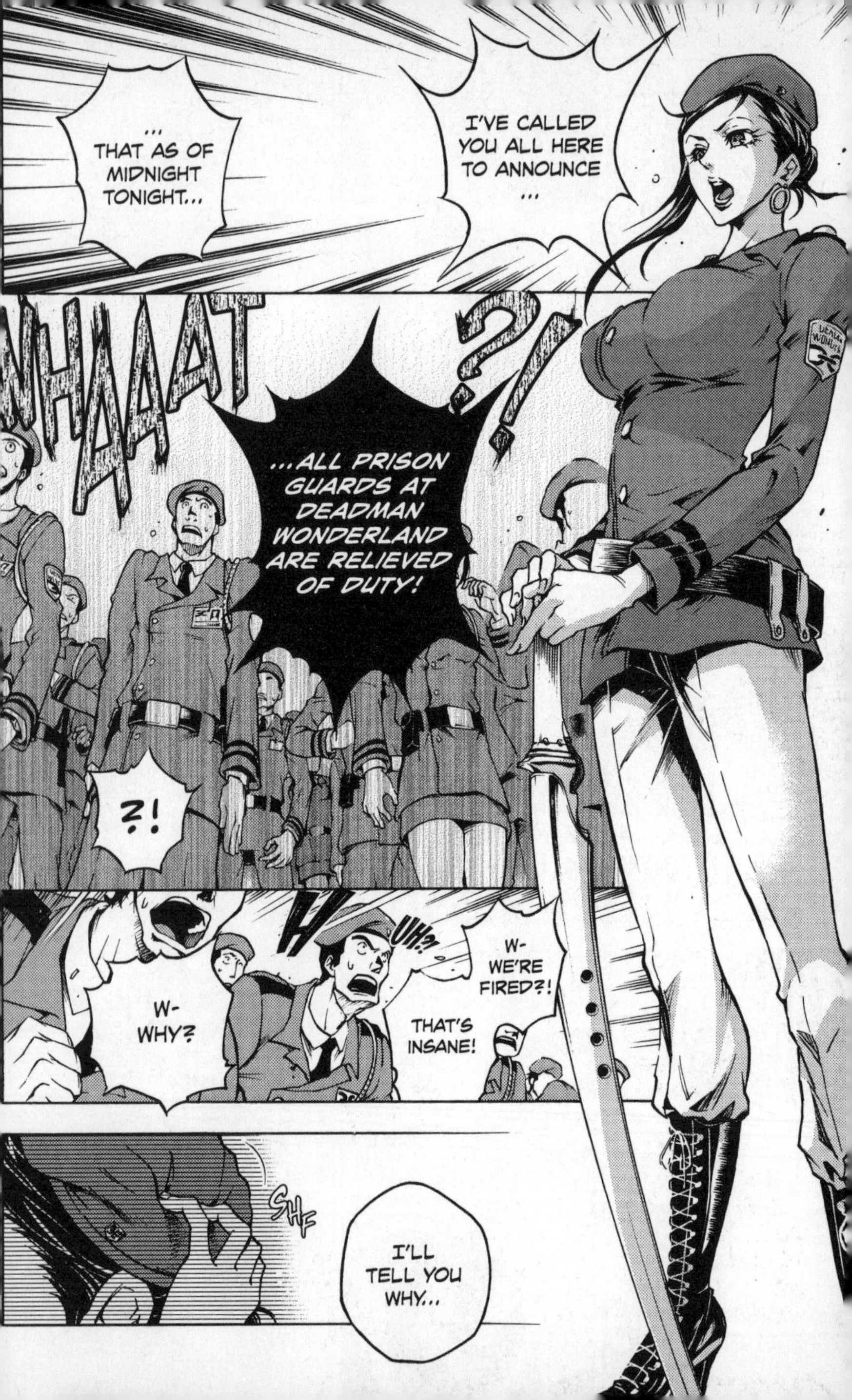
I'VE CALLED YOU ALL HERE TO ANNOUNCE ...
... THAT AS OF MIDNIGHT TONIGHT...
...ALL PRISON GUARDS AT DEADMAN WONDERLAND ARE RELIEVED OF DUTY!
WHAAAT?!
?!
W- WE'RE FIRED?!
UH?!
THAT'S INSANE!
W- WHY?
SHF
I'LL TELL YOU WHY...

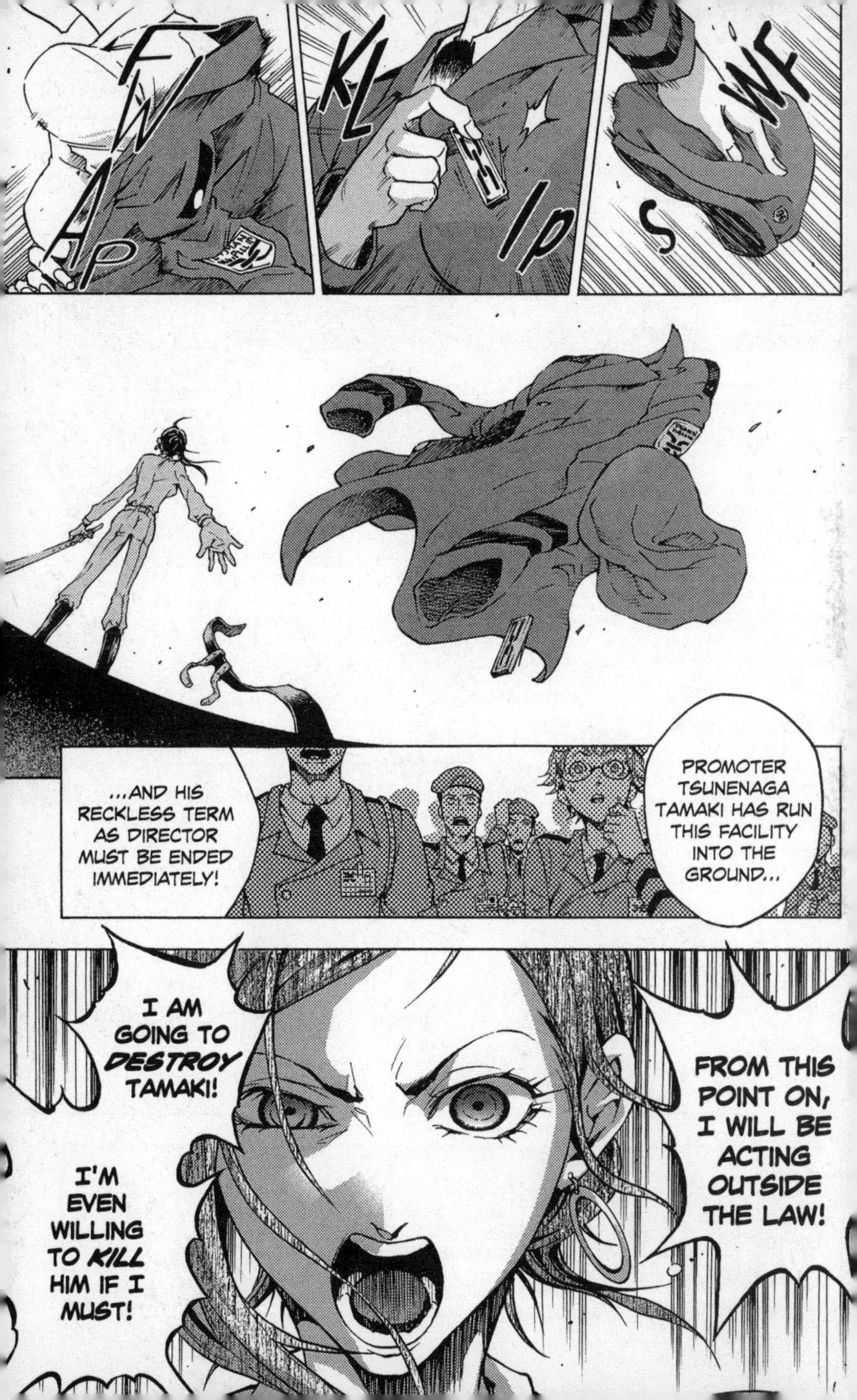
SWF
KLIP
FWAP
PROMOTER TSUNENAGA TAMAKI HAS RUN THIS FACILITY INTO THE GROUND...
...AND HIS RECKLESS TERM AS DIRECTOR MUST BE ENDED IMMEDIATELY!
FROM THIS POINT ON, I WILL BE ACTING OUTSIDE THE LAW!
I AM GOING TO *DESTROY* TAMAKI!
I'M EVEN WILLING TO *KILL* HIM IF I MUST!

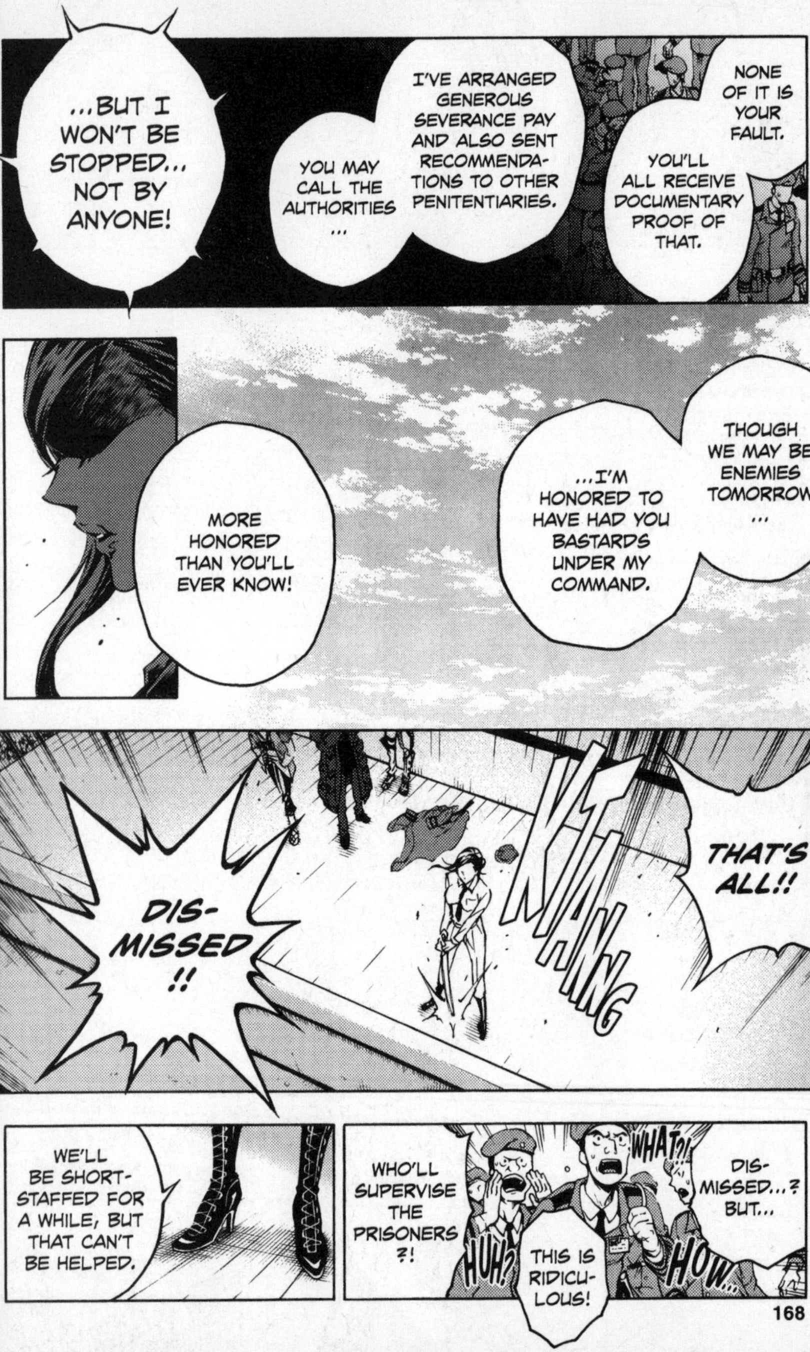
NONE OF IT IS YOUR FAULT.
YOU'LL ALL RECEIVE DOCUMENTARY PROOF OF THAT.
I'VE ARRANGED GENEROUS SEVERANCE PAY AND ALSO SENT RECOMMENDA-TIONS TO OTHER PENITENTIARIES.
YOU MAY CALL THE AUTHORITIES ...
...BUT I WON'T BE STOPPED... NOT BY ANYONE!
THOUGH WE MAY BE ENEMIES TOMORROW ...
...I'M HONORED TO HAVE HAD YOU BASTARDS UNDER MY COMMAND.
MORE HONORED THAN YOU'LL EVER KNOW!
THAT'S ALL!!
DIS-MISSED !!
DIS-MISSED...? BUT...
WHAT?!
HOW...
WHO'LL SUPERVISE THE PRISONERS ?!
HUH?
THIS IS RIDICU-LOUS!
WE'LL BE SHORT-STAFFED FOR A WHILE, BUT THAT CAN'T BE HELPED.

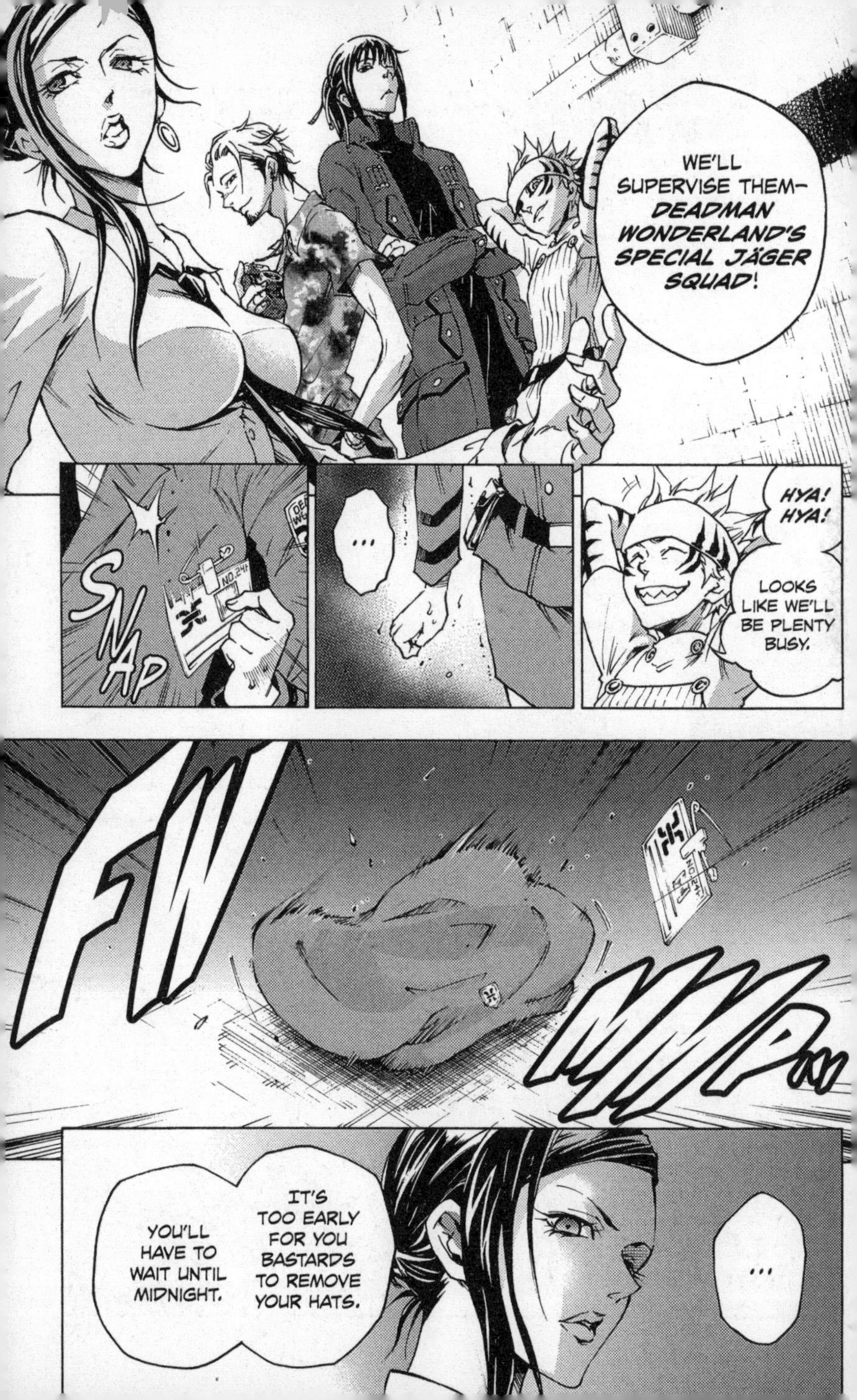
WE'LL SUPERVISE THEM— DEADMAN WONDERLAND'S SPECIAL JÄGER SQUAD!
HYA! HYA!
LOOKS LIKE WE'LL BE PLENTY BUSY.
...
SNAP
FW
MMP!!
...
IT'S TOO EARLY FOR YOU BASTARDS TO REMOVE YOUR HATS.
YOU'LL HAVE TO WAIT UNTIL MIDNIGHT.

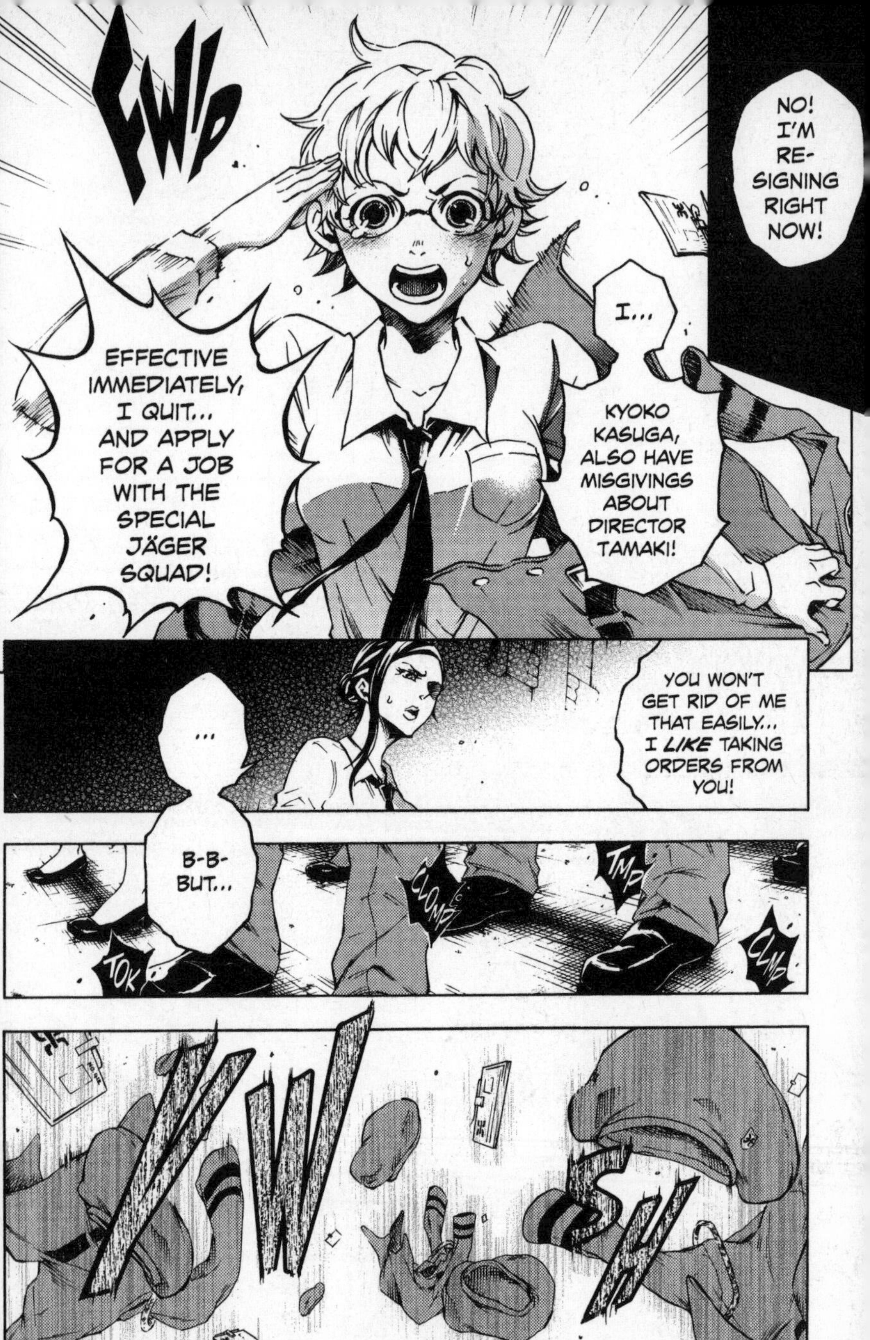
NO! I'M RE-SIGNING RIGHT NOW!
FWIP
I...
KYOKO KASUGA, ALSO HAVE MISGIVINGS ABOUT DIRECTOR TAMAKI!
EFFECTIVE IMMEDIATELY, I QUIT... AND APPLY FOR A JOB WITH THE SPECIAL JÄGER SQUAD!
YOU WON'T GET RID OF ME THAT EASILY... I *LIKE* TAKING ORDERS FROM YOU!
...
TMP
CLOMP
CLMP
B-B-BUT...
TOK

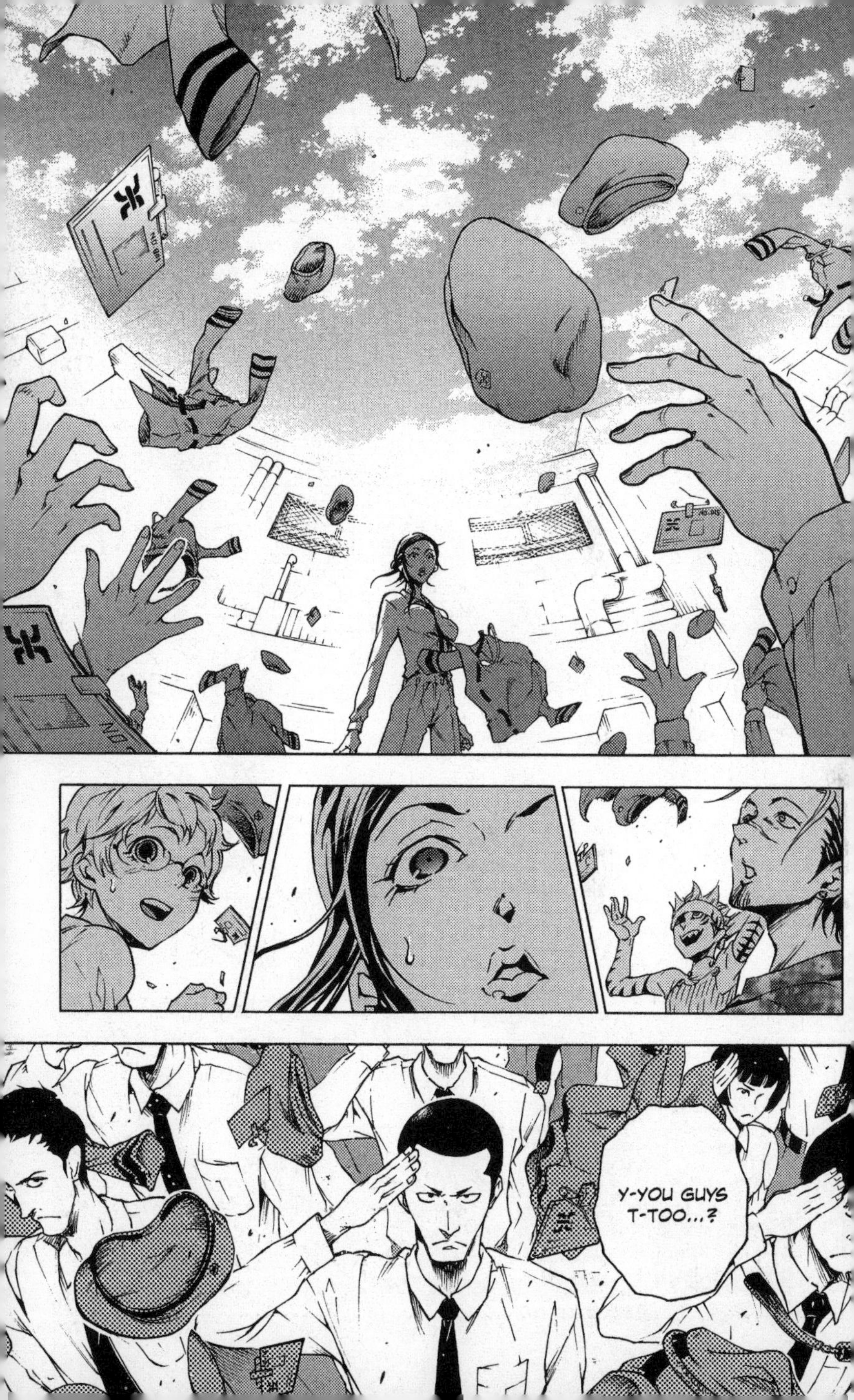
Y-YOU GUYS T-TOO...?

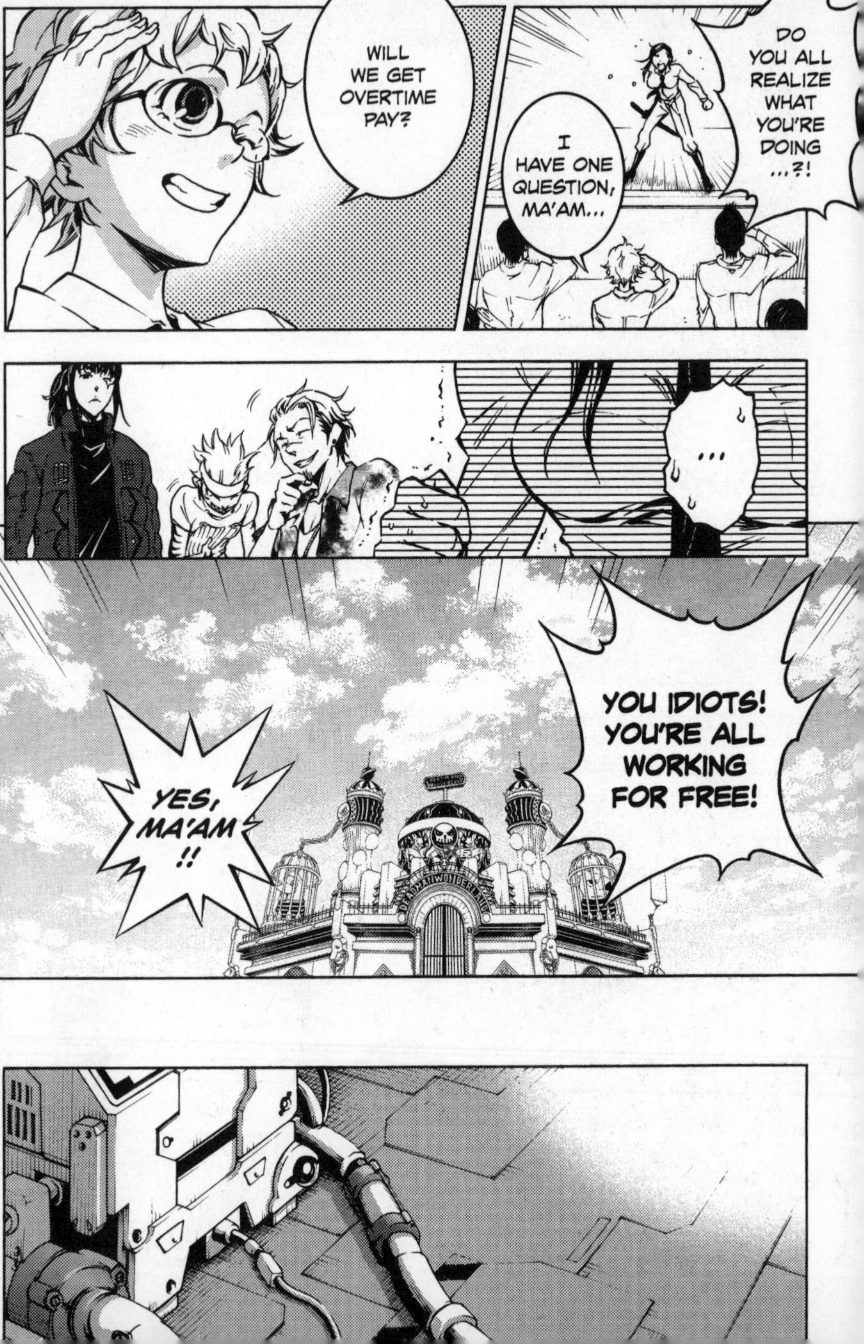
DO YOU ALL REALIZE WHAT YOU'RE DOING ...?!
I HAVE ONE QUESTION, MA'AM...
WILL WE GET OVERTIME PAY?
...
YOU IDIOTS! YOU'RE ALL WORKING FOR FREE!
YES, MA'AM!!

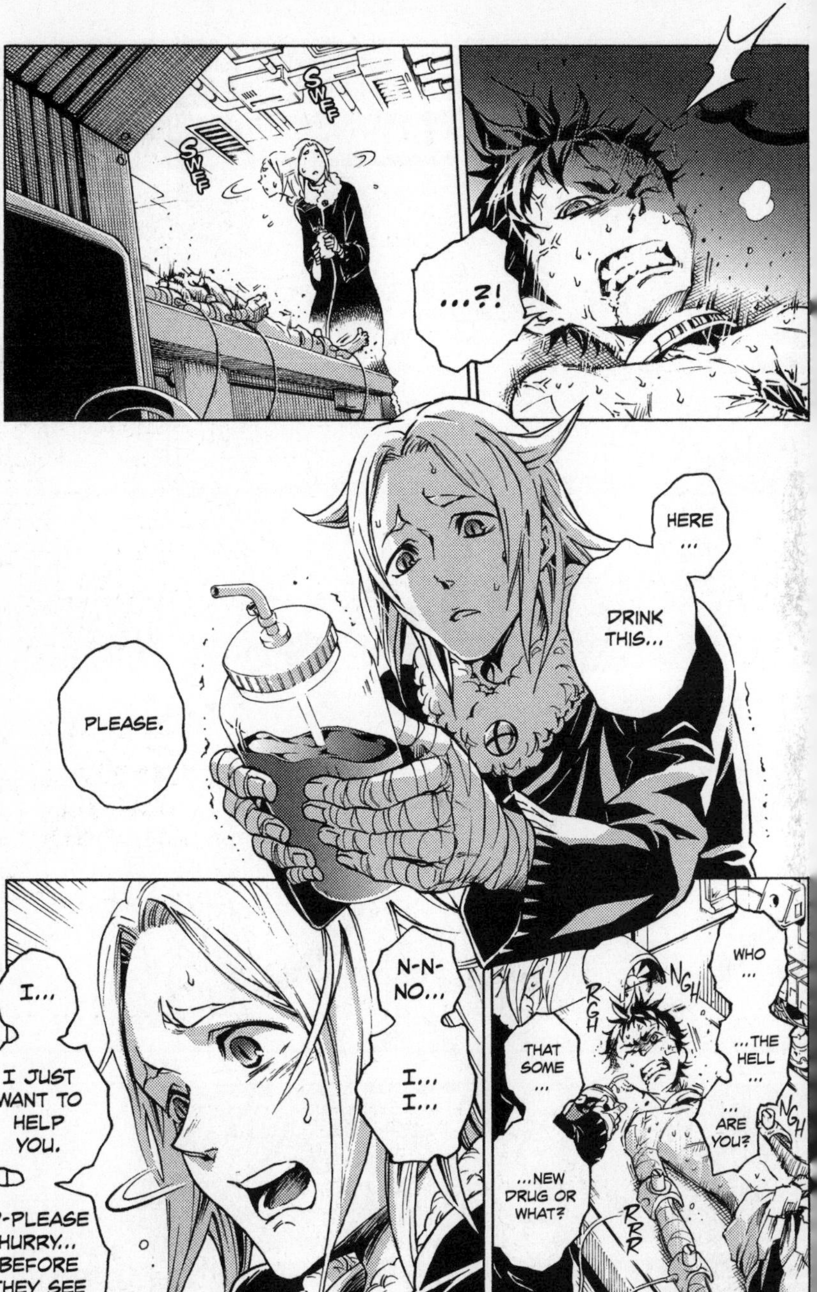
...?!
SWFF
SWFF
HERE...
DRINK THIS...
PLEASE.
WHO...
NGH
...THE HELL...
...ARE YOU?
NGH
RGH
THAT SOME...
...NEW DRUG OR WHAT?
RRR
N-N-NO...
I... I...
I...
I JUST WANT TO HELP YOU.
P-PLEASE HURRY... BEFORE THEY SEE ME...

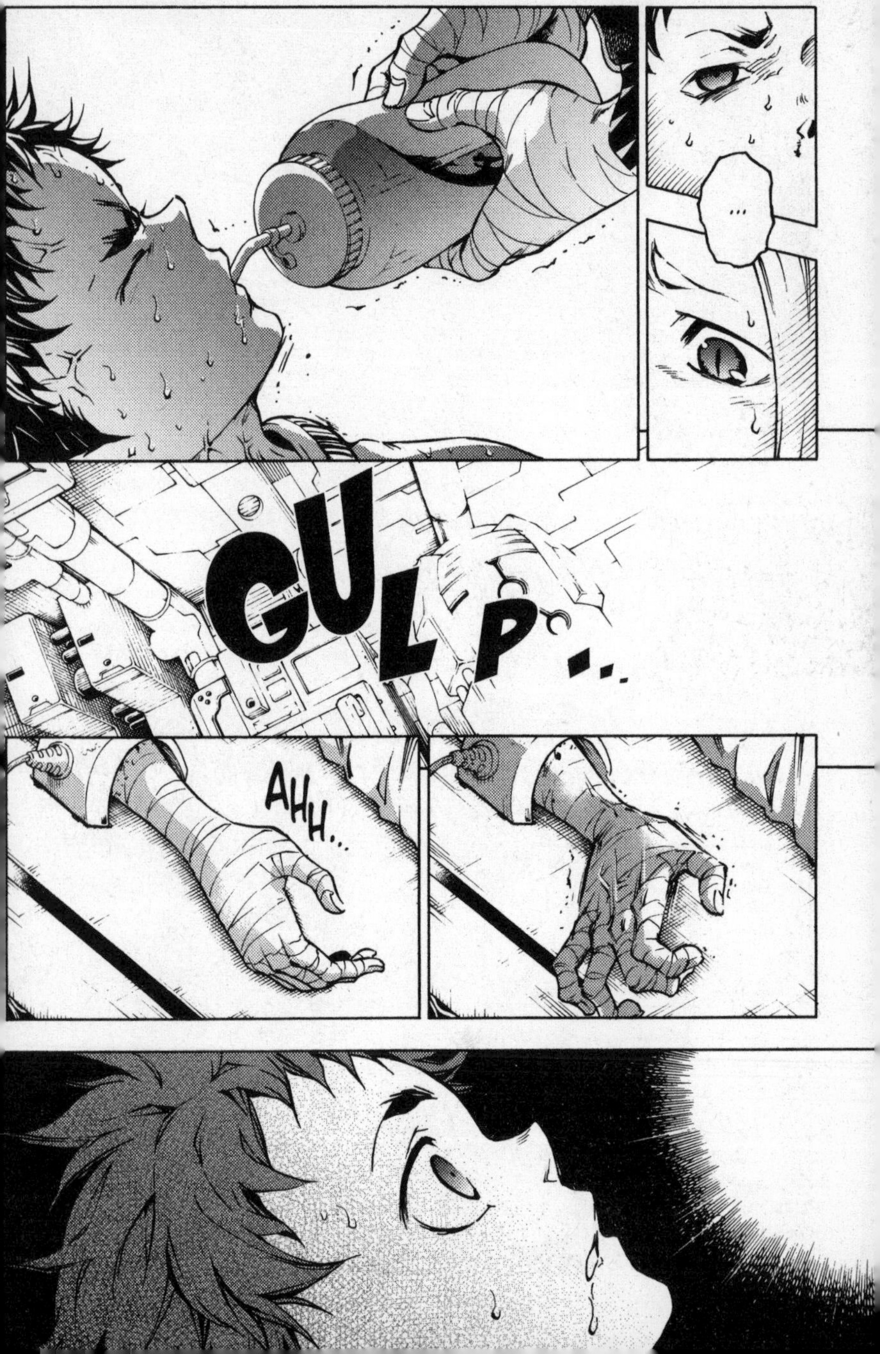
...
GULP...
AHH...

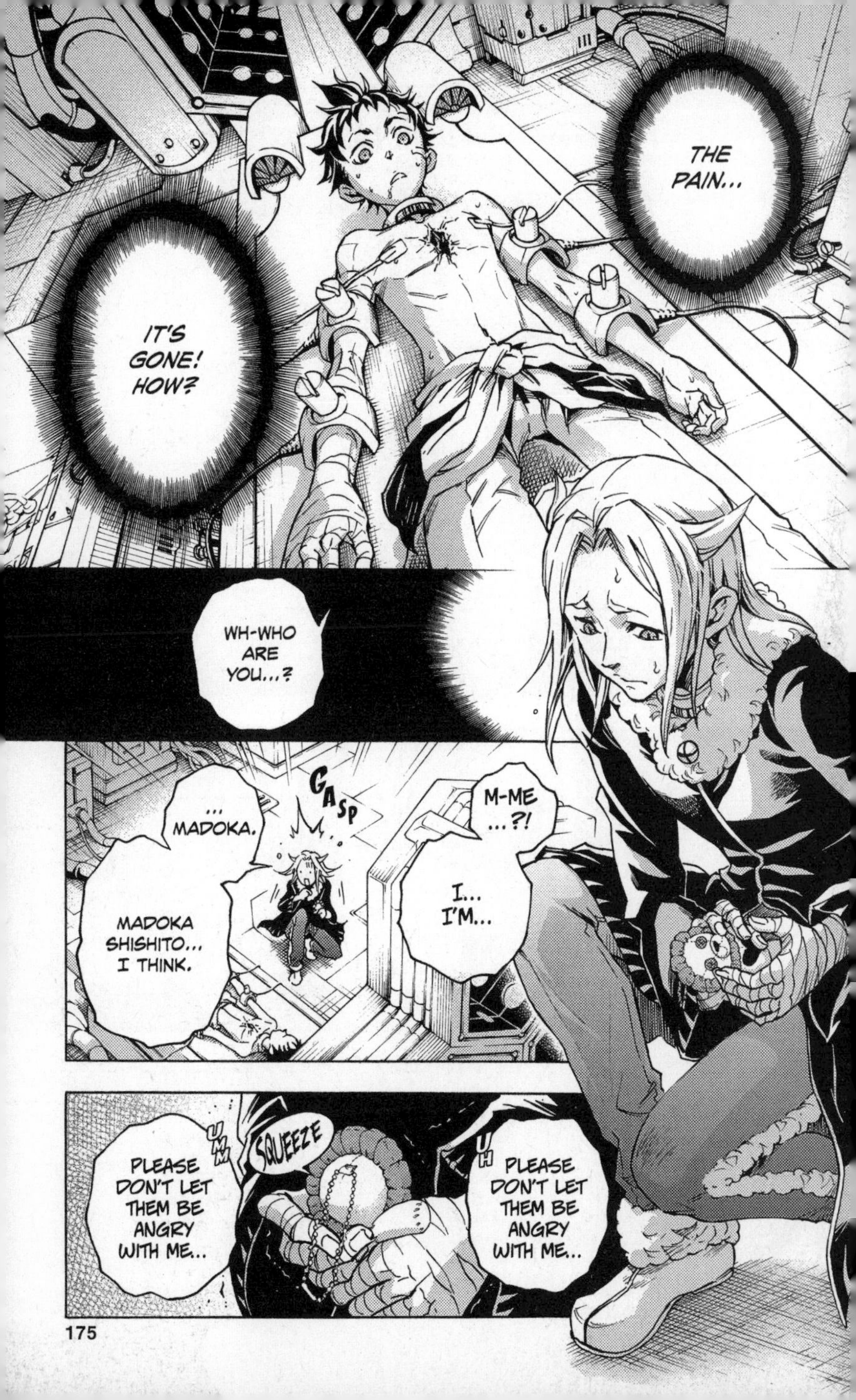
THE PAIN...
IT'S GONE! HOW?
WH-WHO ARE YOU...?
M-ME ...?!
I... I'M...
GASP
... MADOKA.
MADOKA SHISHITO... I THINK.
UH
PLEASE DON'T LET THEM BE ANGRY WITH ME...
SQUEEZE
UMM
PLEASE DON'T LET THEM BE ANGRY WITH ME...

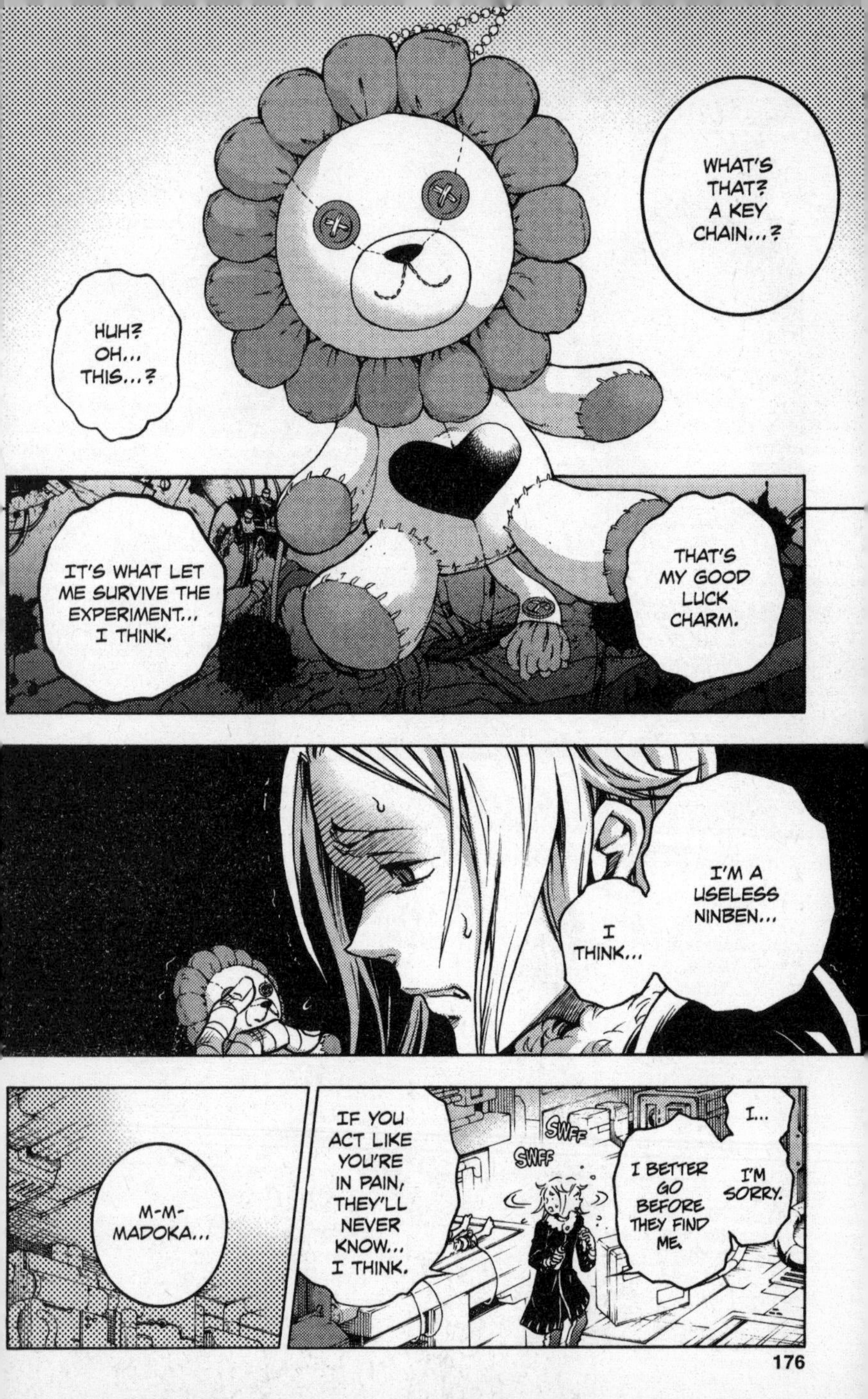
WHAT'S THAT? A KEY CHAIN...?
HUH? OH... THIS...?
THAT'S MY GOOD LUCK CHARM.
IT'S WHAT LET ME SURVIVE THE EXPERIMENT... I THINK.
I'M A USELESS NINBEN...
I THINK...
I...
I'M SORRY.
I BETTER GO BEFORE THEY FIND ME.
SWFF
SWFF
IF YOU ACT LIKE YOU'RE IN PAIN, THEY'LL NEVER KNOW... I THINK.
M-M-MADOKA...

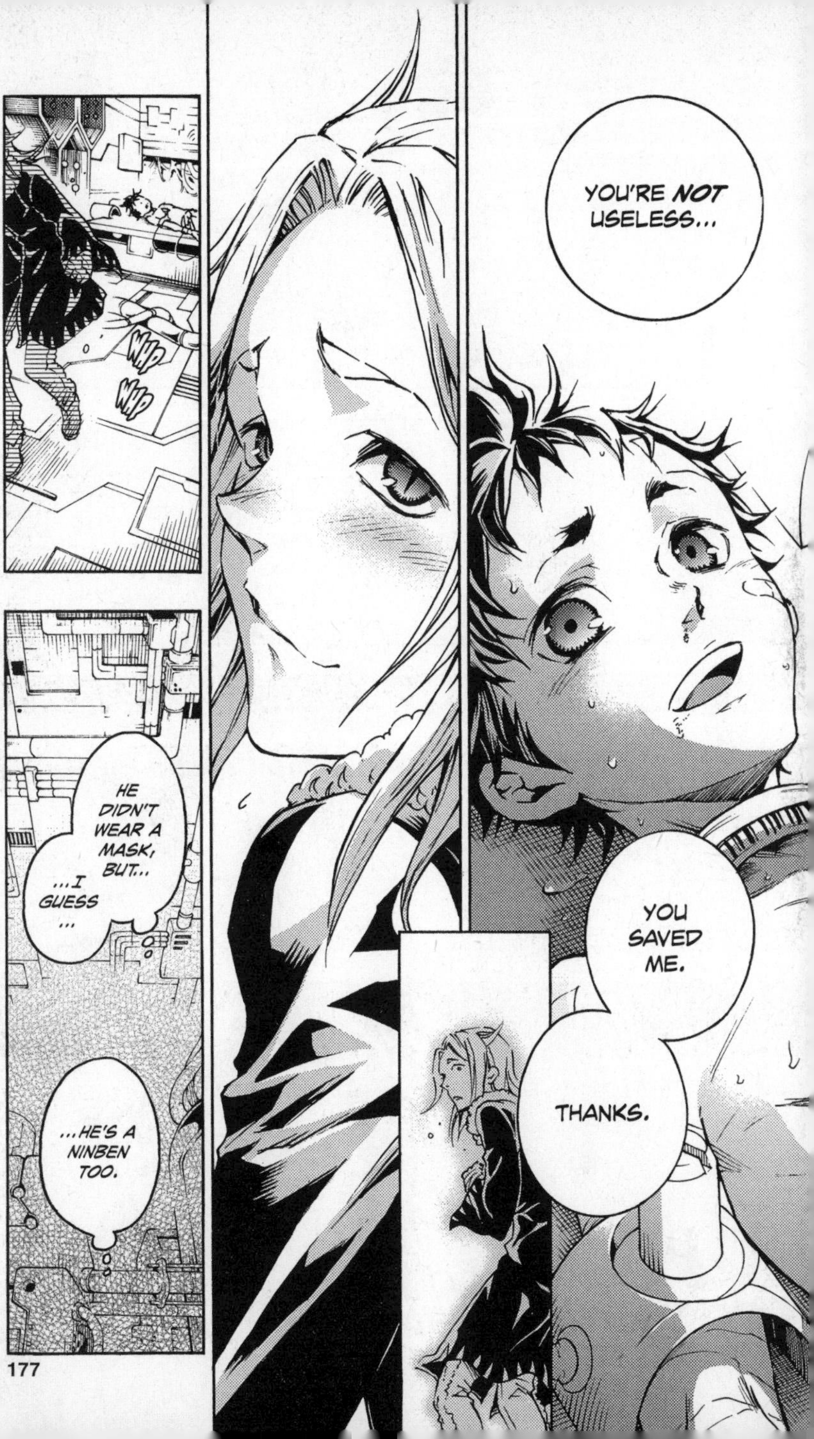
YOU'RE *NOT* USELESS...
YOU SAVED ME.
THANKS.
WHP
WHP
HE DIDN'T WEAR A MASK, BUT...
...I GUESS...
...HE'S A NINBEN TOO.

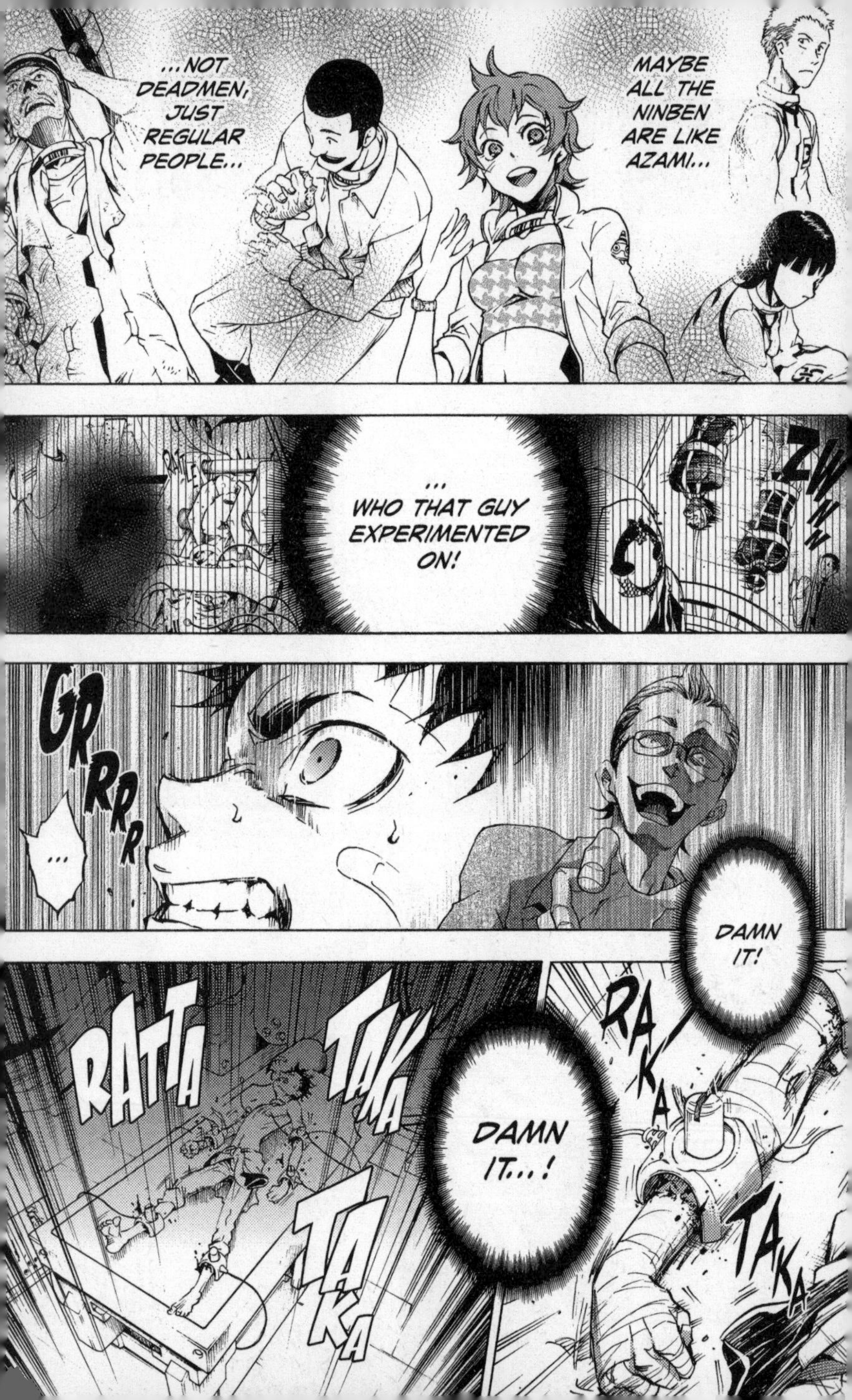

MAYBE ALL THE NINBEN ARE LIKE AZAMI...
...NOT DEADMEN, JUST REGULAR PEOPLE...
ZWN
... WHO THAT GUY EXPERIMENTED ON!
RATTLE
GRRRR
...
DAMN IT!
RAKAKA
TAKA
DAMN IT...!
TAKA
TAKA
RATTA

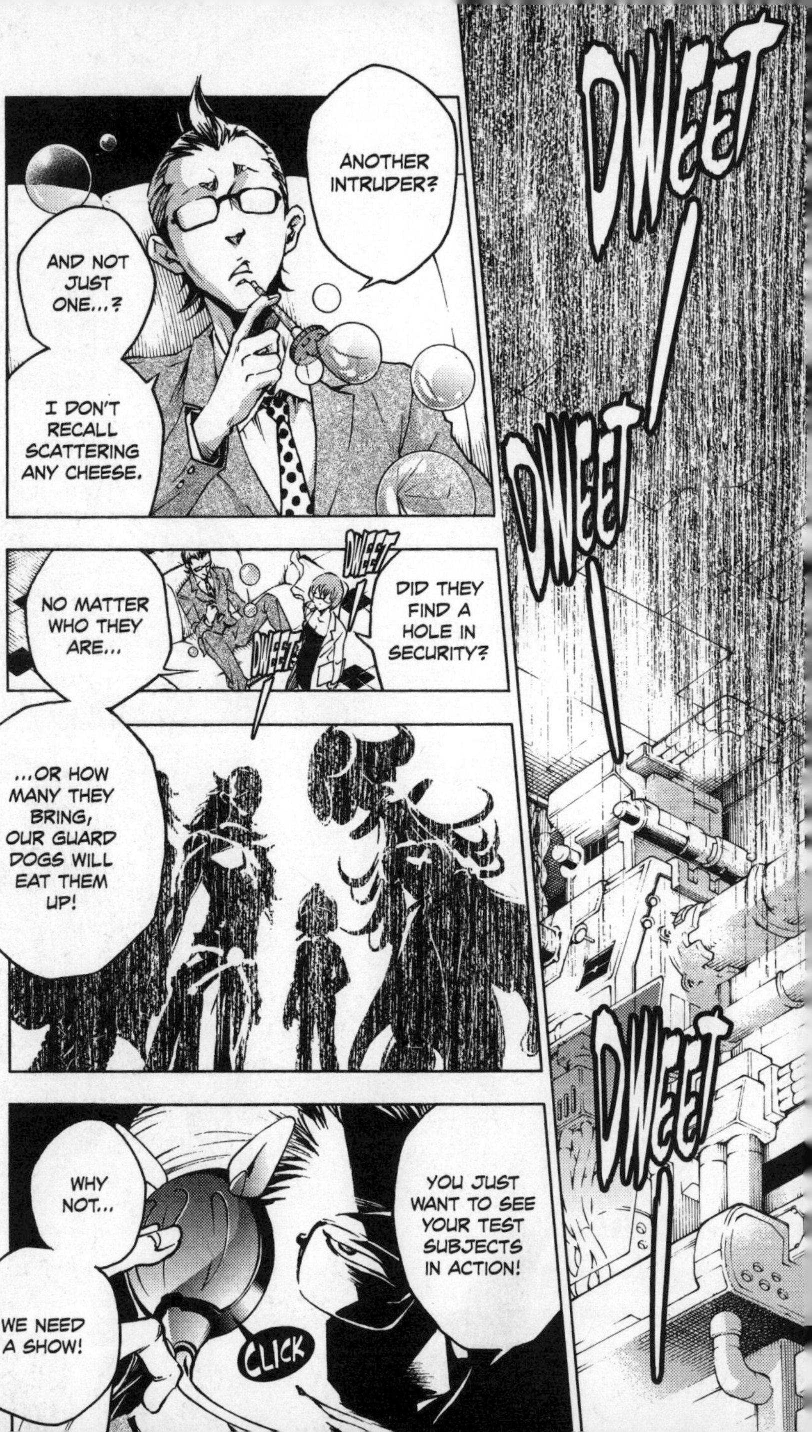
DWEET!
DWEET!
DWEET!
ANOTHER INTRUDER?
AND NOT JUST ONE...?
I DON'T RECALL SCATTERING ANY CHEESE.
DWEET!
DID THEY FIND A HOLE IN SECURITY?
DWEET!
NO MATTER WHO THEY ARE...
...OR HOW MANY THEY BRING, OUR GUARD DOGS WILL EAT THEM UP!
YOU JUST WANT TO SEE YOUR TEST SUBJECTS IN ACTION!
WHY NOT...
WE NEED A SHOW!
CLICK

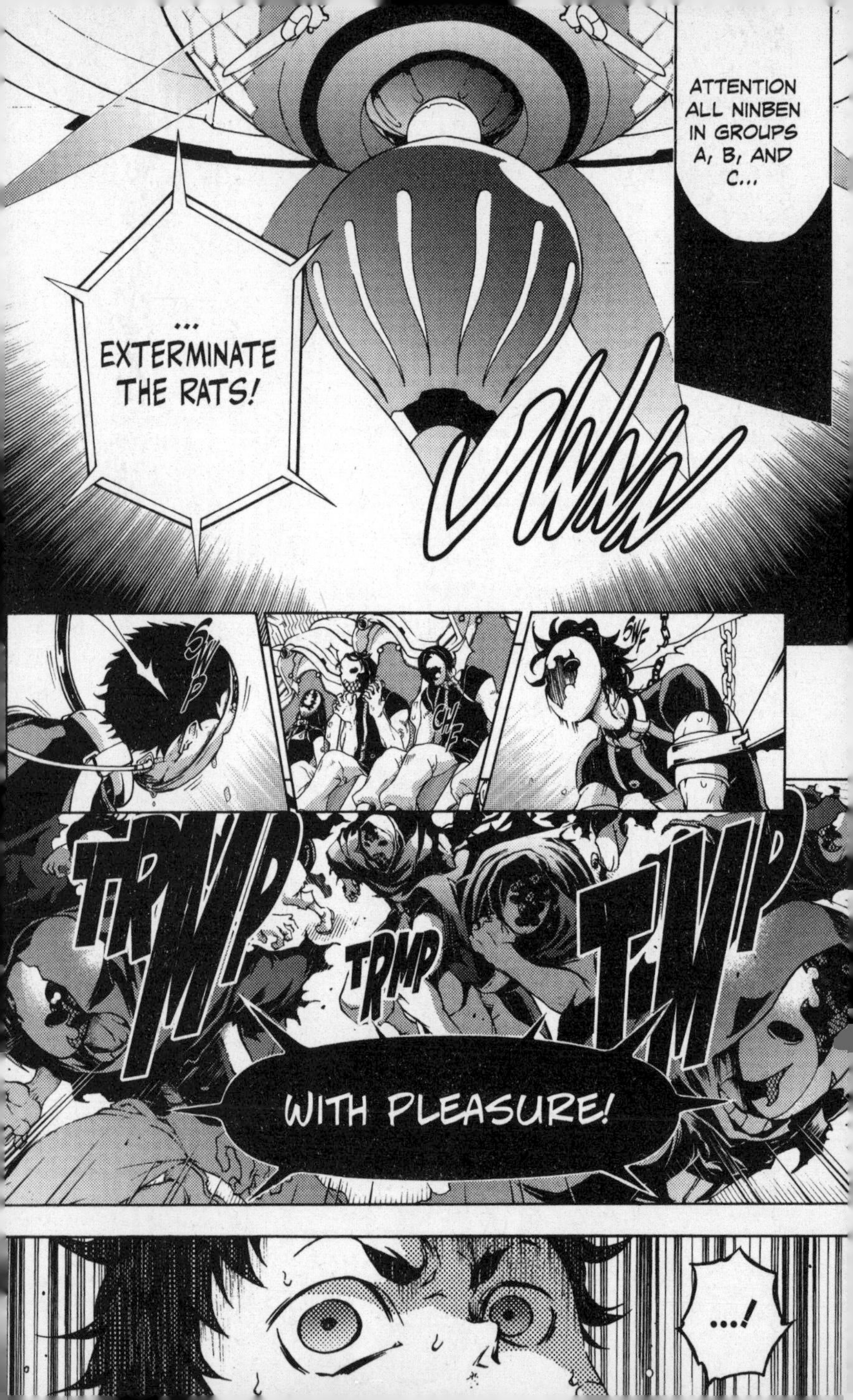
ATTENTION ALL NINBEN IN GROUPS A, B, AND C...
...EXTERMINATE THE RATS!
SWF
CHF
SWP
TMP
TRMP
TRMP
WITH PLEASURE!
...!

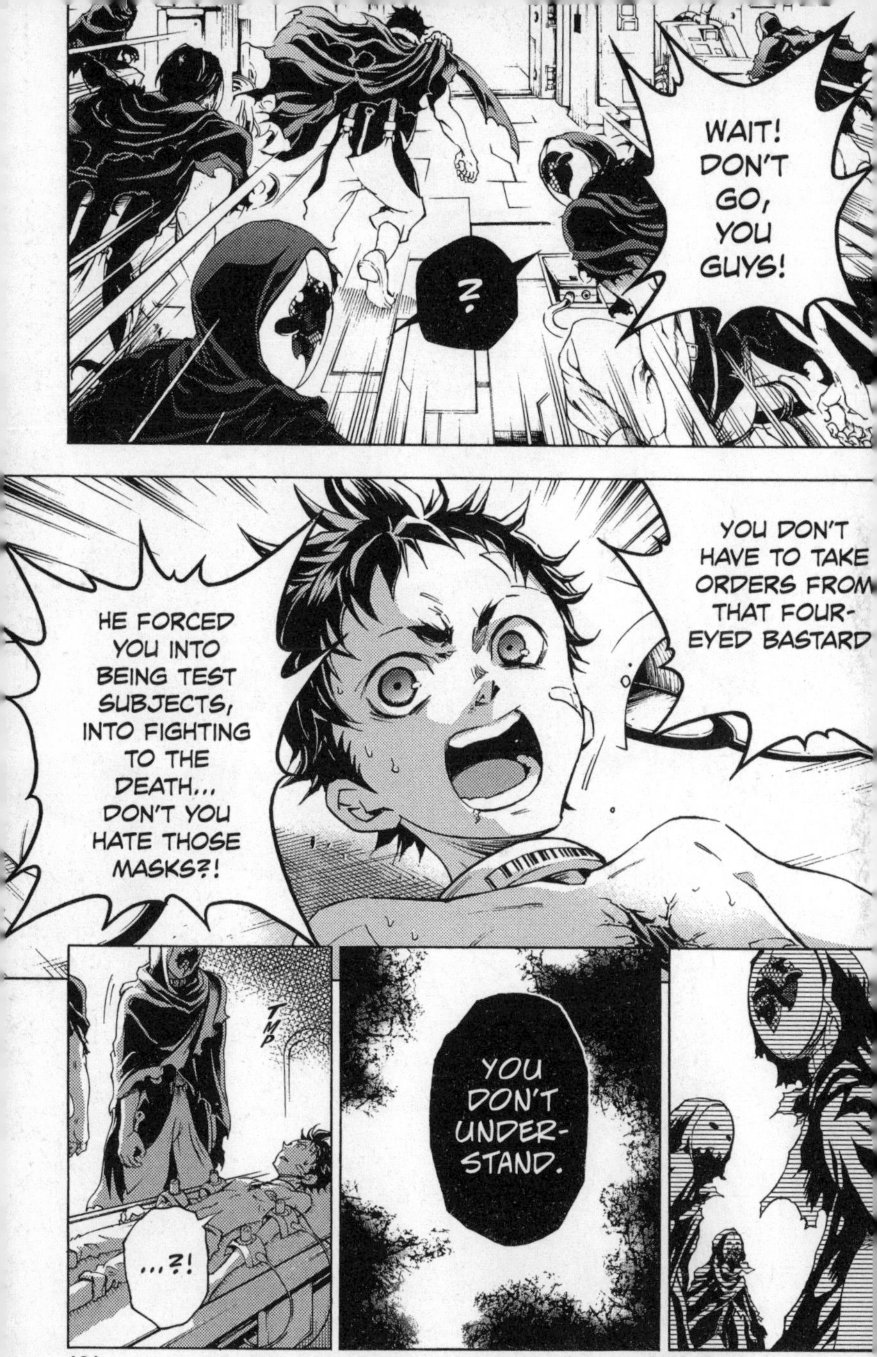
WAIT! DON'T GO, YOU GUYS!
?
YOU DON'T HAVE TO TAKE ORDERS FROM THAT FOUR-EYED BASTARD
HE FORCED YOU INTO BEING TEST SUBJECTS, INTO FIGHTING TO THE DEATH... DON'T YOU HATE THOSE MASKS?!
YOU DON'T UNDER-STAND.
TMP
...?!

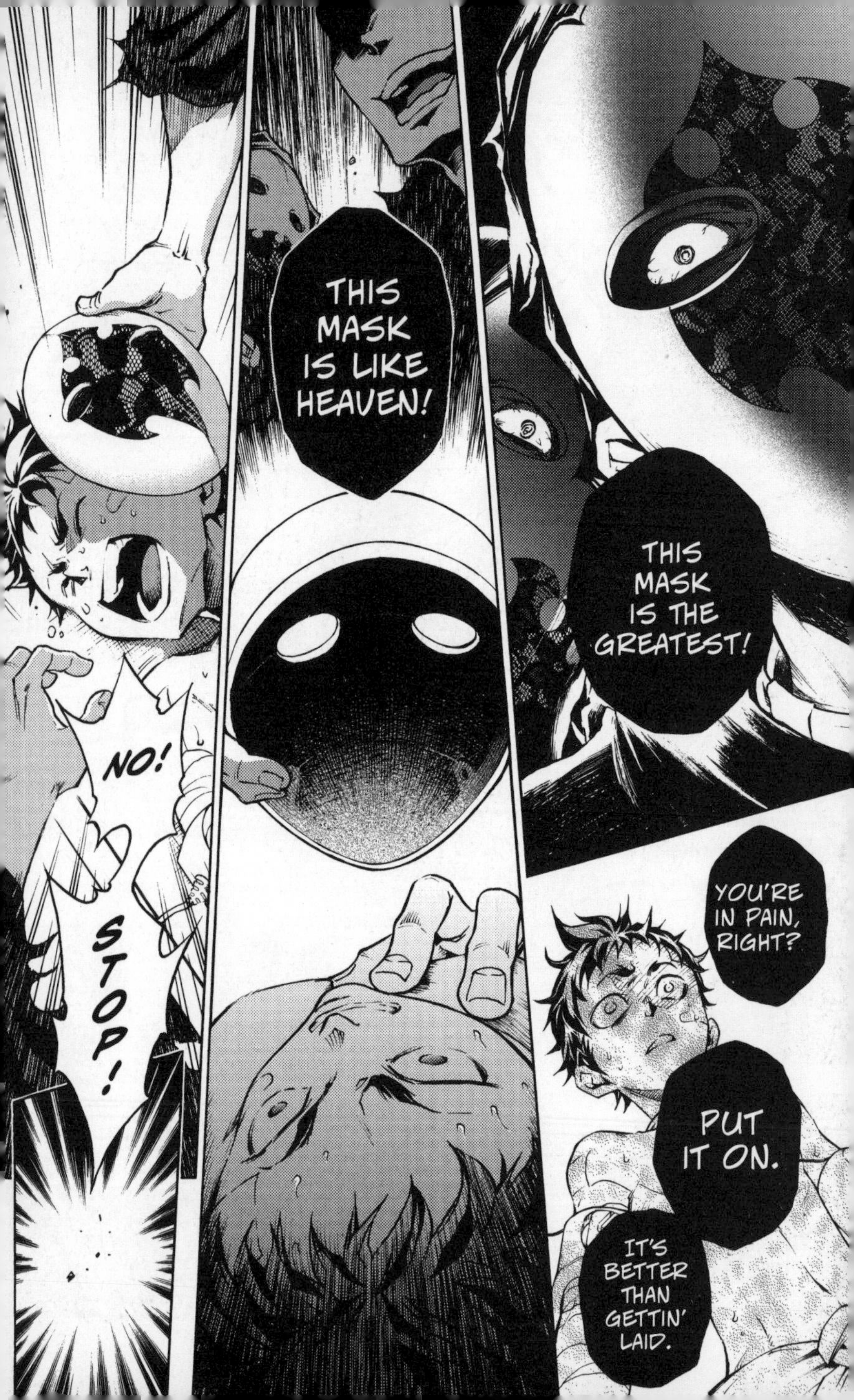
THIS MASK IS THE GREATEST!
YOU'RE IN PAIN, RIGHT?
PUT IT ON.
IT'S BETTER THAN GETTIN' LAID.
THIS MASK IS LIKE HEAVEN!
NO!
STOP!

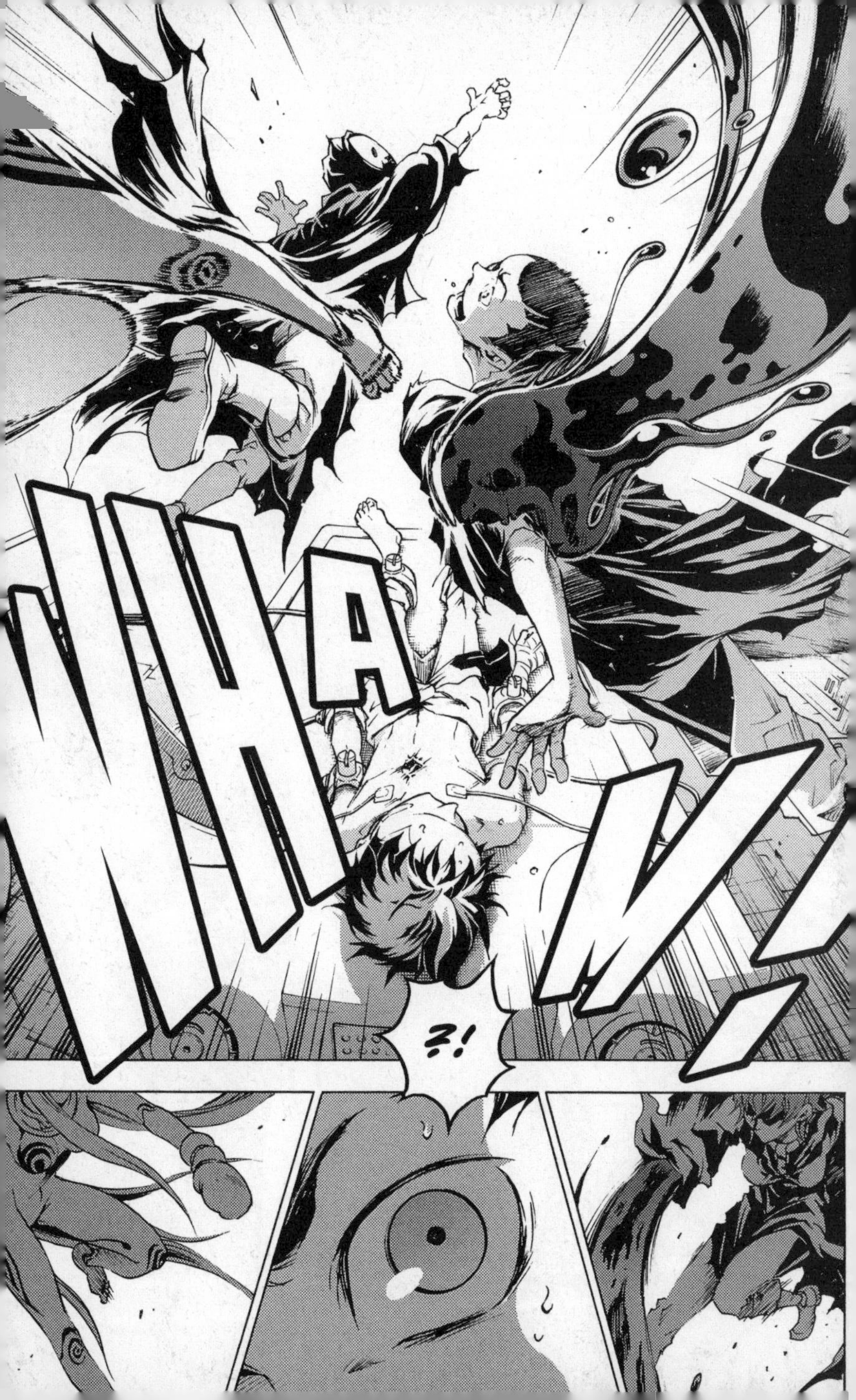
WHAM!
?!

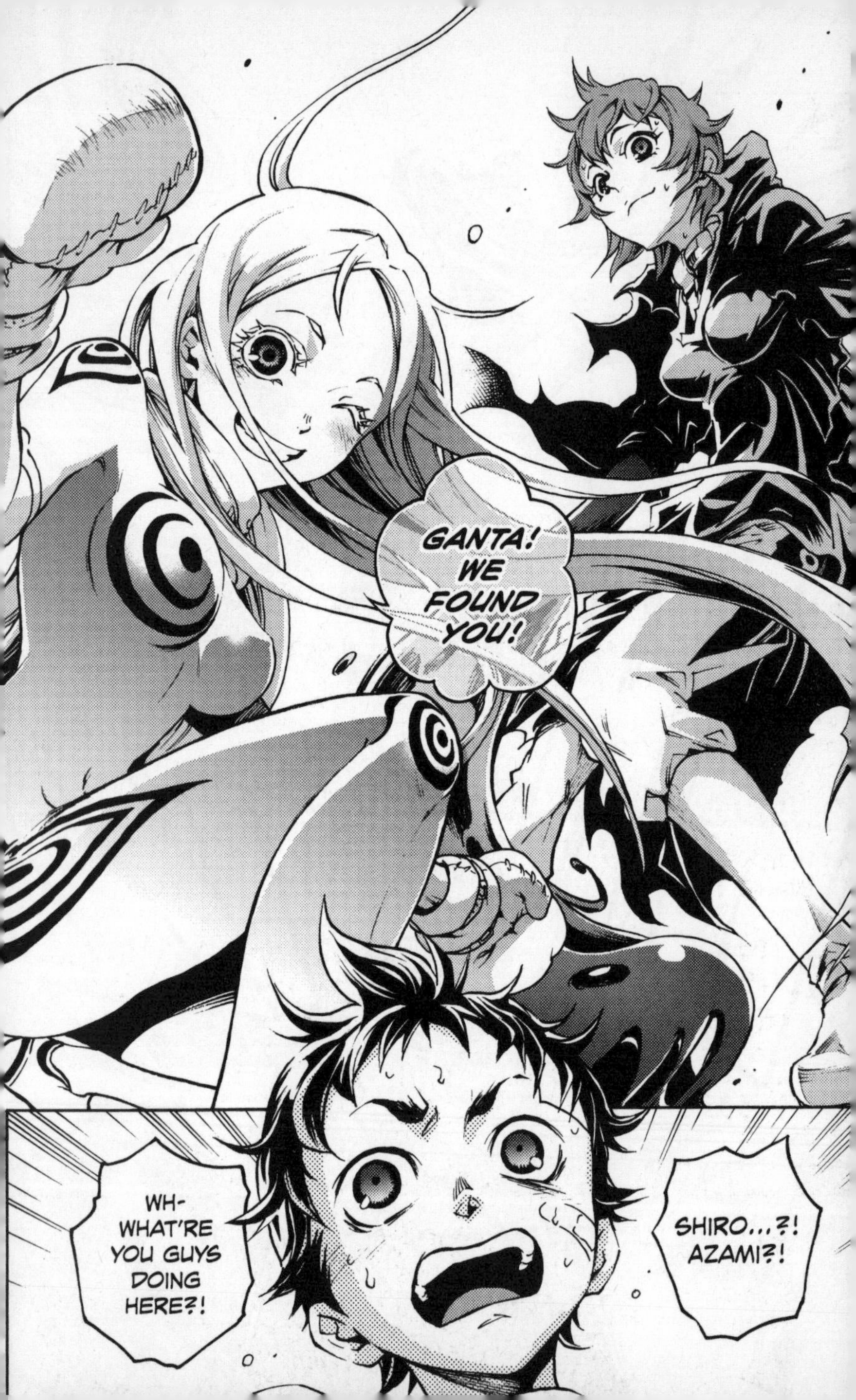
GANTA! WE FOUND YOU!
SHIRO...?! AZAMI?!
WH- WHAT'RE YOU GUYS DOING HERE?!

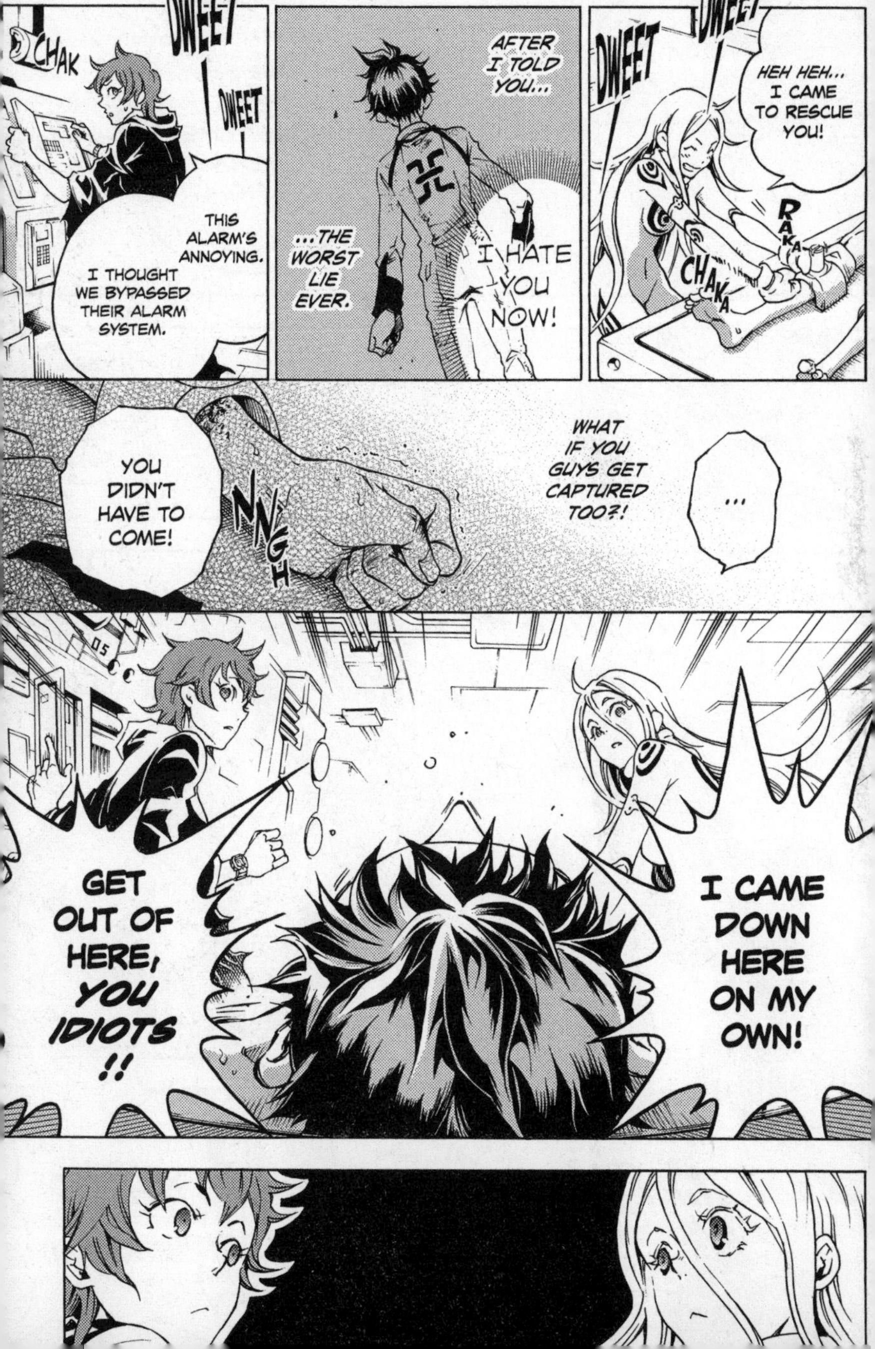
DWEET
DWEET
HEH HEH... I CAME TO RESCUE YOU!
RAKA
CHAKA
AFTER I TOLD YOU...
I HATE YOU NOW!
...THE WORST LIE EVER.
DWEET
CHAK
DWEET
THIS ALARM'S ANNOYING.
I THOUGHT WE BYPASSED THEIR ALARM SYSTEM.
...
WHAT IF YOU GUYS GET CAPTURED TOO?!
NNGH
YOU DIDN'T HAVE TO COME!
I CAME DOWN HERE ON MY OWN!
GET OUT OF HERE, YOU IDIOTS!!

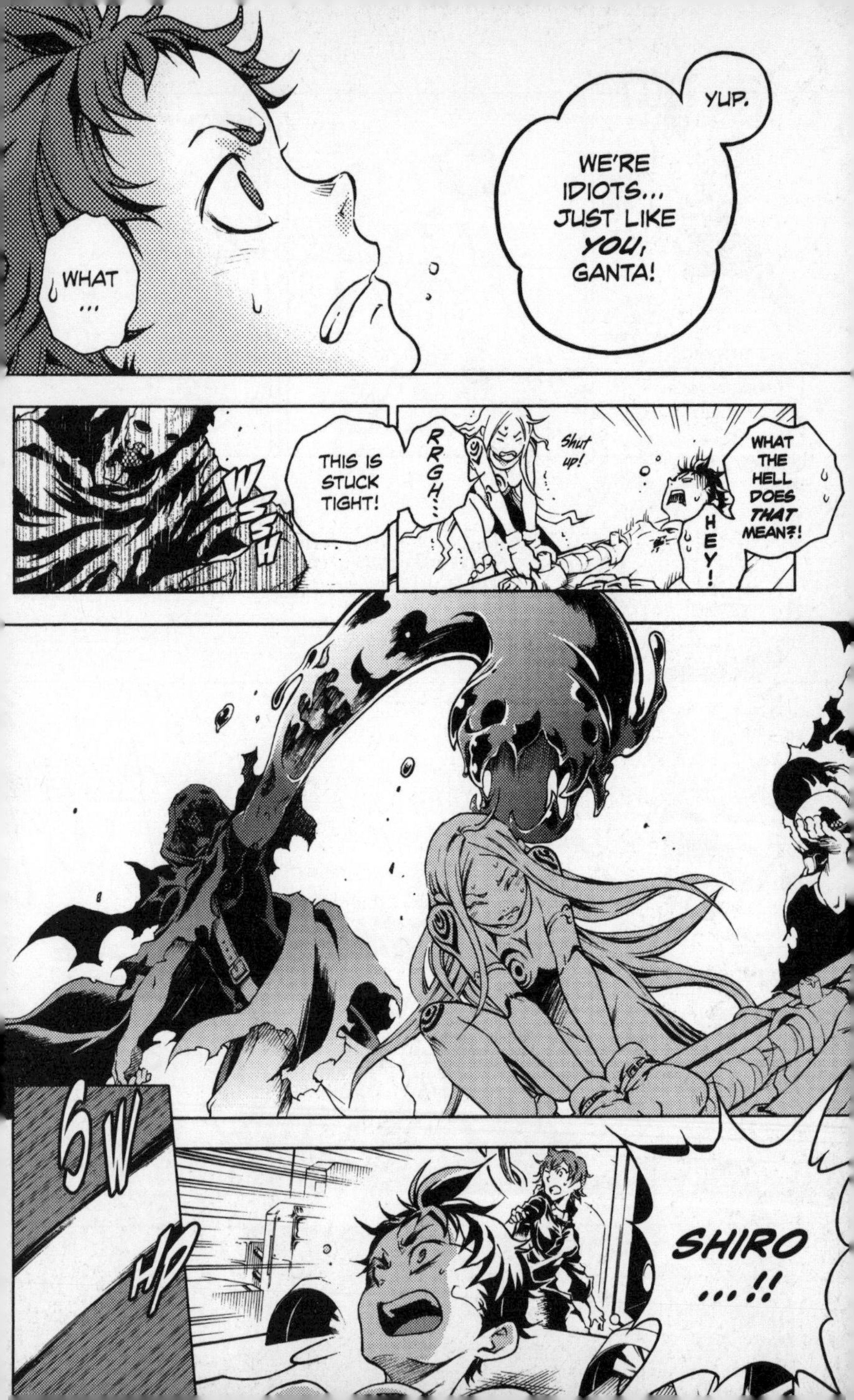
YUP.
WE'RE IDIOTS... JUST LIKE YOU, GANTA!
WHAT ...
WHAT THE HELL DOES THAT MEAN?!
HEY!
Shut up!
RRGH...
THIS IS STUCK TIGHT!
WSSH
SHIRO ...!!
SWHP

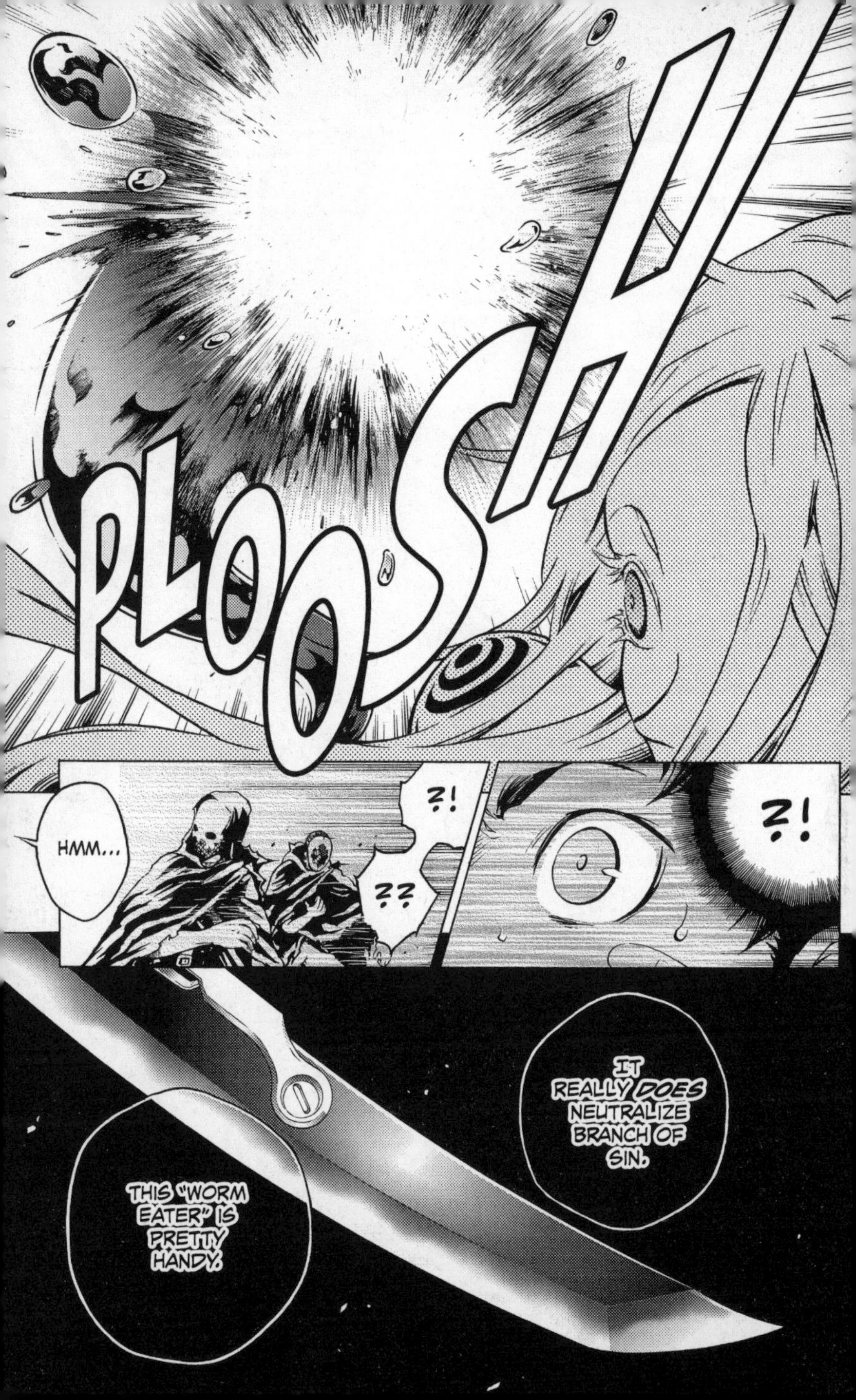
PLOOSH
?!
?!
??
HMM...
IT REALLY DOES NEUTRALIZE BRANCH OF SIN.
THIS "WORM EATER" IS PRETTY HANDY.

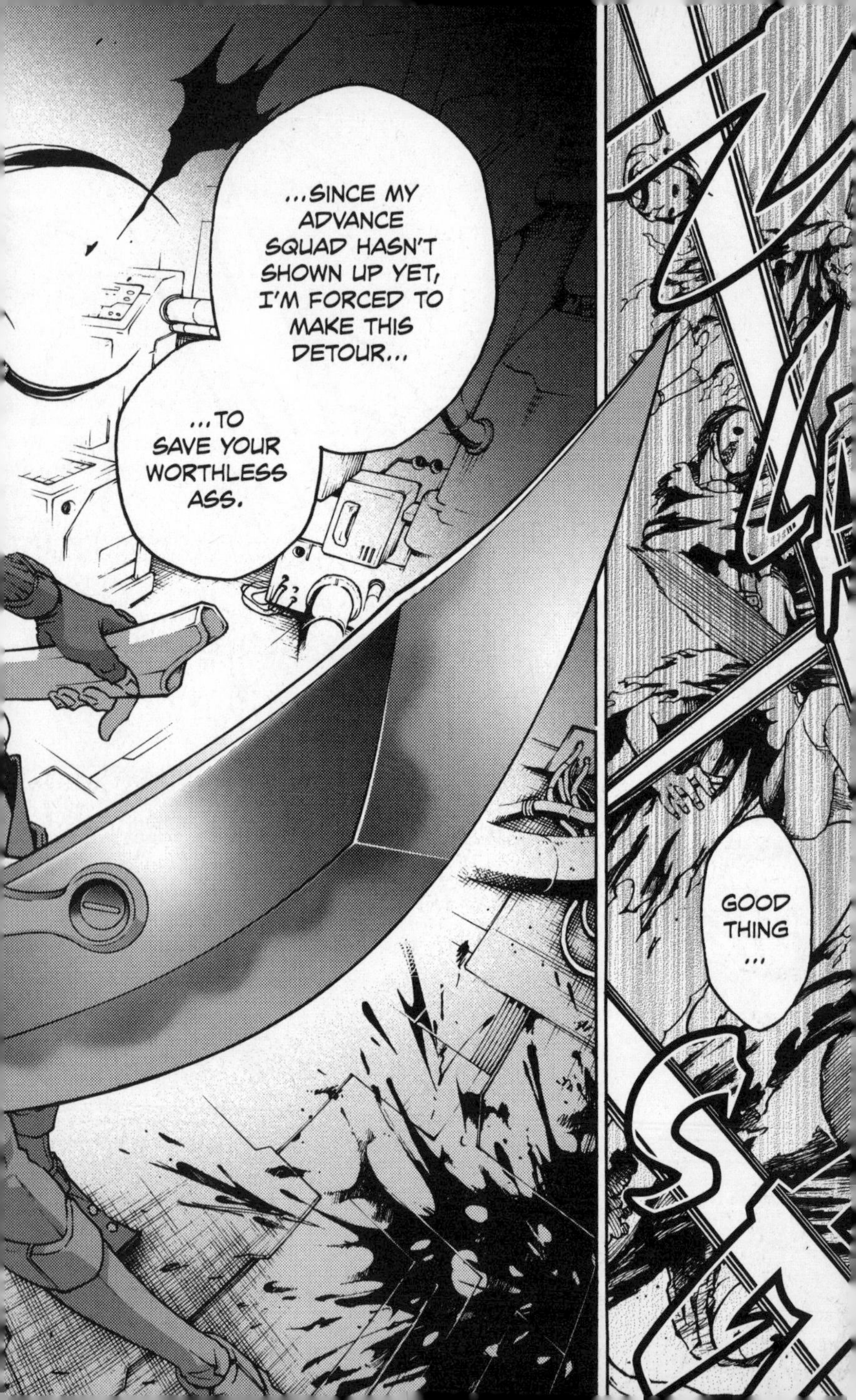
GOOD THING ...
...SINCE MY ADVANCE SQUAD HASN'T SHOWN UP YET, I'M FORCED TO MAKE THIS DETOUR...
...TO SAVE YOUR WORTHLESS ASS.

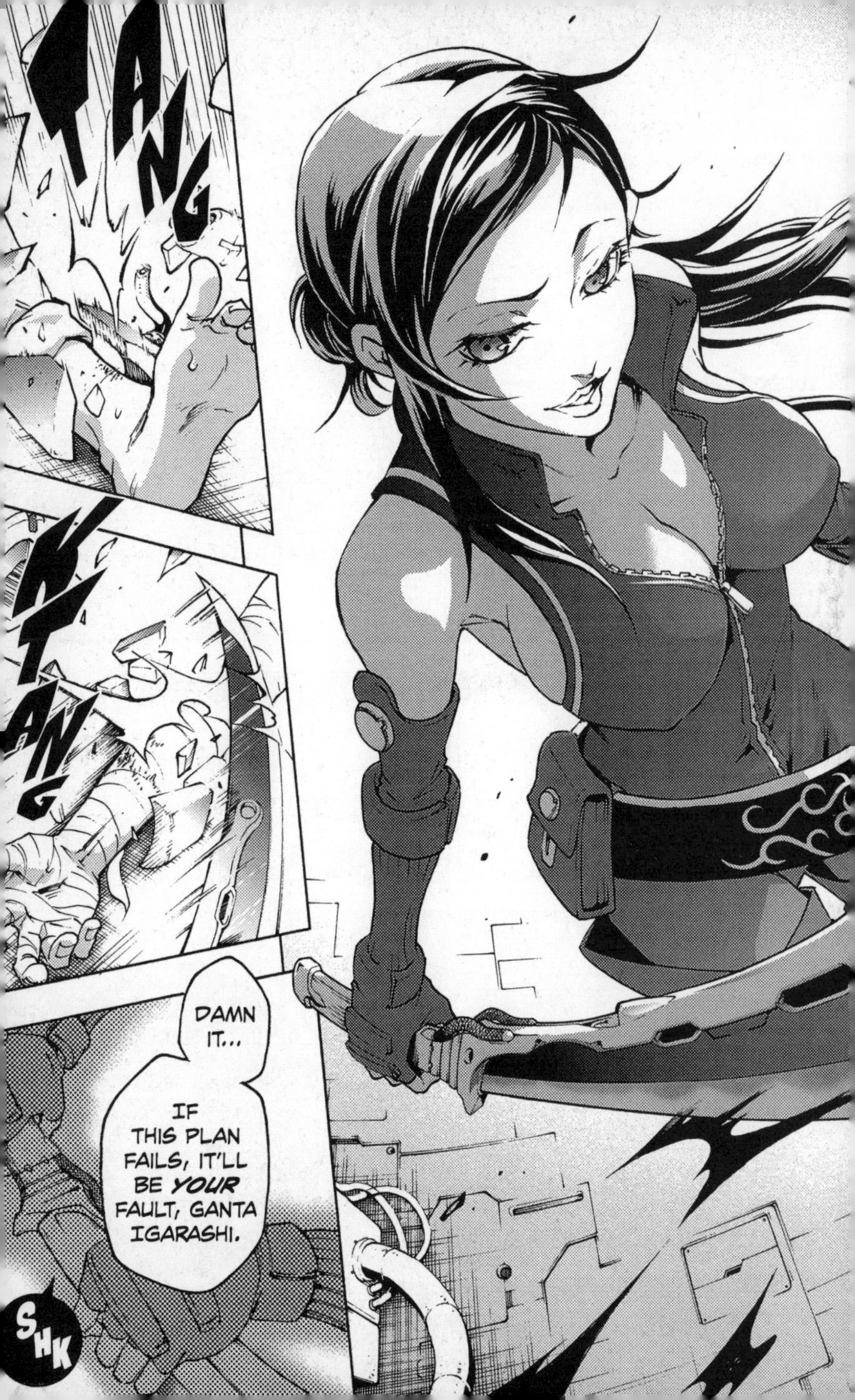
TANG
KATANG
DAMN IT...
IF THIS PLAN FAILS, IT'LL BE *YOUR* FAULT, GANTA IGARASHI.
SHK

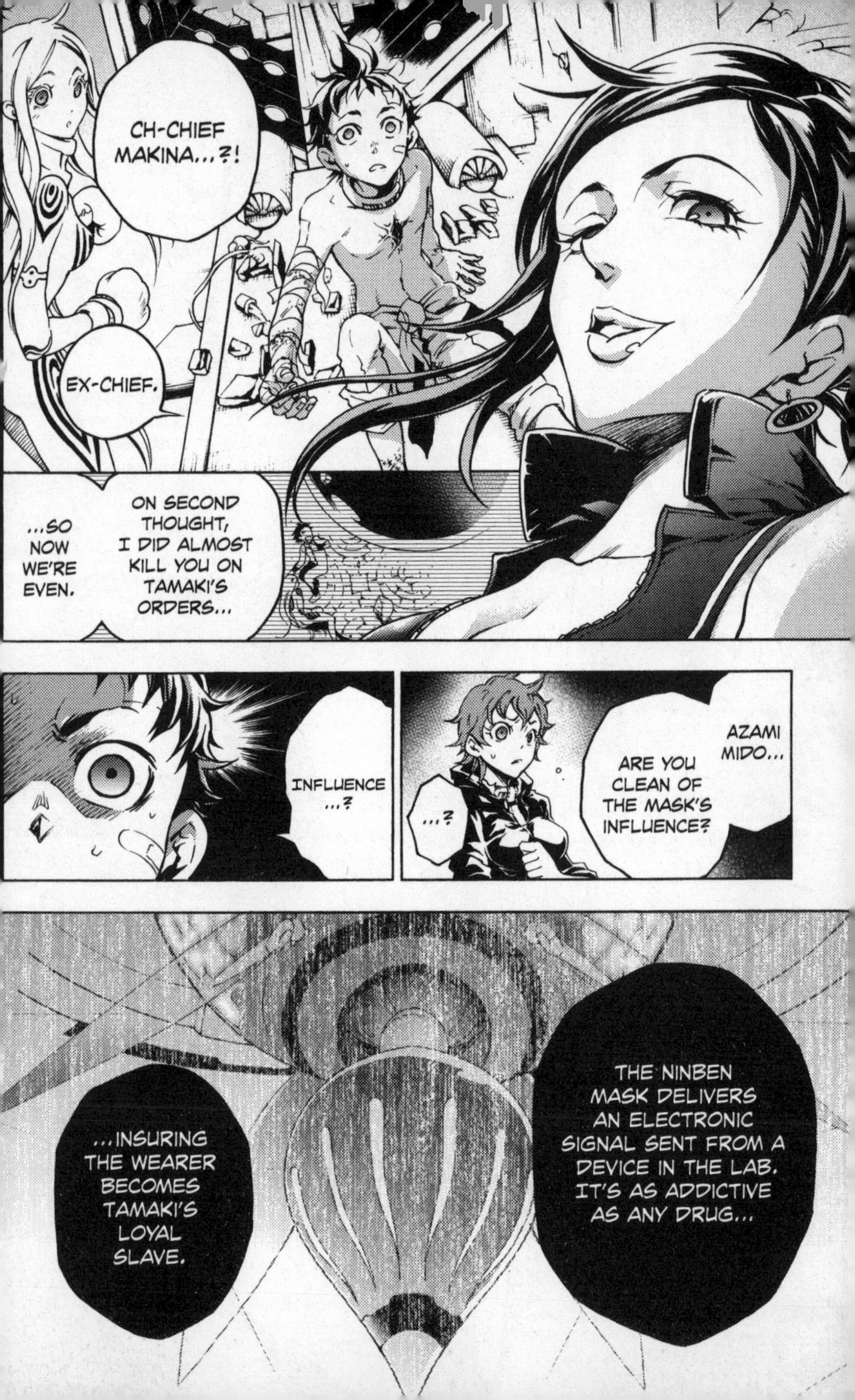
CH-CHIEF MAKINA...?!
EX-CHIEF.
ON SECOND THOUGHT, I DID ALMOST KILL YOU ON TAMAKI'S ORDERS...
...SO NOW WE'RE EVEN.
AZAMI MIDO...
ARE YOU CLEAN OF THE MASK'S INFLUENCE?
...?
INFLUENCE...?
THE NINBEN MASK DELIVERS AN ELECTRONIC SIGNAL SENT FROM A DEVICE IN THE LAB. IT'S AS ADDICTIVE AS ANY DRUG...
...INSURING THE WEARER BECOMES TAMAKI'S LOYAL SLAVE.

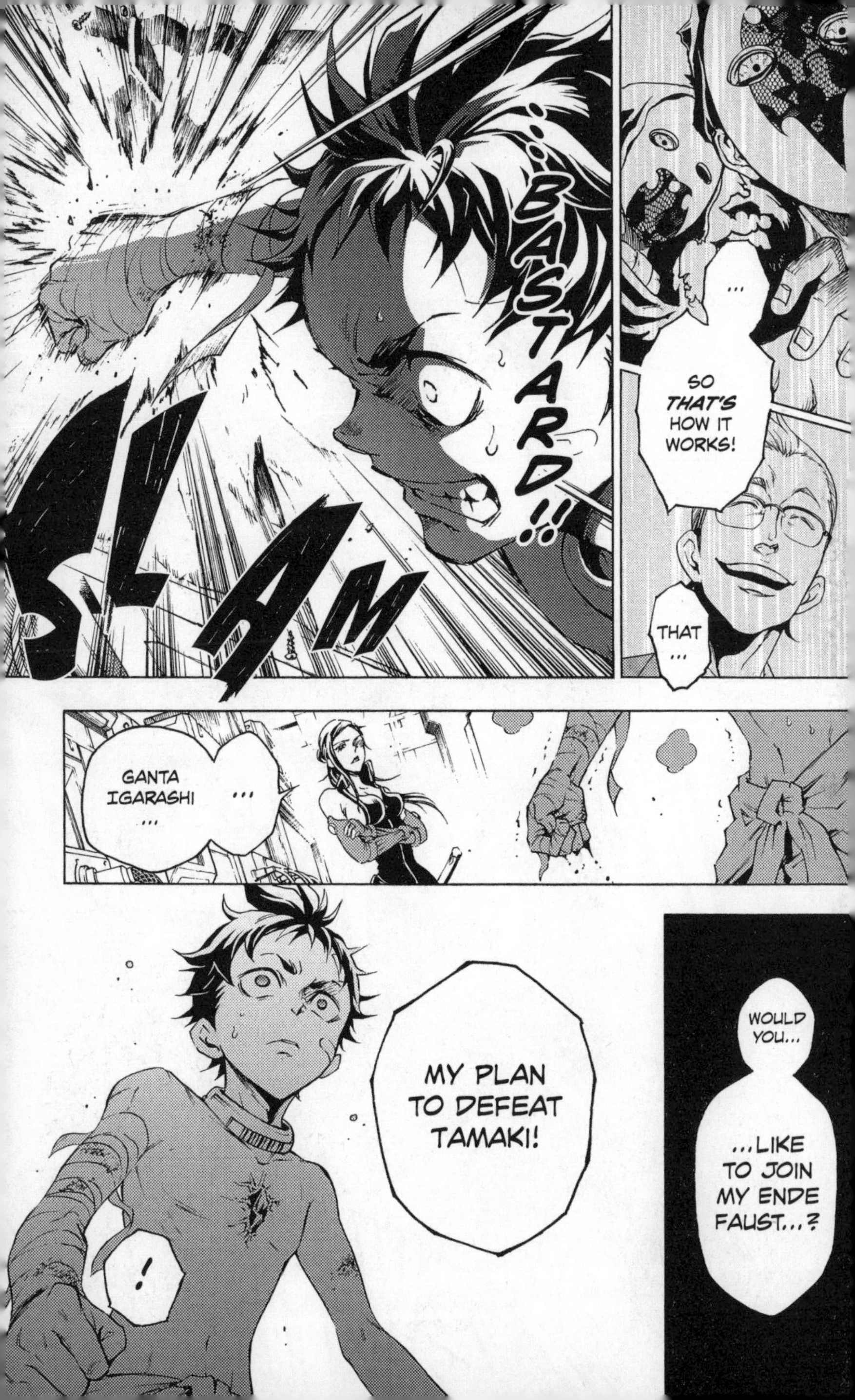
...
SO THAT'S HOW IT WORKS!
THAT...
...BASTARD!!
SLAM
GANTA IGARASHI ... ...
WOULD YOU...
...LIKE TO JOIN MY ENDE FAUST...?
MY PLAN TO DEFEAT TAMAKI!
!

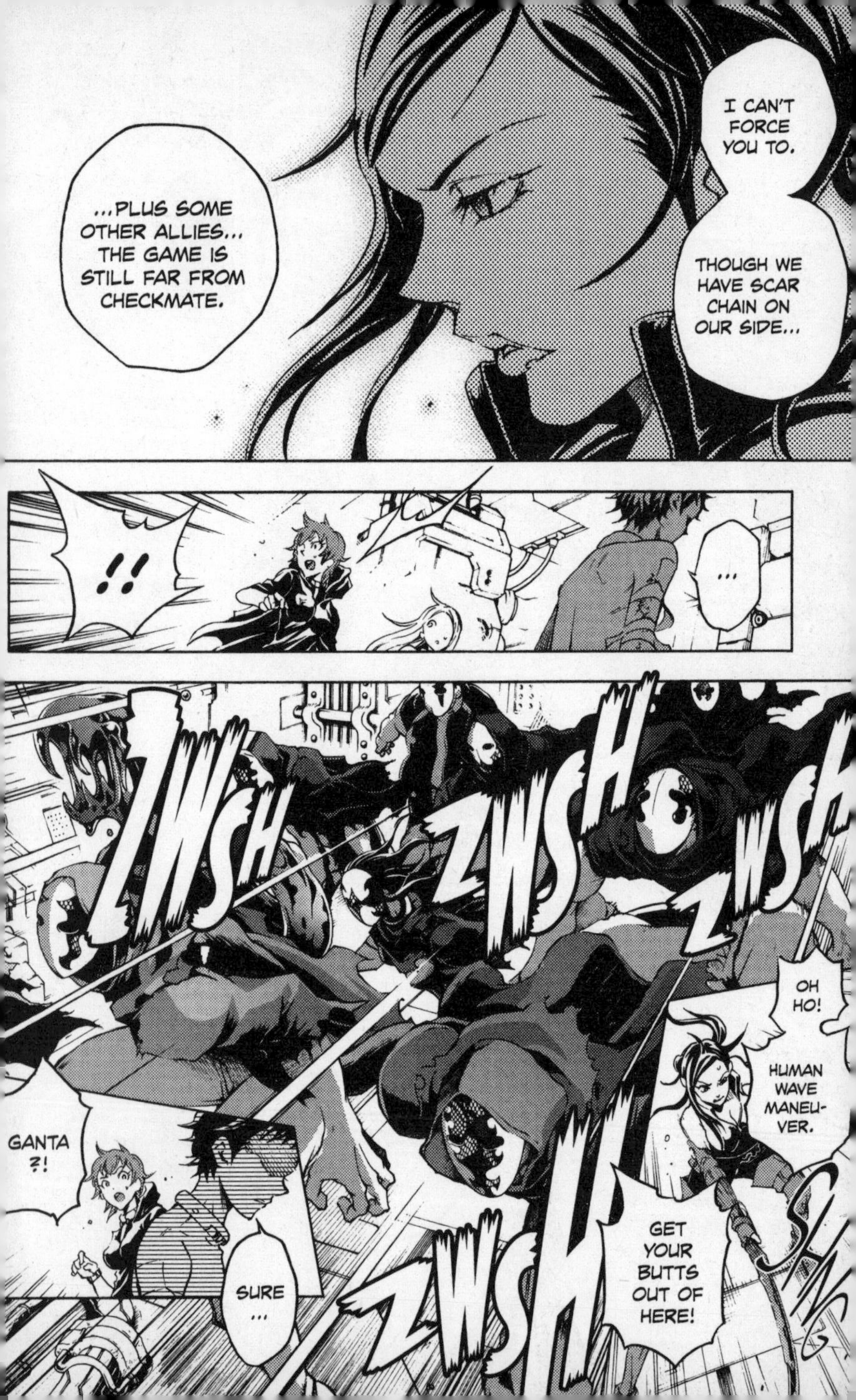
I CAN'T FORCE YOU TO.
THOUGH WE HAVE SCAR CHAIN ON OUR SIDE...
...PLUS SOME OTHER ALLIES... THE GAME IS STILL FAR FROM CHECKMATE.
...
!!
ZWSH
ZWSH
ZWSH
ZWSH
OH HO!
HUMAN WAVE MANEU-VER.
SHING
GET YOUR BUTTS OUT OF HERE!
ZWSH
SURE ...
GANTA ?!

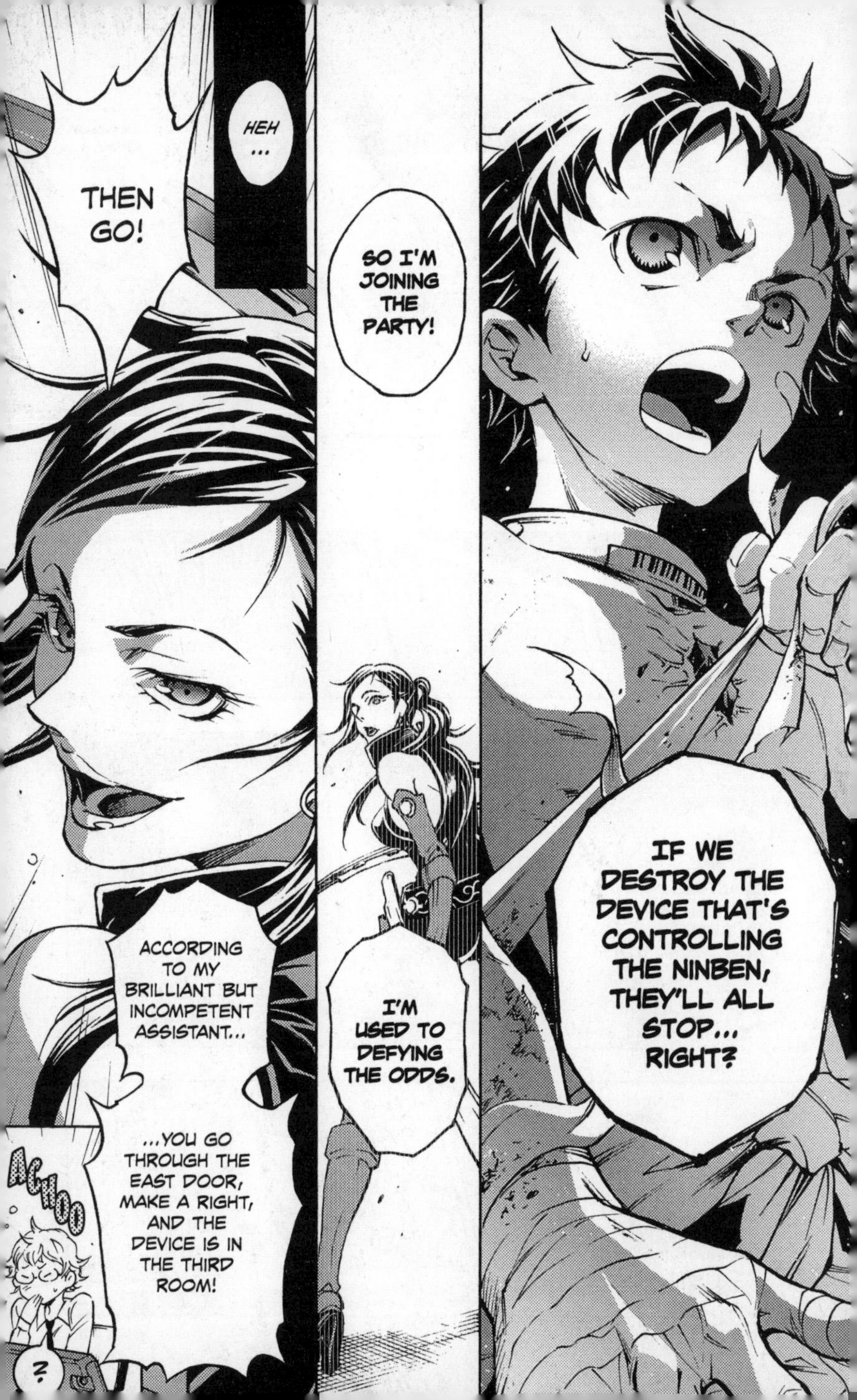
IF WE DESTROY THE DEVICE THAT'S CONTROLLING THE NINBEN, THEY'LL ALL STOP... RIGHT?
SO I'M JOINING THE PARTY!
I'M USED TO DEFYING THE ODDS.
HEH ...
THEN GO!
ACCORDING TO MY BRILLIANT BUT INCOMPETENT ASSISTANT...
...YOU GO THROUGH THE EAST DOOR, MAKE A RIGHT, AND THE DEVICE IS IN THE THIRD ROOM!
ACHOO
?

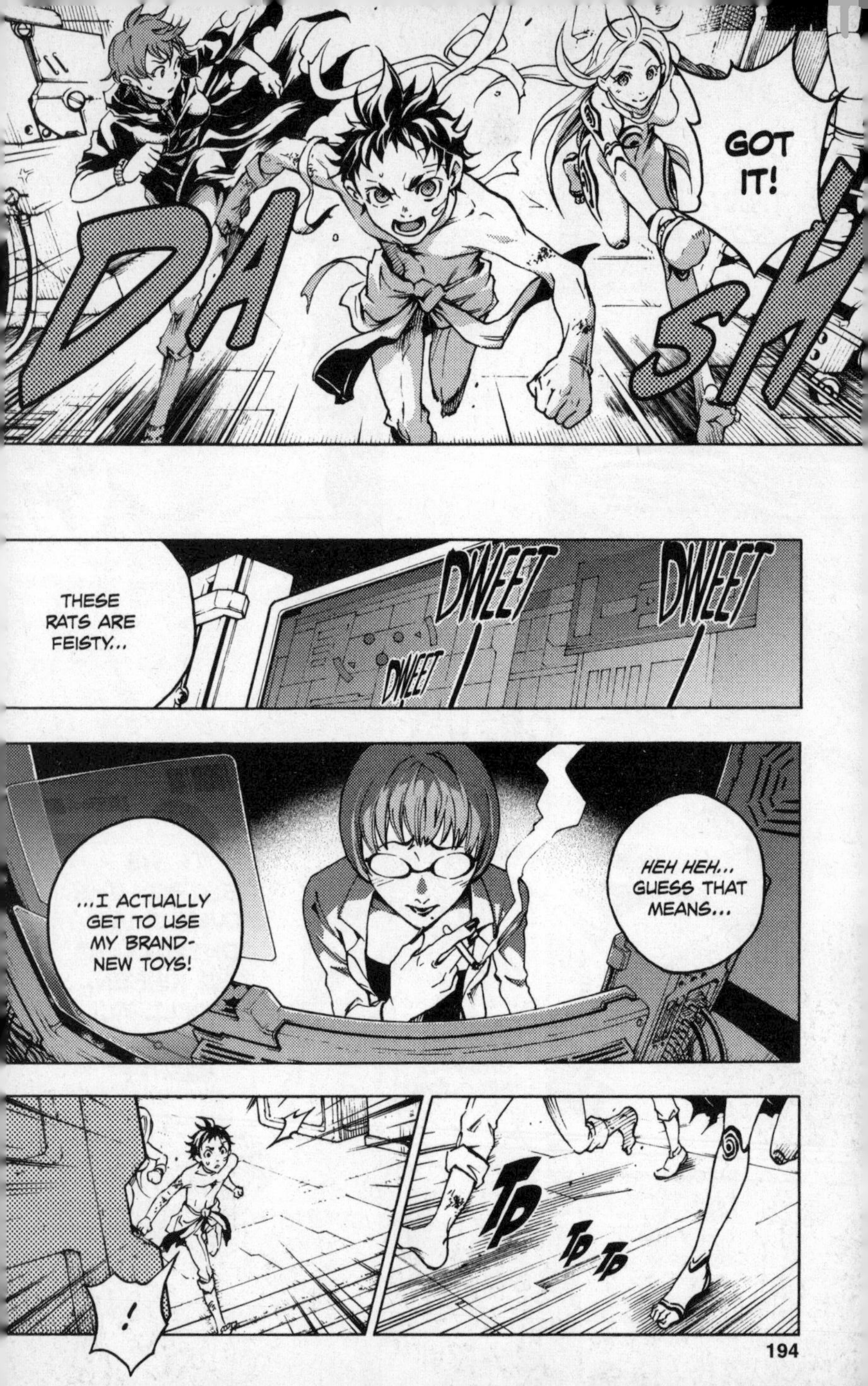
GOT IT!
DASH
THESE RATS ARE FEISTY...
DWEET
DWEET
DWEET
HEH HEH... GUESS THAT MEANS...
...I ACTUALLY GET TO USE MY BRAND-NEW TOYS!
TP
TP
TP
!

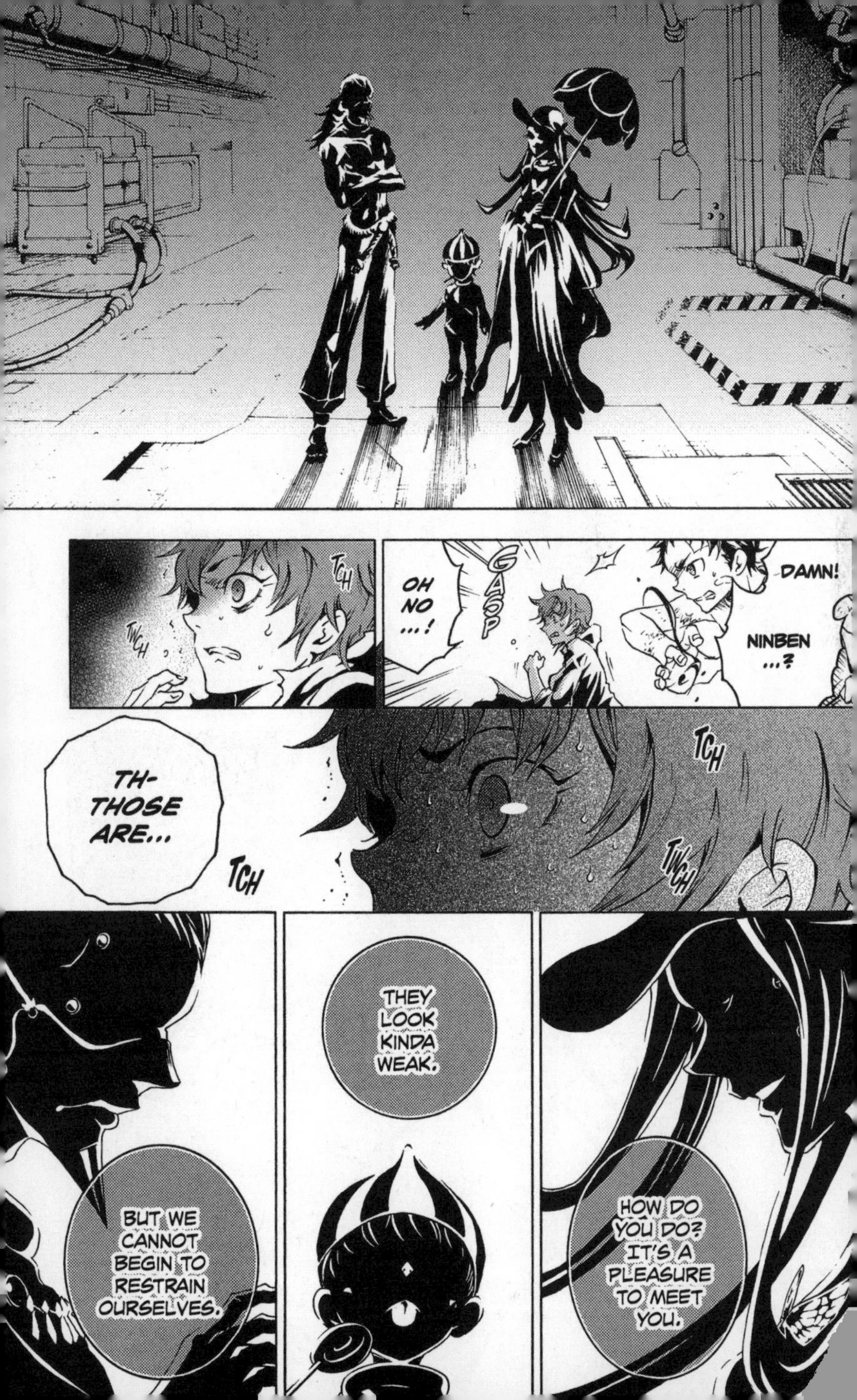
DAMN!
NINBEN ...?
GASP
OH NO ...!
TCH
TWCH
TCH
TWCH
TH- THOSE ARE...
TCH
HOW DO YOU DO? IT'S A PLEASURE TO MEET YOU.
THEY LOOK KINDA WEAK.
BUT WE CANNOT BEGIN TO RESTRAIN OURSELVES.

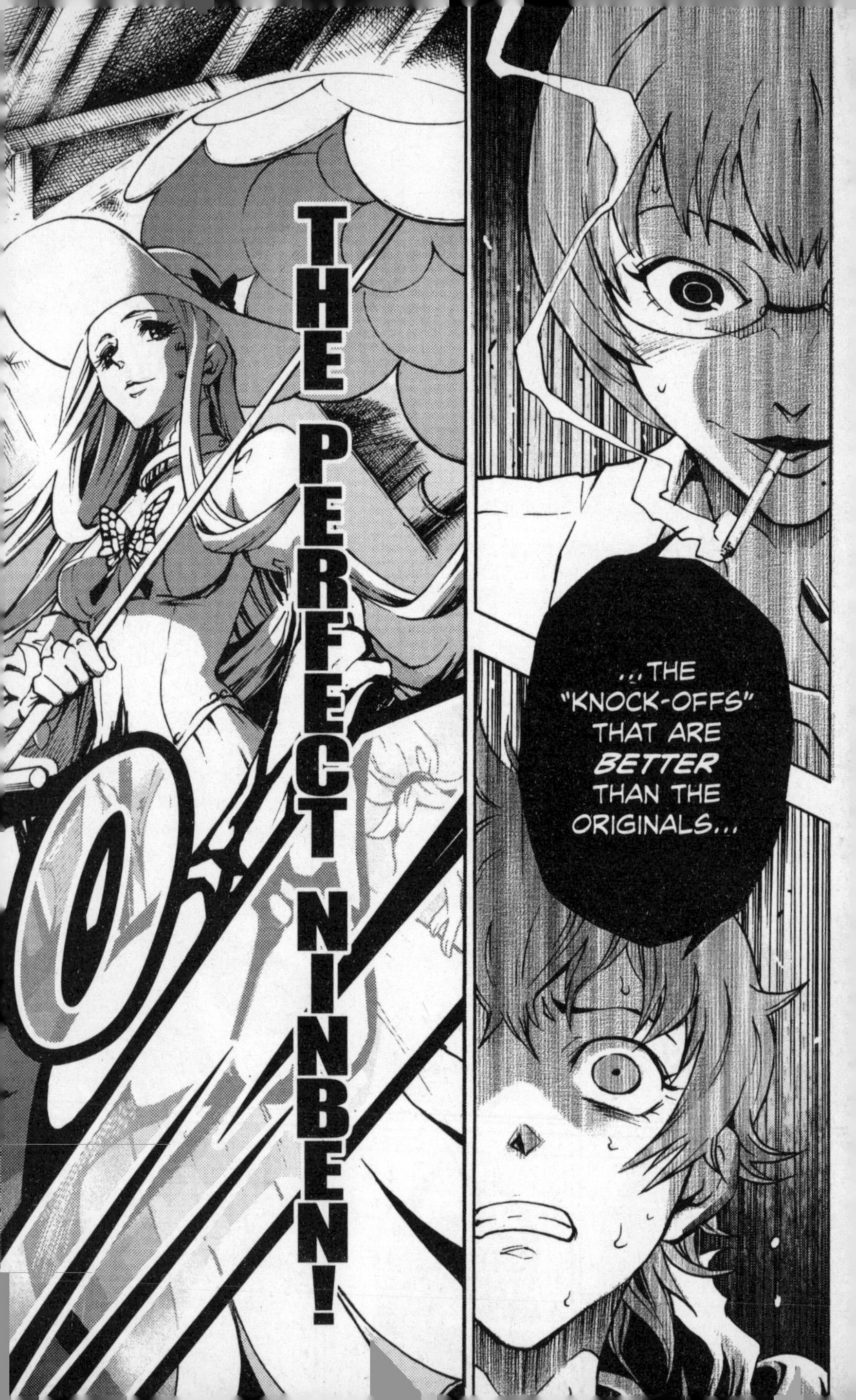
..THE "KNOCK-OFFS" THAT ARE BETTER THAN THE ORIGINALS...
THE PERFECT NINBEN!

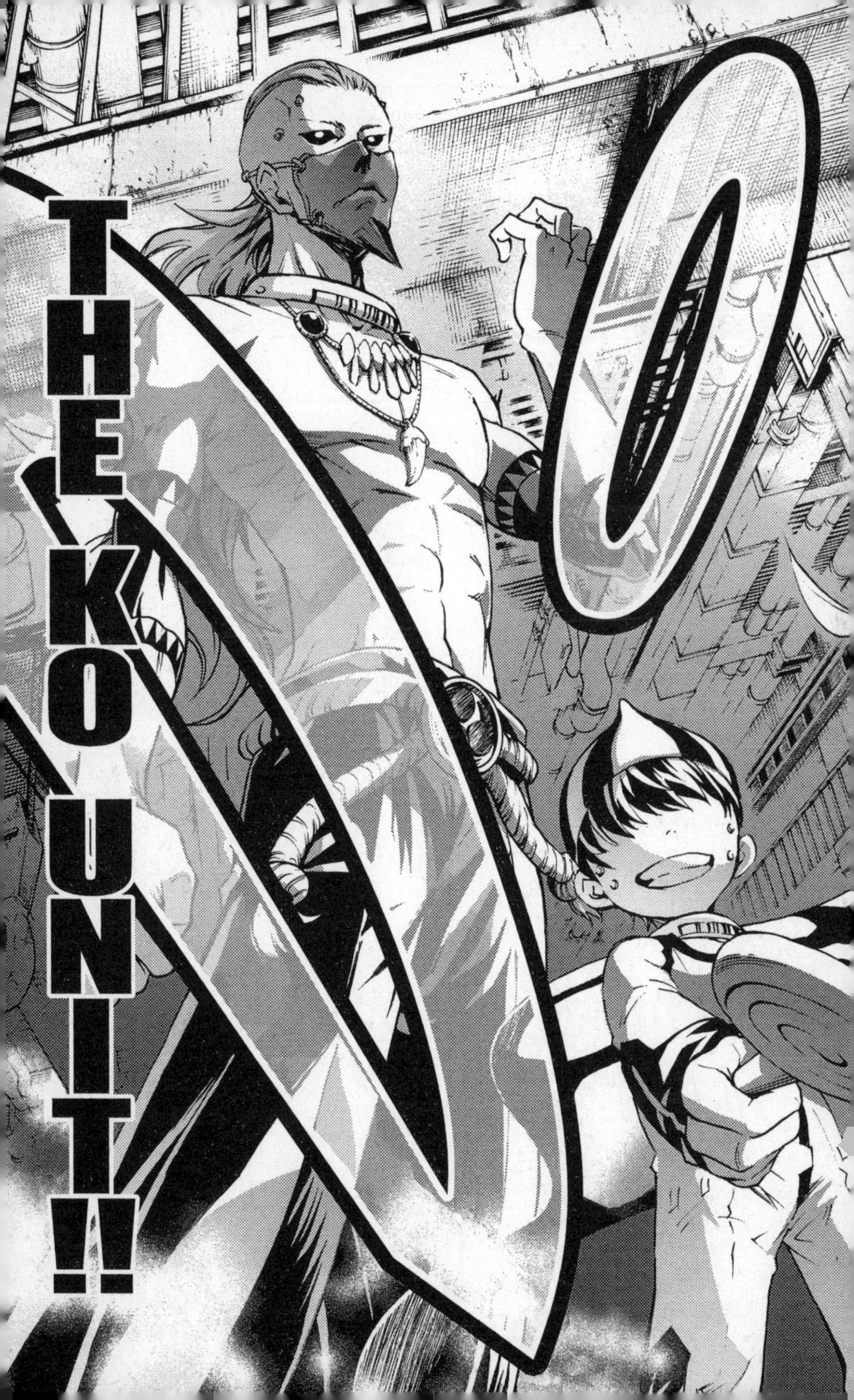
THE KOU UNIT!!

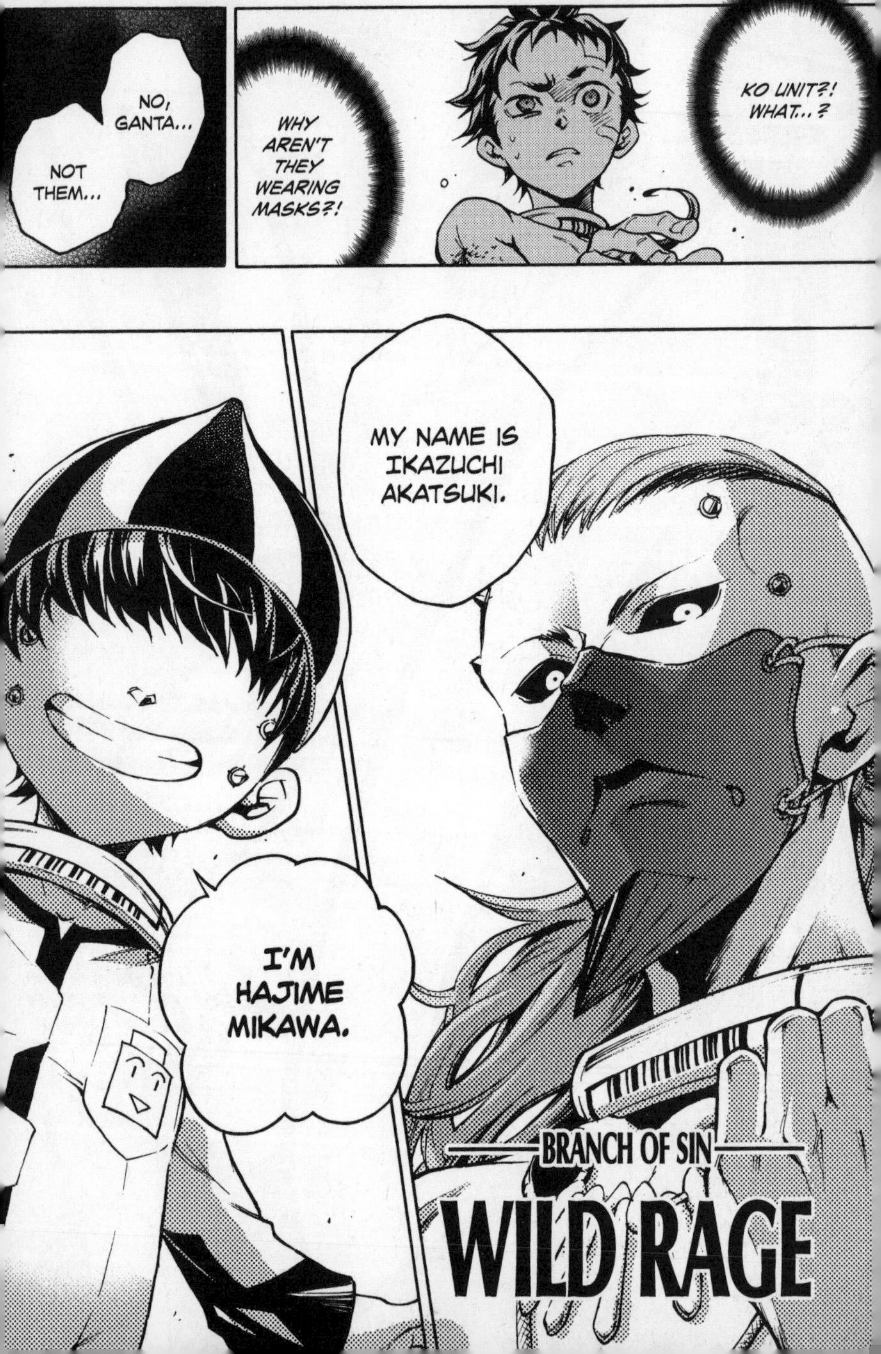
KO UNIT?! WHAT...?
WHY AREN'T THEY WEARING MASKS?!
NO, GANTA...
NOT THEM...
MY NAME IS IKAZUCHI AKATSUKI.
I'M HAJIME MIKAWA.
BRANCH OF SIN
WILD RAGE

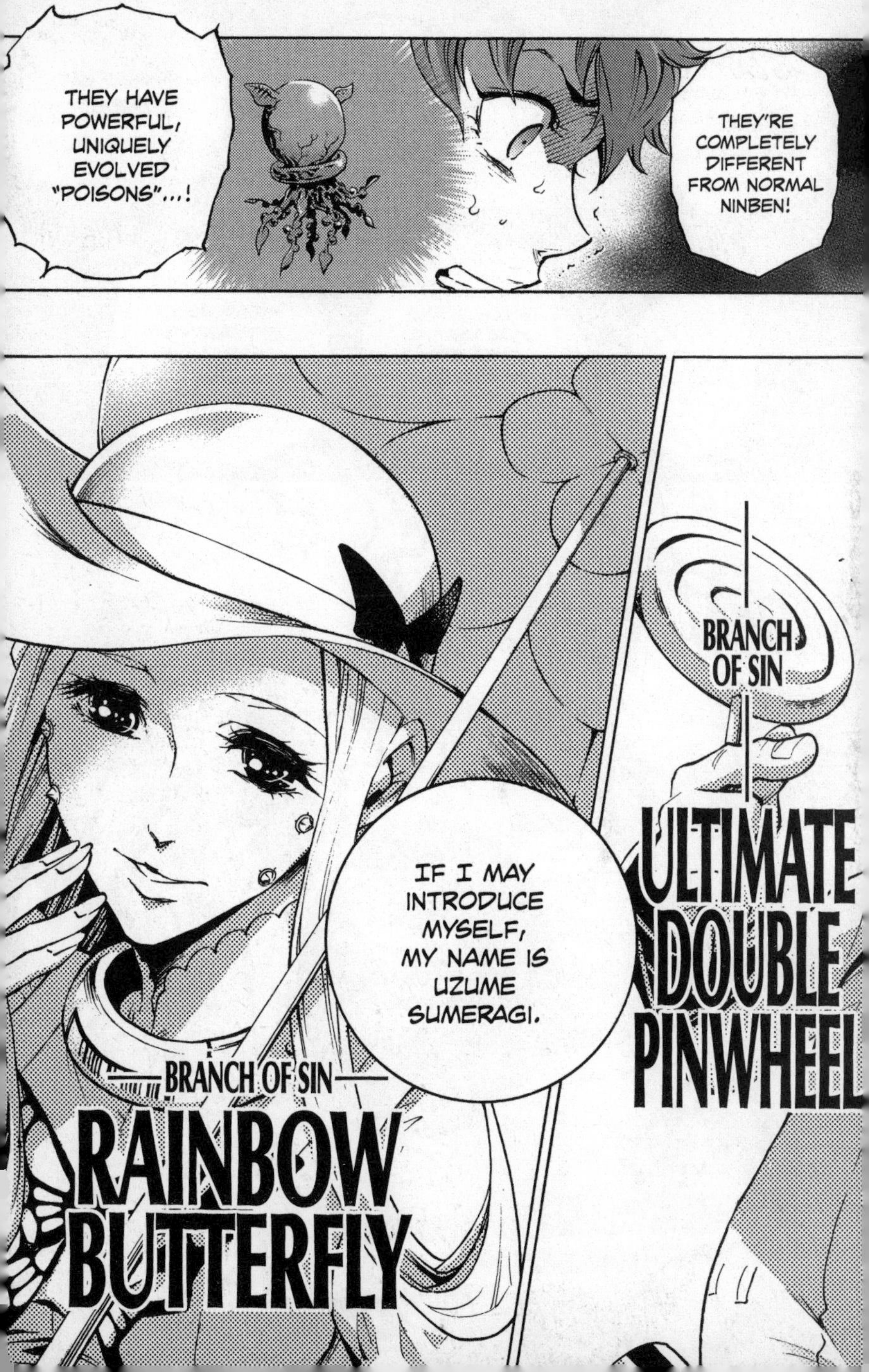
THEY'RE COMPLETELY DIFFERENT FROM NORMAL NINBEN!
THEY HAVE POWERFUL, UNIQUELY EVOLVED "POISONS"...!
BRANCH OF SIN
ULTIMATE DOUBLE PINWHEEL
IF I MAY INTRODUCE MYSELF, MY NAME IS UZUME SUMERAGI.
BRANCH OF SIN
RAINBOW BUTTERFLY

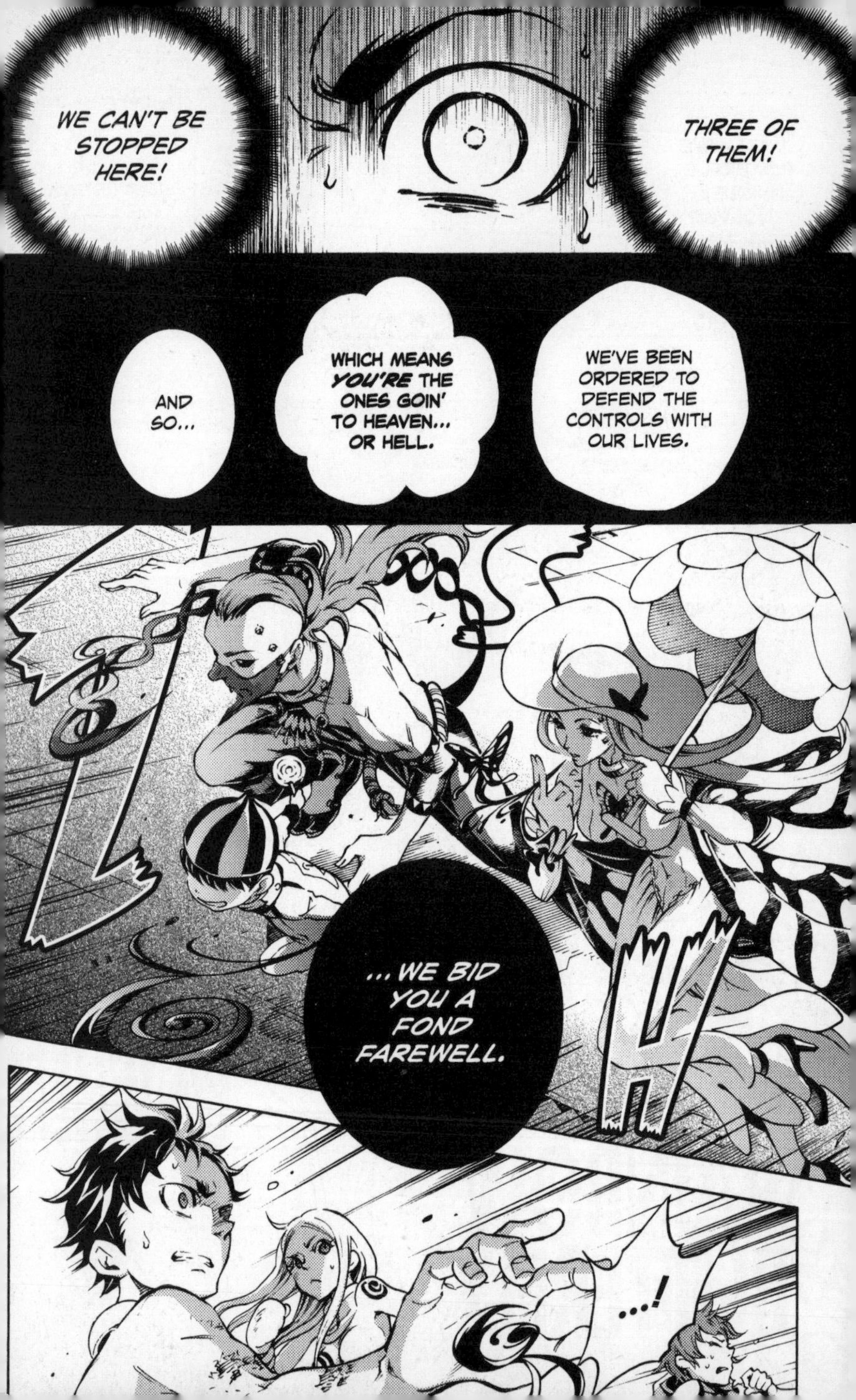
THREE OF THEM!
WE CAN'T BE STOPPED HERE!
WE'VE BEEN ORDERED TO DEFEND THE CONTROLS WITH OUR LIVES.
WHICH MEANS YOU'RE THE ONES GOIN' TO HEAVEN... OR HELL.
AND SO...
...WE BID YOU A FOND FAREWELL.
...!

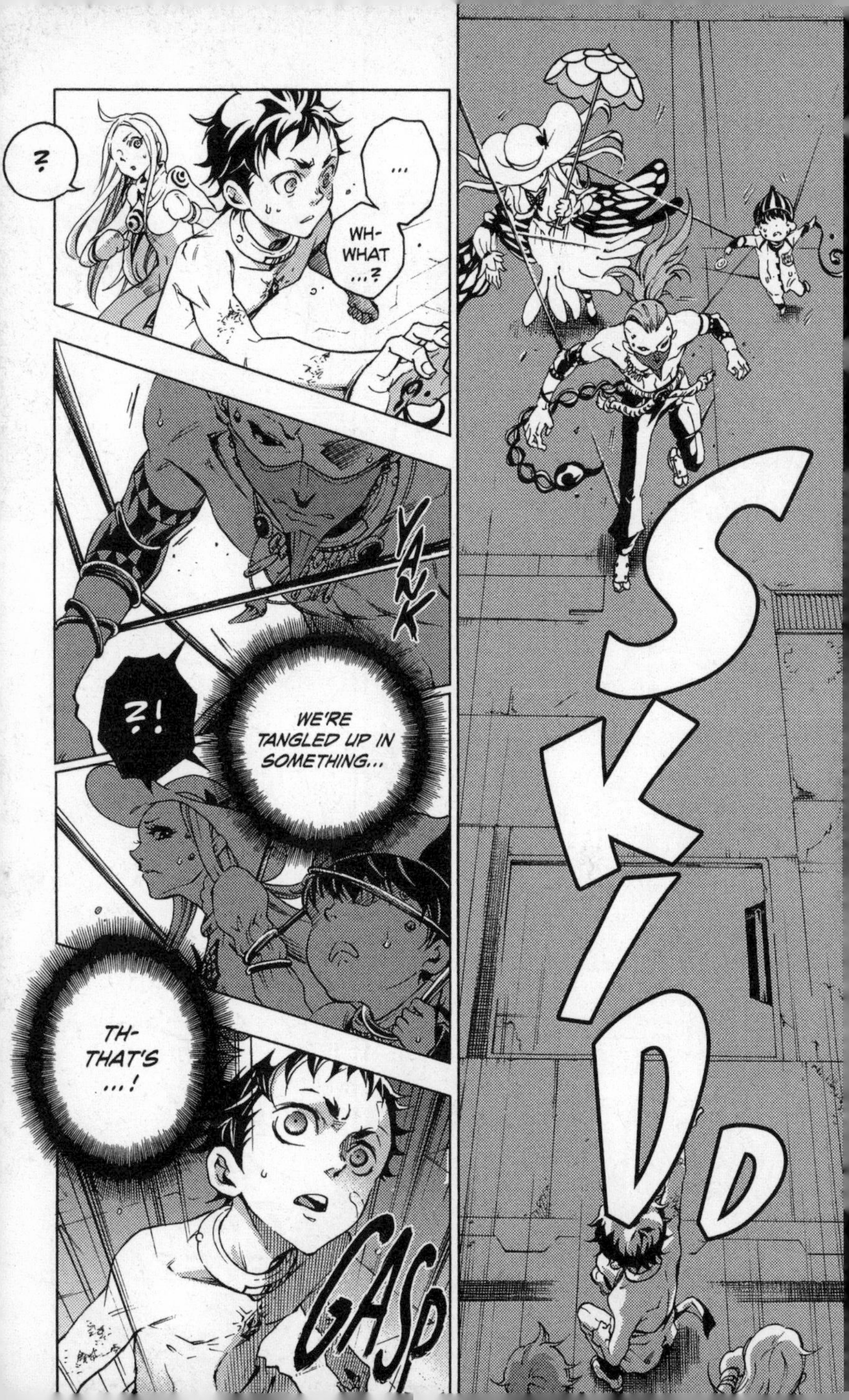
SKIDD
...
WH- WHAT ...?
?
YANK
?!
WE'RE TANGLED UP IN SOMETHING...
TH- THAT'S ...!
GASP

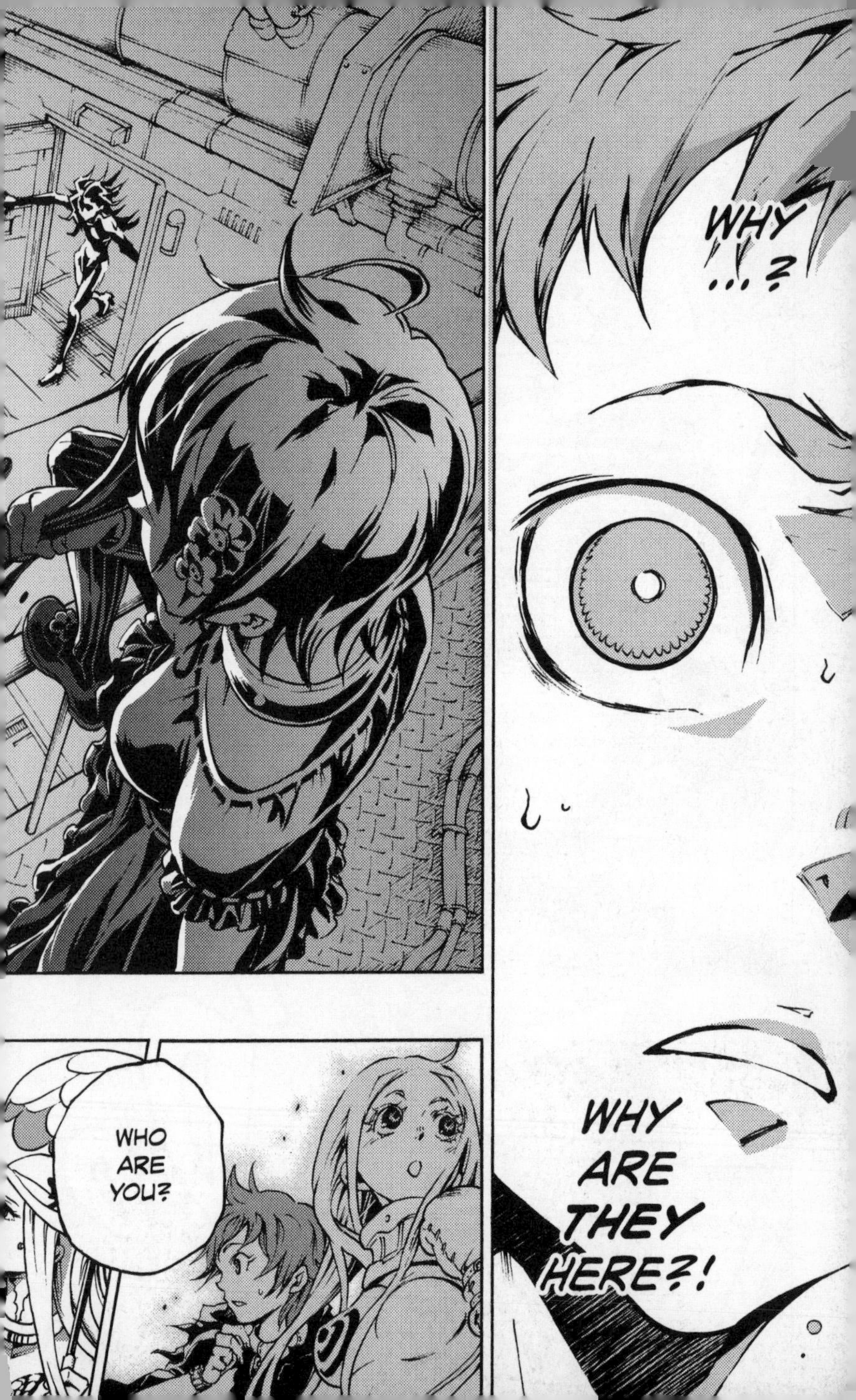
WHY !...?
WHY ARE THEY HERE?!
WHO ARE YOU?

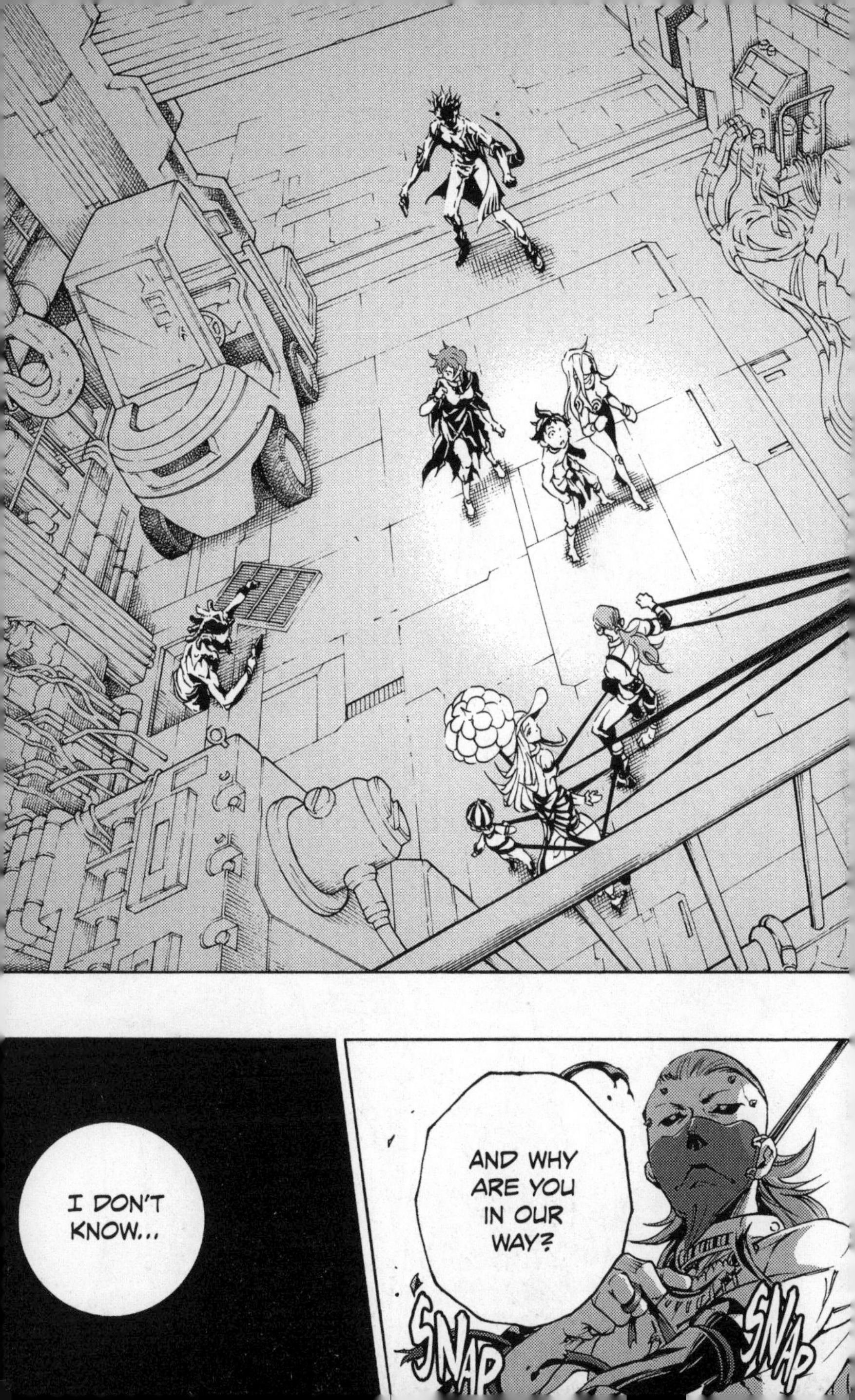
AND WHY ARE YOU IN OUR WAY?
SNAP
SNAP
I DON'T KNOW...

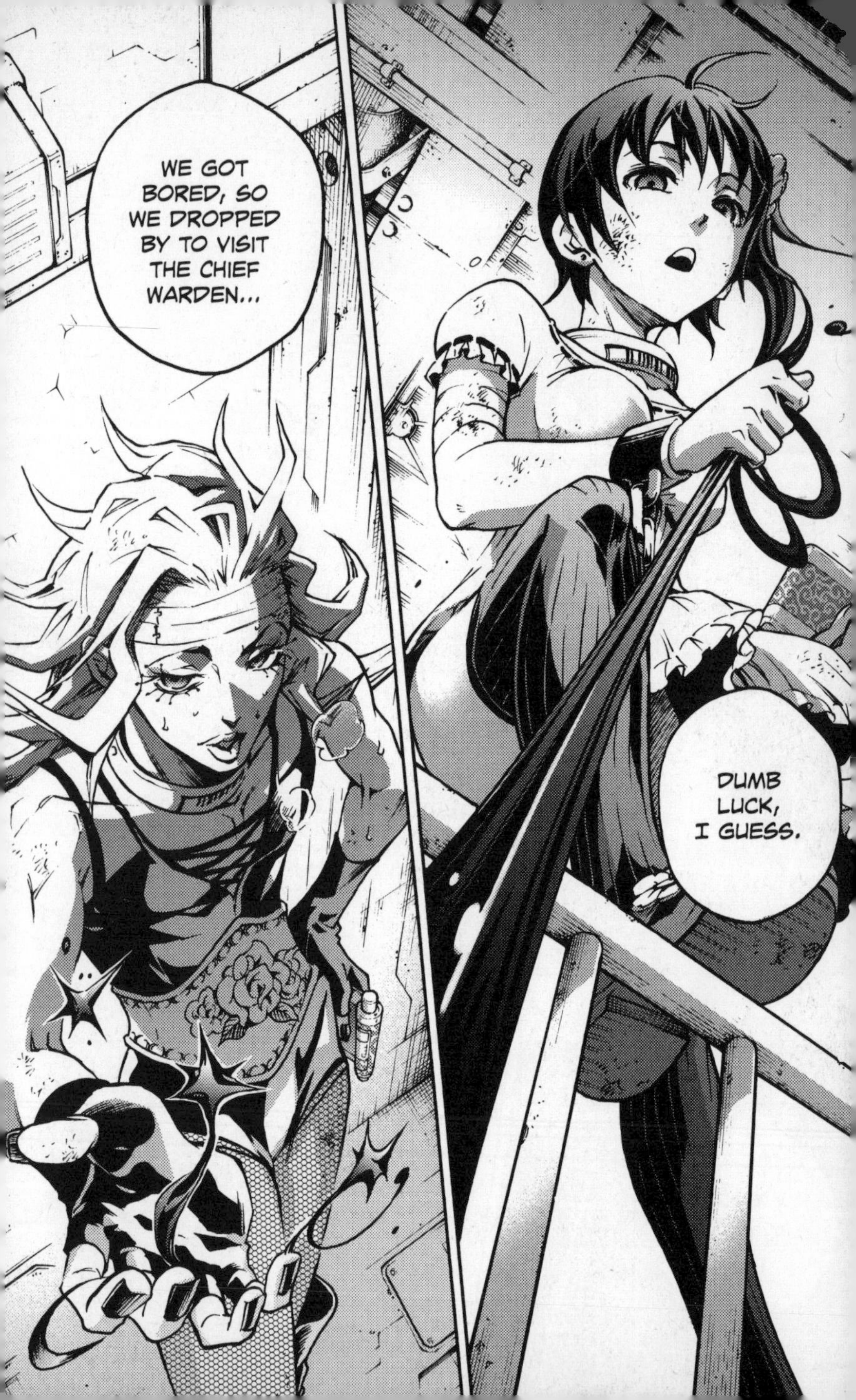
DUMB LUCK, I GUESS.
WE GOT BORED, SO WE DROPPED BY TO VISIT THE CHIEF WARDEN...

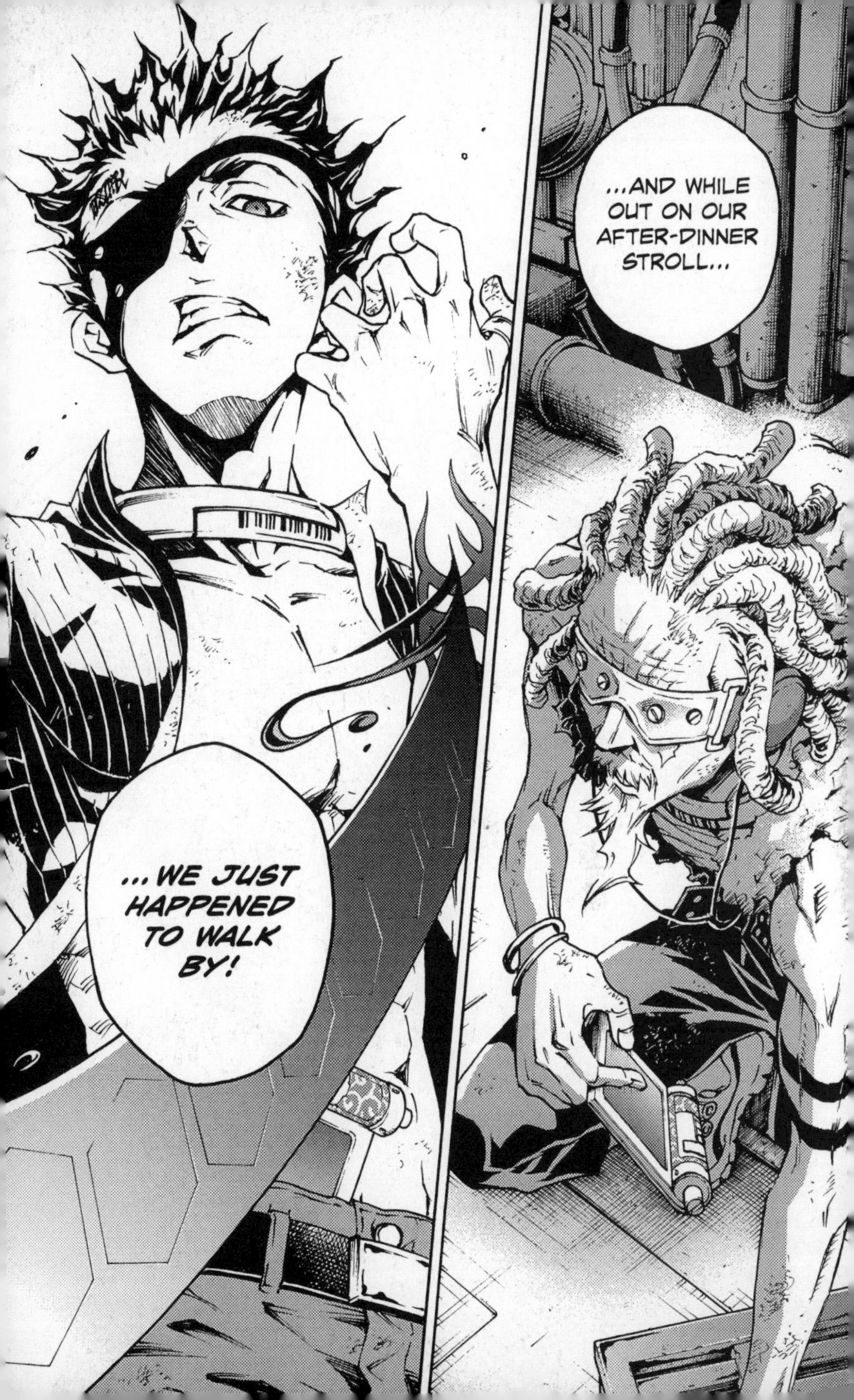
...AND WHILE OUT ON OUR AFTER-DINNER STROLL...
...WE JUST HAPPENED TO WALK BY!

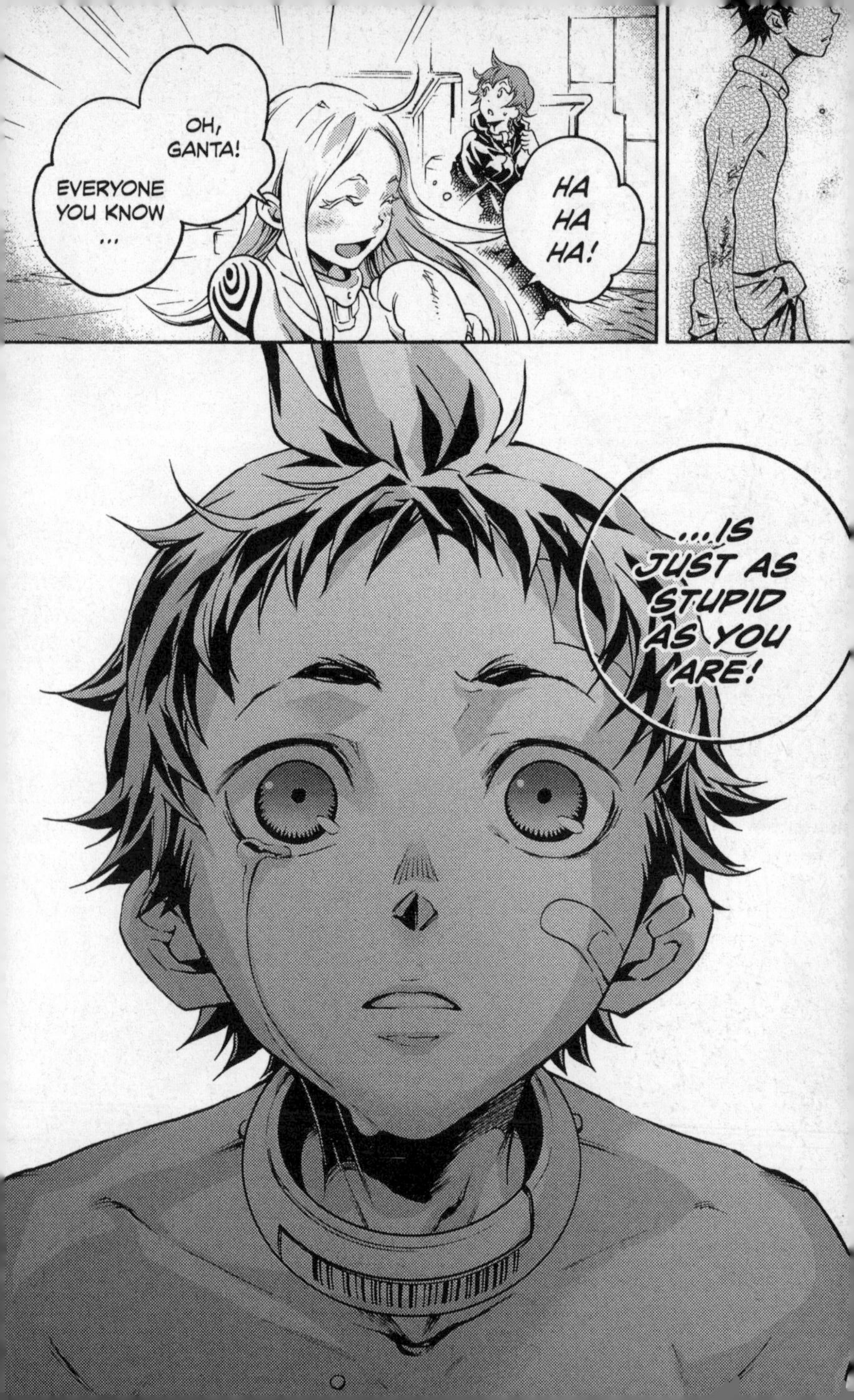
HA HA HA!
OH, GANTA!
EVERYONE YOU KNOW ...
...IS JUST AS STUPID AS YOU ARE!

DEADMAN WONDERLAND 7

Jinsei Kataoka
Kazuma Kondou

STAFF

Yukitsune Amakusa

Karaiko

Shinji Sato

Ryuichi Saitaniya

Taro Tsuchiya

Taku Nakamura

Toshihiro Noguchi

Continued In Volume 8

Take a Guess

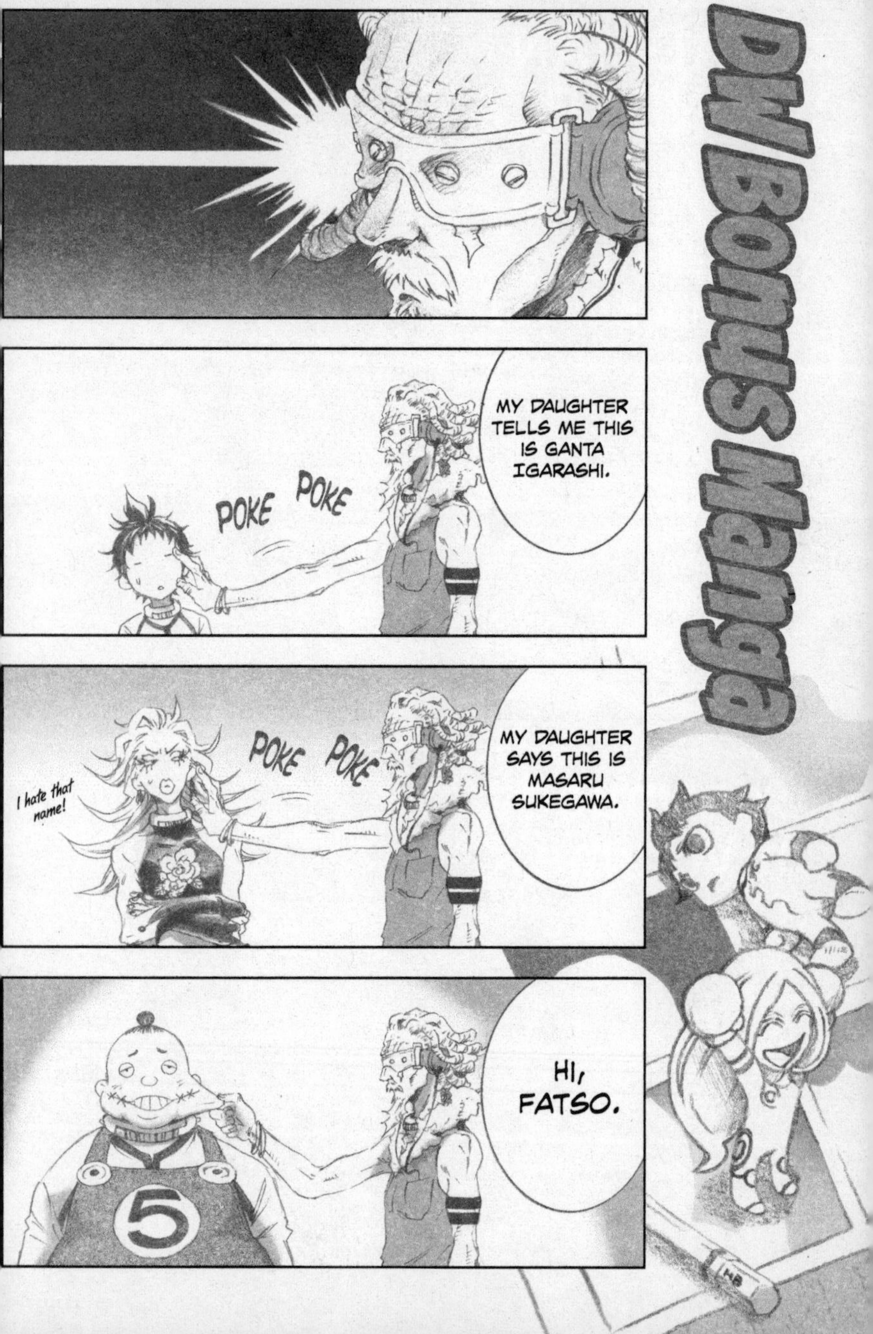
DW/Bonus Manga
MY DAUGHTER TELLS ME THIS IS GANTA IGARASHI.
POKE POKE
MY DAUGHTER SAYS THIS IS MASARU SUKEGAWA.
POKE POKE
I hate that name!
HI, FATSO.

The Known Unknown

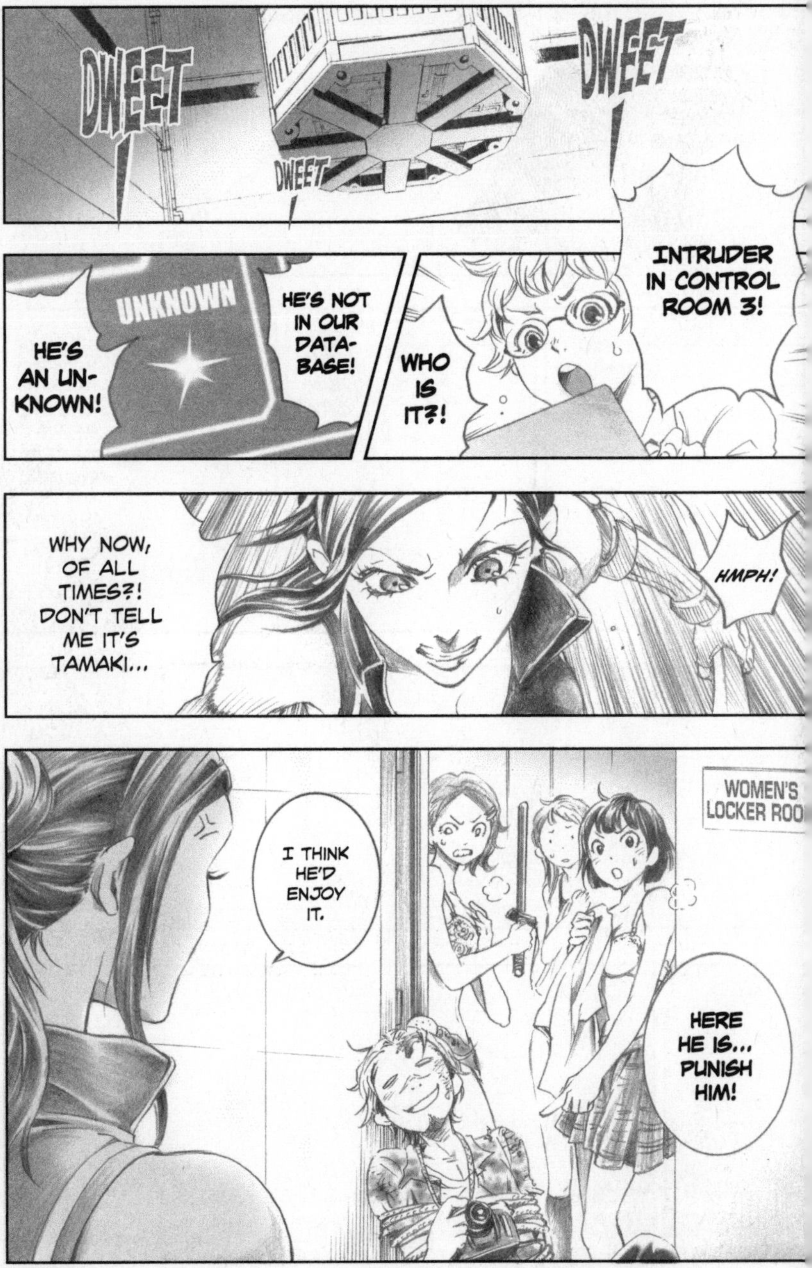
DWEET
DWEET
DWEET
INTRUDER IN CONTROL ROOM 3!
WHO IS IT?!
HE'S NOT IN OUR DATABASE!
UNKNOWN
HE'S AN UNKNOWN!
HMPH!
WHY NOW, OF ALL TIMES?! DON'T TELL ME IT'S TAMAKI...
WOMEN'S LOCKER ROO
HERE HE IS... PUNISH HIM!
I THINK HE'D ENJOY IT.

Kincho's Lament

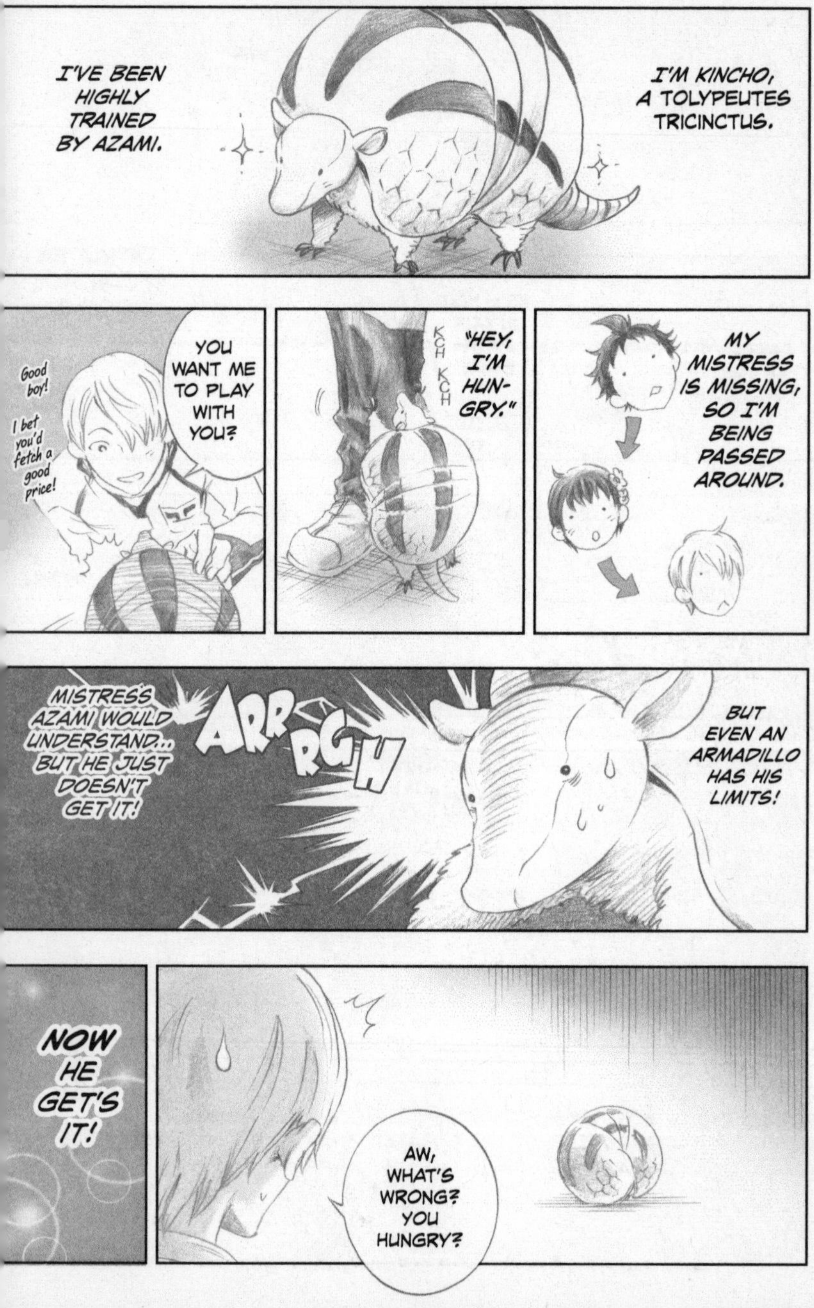
I'M KINCHO, A TOLYPEUTES TRICINCTUS.
I'VE BEEN HIGHLY TRAINED BY AZAMI.
MY MISTRESS IS MISSING, SO I'M BEING PASSED AROUND.
KCH KCH
"HEY, I'M HUN-GRY."
YOU WANT ME TO PLAY WITH YOU?
Good boy! I bet you'd fetch a good price!
BUT EVEN AN ARMADILLO HAS HIS LIMITS!
ARRRGH
MISTRESS AZAMI WOULD UNDERSTAND... BUT HE JUST DOESN'T GET IT!
AW, WHAT'S WRONG? YOU HUNGRY?
NOW HE GET'S IT!

Broken Watch

THIS WATCH CAN BE SOOO USEFUL!

TETRIS...

BEEP

Thursday You'll spend the whole day in your cell.

Lucky Item Key to your cell

HORO-SCOPE...

BEEP

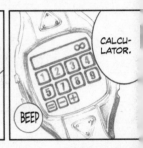

CALCU-LATOR.

BEEP

GAME OVER

SCORE 0

STUPID SMALL SCREEN!

ARGH!

DEADMAN WONDERLAND

DEADMAN WONDERLAND
VOLUME 7
VIZ MEDIA EDITION

STORY & ART BY
JINSEI KATAOKA, KAZUMA KONDOU

DEADMAN WONDERLAND VOLUME 7
©JINSEI KATAOKA 2010 ©KAZUMA KONDOU 2010
EDITED BY KADOKAWA SHOTEN
FIRST PUBLISHED IN JAPAN IN 2010 BY KADOKAWA CORPORATION, TOKYO.
ENGLISH TRANSLATION RIGHTS ARRANGED WITH KADOKAWA CORPORATION, TOKYO.

TRANSLATION/JOE YAMAZAKI
ENGLISH ADAPTATION/STAN!
TOUCH-UP ART & LETTERING/JAMES GAUBATZ
DESIGN/SAM ELZWAY
EDITOR/MIKE MONTESA, JENNIFER LEBLANC

PRINTED IN THE U.S.A.

PUBLISHED BY VIZ MEDIA, LLC
P.O. BOX 77010
SAN FRANCISCO, CA 94107

10 9 8 7 6 5 4 3 2 1
FIRST PRINTING, FEBRUARY 2015

www.viz.com